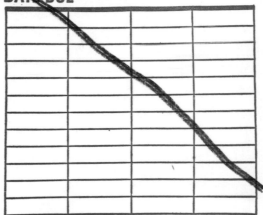

BURT FRANKLIN: RESEARCH & SOURCE WORKS SERIES 125
Philosophy Monographs Series 4

SYSTEM

OF

POSITIVE POLITY

SECOND VOLUME

SYSTEM

OF

POSITIVE POLITY

BY

AUGUSTE COMTE

SECOND VOLUME

CONTAINING

SOCIAL STATICS, OR THE ABSTRACT THEORY OF HUMAN ORDER

BURT FRANKLIN
New York, N. Y.

Published by LENOX HILL Pub. & Dist. Co. (Burt Franklin)
235 East 44th St., New York, N.Y. 10017
Reprinted: 1973
Printed in the U.S.A.

Burt Franklin: Research and Source Works Series 125
Philosophy and Religious History Monographs 4

The Library of Congress cataloged the original printing of this title
as follows.

Comte, Auguste, 1798-1857.
    System of positive polity. New York, B. Franklin 1968?

    4 v. 23 cm. (Burt Franklin research and source works series, no. 125)
    Vol. 2—4 are also Burt Franklin philosophy monograph series, no. 4.
    Reprint of the 1875 ed.
    Translation of Systeme de politique positive.
    CONTENTS.—v. 1. General view of positivism & introductory principles.
—v. 2. Social statics; or, The abstract theory of human order.—v. 3. Social
dynamics; or, the general theory of human progress.—v. 4. Theory of the
future of man, with an appendix consisting of Early essays on social philosophy.
    1. Positivism. 2. Sociology. I. Title.
HM55.C76   1968   146'.4   66-20689
ISBN 0-8337-0640-3

NOTICE.

This volume was published by the Author in May 1852.

It has been translated by FREDERIC HARRISON, M.A., of Lincoln's Inn.

The Marginal notes, references, and the Table of Contents have been added by the Translator.

The references to the ' Philosophie Positive ' are to the second edition of the original.

PREFACE.

In submitting this volume to the reader, I shall only express the hope that it may meet with such serious and sustained attention as befits a subject so important and so difficult. In this epoch of transition, there can be but few who come to the study of Sociology with a previous training in the entire series of the other sciences ; but every reader is bound, at least, to bring to it the same dispositions and habits which are recognised as indispensable for the study of less complex sciences. They who have not acquired this point of view would be wise to avoid speculations about society, so that these transcendental problems may be left to the few, who will eventually make public the fruits of their labour. It may be the more necessary to remind the reader of this duty, inasmuch as this volume is taken up with the most abstract theories of the most difficult of all sciences.

Although these volumes are published separately, they can hardly be understood without reference to each other. It is quite impossible to follow this second volume, without previously mastering the leading doctrines elaborated in the first. And the ideas which this volume presents can only be judged

by the light of the historical illustrations of them contained in
the third, and the practical application of them contained in
the fourth volume.

Note.—The remainder of the preface in the original, relating not to the subject of the present volume, but to the life and work of the author, has been
omitted in the hope that the various biographical pieces may be hereafter collected.—Tr.

CONTENTS

OF

THE SECOND VOLUME.

———•◇•———

SOCIAL STATICS, OR THE ABSTRACT THEORY OF HUMAN ORDER.

GENERAL INTRODUCTION.

CHAPTER I.

THE GENERAL THEORY OF RELIGION; OR THE POSITIVE THEORY OF HUMAN UNITY.

I. *The Functions of Religion, pp. 8–11.*

II. *Conditions of Religion, pp. 11–17.*

III. *The Elements of Religion, pp. 17–20.*

Normal Type of Unity, pp. 20–22.

Intellectual and Practical Basis of Unity, pp. 22–41.

Moral Basis of Unity, pp. 41–53.

Theory of the History of Religion, pp. 70–119.

I. Fetichism, pp. 74–76.

II. Theologism, pp. 76–112.

(A) Polytheism, pp. 80–89.

CHAPTER II.

SOCIOLOGICAL INQUIRY INTO THE PROBLEM OF HUMAN LIFE; (AND THEREIN,) THE POSITIVE THEORY OF MATERIAL PROPERTY.

CHAPTER III.

POSITIVE THEORY OF THE FAMILY.

Moral Aspect of the Family, pp. 155–160.

Political Aspect of the Family, pp. 160–181.

CHAPTER IV.

THE POSITIVE THEORY OF HUMAN LANGUAGE.

Nature of Language, pp. 182–190.

Analysis of Language, pp. 190–198.

Personal Functions of Language, pp. 199–212.

Social Functions of Language, pp. 212–218.

Progress of Language, pp. 218–220.

CHAPTER V.

THE POSITIVE THEORY OF THE SOCIAL ORGANISM.

Positive Theory of the Social Forces, pp. 223–235.

CHAPTER VI.

POSITIVE THEORY OF SOCIAL EXISTENCE, SYSTEMATISED BY THE PRIESTHOOD.

Introductory Sketch, pp. 276–289.

Organisation of Society by the Priesthood, pp. 289–300.

Three Aspects of Social Existence. I. Moral, pp. 300–308.

II. Intellectual Existence, pp. 308–318.

CHAPTER VII.

POSITIVE THEORY OF THE GENERAL LIMITS OF VARIATION IN THE ORDER OF HUMAN SOCIETY.

Introductory, pp. 346–350.

Theory of Social Variations, pp. 350–376.

Theory of their Development, pp. 376–382.

SYSTEM

OF

POSITIVE POLITY.

———⋄———

SOCIAL STATICS, OR. THE ABSTRACT THEORY OF HUMAN ORDER.

———

GENERAL INTRODUCTION.

It is necessary to resolve the positive study of Humanity into two essential parts. The one, the statical, will treat of the structural nature of this, the chief of organisms; the other, the dynamical, will treat the laws of its actual development. Although, in Sociology these two classes of laws are even more intimately connected than they are in Biology; yet the greater complexity which marks the highest of the sciences renders their separate treatment still more requisite in the former, than it was in the latter science. This is moreover the method to which social speculation has naturally conformed during the long era of its growth; for the principles relating to Order were sketched out much earlier than those relating to Progress.

Sociology must be separated into (1) Statics, or the study of Order, and (2) Dynamics, or the study of Progress.

Again, this indispensable division of social philosophy into two parts is a further example of the universal principle, upon which my Positive scheme for the Classification of the Sciences is founded. For the study of social Statics is at once more simple, more general, and more abstract, than that of social Dynamics. Moreover social Statics form the direct link between the final science of Society and the whole of the preceding sciences, and in a special manner between the final science and Biology, of which Sociology now becomes the natural complement. Unless based upon a sound theory of the laws of its *existence*, or fixed

In accordance with the laws of Positive Philosophy.

VOL. II.   B

organic conditions, the study of the *movement*, or organic evolution, of human society would fall short of that scientific coherence,
needed for this study to attain to its full usefulness. Nor is this
distinction of less importance in practice than it is in theory;
for the dynamical laws find their chief application in politics,
the statical, in morals.

But Statics
and Dyna-
mics, Order
and Pro-
gress, are in
intimate
harmony.
Between these two classes of social laws there reigns a sovereign spirit of harmony, by virtue of the general principle,
which here, as elsewhere, combines the study of Movement, with
that of the Existence. The value of this principle was first seen
in the field of mere mathematics; but it is in Sociology where
its full importance and character will be finally displayed. Here
its proper part is to picture Progress as nothing but the gradual
development of Order. Conversely it represents to us Order as
manifested forth by Progress. Such is the intimate union of
these two cardinal notions, equally valuable for purposes of
theory as of practice; for the former defines the Basis, the latter,
the End of all social life, whilst it is animated throughout by
the Principle of universal affection. In Biology we now regard
all forms of life simply as an evolution, and we discard any
notion of creation in the proper sense of that word. But this
great axiom of science has especially its place in Sociology;
where studying a course of development yet more complex,
more extensive, and more gradual, we are forced to recognise
the fundamental unity which runs through all the successive
phases. In this science the statical study, and the dynamical
study tend gradually to unite in one, as the essential spirit of
each more and more distinctly comes out, to illustrate the intimate connection between them; and we explain alternately
the laws of Order by those of Progress, and the laws of Progress
by those of Order.

In the 'Posi-
tive Philo-
sophy' Dy-
namics were
principally
of import-
ance.
But this separation of the two classes of laws in theory,
however necessary there, ought not to put out of view their
intimate relation in fact, and it is such that the main result of
each consists in the reaction, which it naturally exerts upon the
other. Hence arises the change in the position which the two
methods respectively hold, according as the purpose may be to
institute, or to systematise, the social science. In my Philosophical work my main task was to ascertain for the first time,
the natural laws which apply to social phenomena, and these had
not hitherto been subjected to the scientific method at all. It

was consequently the dynamical theory upon which I had there principally to insist, as being alone decisive of the question of Law applying to Society. Then my chief object was to discover and to demonstrate the laws of Progress ; and to exhibit in the march of one unbroken sequence the collective destinies of mankind, till then invariably regarded as a series of events wholly beyond the reach of explanation, and almost depending on arbitrary will. The laws properly relating to Order, which indeed are hardly to be disputed in principle, required examination only so far as their leading axioms bore upon the direct study of the Progress of Man in history. But the present treatise implies an altogether different method of investigation.

The present work on the contrary is addressed to those who are already sufficiently convinced of the certain existence of social laws, and desire only to have them reduced to a true and conclusive system,—a necessity for any reconstitution of general Education in the West. The abstract study of Order must therefore here precede that of Progress, whilst in the succeeding volume Progress will appear as the natural consequence and necessary complement of Order. The statical method of this volume presents indeed more difficulties than did the dynamical method of my former work, because the field of Statics is less clearly defined than that of Dynamics. But the statical method alone can give a really solid basis to a sound Social Philosophy, first because it connects it more closely with the entire range of Natural Philosophy, secondly because it reduces the constituent elements of Social Philosophy to a more truly systematic form. For this special object then I shall consider the laws of human *Order* in the abstract, discarding all question of movement as if that Order was fixed. We shall thus ascertain the primary laws of Society which are necessarily common to all times, and to all places. This will afford a scientific foundation for the treatment of the gradual course of human development, which has been nothing but the growing fulfilment of that System of Life, best adapted to man, whereof the essential form from the first has existed in germ. The present volume therefore will represent the primitive type of society as being without exception the source of the most advanced type; and I shall leave for future examination the long course of preparation, which was requisite to complete so great a transformation. We shall thus form a conception of

The subject of this volume will be Statics, or the Laws of Order, regarded as the source of all Development.

the future of society, so simple and so coherent, as to be equally adapted to meet all visionary schemes of revolution as well as every retrograde tendency. For this conception will at once invest the destinies of the human race with the true character of Continuity in change and also of Unity in nature.

Statics, considered in this volume, prepare the way for the history of the Past in the next, and for the picture of the Future in the concluding, volume.

Such being the general character of Sociology, the present volume will treat human society by analysing it into the various leading elements of which it is composed. In each of these elements it will be my aim, first to ascertain the normal state which most truly answers the conditions of our nature, then to show how it was that a long and gradual preparation was needed for complete fulfilment of that normal state. Working upon this twofold basis of Statics, the study of social Dynamics (the subject of the third volume) will give a new expansion to the laws of Order by adding to them the laws of Progress, which till then had only been considered for the purpose of explaining the phases of the preparation needed for the evolution of Order. The fourth and last volume will then deal directly with the Future of Man, and the concluding phase through which the most advanced among the nations must pass before they can reach it. This general plan of the work shows the importance of the task to which the present volume is devoted, for it exhibits social Statics as the essential foundation of the whole scheme, both in its historical and its dogmatic objects, and as leading up to the Religion of Humanity. The principles then of Social Order on which I now enter, will serve as a guide in our task of conceiving aright the Future, and of estimating aright the Past ; for the former is only the complete maturity, the latter only the transitional development, of germs which are found in the fundamental nature of society.

This analysis of the theory of human order in the abstract will consist of seven chapters, the object and connection of which it becomes necessary to explain.

Chap. I. gives the general theory of Religion.

The first chapter will be devoted to the point of view which alone is strictly universal, the general theory of Religion, so as to exhibit it under its double aspect as regulating and also as combining society. According to the plan just explained, the function and even the character of the final religion will have to be determined, before giving any consideration to the various phases of religion, which have served in turn to prepare the way for the last.

The second chapter will then lead to the regular treatment of the great Problem of human life, as limited by the primary laws which Biology furnishes respecting the conditions of human nature; and herein we shall apply the conclusions arrived at in the preceding volume. Here Social Order appears as the continual reservoir of power, whereby the problem of material life is gradually worked out; and it is the successful solution of this problem which marks the principal Progress of the race.

Chap. II., that of the material Problem of Human Life and the theory of Property.

The third chapter will proceed to explain the Positive theory of the Family, considering it in the abstract, first as a natural element of society, secondly as the primal basis of all moral life. Having treated these two questions which apply to mankind universally without reference to peculiarities of time and place, all the varieties of type which history exhibits will be seen to consist in a gradual approximation towards the true type of the Home.

Chap. III., the theory of the Family.

The fourth chapter will supply a natural transition from the family to society, by treating the fundamental institution of Language, the origin of which is due to the family, whilst the development is due to society. Associated as Language is equally with the feelings, the intellect, and the activity of man, we shall see how it is stamped with a natural unity by virtue of the essential identity of the human race; and it is developed into a scientific unity by virtue of the convergence of all its ordinary varieties to one type.

Chap. IV., the theory of Language.

The direct study of the Social System is thus commenced, and the fifth chapter will treat the elements of its structure and explain the theory of the relations of the various Orders of society. The object is to keep in view amidst all possible diversities the radical unity of all the parts. This truth holds good with every kind of classification in the order of nature, and thus we show that the variations exhibited in history are in the aggregate nothing but the development step by step of a constant set of mutual relations.

Chap. V., the theory of Social Organisation.

After thus treating in the abstract of the Organs of which the social system is composed, the sixth chapter will investigate their proper Functions. When these have been considered in that aspect which is common to them universally in all times and in all places, the outline of Social Statics will be complete. Although the varieties in the forms of social Life are yet more

Chap. VI., the theory of Social Existence.

marked than those in the Structure of the social system, they show still more strikingly the fundamental identity of the natural type, and its continual advance towards realisation in a complete form.

Chap. VII., the Limits of Social Variation.

The order of human society having been thus considered in the abstract under each of its leading forms, the seventh or final chapter will complete the range of Social Statics by adding as a corollary an essential theory, that of the general Limits within which such a system admits of Modification. Unless directly considered in this light, we should be apt to overrate the natural variations which might result from the influence of times or places, or the artificial changes caused by the act of man.

Conclusion of Vol. II.

This chapter will be followed by a short conclusion for the purpose of summing up the contents of the preceding chapters, and so to prepare for the study of human Development, which will form the subject of the next volume.

CHAPTER I.

THE GENERAL THEORY OF RELIGION; OR, THE POSITIVE THEORY OF HUMAN UNITY.

RELIGION, originally Spontaneous, then Inspired, and afterwards Revealed, has at length found its ground in Demonstration. In its full maturity it must satisfy at once the feelings, the imagination, and the reason, as each of these was in turn the source of one of its three earlier forms. But over and above this it must govern directly the active powers of Man, powers which neither Fetichism, nor even Polytheism, nor least of all Monotheism, could adequately control. Now that its ultimate requirements are ascertained, and its preliminary phases are completed, a sound general theory of Religion is possible, which could not begin, so long as narrow views and exclusive sympathies prevailed. The aggregate of the history of the race supplies us now with materials amply sufficient for this task. For the three provisional systems of religion are so contrasted with each other, that the leading features they all contain in common will go to make up the ultimate system; whilst the law by which these systems have supplanted each other will give to that ultimate system its true characteristics. To this general Theory of Religion therefore the first chapter of this volume will be devoted; and thus our abstract study of the social system will start with a systematic inquiry into that institution, which forms the universal basis of all society.

The ultimate form of Religion must rest on demonstration.

In the first place we must remedy the want of clearness and precision which hangs over the term, *Religion*. Very careful thinkers are perpetually mixing up its essential purpose with its temporary means. Its main function in fact is far from being determined; and Religion is referred at one time to the feelings, at another to the intellect. Besides, the constant use of this term in the plural number shows that its primary meaning has never been exactly understood.

Meaning of term, *Religion*.

Religion is the full harmony of Life in all its elements.

Throughout this treatise the term Religion will be used to express that state of complete harmony peculiar to human life, in its collective as well as in its individual form, when all the parts of Life are ordered in their natural relations to each other. This definition, which alone embraces equally all the different phases of Religion, applies equally to the heart and to the intellect, for both of these must concur to produce any true unity of life. Religion therefore gives a natural harmony to the Soul, exactly analogous to that which Health gives to the Body. The union of the moral and the physical nature is so close, and the relation which these two states hold to one another is so intimate, that we may regard the Harmony of the Soul as virtually embracing the health of the Body. Such a notion would be quite in accordance with the practice of the primitive theocracies, in which every direction respecting health was attributed to a religious sanction. The gradual separation of the two sets of rules, as to moral and physical health. was only a passing consequence of the natural dissolution which the ancient systems underwent. But since in the definitive System of Life the connection of these two institutions will be much increased, it will be more appropriate for Religion in that system to assume this comprehensive authority over all life than it was in primitive times.

And is therefore, one, not many.

This definition excludes the use of the plural; it makes it as impossible to speak of several religions as of several healths. In each case, moral or physical, there are only different degrees in the attainment of the true harmony. The natural development of the human race, like that of the entire animal series, exhibits as a whole a Harmony, which grows more and more complete in proportion as it rises into the higher types. But the character of this unity remains always the same, in spite of all the irregularities through which it may actually be worked out.

i. The Functions and Conditions of Religion, pp. 8–17.

Its function is, to *regulate* individual life, and to *combine* collective lives.

The sole distinction which must be constantly maintained is that which relates to the two different phases of our life, individual and collective. Although more and more closely connected, these two forms will never be united in one, and each implies a special quality in religion. To establish a state of complete unity, its task must consist both in *regulating* each personal life, no less than in *combining* different individual lives. Still, however important this distinction is, it must not affect the intimate relation which these two Functions of Religion bear to each other. The conception of their thorough agreement is the first general notion required by the Positive theory of Religion, which never could be reduced to system at all, if these two great ends of human existence did not coincide in fact.

In truth the natural convergence between them springs from the radical identity of the various elements of these two forms of life. The personal and the social life of man can only differ seriously, in extent or duration, or it may be, in rate of speed : never in principle, nor in object, and consequently not in means. This would be far from being the case with a race inherently unsocial in nature ; in which the unity of the individual life and the harmony of collective life might require conditions very distinct and even opposed. Such is the case in fact with many of the carnivorous species, where the unity of the personal powers depends upon an habitual state of mere selfishness, as we had occasion to explain in the former volume. Man on the other hand, more than any other of the social animals, tends more and more to realise a unity strictly unselfish, one moreover which is not so easy to attain as the unity of selfishness, but which is superior in completeness and also in permanence. In his instance, for we need now consider no other, to *regulate* and to *combine* invariably require conditions essentially the same.

In Man, the individual and the social life are naturally homogeneous.

With respect to the intellect, this natural coincidence between the individual and the social form of unity shows itself especially when we consider, that the differences amongst individuals are not greater than those between the successive states, through which each mind passes under the various conditions, external and internal, which affect it. Every doctrine capable of thoroughly regulating any single understanding becomes, thereby alone, capable of gradually combining other minds. The number of these can only affect the greater or less rapidity with which the agreement is effected. This natural test has been the true source of that innate confidence, which different reformers in philosophy have felt in the ultimate ascendancy over mankind of their own system, a system invested with full sanction in their own minds by virtue of this personal experience. The firmness of their own convictions gave them positive proof, that their doctrines would find ultimate acceptance amongst men.

Intellectually, that which can regulate the phases of one mind, can combine the ideas of many minds.

Morally, unity in the individual is only secured by the ascendancy of a social instinct over the personal instincts.

But the agreement natural to these two functions of religion, the individual and the social, is still more direct and obvious in the sphere of Feeling than in that of Thought. I have already shown in Biology, how in all the races capable of social life, the predominance of those feelings which combine several individuals is also the best adapted to regulate each individual separately. The personal efficiency of every animal race, not adapted for social existence, can indeed only result from a full and habitual subordination of the nature to some self-regarding instinct. Hence moral harmony is with them ordinarily very imperfect and very uncertain, owing to the natural antagonism between the various selfish instincts, each of which requires imperatively to be gratified. True control over all the affections, to be complete and at the same time permanent, can only be formed, and certainly can only be developed, by the uniform subordination of all these personal feelings to the feelings which relate to society. This is the ground on which such a harmony is possible in its full measure to man alone.

Practically also, individual unity is dependent on social.

In the sphere of the activity the same connection between combining and regulating is a consequence of that tendency to converge, which we perceive both in the inclinations which determine our conduct and in the opinions which modify it. The activity of every social animal can only be maintained so long as it remains considerate towards others. With the races not capable of social life, action is always devoid of unity, and is too inconsistent to permit any real prevision. It is only capable of control, when the various instincts are concentrated into a single passion, and that is only possible in very inferior animals.

In its full form, Religion must co-ordinate individual and social life.

Now that the intimate connection between these two Functions of Religion has been established, we shall be free to employ in turn either one or the other to explain the unity of man. Their essential agreement is no doubt only fully developed under the final form of Positive Religion, towards which the highest members of the human family are gradually tending. During the transitional era of Theology one Function was supreme over the other, according as the prevalent belief was more or less social in its character. Polytheism was much more capable of combining than of regulating; whereas Monotheism only combined men so far as it succeeded in regulating their lives. Still these temporary differences only brought out into stronger light the natural agreement between the two functions of Religion; for each thus becomes the collateral support of the other.

This leading idea forms the starting-point of a general theory of Religion. It shows a natural agreement between the two permanent conditions which are equally characteristic of a state of harmony. It now becomes necessary to continue the task by one which is more difficult, and for which the ground is less prepared, namely the examination of the two conditions, the one external, the other internal, the complete harmony of which alone makes it possible to regulate or to combine.

To constitute any true religious state there must be a concurrence of two primary elements : the one, objective, and essentially intellectual; the other subjective, and essentially moral. Thus Religion exerts an influence at once over the understanding and the feelings, neither of which separately would suffice to establish a true unity either for individual or collective life. On the one hand it is requisite that our minds should conceive a Power without us, so superior to ourselves, as to command the complete submission of our entire life. But on the other hand, it is equally indispensable that our moral nature should be inspired within by one affection, capable of habitually combining all the rest. These two essential conditions naturally tend to work as one, since the sense of submission to a Power without, necessarily seconds the discipline of the moral nature within; and this in turn prepares the way for the spirit of submission.

ii. Conditions of Religion, pp. 11–17.

Religion implies an objective or intellectual, and a subjective or moral base of unity.

The extreme difficulty which the mental condition of modern times presents to unity, leads us frequently to suppose it possible only in the field of morals. It is, no doubt, only in the moral nature that any agreement at all is consistently sustained in the midst of the prevailing anarchy. But the too obvious imperfection of this as a basis of Order, public or private, is a very good proof of the inherent weakness of this principle by itself, either to combine or to regulate.

A moral base of unity is insufficient.

Even if the nature of the human brain permitted, more completely than it does, the supremacy of the higher instincts, still their constant ascendancy would not establish any true unity within us, especially in the sphere of action, without an objective basis without us, which the intellect only can supply. So long as this belief in an external Power remains incomplete

Our moral nature would be dissipated in aimless effort, if not subjected to external reality.

or unsteady, the loftiest emotions are no check against infinite extravagance and profound disagreement. What would be the consequence of supposing the life of man entirely independent of the external world? In this preposterous hypothesis not only would the activity of our race be at once deprived of any substantial object; but the benevolent emotions also would at the same time lose all character of consistency; and would ultimately be wasted in barren and aimless effusion.

(1) Intellectual condition.

Unity, individual or social, requires subjection to an external Power; for every organism depends for its life on its environment.

In order then to regulate or to combine mankind, Religion must in the first instance place man under the influence of some external Power, possessed of superiority so irresistible as to leave no sort of uncertainty about it. This great principle of social science is at bottom merely the full development of that primary notion of sound Biology—the necessary subordination of every Organism to the Environment in which it is placed. At the opening of the century this truth, of the close dependence of organism on environment, remained still completely misunderstood by the most eminent thinkers. Its gradual acceptance forms the principal advancement in science during our times, although till now it has not been viewed in a manner sufficiently systematic. For its right conception it should in the first place be confined to the Vegetative existence, the primary basis of all the higher types of life. Here it is impossible to mistake, that the continued operation of the surrounding conditions is in three ways indispensable to every being; first, in furnishing the materials of food, secondly in exciting the vital power, thirdly in regulating its exercise. Now the same external influences apply alike to the strictly Animal life, in which the powers of sensation and motion are equally determined by the force without. Lastly passing to the higher functions of man, we find them also equally dependent on the external world, either as supplying sustenance or stimulus, or as regulating the action of the brain. Thus, Man's Moral nature, besides that it rests upon the two lower functions of life, is no less than they are, directly under the limitations of the world without. A sound theory of Biology thus furnishes the Positive theory of Religion with a foundation wholly unassailable; for it proves the general necessity for the constant supremacy of an external Power as a condition of unity for man, even in his individual life.

(2) Moral conditions.

At the same time this reasoning drawn from Biology is

useful as proving, that the moral conditions required by the state of unity are of more importance than the intellectual. In fact the intellectual must be always more or less completely fulfilled in all races of animals, capable of comprehending the first conditions of their life. For the unvarying dependence of the being on its environment has nothing of an accidental character about it, and does not admit at any moment of the slightest doubt. This truth so completely forms part of the life of every organism, that it would require a greater intellectual effort to reject it than to acquiesce in it. Even in the human species the most presumptuous dreamer could never seriously go so far, as to deny in direct terms a subjection to the World without, by which his daily conduct is determined. On the other hand, the moral conditions of true unity, though not less indispensable than the intellectual conditions, are such as are by their very nature more liable to collapse. This moral nature indeed is so little an essential element of living beings, as to be absolutely wanting in a great number of races. Without doubt it is always found wherever there is a capacity for social existence. But as collective life can only be developed in a high form, in our own kind, it is only in man that Religion can control the feelings, in such a way as to lead to real action. Yet the requisite intellectual belief in a dominant Power may be distinctly seen in some of the higher animals. Thus though the importance of the moral unity is not less than that of intellectual, it presents greater difficulties to a scientific explanation ; and none in fact has been given by any school of theologians or metaphysicians.

The conditions of moral unity are more important and more difficult to reach than those of intellectual unity.

That we may understand this more clearly, let us for the moment recall the point of view which more or less prevailed, until the very recent period when biology sufficiently established, that the Benevolent Affections were a real part of human nature. On that assumption moral unity could only exist as the result of an egoistic principle. Now the utter inefficiency of any such influence as a regulating force has been sufficiently shown. The feeling of dependence on a Power without cannot really supply its place. However deep this conviction may be, it inspires at most an enforced resignation, if the Power without is one which obviously offers an insuperable resistance. But this painful moral condition is far removed from a true discipline of the feelings, which must always

Moral unity requires freedom for the life within, as well as the sense of Power over the life without.

be free, to possess real vitality. The difference is seen at once when we compare the moral condition of the dog in a domestic state with that of the lion in captivity. Although long experience inspires the wild brute with a passive sense of resignation, moral unity does not exist within him. He gives way in turn to impotent struggles and to ignoble torpor. On the other hand the moral life of the dog becomes direct and continuous, the moment that he has learnt to submit his egoistic cravings to his sympathetic instincts. The contrast is yet clearer between the ancient slave and the modern proletary. Although in material matters both present a personal existence, whether active or passive, nearly the same, the liberty of the workman renders him alone capable of true moral unity ; for it permits free action to his benevolent feelings. The bitterest circumstance of ancient slavery to all the higher spirits must have been the impossibility of living truly for others, all their tasks being compulsory, or at any rate supposed to be so. It is moreover evident, that an habitual belief in a subjection to an external Power, is far from sufficing to establish unity in man, although it is indispensable for it to a certain degree. For when this sense of dependence becomes too intense it prevents even the discipline of the affections, which is the result of the spontaneous action of the altruistic instincts. The happiness and the dignity of every animate being require therefore the constant action and reaction of an acknowledged external Power without, with free play for the Sympathetic Instincts within.

It maintains harmony with the intellectual unity through the spirit of veneration.

To complete our estimate of the second condition necessary to religion, its Moral unity, we must regard it as the principal means of establishing indispensable harmony with the first, or Intellectual unity. This is by its nature invariable, at least in all essential laws ; and thus the mutual agreement between them must in the main be due to the moral element, which alone can dispose the being to voluntary submission. We have hitherto not properly distinguished submission from a degrading servility, for want of a sound moral theory. Of the three organs of the brain devoted to the altruistic instincts, as we have seen in the former volume, the religious sentiment depends principally on the intermediate one, that of *Veneration*. This is the disposition which accords best with feelings of devotion towards a superior Power. But beside the vital reaction of this inter-

mediate organ upon the two extremes which surround it, these
also must share directly, although in a less degree, in originating that composite feeling of which Religion is the product.
In fact to make submission complete, *Affection* must unite
with respect; and this combination of feelings is indeed effected
spontaneously by the sense of gratitude, which has its origin in
the union of dependence and respect.   This relation at first
seems limited to the most special of the sympathetic instincts,
that which we especially call *Attachment*.   But it extends also
to the highest organ of the altruistic feelings, that of universal
Benevolence, on which the complete unity of the affections
more especially depends.   To this end it is enough, that the
same disposition be observed in the external Power, which
by its superiority demands our submission.   This similarity of
feeling between the external Power and those subject to its
influence has nothing of the fortuitous about it; it is a consequence of the thorough universality of the benefits conferred.
This is such that no one of the various beings whose submission is supposed can claim them for itself exclusively.   In the
second place the profound respect inspired by the Supreme
Power awakens also a mutual sentiment of benevolence, in all
who join in devotion to the same great Object.   This last characteristic again of the religious spirit leads us to comprehend
a further attribute of the external Power.   We must suppose in fact that the Supreme Power admits of a real attachment on our part, an idea which presumes in it a faculty by
which its natural Goodness controls the exercise of its Authority.
By this further condition of the religious state we get a more
complete union between its two principal conditions : Conviction
and Affection.   This existed very thoroughly in the earliest
form of human religion : but in later forms the desire of satisfying this want tended to retard the establishment of the final
phase of Unity, as will be hereafter explained.

Having thus completed our systematic analysis of the religious emotion we can better do justice to the sagacity, deep
although empirical as it was, which in spite of the difficulty of
his task guided the original author of the true theory of the brain.
Gall, when his genius led him to suppose the organ of veneration to be the proper seat of the religious instincts, fell into
important error only in that he regarded as simply moral, a
disposition which is in the same degree intellectual.   But this

Gall was right in making veneration the seat of Religion, wrong in regarding it as the sole seat.

philosophical misconception, though not of great importance in
Biology, leads in Sociology to immense aberration. By withdrawing attention from the objective base of human Unity, it
renders any real history of the entire range of Religion impossible; for it overlooks the unfailing source of all varieties
in Religion, that is, that we are ever modifying our views
respecting the order of the external World. The result is that
this vicious assumption leads us to regard as Absolute, conceptions
which are Relative by their very nature.

Religion is the combination of Love with Belief.

    The religious state, therefore, has for its basis the perma-
nent combination of two conditions equally essential—Love and
Belief; these, though profoundly distinct, must conspire to one
natural end. Each of them, beside that it is itself indispensable,
adds to the other an element, without which its complete efficacy would not be exerted. Such is the instability of our
cerebral organisation that Belief would not be perfect without
Love, however high might be the degree of demonstration
reached. But conversely the best heart would fail in due Love
for any external Power, whose very existence admitted of continual doubt. And thus, whilst Love stimulates Conviction by
overcoming pride, Conviction prepares the way for Love by
counselling submission.

It binds the nature of man within, and connects it with the Power with-out.

    These are, broadly, the respective parts which fall to the
feelings and to the reason in that supreme task of human skill—
the formation by a series of efforts, at first instinctive and then
systematic, of some principle of Unity to govern the active life of
man, individual or collective. Harmony in the moral sphere
results from the subjection of the egoistic to the altruistic
feelings; mental unity is derived from the predominance of an
external Order over us. On the one hand all our instincts are
concentrated under one Affection, which alone can reduce them
to order; on the other hand, all our ideas group themselves
round the contemplation of a Force external to us. At the
same time this Economy of external nature furnishes us with a
direct guide to Action, which consists in accepting this order of
nature with dignity, or in modifying it with wisdom. Our
being is thus knit together, within and without, by a complete
convergence both of the Feelings and of the Thoughts, towards
that Supreme Power which controls our Acts. At that point
there arises *Religion* in its true sense, that is, a complete
unity, whereby all the motives of conduct within us are reduced

to a common object, whilst our conduct as a whole submits
with freedom to the Necessity imposed by a power without.
The mere composition of this admirable word will henceforth
serve to suggest the leading idea of this theory ; it recalls the
fact of two states of unity in succession : the first, the combination of the powers within ; the second, the connection with the
Force without.   This is the issue in which terminates the grand
dualism of positive Thought between the organism and its environment ; or rather between Man and the World ; or, better
still, between Humanity and the Earth.

But in order to complete the fundamental conception of
Unity, we must further suppose that the state of harmony requires for its maintenance the continuous union of the two
principal elements, affective and speculative.   Now, notwithstanding their natural affinity, the harmonious action of Thought
and Feeling must often be disturbed by the tempests which
arise in the complicated system of human existence, individual
and collective.   Sometimes this goes so far as to change for a
time the natural state of coalition, into one of antagonism
more or less violent.   This struggle between the Intellect and
the Heart is the principal feature of all the great revolutions,
whether in the individual or in society.   The greatest of
these revolutions is specially distinguished by that unmeasured
anarchy, both mental and moral, which tortures the West of
Europe, since the irrevocable collapse of the last provisional
system.   Thus the natural co-operation of Love with Faith
does not effect a complete equilibrium, but a state of continuous
movement, tending ever by the law of its action to a better
union.   The degree of completeness, to which by successive
steps this combination of the elements of our nature may be
brought, will be treated in this work as the chief measure of
perfection attained by man.   Human nature then, individual
as well as collective, tends to grow more and more religious,
however strange such a law may seem to our present ideas.

Man grows more and more religious.

Having now sufficiently examined first, the twofold Function
of Religion, secondly the two Conditions which united form its
Basis, to complete the theory of Religion in the abstract, it
remains to define the leading Elements of which it is composed.

iii.—The Elements of Reli- gion, pp. 17–20.

The consti- tuent parts of Religion are :—

The third branch of the inquiry into Religion, to analyse
its Elements, has fewer difficulties than the second, to deter-

1. A dogma or intellec- tual part.

mine its Conditions; and follows from it. Since Religion deals
at once with the Intellect and the Heart, it must always consist of an intellectual part, and of a moral part. The former
constitutes the *dogma*, properly so called, which explains the
aggregate of that external Order to which our unity is necessarily subordinate. In accordance with the principle of classification by means of increasing dependence, this order of nature
will require explanation, first by Cosmology, then by Biology,
lastly by Sociology. The Supreme Power is thus sufficiently
manifested by this ascending series of conceptions; and we
proceed in due course from the first portion of Religion to the
second, and follow the same cardinal rule of progression from
the World Without to that Within. The Intellect having been
reduced to order, order must be established also in the Heart.
From the reign of Faith we pass to that of Love. Such at
least is the chain of systematic reasoning by which Philosophy
would constitute a final state of human unity, collective and
social. Still in Society, as with each one of us, the ordinary
and spontaneous course of development is the reverse. Naturally, we proceed from the internal to the external, from Love
to Faith.

The intellec-
tual part of
Religion is
single, the
moral is
double.

Without stopping to consider the difference between these,
the objective and the subjective methods, we may note that,
the two essential portions of Religion remain always widely distinguished. The only proper subdivisions of Doctrine are due
to the succession, both in logic and in science, of the three
grand stages of Philosophy, Cosmology, Biology, and Sociology.
But indispensable though these be for purposes of classification,
we must never lose sight of the fundamental Unity of the
whole Economy of Nature, which Religion comprehends always
as a whole. This is not the same with the moral part of Religion, in which the radical distinction between feelings and acts
requires a separation of the component Elements.

The moral
part of Reli-
gion deals
with feelings
as well as
acts, hence
2. *worship*
and 3.
government.

Love must alike control Feelings and influence Acts. But
these two direct duties of the governing Principle of life must
not be confounded ; since the former relates only to the internal,
the latter relates also to the external World. In their widest
extension these two functions furnish Religion, the first, with its
worship properly speaking,—the second, with its *government*,
moral as well as political. Viewing Religion as a whole, both
are necessarily subordinate to the *doctrine* which supplies them

at once with the conditions and the laws by which Worship must control the feelings and Government the conduct private and public.   Nevertheless in its turn Affection, with its two-fold domain, reacts powerfully upon Conviction, with its single domain ; and ever recalls Thought to the subjective end, which its objective spirit is constantly forgetting.

Such, systematically viewed, are the constituent parts of Religion, which, undertaking to reduce human life to unity, brings within its sphere the three chief sides of our nature, Thought, Feeling, Action.   In commencing with the first it is especially objective ; the second is mainly subjective ; the last partakes equally of both characters.   This progression of ideas from the external to the internal, serves as a crucial example of true scientific classification.   The Doctrine thus forms the ground-work for the Worship, and the Worship for the Government.   This, the natural arrangement of the three elements, shows the propriety of the universal rule that a religion must be characterised by its worship.   The worship, which holds a middle place, is dependent on the doctrine, and instrumental to the government, and thus is entitled in principle to represent them both.   Taking the worship and the government together we have the true twofold division of Religion into the sphere of Faith and that of Love.   Taking, on the other hand, the worship with the doctrine, we have another combination, that of the theoretic element and of the practical element. Although the latter analysis of Religion is in accordance with the custom of instruction, the former analysis is much more valuable for purposes of teaching.   The principal practical distinction is due to the fact that human action, individual or collective, relates sometimes to our external condition ; sometimes to our own physical, intellectual, or moral, nature.   Now this threefold internal sphere, the human, the necessary object of our highest activity, is the special field of Worship understood in its fullest sense.   If we are to regard Religion as composed of two elements only, we must therefore take it as a combination of Worship and Government.   The other combination of Worship with Doctrine has been mentioned only to bring out more clearly the natural fitness of the second element of Religion, the Worship, to represent both.   But the analysis which I finally choose as the best to express the true series of parts, is that which makes Religion to consist of

Thus the elements of Religion are three : Doctrine, Worship, and Government.

c 2

three essential elements, Doctrine, Worship, and Government.
Thus Religion in its complete form, resumes in itself the
entirety of man's real existence, and is equally scientific,
æsthetic, and practical. It thus combines in their sources the
three great creations of man, philosophy, poetry, and politics.
This universal Synthesis begins by giving system to the study
of the True; next it idealises the instinct for the Beautiful;
and finally it realises the attainment of the Good.

NORMAL
TYPE OF
UNITY, pp.
20–70.
The chief
task is to as-
certain the
character of
human
Unity.

This completes the Theory of Religion in the abstract, its
Function, its Nature, and its component Elements having each
been duly considered. But the great subject of Religion will
hardly be sufficiently worked out, unless by an explanation
of the general Character of the true unity. Taking the
three orders of ideas together, we shall be in a position to show,
what is the synthetic method best adapted to attain the double
End of religion, to supply its two primary Conditions, and to
develop all its essential Elements. This task naturally forms
the leading purpose of the present chapter, which will serve as
a basis common to all subsequent inquiries into the problems
of society. My preceding remarks are designed only to secure
a systematic basis for this all-important construction.

And this
must be ac-
companied
by the his-
tory of its
gradual rea-
lisation.

The importance and the difficulty of this scientific demonstration appear more strongly, when we see that even this
would be insufficient without a justification from history. The
true Religion could not have come into existence without a preparation of vast length, scarcely yet concluded even amongst
the first of the nations. The principle which governs the final
state of Synthesis would be but very imperfectly defined, unless
we were to follow up our direct analysis of it, by a general sketch
of the provisional phases, which prepared the way for the
complete attainment of Unity.

This sketch
of the type,
and of the
history of
Unity will
not interfere
with the sub-
jects of the
two follow-
ing volumes.

At first sight it might appear that this double method of inquiry trenches upon the subjects of the two volumes which are
to succeed :—one of which will embrace the actual course of the
development of mankind, the other the true character of the
final system. Further consideration, however, will show that
this is quite in accordance with the regular connection of the
various branches of Sociology, as stated in the Introduction to
this volume, and in the whole of the General View. What I
am about to do, is only to give special importance, in this the
chief statical theory, to the law stated therein, the law of

constant subordination of the study of Progress to that of Order. The evolution of man can result only from the continuous development of the fundamental organism—Humanity, and this may be defined in the natural type, assumed, in the first instance, to be complete. Thus a statical treatment of the subject will serve as an universal basis for the dynamical explanation reserved for the third volume ; wherein will be drawn out the necessary course of progress, through which the human race had to pass in its path to Unity. The same is true of the relation of this volume to the concluding volume. In fact the Future of mankind can only exhibit the state of Order most conformable to our nature, the germ of which was contained in the earliest state. | This is therefore the place to consider the general Character of the final system ; whilst my fourth volume will treat its ultimate expansion, upon the termination of my volume upon History, or its indispensable preparation.

This outline of the plan of this work will I hope show that the course adopted does not involve any real repetition. The method, which I am here employing for Religion, will be followed in the consideration of all the essential elements of the social system, such as the Family, Language, &c., the subjects of the following chapters. Each of these will be treated here, with reference first to the general Elements of its fundamental constitution, secondly to the gradations necessary for its complete realisation. The next two volumes will treat, the one the actual course which this Development has taken, the other, the normal Type which that development will finally assume. Thus the statical basis I now commence, will facilitate the working out of both these subjects, though it will not render them superfluous. *In this work each element of society will be treated separately.*

This distinction in method is lastly, to reduce it to system, an illustration of the contrast between the concrete and the abstract, which, far from being absolute, admits of various degrees. In this volume each essential Element of the great organism is studied separately from the rest, first in its own nature, and then in its historical development. On the other hand in social Dynamics, the study will always be concerned with the whole of these different elements together, so as to show first their general evolution, and then their ultimate harmony. Thus all the leading subjects of the social science will be treated, first separately without reference to time, *This method illustrates the contrast between abstract and concrete.*

secondly in combination and in order of succession. The treatise when complete will have considered Society, first as existing in space, then as existing in time; but so as not to involve the errors either of repetition or of anticipation. This great principle of logic applies to every case where the statical study can be contrasted with the dynamical. It bears a strong analogy to the relation drawn by Bichat, between the primary theory of the Organism, and the direct theory of Life. The constant use of this method, which in subsequent chapters does not require to be justified, will give no serious difficulty to readers who are duly prepared. Abstract Anatomy, when treating of the vital properties of the various tissues and the evolution of each, is not encroaching on the proper sphere of Physiology; where the tissues are treated only, as combined in organs properly so called. In the same way, in social Statics the study in the abstract, of the existence of each primary element, and its development as a whole, leaves to social Dynamics its special task, that of combining into a whole these various conceptions, and thereby determining the character of the successive phases of Humanity.

Special purpose of this chapter. Having explained the method here adopted, and it will be regularly used for the future in all similar cases, I proceed to the special purpose of this chapter, which will be to establish in the first place, the highest Type of the social union, secondly, to describe the immense course of Preparation required for it.

The highest type of Synthesis principally concerned with the basis of Religion. Of the three classes of abstract notions above stated, the Purpose, the Basis, and the Elements, of Religion, we have now to treat mainly of the second. For it is only the intellectual and moral conditions of the religious state, which are susceptible of great and immediate variations. Thus in order to establish a sound principle of Unity, we must in the first place secure this intellectual and moral Basis; and then its reaction on the other two becomes very important. When the state of harmony best adapted to the nature and the position of Humanity has been determined, it will be time to consider the natural tendency this harmony has, to exhibit in its highest form the true Purpose of religion, and to develop all its general Elements.

Belief is affected by the Outer world directly; affection indirectly. Each of the two component parts which form the Basis of the union of mankind, is directly subject to important modifications, the progress of which, as seen in man's history, exhibits nothing arbitrary. The law which governs all these changes is that which is common to all other forms of evolution ; it consists in the gradual development of the essential principle of the movement—which in morals, is the governing Instinct, in the intellect, is the Belief giving harmony to the ideas. Here however we meet with a radical difference between Affection and Belief, as indeed the cerebral theory established in the preceding volume might indicate. This arises in the following manner. Since Belief refers to some objective foundation, all its necessary modifications are due directly to increased precision in knowledge of the Order of the external world. On the other hand, the subjective impulses are not directly influenced by the increasing knowledge of the world without ; for the emotional organs of the brain are not properly speaking in relation with the outer world at all. The feelings, it is true, tend of their own nature to greater fulness, but their natural expansion requires invariably some external impulse. This can only reach them through the medium of the other two regions of the brain. Consequently all normal modifications of Feeling are the result of the twofold reaction, exercised upon it, first by the Intelligence, and then by the Activity ; whilst it supplies both Intelligence and Activity with constant stimulus. Hence it arises that the external World produces radical modifications in the Affections, although without any direct relation with them. It stimulates some and restrains others, as the speculative or practical condition of man calls out opinions or actions. Thus the Environment constitutes the great regulator of the human Organism ; even in that emotional part of cerebral function, which has no immediate relation with the outer world.

Although our instincts are permanent by their very nature, yet their active development is subject to regular variations in accordance with the progress to be traced in our conceptions and our undertakings. But both conceptions and undertakings tend more and more to conform to the Order without, which is the constant object of our contemplation and of our activity. This is the reason that this Order, which is independent of us, has a twofold part in the regulation of our Instincts ; on the one hand, by stimulating them through the ideas which it supplies, on the other hand, exercising them to make the efforts it involves. It is true that this double external influence is

Moral Progress is determined by the variations in thought and activity.

not the sole source of the biological changes to which the instincts are subject.   The instincts are, besides, affected by the internal impressions conveyed to them through the nutritive viscera, with which they are connected by nerves, according to the general principle already shown in my theory of the brain. But this latter class of modifications of the affections, although very important in the special study of each individual life, remains quite secondary in Sociology, because variations, due to the internal structure of individuals, neutralise each other in the mass.   The external influences only are sufficiently continuous and sufficiently general to produce any great reaction on our social feelings; and accordingly these become more and more bent in conformity to the Order without, which serves them both for an end of Action, and an object of Thought. It thus happens, nor is it merely accidental, that the chief instrument, by which Feeling is modified, is that External influence, which we are best able to study; provided always that we are not pushing our Positive study of Humanity, to enter upon the subordinate career of each individual human being.

The Unity of man within can only arise by submission to an Order without.

Thus, in the true theory of the moral nature, the External Order tends more and more to regulate, not only the progress followed by our intellectual and practical Activity, but the effective development of the Feelings as well.   Hence it is, that the different phases of the unity of mankind in Religion are principally determined by the prevalent belief for the time, respecting this Economy without, which thus dominates our life.   Notwithstanding the slight direct influence of the intellect over the collective system of the brain, yet it is the intellect, which in the end determines the Character of Religion for the individual, and still more for the race, at each phase of our development.   Whilst giving us a truer knowledge of this order of nature, Reason modifies more and more not only the Activity, but the Feelings.   Man reaches more and more fully the state of real synthesis, as he more thoroughly recognises the intellectual, and ultimately the moral, control exercised by the external Order; the effect of which seems limited at first exclusively to practical life.   Since the preponderating influence of this Order is irresistible in all that relates to the Activity, no real Unity could ever be established in human nature, unless our Beliefs and even our Instincts were capable of submitting

to it also. The best mode of producing harmony of all the
faculties, or rather the only mode which is complete and will
be permanent, consists in extending first to the Intellect, then
to the Feelings, that principle of regulation by reference to the
World, which necessarily never ceases to direct the Activity.
Until this essential harmony between the faculties is realised,
Religion must prove insufficient. For the three co-ordinate
forces in human life will remain under the direction of principles, which differ, and often are at variance.   In an organism
so complex as the individual man, and still more the collective
Humanity, entire consensus between all the faculties of life
can only be established, through the subordination of all, to
the uniform influence of an Order external to them : which
shall be simpler than they are, and consequently more regular.
In a word, the great difficulty for Religion is, to provide
that the external Order of the world shall regulate the internal Order of human nature, without interfering with its free
action.

To understand how these two ends can be reconciled, we
must do more than explain the general relation of the external
Order to the three essential Elements of human life. We must
proceed to analyse this Order from the religious point of view,
conceiving it in the first place, as the Basis of submission, in
the second as the End of our activity, lastly as an Object of
affection. This distinction follows directly from my Classification of the Sciences, which requires us first, to study natural
laws inaccessible to our control ; secondly, those which admit of
modification ; lastly, regarded as phenomena of human nature.
The Order of nature cannot establish an influence upon men
of a truly religious character unless it embraces equally these
three orders of phenomena. This only will enable the Affections and the Belief to combine in constant unison with the
Activity ; and thus to establish a condition of complete and
universal Harmony.

Analysis of Laws of the External World.

The whole religious influence of the external Order rests
primarily upon the character of invariability, peculiar to its
several essential conditions, conditions which are wholly independent of us, even where they concern us directly. The constant need of such a regulating force is as yet only thoroughly
felt with respect to our practical life, which would be consumed in vague efforts and indiscriminate activity, unless there

*Both intel-
lect and ac-
tivity need
external li-
mitation.*

existed insurmountable obstacles to form some limits to our schemes. Nor is some such external Power less necessary to the intellect, which would lose itself in an endless play of fancy, unless it were confined within due restrictions.

Hypothesis of an unintelligible solar system.

This need of conforming our Acts and our Thoughts to a Necessity without us, far from hampering the real development of our nature, forms the first general condition of progress towards perfection in man. We shall see what this influence is in a very striking manner, if we suppose the earth to possess an astronomical condition, such as to produce extreme irregularity in its natural order. We need not extend the assumption so far as to suppose for the earth's orbit something similar to that of comets, especially those of quick recurrence ; for in such an orbit all real life, even the merely vegetative, would be rendered impossible, the variations being too extensive and too rapid. Without having recourse to this violent hypothesis, we can easily imagine perturbations which, though they would not render our existence impossible, would prevent us from arriving at any adequate knowledge of the essential Order of our system. Such a result would follow, for instance, from a great multiplicity of planets, almost circular in orbit, very near in position, and almost equal in mass. In that case the entire development of man would be checked by conditions without, from the want of some objective Basis ; whereby alone we can obtain the requisite fixity for our Conceptions, or for our Efforts.

External limitation is still more necessary for moral life.

But the religious influence exercised over man by the Order of nature is still more important, and at the same time less understood, when we turn to the Feelings, than it is, even with the Reason and the Activity. It is through this agency that Belief begins to combine directly with Affection so as to subdue our egoism. In the first place, the compulsory submission, imposed by this external fatality, much assists the spontaneous expansion of the sympathetic instincts, by the check which it places on the whole of the personal desires. Pride and vanity are brought within the scope of this discipline, even in respect to our intellectual creations, which are ever subordinated to this independent power. This universal restraint on man forms in every respect the first Basis of a durable Morality, by forcing us to seek without ourselves the sources of our own actions and conduct ; for that visionary independence, of which metaphysicians dream in their pride, would only lead, if it could be realised, to an incurable assertion of the personal instincts. In the second place this constant external Necessity is just as useful to combine bodies of men, as it is to regulate the individual. As it controls all alike, it tends to unite, in spite of themselves, all who are beneath its sway. It thus fosters in them the dispositions which bring men together, as much as it suppresses in them those, which put men asunder. Mutual union offers itself to each as his principal resource against the Destiny without. Now this spirit of cooperation so induced, never remains strictly confined to passive endurance, even in a case where the external Order remains wholly beyond our influence, as it would be in the hypothesis just made. For in the most irresistible pressure of external circumstances, every living being retains a certain capacity to submit to them, in such a way as to mitigate their force. Even in death an animal so disposes itself as to suffer as little as possible. A great portion of the industry of mankind is directly devoted to enable us satisfactorily to meet laws, which we have no power to modify, as those of the hours, seasons, and climates, all of which call out a continuous exertion of our collective power of action. It cannot indeed be said, that this double influence of the external fatality upon the emotions, can supply the place of a direct appeal to the affections. It does however much assist the special development of the sympathetic instincts ; and I shall have shortly to explain the deep bond of union between these instincts and the full conception of the universal Order of nature.

The existence of an immutable Order is therefore the primary foundation of true Religion, whether in a sponta- neous or a systematic form. This fundamental doctrine, with- out which unity would be impossible to man, must be regarded as the most precious result of our intelligence ; the mind finding Without the only solid ground which can apply to the whole of our nature, individual or collective. The Positive theory of Religion must therefore thoroughly expound a conception which is at once objective and subjective ; which brings into final system the great dualism current throughout all philosophy, and which irrevocably unites Man and the World.

That this Order of nature is a truly objective reality will

An immutable Order is the basis of Religion.

This exter- nal Order is

really objec-
tive.

hardly now be disputed by any thinker. The astronomical hypothesis just employed would of itself prove this fact, as it will serve to show how completely this fundamental notion rests upon external conditions. We can imagine the Order of nature subject to such variations, as to be utterly inexplicable even to minds superior to ours. There is nothing to hinder the supposition of worlds outside of our solar system, totally involved in an agitation of their inorganic substance, without any order at all, to the exclusion even of any general law of weight. Such an extreme supposition should assist us in clearing from the mind the Absolute theories to which it clings so presumptuously, and teach us to recognise how thoroughly Relative is the actual order of nature. At the same time, even if it were actually peculiar to our own world, this would be far from a fortuitous accident there ; since it forms the first condition of our human life. Elaborate investigation shows that this correspondence between our planet and its inhabitants is definite enough, to permit us to say, what must be some of the astronomical arrangements of the earth, as was shown in my previous work on Positive Philosophy.

But our in-
tellect re-
acts on our
conception
of it.

Although the main source of Positive Doctrine, the World, is wholly independent of us, our intelligence directly exercises an influence over the several stages of the formation of Doctrine. In the first place this great notion requires a mind to observe, just as much as a world which may be observed ; and this Kant clearly perceived. For instance, the internal system of the moon is unknown from want of observers ; and we on this earth can only form some vague conjectures about it. On our own planet races of low intelligence are profoundly ignorant of that Order which we see with admiration, and of which they barely gather by experience a few practical details. Secondly, man never remains wholly passive in this work of observation ; it is necessarily modified by the whole of our cerebral system. Nor is this inevitably subjective character of our observations due simply to the power of the emotions or of the activity. The latter in the case before us, as in others, gives to our habitual acts of reasoning, one the motive, the other the end. An influence both more direct and closer arises from this, that our mental activity itself blends its own ideas with the impressions it receives from without ; and thus gives a constant colour to the final result of observation. The organ of comparison in the brain is always looking out for analogies on which to build hypotheses, and with these the organ of co-ordination is always striving after the construction of systems.   Now this tendency of the brain cannot fail to affect the completed notion ; and thus the Conceptions which we form about nature are generally more regular than the external Order they represent.

This notion, that our Belief respecting the Order of nature is to a minor degree subjective, has been much exaggerated by some who pretend to be successors of Kant, and has been carried by some narrow thinkers into an idealism, which is as injurious to morality as it is erroneous in philosophy.   It has led them unconsciously to set up the purely personal existence as the type, and dogmatically to discard any notion of collective life.   Thus the very spirit most adapted to produce a Relative view of philosophy, the study of the various cerebral conditions which all real conceptions imply, is made an instrument of retrogression towards the Absolute.   On the other hand the mere savants, especially mathematicians, from the want of an encyclopædic training, often fall into the very opposite confusion ; when in their turn they exaggerate the objective independence of the Order we perceive in nature.

Our conception of Nature is neither purely subjective, nor purely objective.

Sound philosophy advances with firm foot in a course between these two pitfalls.   It regards all laws of nature as constructed by our minds, out of materials drawn from without.   Objectively considered their resemblance to the reality can never be more than approximative.   But since these laws are needed only to supply our human wants, especially those of the activity, these approximations become amply sufficient, when directed from the point of view of those practical needs, which regularly decide the due measure of exactness required.   Beyond this general measure of precision there is frequently a proper sphere for freedom of speculation, which we can use with wisdom as a means of satisfying our merely intellectual cravings, first of the scientific, then of the artistic order.   In the simplest and best elaborated of all the laws of nature, mathematicians unconsciously apply in many instances this useful method, in order to give the requisite perfection to their leading notions.   For instance they extend this conception of logical precision in order to give to abstract formulæ a character of universality, indispensable for the advance of mathematical speculations ; although at the same time the actual order of nature would

Objectively considered, our laws of Nature are only approximative.

constantly belie that universality if it were carried into too
rigorous application.   Thus we cannot assert that Newton's law
of gravitation does of necessity apply to all possible distances,
any more than we can assert that the law of Mariotte applies
to all possible forms of pressure.   Yet these furnish the appropriate foundation, the one of celestial mechanics, the other of
the mathematical theory of gases.   Unless we could suppose
them thus universally applicable their value as scientific instruments would be extremely slight.

In all con-
ceptions of
laws of Na-
ture there
remains
some subjec-
tive element. Our fundamental conceptions about the order of Nature are
thus the product of a collaboration, between the World without
and the Mind within us.   Laws of nature, that is general
facts, are nothing but hypotheses duly confirmed by observation.
If there did not exist any real harmony without us, our minds
would be wholly unable to conceive it ; but in no case can that
harmony be verified up to the degree which we suppose.   In
this continuous process of cooperation, the world supplies the
matter, and man the form, of every positive idea.   Now the
fusion of these two elements is not possible unless by mutual
sacrifices.   An excessive tendency towards the objective element would prevent any generalisation, which is always based
upon abstraction.   But that analytic spirit which enables us to
form abstract ideas, would be impossible to us, unless we could
suppress the natural excess of subjectivity.   Every man, comparing his ideas with those of others, spontaneously drops from
his observations of himself what is strictly personal peculiarity, in order to reach that accordance between mind and
mind, which is the main function of the contemplative spirit.
But the amount of the subjective element which is common to
the whole human race is ordinarily not eliminated ; nor is its
presence usually accompanied by any serious inconvenience.
We could not reduce it in amount, except by intellectual intercourse with other animals ; this we can rarely resort to,
and then only for subordinate ideas.   Besides, whatever limitations we might impose on the subjective element under a
growing desire to find a ground common to understandings
very different from man's, still our conceptions would never
attain to a pure objectivity.   It would therefore be as impossible, as it would be useless, to determine the exact degree, in
which the External and the Internal respectively contribute to
the formation of our scientific conceptions.

This view of the formation of philosophical ideas amply explains the immense difficulty, which attended the discovery of the laws of the universal Order of nature, a knowledge yet hardly attained fully, even by most eminent thinkers. If this order were completely objective or purely subjective, it would have been long since seized by our observations, or would have arisen from our conceptions. But to grasp it required the joint action of two influences, heterogeneous in nature, though inseparable in result, the combination of which could only be a work of slow development. The various ultimate laws, which compose the scheme of that conception, form a Scale of Nature, in which each branch rests on the preceding, in the order of its decreasing generality and its increasing complexity. Hence a sound comprehension of them could only be obtained step by step. Yet their value in Religion is not truly felt, until they come to embrace those facts, which stand lowest in the series in point of generality, and highest in that of complexity, for these alone can give us any truly universal conceptions. *The Order of Nature could only be understood by successive stages.*

In order to show better the nature and the difficulty of the task of construction thus presented to the mind, I must here point only to three classes of laws, those which relate to the three great functions of man, Affection, Action, and Thought. The most subjective sphere embraces the moral laws, whilst the physical laws form the most objective sphere. Between these two extremes, the intellectual laws form at once the proper connection, and the proper distinction ; for whilst their purpose is objective, their source is subjective. *Moral, physical, and intellectual laws,*

It is certain that the first spontaneous conception of these laws arose with the earliest efforts of the human mind, and were indeed called out by the various wants to which they administer. Although the most complex of all, the Moral laws in the earliest stages of civilisation engross the principal attention ; because they relate directly to the main necessities of man, and are closely connected with the two arts which are then of most importance, that of war and that of government. In all the poetic records of primitive societies, a very considerable empirical knowledge of these Moral laws has been shown to be obtained, whilst the Order of the material universe remains wholly unknown. Yet withal, a knowledge so unsystematic could not provide any permanent Basis of thought, because it *1. Moral laws come first in time, but intellectual laws come first in importance.*

treated the Moral laws independently of the Physical laws, on which they are necessarily dependent. Accordingly the cultivation of these physical laws, in unison with the exercise of the activity, forms the only possible ground of a really scientific course of human development. Hence the decisive construction of Positive Doctrine can only be commenced by the settlement of physical laws, especially mathematical, which are the most completely independent. But this systematisation of the conceptions will never lead to any really religious effect until it is extended to the sphere of Moral laws, which alone directly determine our entire life. Until this sacred task is accomplished, the discovery of the material laws is destined to have but a limited result, that of regulating the Activity. Now the Physical laws do not admit of any systematic connection with the Moral laws. This relation on which so much depends, can only be established by the intervention of the Intellectual laws, which alone are equally connected with the two extremes. This is the reason that ultimately the religious construction as a whole must be mainly determined by the mental laws; though the direct influence of the Intellectual laws is certainly less than that of either the Physical, or the Moral.

2. Intellectual laws can only be learned from society, and are therefore the latest. An empirical conception of the intellectual laws necessarily exists, along with that of the other two orders of law. We can never suppose that the faculty from which we derive all our knowledge of laws either within or without us, was ever regarded as having no laws of its own. The traces of the laws in our mental constitution are found in the least of our discoveries physical or moral; since but for laws of mind, none would be possible. But the scientific understanding of this mental constitution offers more difficulties than either that of the material world, or of our moral nature; because it rests in reality upon the gradual progress of the entire race. The life of the individual gives us enough means of perceiving the main Moral laws by themselves; although they appear at first sight devoid of any connection. On the contrary the progress of the intellect is not perceptible in individual life in so marked a manner as to enable the leading Intellectual laws to be directly studied in individuals. These can only be seen unmistakably in the entire series of the phases through which the mind of Humanity has passed. This important discovery requires therefore that Positive Doctrine should be extended to the social sphere; and

in so doing it is led to form itself completely, and necessarily takes in the moral laws. Thus the establishment of the laws of mind must nearly coincide with that of true Religion.

The principal difficulty, therefore, in the formation of the Positive Doctrine consists in the regular succession of several great phases of thought or sciences; each of which depends on the preceding, and yet they only produce a religious influence when combined in one whole. Each of these successive sciences requires its own special inductions; but they cannot be reduced to a system except by the deductive method called out by all the less complex sciences. Were it not for this natural series, conforming to the mode in which phenomena depend on each other, the laws of nature would be not less incoherent than irrational. When ranged in this classification, the sciences lowest in the scale communicate to those above them that character of regularity and fixity, which is due to their simplicity, whilst they receive down from those above them the dignity, which belongs to those of a higher rank. The religious influence of a Philosophy of Reality arises from this action and reaction between the different elements that compose it. These are the conditions indispensable to a true conviction of the fundamental fixity of the order of the universe. The best type of it is found in the celestial phenomena, for they alone are removed from any interference from man.

The religious effect of these laws depends on their inter-dependence

Notwithstanding, however, that this notion of invariable Order is ever the dominant principle, the Positive Doctrine must also keep in view the natural modifications, to which the Economy of nature is almost constantly exposed. Rightly to understand them, we must recognise from the first that they present nothing fortuitous. These variations follow in fact directly from the general Scale of phenomena, in which each series modifies all those which dominate it. Indeed the universal harmony of nature is dependent no less, upon the reaction exercised by the lower over the superior phenomena, than upon the empire maintained by the superior over the lower. There can be no doubt that total anarchy would ensue, if the special phenomena were not subordinated to the more general. But inversely, were it not for the modifications exerted by the special over the general, all facts would be involved in one indistinguishable sameness. The true distinction between the great Categories of Natural phenomena primarily depends upon

The idea of variation is just as necessary as that of Law.

this necessary reaction of the one order upon the other; and were it not for this reaction, we should have nothing but the most simple laws by themselves. We must therefore conceive the Order of nature as being equally removed from chaos as from anarchy; or in another light, as involving at once both Movement and Fixity. Such at least is the only way in which we can conceive of Order, in any world which admits of Life; and no other case is worthy of examination.

Reaction between Life and Nature.
In fact, the conception of the Order of nature, as being capable of modification in a greater or less degree, is the immediate result of the great dualism, which pervades philosophy, between Living and Inanimate nature. In the first place every living being, though it be limited to a mere vegetative existence, is constantly modifying the environment on which it depends, through the substances which it consumes, and the products which it gives off. Besides, it modifies itself, in order to accommodate its condition to its situation. This twofold power of modification increases, in the degree that the being rises in the scale of life, and becomes more highly developed. Now it is important to notice, that the living being does not produce in the environment, this capacity to receive the requisite modifications. It confines itself to turning this capacity to account. Unless the environment were previously capable of modification in itself, the reaction arising from a force so feeble, as that of the vital power necessarily is, would not succeed in changing the constitution of the medium around it. Again the changes to which the material world is subject, from the mere conflict of the inorganic Forces, are often far greater than all those which come from living Beings. The only part therefore of these beings, is to give to the world without, the impulse which sets in operation a property of matter, necessary to their very existence. But the only proper use, to which this capacity for modification in matter can be devoted, is simply to maintain this relation between the material World and living Beings. Although we cannot conceive Life existing in a sphere which is not capable of Modification, we can readily imagine a sphere of such a kind, provided nothing be supposed to live there, as in some of the uninhabitable planets. The normal capacity for modification, which the material World presents, is therefore intimately connected with the existence of Life; though it is not the product of Life.

Hence the conception of Life alone can found any systematic theory of the changes of Nature, even in the mere inorganic world.   Thus the idea of Order gives birth to that of Progress, of which as I showed in the last chapter of the preceding volume, vitality is always a necessary condition.   Without the reaction continually produced upon an environment, capable of modification by the influence of life, the native power of change in matter would lead to no regular result; and would manifest nothing but fortuitous effort.   It would exhibit change but not Progress.   Progress implies a gradual amelioration of some fundamental Order, by a series of modifications gradually tending to the completion of one design.   Now such a definition of Progress supposes the influence of Life in two ways; it forms at once the indispensable stimulus of the action, and at the same time supplies it with a natural purpose.   Vegetation alone has proved able to establish Progress for the Material substance of our earth; for it has sufficed to modify considerably the solid crust, and the fluid envelope of the planet.   But this influence over matter has been much developed by the Animal kingdom; for in this case, the effect exercised by living beings gains the further stimulus of intelligence and activity.   Its full force is accordingly reserved for Humanity; which, bringing into play far higher capacities, has given to their exercise an extent, and a permanence, which nothing else could have produced.

Progress implies the presence of Life.

We thus see that a sound conception of the Order of nature implies a secondary idea of Variability, as well as the primary idea of Immutability.   It is only in the simplest and the most general of phenomena, that the material World is really incapable of alteration; in those which form the mathematical and astronomical basis of the entire system of nature.   We must observe that even this Fixity is anything but absolute; and results mainly from our position, or the force we possess. We can easily conceive large Modifications in the astronomical condition of the earth, although our material means must always remain insufficient to realise them.   With other celestial bodies these changes are clear beyond question, particularly in the comets, in which physical and chemical laws much affect their planetary condition.   The continual resistance of the entire environment of our system would alone produce gradual changes in it; changes which must ultimately become very considerable at a period certainly remote.   But, although

Variability is as essential as Fixity to our notion of Nature.

we must sometimes fix the attention on this mutability of the celestial system, by which the relative spirit will be much promoted, we must be careful not to attach habitually too great importance to it. For these vast changes in the solar system have not the slightest bearing upon our real future. They will be still very trifling in man's planet, long after the combined effect of the various laws of nature has swept from off its face the highest Type of Progress. We should regard therefore our astronomical condition as not liable to change, during the whole period which we can conceive as possible for the life of the Great Being. Although this general belief in the permanence of our planet is by no means indispensable to our conduct, either individually or collectively, it tends to strengthen the essential fixity of our positive notions, even respecting the higher phenomena. I have only remarked on the want of complete immutability in the celestial order, in order to remove that idea of Chance, which robs our conception of the Variable in nature of much of its philosophical value. The true notion of Progress is, from many reasons, much more recent and more imperfect than that of Order. What is needed henceforth is to establish a precise harmony between these two ideas, either of which requires and implies the other.

Variability increases with the higher scale of Life.

Adequately to represent how essentially modifiable, is the Economy of nature, it must be remembered that the higher are the phenomena, the more completely they are liable to change. There is nothing strictly immutable but the Order of the heavens. The chief of inorganic existences, the Earth, admits of large modifications, which are chemically indispensable to the vitality of living beings. All the phenomena of Life are in a yet higher degree capable of alteration, even in their mere material functions. This natural capacity for change increases incessantly in proportion as a higher form of life is studied; taking first physical life, then intellectual, lastly moral life. The idea of Modification, as an inherent attribute of the Order of nature, is so intimately connected with the idea of Life, that our conceptions of that Modification develop, precisely in proportion as we mount in the Scale of Life.

Religious value of law of Variability.

Now that I have explained, as we find it, the inherent tendency towards Change in the Order of nature, I proceed to point out its special religious value, and the influence which it

exerc⁚ses successively over the Reason, the Activity, and the
Feelings.

These spontaneous Modifications of the Order of nature,
create the first great difficulty which meets the understanding,
in its attempt to reduce all thought to a complete system. We
have in fact to combine this idea of Change, with that of
essential Immutability, with which it appears to conflict. It is
owing to this opposition, that all systematic notions of the economy of nature were long confined to those phenomena, which are
not capable of modification. Even in inorganic truths, the
existence of special laws in complex cases, has only been recognised by the higher minds within the last three centuries.
The greater complication of social phenomena renders their
variations more profound than any others, whilst their harmony
is more important to us. This illustrates the inconsistency
which is shown by legislators, who, whilst refusing to admit in
social subjects the existence of any natural laws, affect to have
the power to maintain by artificial means an unchangeable
order. Since the combination of Order and Movement is more
difficult, as well as more needed, in this sphere than in any
other, a great difficulty here stood in the way of all philosophy,
until my creation of the Social science.

We see then, that an agreement between these two Principles
arises, directly we look upon Progress as being a mere evolution,
according to the biological origin of that notion, discarding all
idea of actual creation. Thus the paramount importance
gradually assumed by the notions of Life, accustoms modern
thinkers to regard Order as always capable of Development, and
to dismiss for ever the old notion of immutability. At once
the two notions, which at first sight seemed incompatible, combine in the closest manner of their own accord, and establish
the principle, by which I have expressed the union of Dynamical
with Statical laws —*Progress is the development of Order.* Social
phenomena offer no excèption to this rule. They only exhibit
the law in a case, which shows its necessary origin, as well as
its principal value. Even in the case of the simplest and the
least variable phenomena the philosophic notion of *law* implies
the perception of Permanence within Variation. Before Astronomy had reached the first stage, the variations caused by the
double movement of the Earth, made the Heavens to appear as
irregular, as the movement of Humanity does now. A true

1. As to
Thought.
The great
difficulty is
to reconcile
regularity
with move-
ment.

Law is per
manence
within va-
riation.

philosopher can no more conceive of a law without variation, than of a law without permanence. Putting aside the special characteristics of animate nature, especially of social life, this alliance between Order and Progress might be traced everywhere, even in the smallest canons of mathematics. It is inherent in the very definition of every law of nature, regarded as a mere general fact ; for law implies a real correspondence between the colligating principle, and the entire subject which it comprehends within it.

Limits of Variation must be determined.
Thus a condition of variability, which at first sight appears contrary to positive doctrines, proves to be essential to their full development. It demands however a general class of investigations, no less important than they are difficult, in order to determine the normal limits of the ordinary variations, to which the Universal Order is subject. This becomes indispensable on two grounds, first for the explanation of apparent anomalies, secondly to give system to our practical efforts. It requires more care, and offers more valuable results, as the phenomena become more complex and of a higher order.

2. As to action. Variability is of still more importance to Activity.
Passing to the second sphere of life, and regarding the natural capacity for modification of the Order of nature, from the side of the activity, we are confronted with features still more important, but more easy to grasp. If the variations proper to Order are looked upon, in all their extension as seen in theory, this coincides with the actual field of our practical existence. We must separate all Progress made in this sphere into the objective and the subjective, according as we modify the World around us, or our own Selves. Although the power of modification possessed by man, whether in his individual or collective character, asserts itself first in his control over the External World ; it exists not less really, and is still more important, over the Internal world of Self. According to the law just stated as applicable to all modifications, it is in fact the latter, the world of Self, which forms the main field for its exercise ; for here the ameliorations possible to us, are both more extensive in scale, as well as more valuable in result. Thus we have the natural Scale of human Progress, at first purely material, then physical, next intellectual, lastly and especially moral. This gradation, common to all human Progress, results directly from the classification of our leading functions, into the vegetative, the animal, the mental, and the social.

Thus a better comprehension of the Great Order gives a nobility to the spirit in which perforce we resign ourselves to its power; for it converts resignation into active submission. Humanity thus assumes the place which belongs to it, as the chief moderator of the general Economy. To bring this Economy to perfection, becomes the object of all our providential labours; and in this task we have the support, in their several ways, of all the agents, organic or inorganic, which are capable of combining in the work. Although the contemplation of this Progress sometimes leads men to misconceive the Order, which reigns throughout nature, such a misconception must be temporary with all who have taken a real part in this noble activity of man. They who have done this must always feel, that our success in modifying Nature is due far more to our prudence, than to our power. Besides the two elements of human prudence, both the moral and the mental, are themselves subject to laws, independent of our will, and yet more modifiable than any of the laws of nature. In a word, the artificial Order in material nature which we ourselves produce, rests necessarily on a natural Order, which we have no power to change; and indeed forms but a rational extension of it, especially in the highest examples of human improvement. Thus the Activity, far from weakening our sense of submission to Necessity, has a great tendency to increase it; for it brings us face to face with the dangers, which result from undertakings ill planned or ill carried out. Our earliest conceptions of the order of nature are due far more to practical wisdom than to lofty speculations. We invariably find that, the need of foreseeing for the purpose of better doing, is the spring of our persistent attempts to discover laws of Nature. This purpose will always afford the best test, of the kind and of the degree of completeness, to which our theories should properly be carried. For it is idle, and indeed injurious, to carry the study of the natural Order, beyond the point needed for the work of the artificial Order constructed by man. But this fundamental rule, though it gives direction to our speculative faculties, does not really restrain them; for our intelligence is so weak, that of necessity it falls short even of this limited task, not only in the greater, but in the lower facts of observation.

The religious influence exerted by an Activity so regulated

Activity ennobles our submission to a fixed Order.

Religious
value of the
activity.

is one that hardly needs explanation. It follows strictly from my mere definition of Religion, as a principle to regulate, as well as to combine. Let us remember that the essential object of this twofold discipline of Religion, is the Realisation of a general improvement ; and not the passive Contemplation of an immovable order. Were it otherwise, Religion would become something abstract, and even something vague, in direct contradiction with its true nature. The fundamental importance of human Unity consists in this, that it supplies us with the only normal Foundation adapted to man's Activity, in the entire range which Philosophy assigns to it.

3. Emotional
influence of
Variability
of Nature.

It now remains only to complete this analysis by examining the influence over the Emotions, exerted by the principle of Variability as a constituent part of Law.

It stimulates
the tendency
to joint ac-
tion.

If the primary conception of the Fixity of the Order we behold naturally calls out the affections, by controlling the selfish instincts and by enjoining union, the secondary conception of its Modifiability must increase both forms of this influence on the moral nature. Unless indeed the Activity thus called out be properly regulated, the power of modifying nature may easily degenerate into a merely Personal motive. But naturally it always stimulates the Social instincts, by suggesting a joint action. This tendency is so strong in the principle of activity, that it often shows itself, even where the aim of the activity is destruction ; for this motive, with the animals, as with ourselves, often induces combination. A life of Action is a greater stimulus to the affection than a life of Thought ; because combination makes itself felt as more indispensable in Action, than in Thought. When adequately developed, active life gives a sense of the Continuity of generations in history, no less than of the Solidarity of contemporaries now. Again, a deeper and more immediate moral result arises, from the reaction exerted by the Activity upon the Sympathies, to which it affords a constant gratification. For in every true society, each member does habitually labour for others, though frequently with no right perception of the function he is really filling. It is true that this stimulus of the sympathies, however constant, is not sufficient, without a more special cultivation of Universal Love ; which no cultivation would be able to awaken unless it originally existed. But this stimulus of joint activity has an inherent aptitude to second the moral growth. An habitual interest in Human Progress forms the best preservative against a mere emotional Quietism or a mere speculative Asceticism. Our smallest acts thus acquire a continual charm; which tends to bring out all our good inclinations. In a word, we cannot reflect on the modifications peculiar to the great Order around us, without recalling the Great Being, who is at once the author, and the object, of all attempts to regulate them. The close affinity which exists between the different kinds of Progress further enlarges the moral influence, exerted by the most simple efforts at the improvement of our condition. All must feel how completely any one of these is bound up with the improvement of the moral nature, without which they would all be worthless. Lastly, the sense of imperfection in all our dealings with material nature, adds to the religious uses of the activity, when thus controlled; for it irresistibly forces upon us a spirit of humility, especially in respect to the higher attributes of man, and these are also the most imperfect. This disposes us to conceive the constant subordination of Personal to Social instincts, as the most important and the most difficult, of all those kinds of Progress, which are compatible with the Order of nature as a whole. If the imperfections we perceive in that Order were wholly beyond remedy, we should feel them much less; because we should not be, as we now are, constantly urged by an active desire to remove them.

I have now considered far enough the two essential attributes of General Order: first, its primary attribute, that of Immutability, and next its secondary, that of Perfectibility. These two notions, which seemed so long incompatible, may be henceforth looked upon as inseparable; since each can be deduced from the other. Systematic reasoning alike rejects an unchangeable order of nature, and a perfectibility without any limits. To establish this harmony between Stability and Movement, is the work of the Positive Doctrine. Regarded as a theory only, it combines the two aspects of every science, statical and dynamical, especially of any relating to life and to society. Applied to practice, it determines the normal character of our permanent existence; which we may call an active Submission, or, in other words, an ordered Activity. *We must reconcile Stability and Movement.*

Possessed of this double power, Positive Doctrine becomes the intellectual Basis of Religion, the purpose of which is to unite *Moral Basis of Unity, pp. 41-53.*

Relation of
Doctrine
with Emo-
tion.

in order to direct.   But, however indispensable this basis be,
it is still not adequate ; since it only deals directly with two
out of the three essential sides of human nature.   Treating
exclusively of the Intelligence and the Activity, it would seem
to leave no place in the doctrine for the Emotion, the one true
stimulus of our entire life.   If this great want were not supplied,
human Unity would become impossible, for there would be no
adequate combination between its two necessary conditions :
Belief, and Affection.   We have just seen how much sound
notions respecting Order and Progress tend, when brought into
thorough unison, to promote the natural play of the sympathies.
But this indirect influence will not suffice to bring out all the
religious efficacy of Positive Doctrine.   Nothing can take the
place of a special and sustained cultivation of Universal Affection, the only internal spring of true Religion.   Nor can we
forget that this influence of the Doctrine upon the affections is
seriously counteracted by other tendencies, equally a part of
the Positive Doctrine.   I have already had cause to deplore,
and I shall again have to point out, the disastrous moral effect,
which almost always accompanies intellectual culture, especially
in science.   It may indeed be described as the expansion of the
individual instincts, by the scope it offers to pride, and the
suppression of the sociable instincts, by concentration of the
energies in solitude.   Although these two tendencies ought
to be properly restrained by a wise education, they must always
accompany the intense efforts required by individual minds,
in the laborious working of the intellect.   In a less degree
practical life offers us naturally the same moral dangers ; for it
exalts the pride and restrains the sympathies.   If the activity
disposes men to combination better than the intelligence, it
leads also to an engrossment, more habitual, and certainly more
universal ; under which the special cultivation of the feelings
is too easily neglected.   These evils, both in theory and practice, can only be corrected, when Religion supplies some systematic stimulus to the benevolent affections.   The Positive
Doctrine must therefore directly fulfil this sacred duty.   We
first laid down that it must regulate the Intellect ; secondly
that it must guide the Activity ; it must lastly show its power
to give unison to the Emotions.   This last attribute of Religion,
the one which most truly characterises its nature, is at once
seen to belong to it, when we give its full and proper exten-

sion to our idea of Positive Doctrine.   All that is needed is that this doctrine should be expanded till it embrace the most complex and the most elevated portion of the whole system of nature, that which controls the Life of Humanity, both in its Essence and in its Progress.   This is the third fundamental attribute of the positive belief, which it remains to explain ; and Doctrine will then be intimately associated with universal Affection, and so together these will directly constitute true Religion.

We shall more clearly understand the leading idea, if we remember that the object is not by any means to base Affection on Belief.   On the true theory of human nature, these two great conditions of Religion are wholly independent of each other ; and each develops of its own accord.   It is especially owing to this spontaneous nature of both, that the difficulty and importance of their due combination arises, whether under human training or of their own nature.   In a truly rational system of education these two qualities rise and develop together ; and then give each other mutual support.   But the existing anarchy exaggerates their natural independence ; and even converts it into a settled antagonism.   The case where Love conduces to Faith, is more usual and certainly more efficacious, than the converse.   Still the case of the reaction of Belief in kindling Affection would not be so rare as it is, were it not for the radical incoherence of modern Belief.   Those who have reached a condition of real intellectual synthesis, find themselves strongly drawn towards a moral Unity, unless their moral nature is deficient.   Although Positive Belief is unable to create Universal Affection, it possesses a direct capacity to second the instinctive growth of that feeling, over and above the tendencies just stated, which indirectly foster it.

Belief does not directly form Affection, but it indirectly fosters it.

This precious quality appears in Belief even when its sphere is merely that of Natural philosophy ; that is, the aggregate of the theories which precede and prepare the final science of Society.   The lower mathematical studies even may thus possess a truly moral attractiveness for all the healthy spirits who cultivate them with a noble purpose.   It flows from the gratification which it gives us, to experience in the plenitude of conviction, an indisputable reality, such, that humbling our personal, and even our intellectual dignity, it can dispose us to a willing submission to the Order of nature.   This feeling is

Scientific truth inspires a sense of gratitude.

sometimes, and especially in our day, degraded by the pride which fills us upon the discovery or acquisition of such positive knowledge. But it may exist free from any such alloy, even in our own days. All those who have, to any degree, freed themselves from the metaphysical welter, have certainly experienced the tranquillising effect upon the heart, exerted by this unfeigned submission of the intellect to fact. Hence a true Affection may arise, not very intense it is true, but very abiding, towards those general Laws, which dispel the sense of hesitation natural to our ideas. For man is so much by nature disposed towards Affection, that he extends it easily to inanimate objects, and even to mere abstract rules, so soon as he can see in them any real relation to his own existence. In proportion as positive Belief is developed and ennobled in us, we feel more and more Affection for the Order of nature and especially for the Progress proper to it. This fixed Order, gradually ascending into a capacity for perfection, grows more and more precious as it comes to regulate more fully our active and passive existence. As the phenomena we deal with become more special and more complex, and harmony in them becomes both more essential and more difficult ; so we come to feel how vain would be our knowledge and how illusory our power, without some such external ground of Belief. Thus we learn to prize more and more this essential foundation of all human Progress, in the degree that we recognise more fully its services, both to Thought and to Action. A true humility, even be it but that of the intellect, brings us at length to acknowledge, as we must, that all man can hope for is to understand that which *is*, in order that he may improve that which *is to be* ; renouncing for ever any notion of creating.

The more so, by its objective character.

All these instinctive feelings of submission and gratitude are even increased by the essentially objective character of the Positive Doctrine. For this Faith, which we prize so highly, becomes a service continually renewed ; and inspires a gratitude ever fresh. Its original Basis will always remain inductive ; since it results merely from a continual course of verification, never contradicted, it is true, by any real exception, but not such as to afford logical guarantee of its necessary universality in all time or space. Although this conviction may not be widely shared in times so little removed from the Absolute period of philosophy, it is by its nature as completely com-

petent to develop true Morality, as it is to consolidate sound
Reason.

Lastly, besides these different modes in which true Faith
reacts upon the Affections, there is a further direct stimulus
which it gives to the benevolent feelings. This is due to the
reflection—what is the necessary source whence flow to us so
many important acquisitions? The most self-sufficient and
narrowest of savants cannot long conceal from himself, how
completely his own discoveries depend, on the united labours of
mankind, either in the past or contemporary with him. True
Philosophers, we know, will never forget, that the personal efforts
of the most potent reformers, are small indeed in comparison
with the labours of the multitudes, by whom the way has been
prepared for them ; and the relative importance of these previous
labours is ever greater and greater. High success in practical
spheres, which requires cooperation of numbers in a manner
still wider, and even more unmistakable, instils into leaders of
Action this wholesome conviction in yet stronger lines. Thus
personal pride in all our achievements is gradually absorbed in
a reasonable pride in the race ; moderated though it ever be,
by the continual sense of imperfection in all our triumphs, even
those of the smallest difficulties of thought. Thus each step of
sound training in positive thought awakens perpetual feelings
of veneration and gratitude ; which rise often into enthusiastic
admiration of the Great Being, who is the Author of all these
conquests, be they in thought, or be they in action.

It recalls to us its true Author, Humanity.

Such is the power over the Affections possessed by Faith in
realities, even in its introductory stage alone. If this power
has not hitherto been much experienced, it is from the thorough
irrationality of the prevalent instruction, which has been almost
ever characterised by the disastrous rebellion of the Intellect
against the Heart. But this quality of science will be amply
and worthily developed, when a reformed system of Education
aims at directly embodying human Unity ; and calls to a share
in the work all our faculties in accordance with their true laws.
Nevertheless, even then, Positive Doctrine would remain morally
insufficient, unless it had a still more direct action, in causing
all our feelings to converge towards universal benevolence. Now
true belief completely developed, naturally satisfies this all-important condition beyond all that we could have anticipated.
For it compels the Mind to rest the unity of its conceptions, on

But there must be a more direct appeal to the emotions.

the same Great Being, who also appears to be the sole source
of unity in Feeling, as of unity in Action. I have now only to
examine this last element of Religion, to which I pointed
above, when explaining the moral influence exercised upon human
progress by successive discoveries in positive knowledge.

There must
be a union of
Faith with
Love.

When Belief directly conspires with Affection, human unity
will be fully established. The essential alliance between these
two can only be effected by a fundamental notion, at once
instinctive and systematic, but capable of giving unity to the
whole range of Positive Doctrine. We thus perceive the
extreme difficulty of reconciling the two, a difficulty which
forms indeed the crucial problem to be solved by true Religion.
But this final statement of the problem also indicates its
natural solution. It is this: to invest with a moral purpose
that natural Economy; which at first is to us but a merely
physical, and then becomes an intellectual system.

Only to be
satisfied by a
Being like,
but superior
to, man.

The positive doctrine of Law which at first was necessarily
limited to the simplest and most general phenomena, is long
before it exhibits to us the existence of a Being, really possessing
affections and wishes analogous to our own, united to a power far
greater than ours. Now, until this condition has been really
fulfilled, the qualities of affection, just attributed to Belief in
the real, will not be adequately brought out. However valuable
to us be the primary fixity of the Order of nature, and its
secondary capacity for improvement, the satisfaction we derive
from its majesty will never rise into true gratitude, whilst we
see around us only inanimate beings as the objects of our
acknowledgments. So long as the contemplation of the external
World fails to show us powers capable of true sympathy with us,
the Positive Doctrine must fall short in supplying the wants of
our moral nature. From want of real objects, the veneration
and the gratitude inspired in our hearts, by the continual benefits
bestowed on us by the Order of nature, must be expressed to
beings who are imaginary, however much they seemed to
answer chords in our souls. Unity of thought was, no doubt,
impossible under the provisional reign of these creations of the
mind; for these subjective beings were unable to give the
stamp of objective reality required for ideas as a basis of action.
Nevertheless the superior importance, natural to moral requirements, favoured the long continuance of these simple fancies;
without which we should never have risen to our highest

culture.   Although these supernatural hypotheses never satisfactorily accounted for the World we saw around us, they have
ever given free scope to the feelings, with which it inspires us.
Now this first primary phase of Religion, since it bears directly
upon the moral sources of human unity, was of more importance
than the systematic development of our speculative and even
practical ideas.   Thus exercise, constant even if ideal, fostered
all our higher instincts, in spite of their natural weakness, and
the difficulties to which our material existence was exposed.
Besides, before the true Order of nature had begun to be
scientifically understood, the theological fictions which inspired
the affections did not prevent the formation of the necessary
body of convictions.

As soon as positive doctrines acquired a systematic form in
the simplest phenomena, especially in the celestial, the intellectual conditions of man's Unity were soon found to be incompatible with the religious system, which still remained in
harmony with the moral conditions.   This inevitable separation,
which grew deeper and deeper at every epoch, from the first
rise of Greek science and philosophy, forms the principal source
of the complete anarchy, peculiar to the modern people of
Western Europe.   From it proceeds the downfall of the Theological system; which has continued step by step as Positive
belief has made new and important advances.   But this system
of life in spite of its real decrepitude, has always maintained its
apparent ascendancy, by virtue of its moral power; so long as
the Order based upon reality, was unable to satisfy the emotions,
so well as the Order based on fictions.   Now from the regular
progress of positive ideas, gradually advancing from the world
to man, the Positive Belief has only been called on to discipline
the Feelings, in this its latest phase, which alone deals with the
moral and noblest phenomena.   Since then scientific doctrines
have advanced at length to the world of Man, by the foundation
of the true Social science, the Real, can now take the place
entirely of the Fictitious, Order, both in the sphere of Love, and
in that of Faith.   From thence sprung once for all the true
unity of human nature.   It rests upon the fact, that the entire
system of Positive Belief points to the existence of a single
dominant Power; whose real and incontestable attributes appeal
directly to the Affections, in no less measure than they appeal
to the Intellect.

*Unequal
Progress of
moral and
intellectual
conditions of
Unity.*

The indi-
vidual feels
the power
exerted over
him by Hu-
manity.

In fact, as we gradually learn to comprehend the great Order around us, we come to perceive a last class of natural laws, less obvious than any of the others, although they even more nearly concern us. The sum of our actual existence, although directly circumscribed, first by the Cosmological, then by the Biological laws, is far from being adequately represented by them. Our chief functions must be obviously explained by a different class of laws, the special need of which is apparent, so soon as their full development takes place. Each of us finds himself under the constant influence of the laws of Mathematics and Astronomy, of the laws of Physics and Chemistry, and of the laws of Life. But a deeper study reveals to him a still further influence, not less dominant than the former, though far more capable of modification. These are the series of laws, statical and dynamical, belonging to the Social system. Like all the others, this last body of law impresses us, in the first place by its physical results, then by its intellectual influence, and lastly by its moral authority. Ever since the real rise of civilisation, each has felt that his own lot was materially bound up, with that of his contemporaries as a whole, and even with that of his predecessors. The mere reflection on the ordinary products of human Industry would instantly dissipate the sophisms, which might arise from any ignorant sense of independence. In a higher degree, the spontaneous comparison of various social states, whether simultaneous or successive, manifests the intellectual dependence of each individual upon all the rest. The most self-sufficient dreamer could not now deny the great influence of places and times over individual Opinions. Lastly, even in the most spontaneous facts of our life, further reflection incontestably proves, the constant subordination of our personal Sentiments to those of the collective body of mankind. Although everyone can modify his Feelings more thoroughly than he can his Thoughts, he is sensible at once of the influence over his own Moral condition, which is exercised by the general character of the moral tone around him. Thus under all aspects, since social changes have been sufficiently manifest, Man feels himself subordinate to Humanity. Language alone might suffice to recall to the mind of everyone, how completely every creation of man, is the result of a vast combination of efforts, equally extended over time and space.

Although this constant dependence of the individual upon the race must have been practically felt for several centuries, it is only after the discovery of the laws which affect human society that it exerts any systematic influence. Until these were known, all that results from this dependence was supposed to be the work of those arbitrary beings, by which Theological philosophy explains all social facts. But, when these latter phenomena had been at last brought under invariable laws, the Positive Doctrine becomes complete. The existence of the individual is dependent on the existence of society; as that of society is upon the laws of life; and these upon the laws of matter. From the time of Thales and Pythagoras a long succession of philosophers has gradually built up a systematic conception of the Order of nature in its entirety; extending the primary idea of science to an order of phenomena gradually rising in complexity and speciality. This long mental preparation is evidently brought to a close by my discovery of the leading laws of Sociology. Thus the difficult step in objective thought from the World to Man is sufficiently conquered to create a complete and uniform faith. Beginning with the first notions of Mathematics, it rises by imperceptible steps to the loftiest conceptions of Morality; raising a succession of sciences each more noble and more complex than the one that precedes it. The highest of all these sciences becomes the immediate controller of our existence. It must therefore hold the principal place in every regular study of the individual human existence. And its prominence is still increased by the fact, that, in accordance with the general character of the graduated system of Nature, the last necessarily combines the features of those, on which itself depends. Each of us without doubt, is directly subject to all the influences without, which can only reach our species, by affecting the individuals who compose it. Nevertheless the principal action of these external forces is only felt by individuals indirectly, through the medium of Humanity. It is especially as a member of the social system, that each man has to endure the weight of the material system, and of the vital system; and to the influence these exercise over him, must be added all that which they exert over the whole of his contemporaries and even of his predecessors. Besides, the providential efforts of Humanity protect each of its servants against less worthy influences, ever modifying them more and more.

But this power is only felt in full through the medium of society.

In the Scale of Nature, each order is affected mainly by that next below it.

Furthermore this indirect transmission of influence appears to be in entire conformity with the fundamental law of the classification of nature.   When the system of individual existence is distinguished from that of the social existence, in the strict sense, that is the collective, we add a final step to the general Scale of phenomena.   Although this new step differs much less from the preceding than any other, it is still their appropriate sequel, as being the most special of all, and the most dependent of all.   I shall often have occasion to show the necessity of continuing to its last term the long series of the sciences, which commencing with the World considered under its widest aspect, terminates with Man regarded in his most special character.   This the final completion of my Classification of the sciences is now referred to only to show, that the preceding remark applies to the normal relations of all the terms in this series of Nature.   In fact in the Scale of Nature each order of phenomena is especially dependent upon that to which it succeeds, and through which it receives the influence of those which precede.   Thus the graduated system of Nature becomes more like those systems of classification which we create ourselves.   If it is especially through the medium of the social system, that the individual system receives the influence of all the rest, the main effect of the material system on the social is due to the intervention of the vital system, which at once separates and connects them.   This is true of all the subdivisions of the general classification, as my Philosophical treatise suggests.   Thus the vital system, though directly dependent on the physical system proper, is affected by it principally through the agency of chemical laws.   In like manner the chemical phenomena, although directly dependent on the astronomical, are mainly affected through the medium of the physical phenomena.

Sociology is thus a condensation of all science.

This view need not be now any further expanded ; but it serves to justify the final concentration of the Positive Doctrine in the sphere of Sociology.   So whilst seeking only to complete our conception of the Order of nature, we have spontaneously realised the only unity of which it is capable.   In accordance with the objective fact of the subordination which runs through the entire Scale of phenomena, the Order of the World may be in essence reduced to the order of Man, the last term in all the influences which we can estimate.   This concentration is the more appropriate from its embracing at once the Order of nature and the order created by man ; for it treats the external economy of the world, first as independent of us in all its principal features, then as capable of improvement through our wise interference.   At the same time our intelligence is thus placed at the only point of view which can combine all our speculations, for these in their subjective aspect form simply phenomena of human effort, either personal or social.

The Positive Belief thus attains its true unity both objectively and subjectively by that which is only a necessary consequence of its own normal evolution.   The laws of thought in fact lead to the grouping of all the laws of nature round that aggregate Being, which is the direct controller of man's destiny ; submitting itself to the conditions in which it exists, but modifying them by its own wisdom.   When such a point is reached, this belief becomes thoroughly in harmony with the affections ; for it directs towards this Great Being, whose property is sympathy, all the homage which is due to the beneficent control of the Order of nature.   This Being, it is true, vast and relatively eternal as it is, has not really created the materials which in its sagacious activity it employs, nor the laws by which its results are determined.   But an absolute view of facts is still less natural to the feelings than it is to the mind.   The Order of nature is certainly so imperfect, that its benefits are only dispensed to us in an indirect way, by means of the loving ministry of that active and intelligent Being, but for whom our existence would be scarcely tolerable.   Now this belief alone would justify us, in offering the whole of our dutiful feelings of gratitude to Humanity ; even although there did exist a still higher Providence, the source of all the powers of our common mother.   The consensus of positive philosophy essentially excludes this last hypothesis.   But, strictly speaking, this particular problem has become just as idle with respect to the Heart as it is for the Head ; or rather it implies similar risks to both. Our true intellectual wants, both theoretical and practical, are satisfied by the simple understanding of the general Order of nature to which we have to submit ; and which we are enabled to modify.   If the authorship of it were indeed within the reach of our understandings, we should still be right in abstaining from the search after its creation ; for our duty is to reserve

The conception of Humanity satisfies all the conditions of Religion.

the whole force of our speculative powers for their true task, the perpetual improvement of our condition, and of our nature. It is the same with the moral question, and that in a still higher degree. Our gratitude, whether in our individual or collective capacity, for the benefits which we receive from the Order of nature, should be restricted to their immediate Author ; and this is one whose existence and whose activity are constantly before our eyes. Thus regulated, our gratitude would inspire in us that high moral improvement which this tribute of duty involves. Even supposing that our general parent, Humanity, were to find in the Order of nature a Providence, still higher than its own, yet it would not belong to us to offer up our worship to that Providence directly. Nay, such a great violation of moral continuity, apart from its manifest injustice, would prove at once contrary to the main object of our worship ; for it diverts us from the act of direct adoration, which is alone thoroughly natural to our emotional nature. The intermediate religion, which we see in its decline, has shown, only too distinctly, how serious this danger is, since the thanksgivings it addressed to an imaginary Being, for the most part were simply acts of ingratitude towards Humanity, the only real author of the benefits received. In a word our gratitude should be awakened by productions not by materials ; which latter have hardly ever a value worthy of our praises. Even in the Order of realities it is of still greater importance to the heart than it is to the intellect, that no essential intermediate element in the series should be passed over. It is even more necessary to preserve our affections from working towards a chimerical object, than it is to preserve our thoughts, now that their true object has become visible. If the adoration of imaginary powers was morally indispensable so long as the true Great Being was unknown, now that its existence is proved manifest, it would only serve to turn us from the one Worship, which is capable of improving us. Those therefore who strive to prolong it in our day are unconsciously turning it against its legitimate purpose, which was, to regulate for a time the expansion of our higher feelings under the Regency of God during the long minority of Humanity.

It furnishes the Supreme Power towards which human life is directed.

Thus real Faith harmonises entirely with true Love directly that the Positive Doctrine is complete, and is reduced to a system. The unity of man rests solely on a sound general conception of our condition and our nature. A deeper study of the great universal Order reveals to us at length the ruling power within it of the true Great Being, whose destiny it is to bring that Order continually to perfection by constantly conforming to its laws; and which thus best represents to us that system as a whole. This undeniable Providence, the supreme dispenser of our destinies, becomes in the natural course the common centre of our affections, our thoughts, and our actions. Although this Great Being evidently exceeds the utmost strength of any, even of any collective, human force, its necessary constitution and its peculiar function endow it with the truest sympathy towards all its servants. The least amongst us can and ought constantly to aspire to maintain and even to improve this Being. This natural object of all our activity both public and private determines the true general character of the rest of our existence, whether in feeling or in thought; which must be devoted to love, and to know, in order rightly to serve, our Providence by a wise use of all the means which it furnishes to us. Reciprocally this continued service, whilst strengthening our true unity, renders us at once both happier and better. The last result which is its property is that it finally incorporates us into the Great Being, in the development of which we have had a part to bear.

Such then is the general spirit of the true religion which I have already indicated in my General View of Positivism. I must reserve for the fourth volume its direct and special explanation, having prepared the way for it in the third by an historical basis as the ground of a comparative judgment. I must however still more accurately define the fundamental conception which crowns the entire system of positive thought; and I must still further set forth the composite and relative character of the highest existence we know. Analysis of Humanity, pp. 53–58.

This vast and eternal organism is peculiarly distinguished above all others by reason of its being formed of separable elements, each of which is conscious of its own cooperation, and consequently can give or withhold it, at least so far as its cooperation is direct. Its essential attributes as well as its necessary conditions are both alike the consequence of this partial independence; for it admits of combination on a great scale, but at the same time of profound antagonism. In a word, the chief superiority of the Great Being consists in this, Humanity is a Being itself composed of separable beings.

that its organs are themselves beings, individual or collective. All the functions belonging to it, whether those of the affections, of the intellect, or the activity, are therefore ultimately exercised by certain individuals whose free intervention is indispensable, although the refusal of any single individual will generally be compensated by the assent of others. But to illustrate this point, we will now consider separately the two existences belonging to each individual human unit, which in the General View were considered together, without any difficulty thereby arising.

The subjective life after death, is the period of true incorporation with Humanity.

The Supreme Power is the continuous result of all the forces capable of voluntarily taking part in the amelioration of the race, even without excepting our worthy helpmates amongst the animals. Each individual member of this great whole has two successive existences, the one, objective, and always transitory, in which he serves directly the Great Being by using the entire series of the previous labours of our race; the other subjective, and of its essence perpetual, in which his service is indirectly prolonged, by the results which he leaves to his successors. Strictly speaking, scarcely any man becomes an organ of Humanity until this second life has begun. The first really forms nothing but a trial of his worthiness for the final incorporation; which ordinarily should not be recognised until the objective existence has been completely ended. Thus the individual is not yet a real organ of the Great Being, though he aspires to become so by his services as a distinct being. His relative independence exists only in this first life, during which he remains immediately subject to the Order of nature; to the laws of matter, of life, and of society. Once incorporated with the Supreme Being he becomes truly inseparable from t. Thenceforth he is removed from the influence of all physical laws, and remains only subject to the higher laws which directly govern the development of Humanity.

The subjective life is the more dominant.

It is by means of this passage to a subjective life that the chief extension of the great organism is maintained. Other beings increase only by the law of the renovation of their elements, by the preponderance of absorption over exhalation. But beside this source of expansion, the Supreme Power increases especially, by virtue of the subjective eternity to which its worthy objective servants rise. Thus the subjective existences are necessarily more and more in preponderance, both in number and in duration, in the total composition of Humanity. It is on this ground that its power always exceeds that of any collection of individuals. Even the insurrection of almost the entire living population against the combined subjective influence of the past, would not prevent the evolution of the race from following its course. Those servants of Humanity, who remained loyal, could easily overcome this revolt, by basing their efforts upon the old principles, which, in spite of anarchy, would be left in all hearts and intellects from the labours of all former generations, they only being the genuine successors. In a word, the living are always more and more ruled by the dead. But to meet the metaphysical error which would result from too abstract a conception, we must never lose sight of the real nature of this preponderance of the subjective organs of Humanity. Each subjective organ is the product of a previous objective existence, and it requires the alliance of another objective existence for its exercise. Thus man serves Humanity as a being during his life strictly so called, and as an organ after his death, which finally transforms his objective into a subjective life. In his first existence he freely receives and spontaneously employs the resources of all kinds accumulated by the Great Being. In the second, if his personal office has been worthily filled, he takes part in the work of directing the continual use of the collective material of mankind. His individuality is at once the essential condition, and yet the principal danger, of his objective cooperation; for the problem is, how to place the egoism which is unavoidable under the guidance of the altruism which is indispensable. When his service has become subjective, the constant ascendancy of the sociable over the personal faculties is a spontaneous consequence. For, not only is Humanity composed only of existences capable of assimilation, but it assimilates only from each, that portion of his life which is capable of being incorporated; and rejects every individual shortcoming.

In this general sketch I cannot hope to explain entirely, even to minds already well prepared, the most extensive and most difficult of the positive conceptions, the sum of the whole system of real doctrine. Still it will be proper to define exactly this the essential centre of the true religion. All the rest of this treatise will illustrate still further this radical notion, and show its applications in a manner more or less explicit. The

Humanity represents the sum of positive truth.

last volume will complete the theory as the general basis of the final system.

Is it capable of personal representation?

It is obvious that it is the leading characteristic of the true religion, that everything in it relates to Humanity. But the composite nature of the Great Being produces a difficulty which, whilst applying chiefly to the worship, affects the doctrine, and even the regimen. In fact this centre of human unity seems incapable of receiving any personal representation. This point which will be hereafter dealt with, I will at once endeavour to clear up.

Every worthy individual is in a sense a representative of Humanity.

This objection is removed by reflecting on the nature of the true Supreme Being. Although it is really composed of subjective existences, it can act directly only by means of objective agents. These are individual beings, of the same nature as itself; though less eminent, and not so permanent. Each of these personal organs becomes therefore capable of representing the Great Being in many ways, when duly incorporated therein. Thus the veneration of men of real greatness forms an essential part of the veneration of Humanity. Even during his objective life, each of them forms a sort of personification of the Great Being. It is however essential to this representation that they be conceived as free from the serious imperfections which often obscure the best characters. The variety of the individual types, and the connection between their social duties, make this essential point of conception easy; especially when a sound education enables the true qualities of Humanity to be universally understood.

Women, in a special sense, represent Humanity to men.

As examples of the highest attributes of man there is no lack in the world of living personifications of the Supreme Being. Every man of feeling can recognise them in the special qualities of the tender sex ; and see them as the natural prerogatives of every woman worthy of the name. When by a true system the instinctive tendency of our nature is brought to its perfection, and our artificial Order has developed the natural Order of the world, this quality in woman will enable us to meet all the difficulties which arise from the subjective nature of the Great Being. Superior in power of affection, more able to keep both the intellectual and the active powers in continual subordination to feeling, women are formed as the natural intermediaries between Humanity and men. This is their high mission in the Religion of demonstration. The Great Being confides specially to them its moral Providence; maintaining through them the direct and constant cultivation of universal affection, in the midst of all the distractions of thought or action, which are for ever withdrawing men from its influence. The uniformity in their natures and position shows still more clearly this quality in woman. Lastly, this high office is that which best sustains the objective action of the living by the subjective influence of the dead. For a true woman cannot really die in the chief of all her functions, that of forming men.

To proceed from the general to the special consideration of this subject. Beside the uniform influence of every woman on every man, to attach him to Humanity, such is the importance and the difficulty of this ministry, that each of us should be placed under the special guidance of one of these angels, to answer for him, as it were, to the Great Being. This moral guardianship may assume three types : the mother, the wife, and the daughter ; each having several modifications, as shown in the concluding volume. Together, they form the three simple modes of solidarity, or unity with contemporaries— obedience, union, and protection,—as well as the three degrees of continuity between ages, by uniting us with the past, the present, and the future. In accordance with my theory of the brain each corresponds with one of our three altruistic instincts : veneration, attachment, and benevolence. This theory shows that for a complete protection all three types of angels must be constantly conjoined ; and where deficient naturally, they must be supplied by types of our own choosing. The union of all three forms that first ideal in the gradually enlarging spheres, both moral and mental, through which we rise to the conception of the Great Being.

The Mother, the Wife, and the Daughter.

Thus completed, the fundamental notion, wherein we sum up the entire Positive Doctrine, no longer presents anything to impede its full religious efficacy. Being united by a series of intermediate beings, both subjective and objective, to the aggregate Power above all beings, we are more ready to feel, and more able to cultivate, entire sympathy with this uniform and complex whole. The preponderance of the true Great Being is relative only to our weakness as individuals or as a race. By itself, its whole existence is subject to the general Order of nature ; of which it is nothing but the noblest element. Still this, its necessary dependence on the External

The correlations of Love, Order Progress.

World, whilst it in no degree affects its relative superiority to man, forms the chief source of its religious function. For, by reason of this dependence, its destinies can be on the one side foreseen, on the other side ameliorated. Belief and Affection are thus confirmed and developed in man, by a constant life of action ; every phase of which forms an act of religion. At every phase or mode of our existence, individual or social, we should always apply the honoured motto of our religion :—The Principle, Love : the Base, Order : the End, Progress. True unity is therefore finally formed by the religion of Humanity. This, the only doctrine truly universal, may be equally regarded as the religion of Love, or the religion of Order, or the religion of Progress, according as we consider its moral value, or its intellectual character, or its practical object. Everything being referred to Humanity, these three general ideas necessarily tend to fuse in one. For Love craves Order, and instigates Progress : Order again gives consistency to Love, and direction to Progress : lastly, Progress is the development of Order, and the renewal of Love. Thus affection, speculation, and action, tend equally to the constant service of that Great Being, of which each individual may become a perpetual organ.

OBJECT OF RELIGION OF HUMANITY, pp. 58–66.

I have now adequately set forth the only system of human Unity which thoroughly fulfils all its conditions. To complete my sketch, I must consider this system, first, as regards the object of religion, and then as regards its composition.

This Object, must be both individual and social Unity.

The object aimed at by religion is twofold ; it is the unity of the individual, and the unity of the society. Now in both of these it is easy to see that the Synthesis, which has Humanity for its base, is the only one that is complete and durable ; for it is the only one in true conformity with our nature.

Humanity, as the centre of Unity, harmonises (1) Affection, (2) Intellect, and (3) Activity.

No other principle could establish an equal degree of harmony between the three essential elements of our existence. When everything refers to Humanity, the affections, the intellect, and the activity, at once assume their natural relations. The activity, directly devoted to the service of the Great Being, is kept in due subordination to the feelings. At the same time the intelligence fully accepts its true office, that of enlightening the activity. Thus the heart is supreme both over the mind and the character, in a way far more simple and systematic than under any other mode.

And from this harmony of the whole, harmony of the parts

equally results; whereby the different powers of our various faculties are confirmed and developed.

It establishes the discipline of the affections when it secures a direct and continual appeal to the nobler instincts; which although, in themselves, the less active, are at once the most delightful to experience, and the most capable of a great expansion. Without doubt this form of discipline implies a constant struggle against the ascendancy of the personal instincts. But this conflict within would be far more desperate, and far less capable of conclusion, under a system of personal gratification. For beside the constant effort to repress the benevolent emotions, it would be necessary to restrain the antagonism of the various lower inclinations. Even when one of the personal instincts had succeeded in effectively crushing the benevolent within, the energy of the individual would still fail in the vain task of resisting the world without, against which the ascendancy of egoism necessarily forms a permanent rebellion. On the contrary the altruistic system of discipline, which holds a continual rein upon the personal instincts, is the only one destined to true success in the task. Beside the important help which the world without supplies, it is far from requiring the sacrifice of personality—but requires only its due subordination to sociability. The religion of Humanity ennobles indeed our lower instincts; even whilst training them to discipline. For the cares of every description, required day by day for the preservation of the individual, find in this religion a sanction, as the means which enable each to accomplish better his social duties; so long as they are not pushed beyond the natural limits, which men are too ready to neglect. Sound religion especially condemns all habitual austerities; which, however respectable in intention, would lessen the general force of every servant of Humanity, and hamper the exercise of his ordinary duties. It must be said also for the system of altruism, that not only does it sanction all reasonable regard for the person, but it largely assists such regard when treated in the whole; for it does much to strengthen the physical health, as several physicians have judiciously remarked. The entire freedom from anxiety, and the sweet sense of expansiveness, which invariably follow the active cultivation of the nobler feelings, have a direct part in producing a balance in the physical nature. When I come to develop further the connection in the

And it also strengthens each subordinate element of our nature. (1) Morally, it restrains without suppressing the lower instincts.

Indeed, it ennobles them.

nervous system, as indicated in the preceding volume, between the vegetative organs of our body and the emotional region of the brain, I shall reduce to a system this unquestionable re-action, and found thereon new modes of improving the mutual influence of the moral and the physical nature.

(2) Intellec-
tually, it ex-
pands the
power of
speculation,
especially in
the sphere of
Art.

With respect to intellectual harmony, it might at first sight appear that the altruistic system was not favourable to it, if we argue hastily from the long insurrection of the mind against the heart in modern Europe. But this disastrous con-flict is far from implying a permanent incompatibility between the two ; for it is the reason itself which has discovered a regular method of conciliation, by carrying the positive study of the external world to the point, at which Belief becomes the immediate fellow-worker with Affection. The Religion of Hu-manity arose originally as nothing but a system of philosophy, with no other object but that of founding a real and durable harmony, throughout the entire series of our positive notions, whether logical or scientific. If it recalls the intellect to the due control of the heart, whilst respecting its freedom ; it does so after amply satisfying all the reasonable demands, which the intellect has put forth in its struggle for freedom in modern times. Indeed the indispensable preponderance of the heart, far from restraining the legitimate exercise of the speculative faculties, strengthens and improves them whilst subjecting them to discipline. Thus preserved from wasting itself in hopeless problems and idle disquisitions, our entire capacity for meditation or contemplation is free to satisfy our true specula-tive wants, whether to organise our knowledge or to extend it. Logical harmony is finally established upon the direct agree-ment between the objective and the subjective method, in accordance with the twofold nature of the Positive Unity, which is at the same time within and without the individual mind. For objectively, the Great Being is as much external to each of us as another real existence, whilst subjectively we form part of it, at least in hope. This Unity coordinates in their natural way all our scientific theories : since the social order evidently supposes an anterior vital order, and that in turn supposes a preexistent material order. The altruistic system directly recalls our intelligence to the constant pursuit of the most valuable and most difficult speculations ; though without neg-lecting the lower studies, which are not less indispensable

both for method and for doctrine.   Lastly this continued exercise of the reason harmonises perfectly with the free play of the
imagination.   Art is profoundly incorporated with the essence
of the religion of Humanity ; it serves to idealise and ennoble
its doctrine, its worship, and even its discipline.   When devoted
to the animated expression of our highest feelings, which alone
are capable of habitual expression, this idealisation in Art will
form the intellectual exercise best adapted to the sum of our
composite nature.   Our religion sanctions its assiduous cultivation by all in unison, as the means of moral improvement,
which, though indirect, is full of power.   It supplies the mind
with the best mode of preserving it from, or correcting in it,
that unloveliness inherent in all scientific speculations, however carefully we seek to purge them from the spirit of vain-
glory.

Turning finally to the activity, it is evident that the altruistic system is more capable of giving it grandeur, than any
other.   Practical life necessarily eluded the grasp of all the
provisional systems of religion, by reason of the reality which
is the characteristic of action.   On the contrary, it was from
the practical life that the Positive principle first arose, and was
then extended to the contemplative, and lastly to the affective
life.   Under the true religious discipline, the activity forms the
connecting link between belief and affection, as being the
object of the former, and the result of the latter.   The smallest
actions are ennobled when they are referred to Humanity.   The
reaction which they exert over the moral nature, naturally
seconds the familiar expansion of the good feelings ; for an intimate connection necessarily exists between all kinds of progress.   It is only thus that *to live for others* can really become
for all the supreme happiness ; since the ordinary labours of
each are thus essentially destined for the good of others, so that
each servant of Humanity may attain to happiness when he
feels that he is filling his own duty worthily.   But beside that
each in his vocation will be naturally working towards this
common end, there will be cultivated in all the same spirit of
eagerness to help forward the work of general advancement.
Although the grander services in this Cause require systematic
organs, each joins himself to this supreme part of human life,
taking thought first towards himself, then towards others.
Thus the activity which has its source originally in the affec-

(3) Practi-
cally, it dis-
ciplines the
activity, re-
ferring
every action
to a common
end.

tions, tends at length to awaken the affections. At the same time it forms the best means of regulating the intellect ; for it ever impels the intellect to study the Order of nature with a view to bring it to perfection.

The conditions of personal Unity and of individual happiness are, Love, Faith, Hope.

On all three sides it thus appears, even looking to personal unity alone, how blessed a thing to us is that external Necessity, which imposes on us the altruistic discipline as the sole basis of a harmony at once real and stable ; for this discipline for others becomes the sole guarantee of true happiness for any individual. A rational philosophy sanctions and perpetuates those vague yearnings that arose in the last provisional system of religion, and marks as the highest boons that man can know the three grand conditions of all social life—*Love—Faith—Hope*. The first of these forms the inward impulse of unity ; the second supplies us with its external basis : the last, closely connected with the activity, becomes at first the result, and then the stimulant of each of the other two. This simple order seems indeed disturbed on occasions of anarchy in public or private life ; and it would then appear that Hope only is left behind ; without which indeed any life is impossible. But a more careful study shows us how, even in these cases, Hope is then dependent on an earlier system of Affection and Belief, a discipline of life, which insensibly remains after its foundations have been removed. Besides, the too common tendency to despair in nations or in men proves how much, in such exceptional cases, Love and Faith are indispensable to Hope. In every case, however, the union of these three qualities is the distinctive mark of our true unity, be it affective, speculative, or active. As Order is gradually restored in the West, it will be felt, even better than it was felt in the Middle Age, how completely these three essential conditions of all public good furnish also the chief sources of our individual happiness.

Condition of Social Unity, common work to one end.

If it be admitted that the Religion of Humanity alone can adequately produce any true personal unity, its superiority is still clearer when we turn to social unity. For its power to restore harmony in society is a consequence of its Principle of affection and its Basis of speculation ; both of which tend equally to reunite men universally, in the same feeling and in the same belief. Both the Positive theory of human nature and the historical analysis of human progress forbid us to look to any other system of discipline, as being able to establish any practical communion of Love and Faith amongst all the members of the human race. Children of the same Great Being, we all become at first his objective servants in life ; and then his subjective organs after death. The communion of this vast whole is far from being confined to the present : Intellect and Feeling combine in comprehending in the same circle, the entire sum of the Past, the entire sum of the Future of mankind ; the Past being the source, the Future being the aim, of the vast consensus of Man. It is this spirit of *continuity*, or communion between successive generations in time, which is more characteristic of the true Religion, even than the *solidarity* or union of the whole living race now contemporary in space. It is here that we gather most distinctly, the true purpose of our objective existence in life : which is, to transmit, improved to those who shall come after, that increasing heritage, we received from those who went before. Thus regarded as a whole, the service of Humanity appears to be in its essence truly gratuitous. Each generation is bound to restore freely to the succeeding, that which itself has freely received from the preceding. The improvement, which it adds to the sum total itself, forms never more than a trifling fraction of the worth of the whole ; and it is, moreover, a constantly decreasing fraction. We must extend this notion of the collective transmission of each age to the personal cooperation of each individual. In stating, in the second chapter of this volume, the Positive theory of wages, I shall be able to show that wages never recompense the essential part of the service given, but merely the material part. Every act of human labour uses up certain materials, which require to be continually renewed, whether to replace the provisions consumed, or to restore the instruments worn out. Wages form the fund whence this twofold restoration takes place, and have no relation with the service given : a service that could only be recompensed worthily by means of complete reciprocity, between the producer and him who enjoys his product. This notion, which is already recognised for all the higher social functions, is extended by the Religion of Humanity to real labour of every kind. The new view of labour will tend to remove those moral evils of industry, the result of the egoist system ; evils, which would seriously embarrass the altruistic system also, were it to suffer appeals to the selfish instincts in place of steadily restraining them.

All active
associations
tend to be-
come reli-
gious if suf-
ficiently
wide.

Such is the social affinity of the true Religion, that every durable association of men has always spontaneously tended towards this form of union. It is only the higher Feelings which can unite men ; and common interests have never secured permanent bonds of community, even in small spheres. We thus find everywhere that consecration of individual efforts under the sanction of an ultimate purpose in human good, at once collective and continuous. Thus arose the notion, which widened by successive generalisations, has gradually led up to the conception and sentiment of the Great Being. Even where the association has only destruction as its object, it still rests on mutual attachment ; only this attachment is then limited to a special population. At the same time this military activity is directly opposed to moral unity ; because it constantly arouses feelings of enmity towards the greater part of the human race. For this reason it is still more necessary, for the heart than for the head, to conceive the community of mankind as coextensive with the entire race. Any sense of national antagonism between the different servants of Humanity is totally incompatible with true conception of, and certainly with true feeling for, the Great Being. Nevertheless the Order of nature is such as always to prevent any absolute empire in the altruistic system. For the broadest sense of union can never extend beyond the limits of our race ; except to such of the animal races as can really be associated with us. Outside the circle of this vast confederacy, whose destiny it is to improve the earth as its domain, our planet possesses a variety of animate beings, who cannot be assimilated. Towards them our activity will always remain one of destruction ; and no sophistry should blind us to the reality of this cruel necessity we acknowledge. This bond of Unity in a common attachment must therefore always remain a relative conception ; although it is true that its sphere is continually widening. Even when our personal, have been thoroughly subordinated to our sociable, faculties, the egoism imposed by facts on the totality of Man must forbid the feelings of Love to embrace all Nature. Necessary as such limits to Love may be, they should in no way impair our enthusiasm ; whilst we ought fairly to admit their force, as a good check on indulgence in absolute ideas. We can only regret that the imperfections natural to the Order of nature bar us from unlimited expansion of affections, which of themselves would desire to embrace all things alike in their Love.

To complete our view of the social efficacy of the true Synthesis we must turn to its power to unite without coercing. For a sound conception of the Great Being makes the independence no less sacred than the cooperation of the members: both are equally necessary to the essential service; since the parts performed by an aggregate are impossible without individual organs. It can only be an unintelligent, and even a narrow, view of social duty, which can ever lead an honest social reformer to undervalue personal liberty. The supposed antagonism between individual liberty and social combination comes from a crude attempt to found an altruistic Unity, with only one mental and moral condition. These socialist visionaries thought only of the solidarity of living men, and forgot the continuity of ages. We need apprehend little from this misconception which is directly contrary to the ideas and the feelings which characterise the systematic Religion of Humanity. As regards the Great Being the subjective service after death constantly becomes more and more important, compared with objective service in life. Now subjectivity invariably supposes individuals as its authors; and their free cooperation alone can endue them with an aggregate influence. Far from lowering the freedom of the individual, the Positive religion sanctifies and develops it afresh; for it supplies it with a noble destination. This freedom is a condition indispensable to personal dignity : it is in no less degree indispensable to every service of society, which any form of oppression would paralyse. True cooperation ought always to be wholly voluntary; allowance being made for the motives which cause it to be withheld. In a word the altruist regimen supposes and produces the spirit of trust, as it exacts and increases the habit of responsibility. On the other hand it directly sanctions every real form of superiority, be it natural or be it acquired; for it devotes on system the strong to the service of the weak. Far from breaking up and subdividing Power, whether spiritual or temporal, the Religion of Humanity habitually concentrates Power, to enable it better to fulfil its social function. In its judgment on the Past, it gives the amplest honour to the illustrious characters, each of whom has done so much to influence the destinies of men. The Positive Religion inspires all the servants of the Great Being with a sacred zeal to represent that Being as fully as possible. It invokes the

The Religion of Humanity sanctifies, and does not suppress, individual Freedom.

veneration of all towards every truly worthy individual. The full acceptance of this Religion alone can check that spirit of blindness or of envy, which in our day would seek to crush out the real inequalities, which exist amongst men ; instead of turning the inequalities to account. A healthy sense of individual merit should invariably sustain our Positive morality, and dispose us to combat all those miserable attempts to discredit the power of individuals—a power for ever consecrated to the service of the Great Being.

THE CON-
STITUENT
PARTS OF
THE RELI-
GION, pp. 66-
70.

The essential superiority of the altruist synthesis in the great twofold object of religion, to *regulate* the individual and to *combine* society, must render it also the best adapted to develop all the essential parts of a Religion. This subordinate inquiry will appropriately follow the main argument, and can be now treated with brevity.

In the Reli-
gion of Hu-
manity,
Doctrine,
Worship,
and Disci-
pline coin-
cide in one
work.

We must first recognise the complete harmony which is produced between the three general elements of religion. *Doctrine, worship,* and *discipline,* were never truly combined, save under the original theocracy. This ancient connection of all three, which the institution of caste confirmed, became speedily incompatible with progress : first, politically ; next in poetry ; and finally even in philosophy. These could only develop their powers as they separated from the system. In the Positive organisation they are finally combined, without being confounded : the instrument being the natural harmony of their respective ends. Under the permanent inspiration of universal Love the business of Doctrine, Worship, and Discipline, is to study, to honour, and to serve, the Great Being ; the crown of all human existence. To discriminate between their functions is not to disguise their natural relations. For, the mind, the heart, and the character necessarily cooperate in all our principal labours, though in a way more or less direct. The Positive Religion adopts the conception of this synergy, or common action, of our cerebral forces, develops it, and turns it to account.

(1) The Doc-
trine, thus
supported by
Worship and
Discipline, is
most favour-
able to in-
tellectual
Progress.

It is for the Doctrine especially that this union is most important ; in order to undo the disastrous consequences which the isolation of Thought from worship and from discipline has produced on speculative progress. Already every true positivist feels the essential reconciliation between the Heart and the Intellect, to the common gain of both. Although but recent it has already produced a great influence upon thought. It led me to found the system of positive logic, which rests, as explained in the first volume, on the double use of the subjective and the objective method : both of them equally essential to any great abstract creation.   Both methods are equally appropriate to the nature of the Great Being, regarded first, as dependent upon Nature, then as preeminent over other real existences.   The former method shows us the necessary foundations of the great Order of Nature ; the second method supplies us with its principal laws.   Both are equally indispensable to the activity of that Being, for the former directs our earliest progress in living, the latter our highest progress in religion.   When this natural reaction of the Heart upon the Mind has become sufficiently familiar to us, it will produce results upon thought impossible in the Middle Age, under a system repressive to the intellect.   It will be felt hereafter, better than it then was felt, how completely our grander moral effusion may in practice come to second true intellectual efforts.   Science, the systematic basis of Belief, thus acquires a sanctity, higher than that which it received when it was first consecrated under the Theocratic system.   Even the lower branches of thought will acquire a charm and a dignity which now seems scarcely possible.   We shall give new expansion to that profound action and reaction, which causes the simplest and the most general laws directly to operate upon each other.

The invariable connection which exists between the various elements of the true Religion is not less obvious, and has an equal importance, in the Worship as in the Doctrine.   For the natural relations of the feelings with the intelligence, and the activity, are by it systematised and brought out with their full moral force.   Poetry more than Science needs thus to be consecrated to its office by positivism ; since it had a smaller space in the consecration given to all intellectual effort of the Theological systems.   But the sanction, which it receives from the final system, is still more direct ; for Poetry has a stronger affinity than Science with the principle of affection in our Altruistic system.   If science becomes the basis of the Doctrine, poetry remains the soul of the Worship ; and its effect, moreover, is more immediate, and more pure, as well as more habitual, than Science can ever give.   Next to the practice of good deeds, nothing tends more to develop the sympathetic

(2) The Worship calls out all the faculties by Prayer.   To pray, is to love, to think, and to act, in one.

F 2

instincts than due expression of the emotions as a familiar use.
Purged from any character of egoism, Prayer may henceforth be
made use of to give a free and direct expansion to our higher
feelings. And thus, whilst it acquires a fresh moral value,
Prayer becomes at the same time more natural; for it is
addressed to beings better known to us, and more sympathetic,
than of old. To pray, is to love and to think in one, whilst
prayer remains purely a mental act; for it is either to love
whilst thinking, or to think whilst loving, as one or the other
element prevails. But when Prayer finds utterance, and this
is its true nature, then to pray is at once, to love, to think, and
even to act. Thus prayer in its purest form offers the best
type of life, and conversely life in its noblest aspect consists in one
long Prayer. The humblest home in Positivism, should contain
better even than under Polytheism, a sort of private chapel, in
which the worship of the true guardian Angels would daily
remind each positivist of the need of adoring the finest personifications of Humanity. Now this sacred effusion of spirit
requires a constant use of some beloved types; and thus continually promotes a true poetic effort. The memory the best
stored with poetic images can never do more than assist the
original inspiration of the worshipper; since each special
object of Love requires to be separately idealised. Whenever
General Education has assumed a character sufficiently esthetic,
the special Arts will continually join with the main art of
Poetry, in giving a more tender and more effective character to
this form of domestic worship. Thus the higher affections will
enable each positivist to carry the sense of subjective existence
to a point, which hitherto it has been impossible to reach. Its
peculiar importance in the scheme of the Human Religion will
obtain for it a public and private support, which will speedily
give it a higher and more regular form. A better acquaintance
with the different Positive laws of our nature will enable us to
base this great advance on the general agreement between all
parts of our objective knowledge. By this blest interchange of
work between Science and Art, the reaction, which the intellect
exerts over moral life, is nobly repaid by the influence, which
the Heart exerts over the Mind.

(3) The Dis-
cipline em-
braces the
whole sphere
of Life, se-

Lastly with respect to Discipline, it would be superfluous
now to give proofs of the necessary tendency of the Positive
Religion to develop it. Positivism reduces Discipline to a

system, establishing its true relations with Doctrine and with Worship. Now it is as respects the activity, that our Synthesis of Life shows best its natural and direct superiority over others; for it was the practical life which always resisted the organising skill of all former systems, even under Polytheism. The activity, henceforward made a substantive part of the true Religion, takes its place, as it does in real life, as the ultimate object both of the Doctrine and the Worship. It protects both Doctrine and Worship against ever deviating into asceticism on the one hand, or quietism, on the other; for our activity will be urged on continually by true Affection, itself for ever yearning after practical Good. Religious Discipline, thus regulated, will acquire a character at once more rational and more noble, even in its more material part, thenceforth regularly connected with the highest part. This connection between the lowest bodily good and the highest perfection of the Soul gives a general and constant impulse to every form of actual improvement. I might here point out the direct union of the Discipline with the Worship, and even with the Doctrine in its higher forms. In fact, although morality looks to actions as its final result, it directs its influence in the first place on the emotions, which are the mainsprings of action. From this point of view Morality is connected with the Worship, which is devoted to the expansion of the higher affections, and so indirectly increases their force. Although this influence of Art upon emotion has not the same moral value as the actual practice of good, the more continuous exercise of Art is so natural, as to give it no small part in the most important and most difficult of all forms of improvement—moral elevation. On the other hand, the Discipline, apart from the subsidiary operation of the Worship, is connected directly with the entire scheme of Doctrine; in accordance with the profound dependence of the theory of Progress on that of Order. The general rules of morality thereby acquire a systematic authority; which tends to increase as well as to strengthen their practical effect. This is especially true with respect to the highest dictates of the moral law, which are so much exposed to all those sophistical attacks, prompted by the rebellious instincts. Positive morality taken as a whole becomes even a sort of necessary continuation of the positive Doctrine, when we extend the graduated Scale of the sciences to the life of the individual:

and this, as I have already remarked, is its natural limit. For the constant subordination of Personality to Sociability, is nothing but the last grand application of the great law—that in every objective theory the more special, is subordinate to the more general, order of Science. This dependence of the particular on the general, which has been already shown under its theoretical aspect, is no less true under the practical aspect. Thus Individuality is subordinate to Sociability; as this latter is to Vitality; and this Vitality has been shown already to be subordinate to Materiality; itself the first stage of the objective world, proceeding from without, and the final term of the subjective world, proceeding from within, in the universal harmony between Man and Nature.

THEORY OF THE HISTORY OF RELIGION, pp. 70–119.

I have now adequately examined in all its leading aspects the only form of Religious Unity, which is thoroughly adapted to human nature. The direct and special development of its character belongs to the last volume of this work, when after a regular philosophy of the history of the Past, I shall have formed a basis whereon to consider its final advent. But to complete the general Theory of Religion it is, as I have said, necessary to examine summarily the long and difficult course of Education, required for the establishment of the true Unity.

The evolution of true Religion must have been gradual and protracted.

The preceding remarks will have sufficed to show, that a Synthesis, such as I have described, could never have had an immediate development; much as our natural instincts constantly tend towards it. It will be easy then to explain the necessity for steps in its preparation. This gradual evolution was required at once by the intellectual substance and by the moral impulse peculiar to the true Religion.

Belief must be constructed objectively, from the World without; and therefore slowly.

In the first place the requisite Belief must be essentially objective; since the Positive Doctrine consists in a real knowledge of the Order of Nature. Subjective ideas have only a secondary influence in the full elaboration of such materials of thought. They form, as I have already pointed out, hypotheses destined to result in laws, when properly verified by facts without. It is only when positive Science has succeeded in reducing these laws to a shape admitting of system, that subjectivity takes a prominent part; for it alone is capable of coordinating the materials obtained by Science, as explained in my first volume (Introd. Princ. ch. 1). But this point is

not reached until the scientific spirit has embraced the least
general and the most complex of all phenomena. Until this
condition is fulfilled, to give the leading post to the subjective
method would vitiate all our theories. Now, this involves a
long and continued labour; for the laws of nature can only be
discovered by successive stages, progressing constantly from the
World to Man, or from the most general to the most particular
phenomena.

But on the other hand, even by reason of this peculiar
character of all natural science, no Synthesis whatever can be
constructed by the objective method itself. If we are now
convinced how impotent this is to systematise after twenty centuries of barren attempts, the task must have been still more
hopeless before the construction of positive materials. Every
Synthesis, or system of unity, must be *subjective*; although to
give it reality, an *objective* basis is required, and the construction of this basis requires the labour of time. Still man
never can dispense with some Synthesis; in order to give order
to his ideas, and thus to regulate his conduct. These being
the conditions of our intellect, no alternative remained, but to
erect a system of Unity entirely ideal—right in instinct, but
unreal in fact; and therefore simply provisional.

The objective method itself is incompetent to construct a Synthesis.

This, the primitive solution of the dilemma, without which
our reasoning powers could not have arisen to maturity, is the
natural result of our inherent tendency to absolute views. It
is so strong as to lead us to dispense with investigating into
special facts; and it prompts us to proceed at once to Deduction without having any previous basis of Induction. Laws of
nature, that is general facts, can only be demonstrated after a
long course of thought, even in the case of the minor celestial
phenomena. Whilst laws remain unknown, the human mind
necessarily follows the vain search after *causes*; that is, the
absolute Origin and the absolute End of things. This investigation, prompted by the hope of attaining an unlimited command over a world which appears to be subject only to arbitrary
rule, is the only impulse capable of overcoming the primitive
want of curiosity in the mind. The supposed problem indeed,
admits, even in our day, only of the actual solution, which was
originally proposed, the explanation of the World by Man, by
assimilating inert nature to living Nature. Thus at once
begins the subjective method of reasoning; and its free expan-

The natural and primitive Synthesis is subjective, searching for Causes.

sion meets with no objective difficulty in reality. In a word, in this spontaneous philosophy, in which man seeks after the essence of things, *wills* take the place of *laws*. This Synthesis, which now is as little adapted to speculation as to action, was for a long time no less indispensable to the one, as to the other. We continually fall back upon it, whenever we seek to act regularly upon phenomena, of the special laws of which we know nothing. In the absence of knowledge of these external facts, we are forced to follow the suggestions within us ; suggestions, the products rather of our moral dispositions, than our intellectual efforts ; unless we altogether abstain from action, and this we are very frequently unable to do.

Gradually, the objective and the subjective methods are combined.

The earliest state of the intelligence does not therefore admit of any permanent agreement between practice and theory. The one, entirely objective as it is, offers nothing but unconnected facts ; the other, entirely subjective, presents the mind with generalisations, which have no power of connecting the particular observations of facts. Still, however much influenced by false analogies, the subjective tendency to theory continually guided Man towards regular prevision ; even in spheres where prevision was subsequently renounced. The practical instinct on its part objectively prepared the ground for an improved system, by discovering in each department some empirical laws, sufficient to permit real prevision in several ordinary cases. Our mental training consists in learning to combine these two simultaneous tendencies ; so as to attain reality in our observations and generality in our conceptions. This combination is only possible by correcting excessive objectivity on the one hand, and excessive subjectivity on the other. Now our practical instincts as a whole constantly incline us to apply such a corrective ; for they show us more and more distinctly, how these opposite errors alike prevent us from foreseeing as a means of acting. Excessive objectivity is an obstacle to any general Induction ; Excessive subjectivity, to any real Deduction. Under these influences the *study of laws* gradually asserted its superiority, both over the *knowledge of facts,* as well as over the *search after causes.*

The primitive Synthesis, or Fictitious, like the Final Synthesis, or Positivism,

When compared with the final Synthesis, this preparatory system of Unity shows essential points of likeness combined with profound points of difference. The spontaneous nature peculiar to the first system makes it entirely subjective ; but its purpose as a guide to action requires it to be conceived as objective. This points to, and even prepares for, the final union of these two great speculative methods. The primitive like the final Synthesis rests on the predominance of the Human type : only, the type is personal in the one case, and social in the other. The principal difference between them is due to the Absolute character of the first, and the Relative character of the second. The contrast between the Scientific nature or positive results of these two systems is carried out in the contrast between their Logical methods. For the primitive hypotheses of the one system are never capable of proof ; whilst the final hypotheses of the other are invariably capable of verification. All these points of difference together render the antagonism between the two methods more and more complete, as the final system gradually develops its true character.

rests on the Human Type.

Secondly from the social aspect, we see even better how impossible it was for the true system of Unity to arise at the outset of society, and the necessity which nevertheless existed for a preparatory stage. Not merely was the Great Being then unknown ; but it had not been even adequately developed. Its final advent supposes a long preparation, which could only be under the empire of spontaneous fictions. The Spirit of Love, which hardly yet is sufficiently developed, is at first so thoroughly stifled, that enmity is the rule towards the great bulk of the human race. In that stage all the joint activity of men as social beings is due to the lower instincts. Unable to undertake the subjection of the Earth, which they feel as little able to conquer as to explain, each local association of men turns its whole efforts towards subjugating others. But this tendency, at first blindly destructive, becomes regular as it develops. It gives play to a spontaneous capacity for association : and this prepares the way for association more systematic, for it strengthens union within the special body, and induces them to aim at incorporating others from without. Thus Country prepares the way for Humanity ; and the narrow love of the nation tends to expand into affection for mankind. .

Gradual Evolution was necessary also, from the social point of view.

This Civilisation of War, like the Philosophy of Fictions, remains always incomplete ; by reason of the antagonism of both to practical requirements. Industrial activity arose from beneath the shelter of the one as the Positive spirit from the impulse of the other. Thus the elements of the final system

Industry had to develop under the system of War ; as Positivism, under the system of Fiction.

are formed during the imperfect ascendancy of the primitive elements; until at last the progress of the new elements and the decline of the old bring on conflicts which accelerate the inevitable Advent of true Unity.

The Absolute system of Religion and the civilisation of War have a natural affinity.

The two preparatory systems have a constant tendency each for itself to claim exclusive power over human life. Nevertheless their natural rivalry to a certain extent may be modified by a spontaneous affinity between them, which enables them for some time to combine. The Absolute spirit of the philosophy of Fictions and the Egoist spirit of the system of War, have too much in common to remain in perpetual hostility. By combining, the former extends its ascendancy over minds, whilst the latter strengthens its power over life. By this means Opinions incapable of proof, and Authorities which are above question, give to each other a mutual support. Their alliance produces at first, a consolidation in the preparatory order of society; but then, its spirit of domination urges this social phase to prolong its rule beyond the natural limit set to it. Still its temporal element is less incompatible with the growth of the ultimate system, than is its spiritual element. It is not, like the spiritual, destined to final extinction; for it may lose its ascendancy without losing all its value. Warlike activity will always retain a subordinate duty to be performed towards those members of the human or animal body, who violate the general Harmony, or obstinately refuse to conform to it. But Preternatural Belief has already lost all true utility amongst the more advanced races. It must eventually cease to exist everywhere; since its pretensions prevent it from accepting a subordinate position.

Phases of the earlier Religion.

Having viewed the preparatory system as a whole, I will proceed to examine the principal phases through which it had to pass before the era of the final system.

FETICHISM, pp. 74–76.

In the first stage, the supposed human will in objects resides in the thing; in the second it resides in the God who directs it.

The method of the Philosophy of Fictions is to explain the World by Man; and to attribute everything in nature to *wills* similar to our own. Now this primitive philosophy admits of two very different modes; the one direct, and the other indirect, according as these governing wills are supposed to reside in the objects themselves, or merely in supernatural Beings. This is the feature which distinguishes the two principal successive forms of the Absolute Religion; the former pure Fetichism, the latter Theologism, strictly so called, the two being the necessary precursors of Positivism. Both attempt to interpret inanimate nature by means of living nature; and supply the place of laws of the physical world, by means of ideals immediately derived from the laws of the moral world. But they differ essentially in their conception of matter; which, in the first case is supposed to be living, in the second to be inert. The step from the one to the other is in fact the most important transition in the whole of the provisional Synthesis. Nevertheless this step is quite consistent with the character of the system; as the tendency to observation in its concrete form, leads to observation in its abstract form. What is really done by the human intellect is, to extend to the *properties* of things the original explanation, which it limited at first to their *substances*. Now more general conceptions, such as these, can only be maintained, by referring the governing wills to Beings distinct from the bodies themselves. Each of these Beings personifies the common property, apart from the particular objects, which have originally suggested the analogy. Thenceforth, all bodies are conceived as passive in themselves; each as depending for their whole existence on the God who directs it, though he be not residing within it.

When we watch the ways of children, and even of animals, we at once perceive that only the Fetichist theory could be the natural starting-point of the Absolute Religion; which itself precedes and prepares the way for the Relative Religion. As a philosophy it is wrong only, in confusing, as it could not but do, the inorganic world with living nature: and the true distinction between them is still misconceived by so many of the teachers of the day. At bottom the fetichist reasoner, who fails to distinguish activity from life, is less distant from scientific truth than the theological dreamer who in spite of all the evidence, persists in taking matter to be passive. The observation of the one is doubtless too superficial; but the other admits an exorbitant influence to the imagination. In Fetichism, the spontaneous Religion of Nature, the subjective element does nothing more than supply the place of *reasoning*, (then from want of materials impossible) by *feeling*, the natural preponderance of which is at first so decided. But theology, the Religion of Inspiration, gives a direct authority to the subjective element, far beyond what was needed for the original search after causes. It is true that it thus becomes better

Fetichism, is the early and natural form of Absolute Religion,

and is, in some respects, superior to Theologism.

adapted to give scope to the human imagination. Still Fetichism also, admitted under other forms a complete esthetic development ; and it guaranteed more effectually the ascendancy of the Heart. So that, had the Absolute Religion been destined to endure, it would certainly have retained this, its original and spontaneous form. It is to Fetichism, and not to Theologism, that men return when an overpowering feeling temporarily recalls the strongest minds to the vain search after causes. Thus the fact that Theology took the place of Fetichism, is itself a proof how thoroughly provisional was the part taken by the Absolute Religion, which was unable in any case to maintain that one of its forms, which was best fitted to its nature. Theologism assisted intellectually in preparing for Positivism ; were it only that it denied matter to possess life. But this function of Theology, though indispensable to the first progress of thought, would be far from being essential to that progress which is either communicated or directed from without. In the latter case it would be possible to pass at once from Fetichism to Positivism, and omit any sort of Theologism, if any important cases of individuals or bodies arose really requiring this systematic attempt to dispense with the intermediate phase. It would be enough to enforce the true distinction between Activity and Life, as I shall explain hereafter.

Fetichism had much moral power, but only in private Life.

This remark is of value to us now, as proving that the importance of Theologism in the Past is concerned with man as a social, rather than as an intellectual being. Its great value indeed must be considered to be a political, rather than a moral one. For in this latter aspect Fetichism is not inferior to Polytheism. The harmony which it creates in the affections, is more direct and more complete ; and this is shown by the long and obstinate attachment of our race to this simple faith, of which so many traces still remain. This moral superiority of the spontaneous system of religion is however necessarily confined to private life. Public life could not develop, nor even commence, except under Theologism.

THEOLOGISM, pp. 76–80.

Polytheism introduced new power, by extending its sphere to Society.

In fact the Fetichist Worship is too special to give rise to any Belief, really common to many. At least it never acquires this power until its last phase, when it reaches the stage of Astrolatry ; and from thence it rapidly passes into Polytheism. Besides the Absolute Doctrine remains very incomplete, so long as it does not get beyond its first natural stage. In that state it does not extend its explanations beyond the World without, and it does not embrace the World of man; but rather draws from Man its explanation of Physical facts. But when Polytheism refuses to admit any Activity in matter, and refers the wills supposed to govern it to imaginary Beings, having no exclusive abode, then these Beings are made to control the facts of man and of society; and this is soon regarded as their principal sphere. Thus moral speculation, spontaneous at first, begins to assume a more systematic character; just as speculation upon material laws did also, when it passed out of the earliest Fetichist form.

Indeed all our general notions respecting material laws were subject to a very important influence from this great revolution in thought. We get from it the first direct conception of the Material Order, which is artlessly likened to the social Order. For the two very different meanings we give to the word *order*, are in the minds of the first thinkers essentially the same: for they supposed that every *arrangement* must be the result of a *command*. The supreme *wills*, which everywhere supplied the place of *laws*, were the origin at once of *causes* in philosophy and *rights* in politics. Without at all abdicating their rule over the material world, the gods were supposed to be usually occupied with the moral and social world, and to leave the ordinary course of Physical phenomena to certain regular customs, established by the deities as much for their own convenience as for the benefit of man. *(margin: Theologism regularly extended thought to things social.)*

Lastly, this first attempt of Theology to systematise our highest conceptions possesses also a profound political importance. It consolidates all the authorities which spontaneously arise, and it gives them a Superhuman sanction, the earliest germ of which is found in Astrolatry. Still to give full effect to this influence, men must have already risen to the capacity for collective action; and this was supplied by the habitual tendency towards conquest. This however supposes an agricultural, or at least a pastoral, form of existence; and especially the establishment of slavery, which at last replaces the original practice of massacre. *(margin: Political uses of Theologism. Conquest, and Slavery.)*

It is on this twofold ground, intellectual as well as social, that Theologism is shown to have been indispensable to the entire course of human Civilisation. Such is their close connection with man, that these imaginary Beings could very easily *(margin: It formed a Regency during the minority of Relative Religion.)*

serve to represent in an artless way the true great Being during
its unavoidable period of tutelage.   Although their supreme wills
must necessarily have appeared arbitrary, the desire of penetrating to that which guided them gradually introduced all
the regularity required by our peculiar conditions.   The indefinite character which was due to their purely ideal origin admitted that every healthy impulse, suggested by the growing
force of the social instincts, should be referred to the gods.
The gods were thus unconsciously made the mere organs of the
affections and notions of men in the aggregate, and thereby
gave to those moral and mental tendencies in their infancy a
consistency that they could not have otherwise acquired.   This
invaluable sanction was almost exclusively confined to those
sound instincts, which alone could attach men around a faith so
vague.   In a word the assembly of the gods formed a sort of
council of Regency, charged for a time with the guardianship of
Humanity.   This regency also was a general type of the real
Inspiration given to men by the Great Being, although conceived under a confused and indistinct form ; and in the second
phase of incomplete Religion an ideal symbol of this Inspiration
was imagined and worshipped.

Fetichism
led the way
for Religion,
and opened
the Subjec-
tive Method.

    The task of Fetichism was to initiate everything; but it
could very rarely establish anything; for its conceptions were
as floating, as they were special.   It only succeeded in completing one great step in human progress, one quite in accordance
with its nature, and the necessary starting-point of our whole intellectual advance.   This was the Logic of the Feelings, by which
I mean the colligation of ideas in accordance with their connection with the sentiments.   This is the origin of the strictly
Subjective Method of thought.   The human intellect required
this first step to awaken it.   It drew from our natural affections
the earliest hypotheses which were capable of connecting and
guiding our observations ; these having at that time no rational
guide whatever.   The highest cultivation will never prevent
our falling back into the same tendency, whenever we choose to
speculate about events, with the laws of which we have not
even an empirical acquaintance.   We are obliged to leave it to
our emotions to dispel the uncertainty which exists in our
speculations; for, on the other hand, it is not always possible
nor desirable to suspend our judgment.   This Subjective
Method which is the intellectual foundation of Fetichism,

acquired by constant use, a rapidly extending power. The
influence which it spontaneously acquires makes us familiar with
the most essential precept of true wisdom :—the constant preponderance of the Heart over the Intellect. The Theologism,
which followed, never could give the Heart so decided an influence, even under the system of Monotheism. Positivism
alone could give to this principle a consistency really systematic,
and that without at all affecting its primitive simplicity.
Thus the principal foundation of the Relative Religion, the
paramount office of the Heart, was established spontaneously
even by that form of Fetichism which the Absolute religion was
forced to assume in its origin.

But whatever be the importance of this first step, and it has
been till now but little recognised, the work of religious Progress
was in the main effected under the guidance of Theology in
the proper sense of the term. Theology itself was the offspring
of the original Fetichism, which never wholly lost its direct
influence even amidst its palpable decline. The great superiority of the Theological type of Religion was a consequence
of its always favouring the formation of a distinct Priesthood,
an institution which was destined to form the nucleus of the
entire subsequent development. Until Fetichism had reached
the form of Astrolatry, the worship it needed, although highly
developed, required no special priest ; for each worshipper
could address, without any minister, powers supposed to be always
present and within the reach of the senses. But as soon as
the notion of gods became prevalent, the assistance of a Priesthood was required to expound the will of the divinity, and
offer up to him the ˉhomage of the worshipper. Thus arose,
and often even during the nomad period of existence, a regular
body of men, devoted to Speculation ; and they were naturally
invested with a high social authority. It is indeed to the
Government, more than to the *Creed*, or even the *Worship*, of
the Theocratic system that the religious Progress of mankind
was really due, upon the decay of Fetichism. It was from the
Theocracy not from the Theology, or the Theolatry, that all
the main powers of the State obtained the sanction they
needed, and it was from this that all the main institutions
originally sprang. Fetichism never equally succeeded in acquiring the full power of which it was capable except where
it assumed the form of a highly developed Astrolatry. Then

Marginal note: Theologism, however, took the great step by instituting the Priesthood.

it gave rise to a true Priesthood, with no difference but one of doctrine.

Theologism is, (1), Polytheistic. (2), Monotheistic.

To understand the peculiar influence of Theology, social and intellectual, we must separate it into two successive types, the Polytheistic and the Monotheistic. The former is the immediate successor of Fetichism, which readily merges into it. Polytheism is on all grounds the principal form of Theologism ; since Monotheism marks the inevitable decline of it. It is therefore under Polytheism that the great Progress of man was principally effected, although Monotheism becomes subsequently indispensable in order to direct the great concluding period of training.

POLYTHE-ISM, pp. 80–89.
The principal work of Polytheism was to cultivate the Imagination.

The principal intellectual influence of Polytheism consists in having aided the free expansion of the Imagination. Besides its immortal achievements in Art and Poetry, its special value was due to the way in which it prepared the way for the final Religion, by virtue of the importance it gave to the Subjective Life. During a long series of ages, every individual maintained familiar relations, to a degree often amounting to actual illusion, with purely imaginary Beings. This fact alone serves as a conclusive proof, how much more vivid and distinct the subjective existence will become, when made dependent on a previous existence in Objective Life. These conditions are fulfilled now in the Positive system by its public and private Commemoration of the Dead.

Intellectually, it founded the Objective Method, as Fetichism founded the Subjective.

The intellectual ascendancy of Theologism exhibits the natural rise of the Objective Method. Fetichism, which proceeded always from within outwards, employed the Subjective Method exclusively, that is it explained the World by means of Man. But Polytheism, notwithstanding that it introduced fictitious Beings, which were however supposed to be real, was able to follow an opposite course. The essential feature of its whole system was the practice of reasoning from without inwards, that is to say, it gradually extended to Man, the hypothesis which it created originally in reference to the World. During its entire period, the principal gods were supposed mainly to control the movement of inorganic Matter ; and the events of Human Life formed the exclusive sphere only of the inferior divinities. Intellectual and moral attributes assumed great importance only during Monotheism, when Theology began to give way. Thus Fetichism and Theologism, in their respective spheres, instituted first the Subjective, and then the Objective Method. It was reserved for Positivism to bring about the natural combination of the two.

In its social aspect, the system of Polytheism is based on two institutions, which are naturally related. The first is the complete union of authority in the Spiritual and in the Temporal domain. The second is, the common Slavery of those who produce material wealth. The former, which is sanctioned by the divine origin assumed for every family in the possession of power, is indispensable to the Religion of Inspiration, in order to check the intellectual extravagances and the political confusion, incident to complete freedom in speculation, unless controlled in practice. Slavery, which is a consequence of the general features of the system, speedily becomes a condition necessary, no less to warlike Activity, than as a training in Industry.

Socially it is marked (1) by Union of Temporal and Spiritual Power, and (2) by Slavery.

To ascertain the part which Polytheism had in guiding the principal education of man, it is not sufficient to consider its common properties. It will be necessary also to examine separately its leading forms. These are marked by the relations between the influence of the Priests, and that of the Warriors; for although the influence of these two classes spontaneously combined, they still retained their natural diversity.

Polytheism was divided into, (a) the Priestly, (b) the Warrior, types.

The rule of the Priests invariably obtains the ascendancy at the outset, and thus Theocracy was everywhere the original form of government. Its influence has indeed subsisted down to the existing mental condition of the advanced races, however much modified by subsequent revolutions. Wherever this form of government is permitted to come to maturity, Polytheism takes an essentially conservative form. It is especially marked by the institution of Caste, the rule of an hereditary Priesthood forming the chief political bond of union. This system is so obviously well adapted to preserve the earliest acquisitions of every description, obtained by man, and so entirely conforms to the tendencies then prevalent, that it rises to an admirable degree of completeness. But ere long the Order which it enforces becomes hostile to every kind of Progress; and Progress can only begin, when men escape from the oppressive rule of the Priests.

The earliest form is Theocracy, with Caste.

This result is naturally brought about by activity in War; and so this is the distinguishing feature of the second form of

The later form is warlike, offen-

sive or defensive.

Polythelsm. This warlike form assumes two very different types, according as the general conditions, internal and external, favour or prevent a full expansion for the system of Conquest. This is the normal tendency of the military form of existence.

Greek, or intellectual, form of Military Polytheism.

In the first case this activity in war indirectly produced an important intellectual result ; which was nothing less than the foundation of the entire mental Education of the West, through the various labours of the Greeks. After successfully overthrowing the theocratic yoke, the military spirit, under the pressure of the peculiar conditions of the case; urged all the higher minds towards intellectual cultivation, first in Art, then in Science, and finally in Philosophy. The Greeks retained no more of the actual military activity, than was required for the proper protection of the Home of Free Thought against the invasion of the Eastern Theocracy. But, whilst sustaining the noble thinkers, on whom the future advance of mankind depended, the Greek, or Intellectual form of Polytheism involved profound degradation in the general population of Greece, for it committed them to that form of existence, the intellectual, which is the least in conformity with our nature. Whilst deploring this fatality, and it is one yet unredressed, we must estimate at its full worth the gain, which the system was for the Future of Man ; and when the Providence of the Great Being assumes a regular form, it will know how to protect with special care the Nation, whose welfare has been so sacrificed to the Race.

It instituted the Logic of Images.

The esthetic influence of Greek Polytheism is not confined to those admirable productions, which then for ever illustrated the Poetic and Artistic powers of man. It consists in that innate and popular spirit which led to the second element of the true logical method. Polytheism alone was competent to produce the Logic of Images, a method which strengthens and perfects the Logic of the Feelings, created by Fetichism. Apart from its artistic purpose, this new element in logic long exercised a powerful reaction upon thought by the impulse which it gave to the inductive process, during the objective construction of Science, effected by Polytheism. The constant employment of Images to facilitate fictitious inductions, prepared the way for their use in real inductions. We thus see an additional proof of the power in the provisional Synthesis to initiate all the forms of development, which the final Synthesis has to systema-

tise. In spite of the *ex cathedra* pretensions of our self-sufficient Philosophers, the principal Institutions of civilisation are
due to the united thoughts of all mankind, directed only by such
simple beliefs as were able to arouse the natural inactivity of
the human understanding.

In the sphere of Science, the work of the Greeks had an
importance other than that of its particular achievements, important as they were. After an adequate training in Concrete
study, the Positive spirit of their minds laid the foundation for
Abstract thought ; and constructed the first mathematical, and
still more the first astronomical, rudiments of Positive belief.
Although necessarily confined to the simplest element of the
Natural Order, this remarkable achievement led to a wonderful
influence upon Thought ; and with this Type of true reasoning
to work from, the mind sought on every side to substitute Laws
for Wills.

Also commenced Abstract Science, in Mathematics.

But the special character inherent in Science prevented it
from becoming the organ for developing this tendency, to find
law in all things ; and it ended in leaving this task to the
metaphysical spirit. This differed from the Theological only
in this : it replaced the *gods* by *entities,* but tried to solve the
same Absolute problem. The change, by depriving the earlier
solutions of their whole mental coherence, destroyed their
utility especially in the sphere of Society, and even in mere
Speculation, into which it introduced doubts that it could not
solve. This negative power of the Greek Metaphysics was
subsequently used to counteract the excessive Theologism,
which interfered with the latest phase of the preparatory
era. The metaphysical spirit was also of importance to Progress, in its attempts to form an Objective system of Thought,
on the basis of the earliest achievements of science. These
ambitious attempts being renewed with untiring energy, in
spite of their constant failure, the want of a sounder system
became thus continually more and more manifest ; and this was
impossible without a further extension of rational Positivism.
These endless divergencies in philosophy gradually raised into
prominence the Logical Theory, the most valuable and most
permanent element of previous Thought. Thus appeared, con-
fusedly, in the midst of many Objective systems of Unity, a
growing tendency in the mind towards a Unity essentially Subjective, which alone was able to replace the Theological systems.

The Metaphysical spirit had also an important influence on Thought.

But these various advantages to speculation were confined to a few thinkers, and were in them seriously impaired by the vanity which they induced. Nor must it be forgotten, that this philosophy was on the other hand the source of great moral degradation ; inasmuch as it raised the intellect to the highest place, and even exalted the minor intellectual faculties, for Expression speedily was preferred to Conception.

Roman, or Social form of Polytheism.

These were the three modes in which the intellect was influenced by Military Polytheism, succeeding to Theocracy in a people, amongst whom the system of conquest could not be adequately developed. It remains to explain the direct influence of military activity, where circumstances admitted of its being carried to its natural limit. In Rome its influence becomes more unmixed and more complete, as it relates specially to Social qualities ; although it ultimately reacts also on intellectual progress, when its duty was to disseminate the achievements of Greece in thought.

Rome, by incorporating nations, checked War, and founded Industry.

Thus took place the most important, and the most difficult of the various preparatory stages, needed for the final growth of the Great Being. At first each people aims at becoming the central race. But these incessant efforts lead to no great social result, until the gradual supremacy of one nation is achieved, and by the combined influence of the requisite conditions within and around it, she becomes the mistress of all the races capable of being assimilated. Some centuries of an admirable military activity, at first spontaneous, and subsequently reduced to a system, were enough to unite in one whole, the greater part of the white race round a provisional centre. The best way in which Polytheism could prepare the way for Positivism was, by directing this, the first real formation of the Great Being, which then began practically to replace its divine predecessors. This result was the more remarkable, as it indicated the natural activity of regenerated Humanity. Rome, by incorporating the nations everywhere, checked the aimless love of war, and insensibly substituted for it an industrial activity, which is alone capable of universal adoption. Thus the final condition of our race was thenceforth foreshadowed, and even directly aimed at, by all the nobler characters of the age.

The Roman system of incorporation

Apart from these vast results, so great a social effort could not fail to elevate the people who accomplished it, whilst their intellectual labours had utterly demoralised the Greeks. The required a high standard of social activity. work could in fact only be achieved by the active and constant participation of every citizen. The union of the Roman people within formed the first condition of incorporating nations without. The Roman system of Polytheism thus went far to realise the form of existence normal to man; for it continually placed Speculation in subordination to Action, and impressed on Action a deeply Social character. When the work of political assimilation had so far advanced, as to draw general attention to the intellectual movement, this admirable Roman system promoted that Greek cultivation, which it had till then neglected. The natural capacity shown by Rome to welcome all forms of further progress, contrasts with the inherent feebleness of the Greek civilisation, which, contrary to the natural rule, never succeeded in finding a fresh career, when its own special work was exhausted.

To estimate this, the Social form of Polytheism, we must And also, a severe type of personal discipline. also directly estimate its moral value. For in this respect it was as far superior to the Greek, or Intellectual form of Polytheism, as the latter had been to the Theocratic or Conservative form. Although all morality under Theology is naturally based on egoism, the real influence of its morality depends more on the situation, than on the doctrine. It was thus in the ancient Polytheism, in which the simple instincts that had given rise to the Belief, had never succeeded in any direct attempt to regulate Human Life. The natural encouragement given by the Polytheistic creed to our various instincts, was even indispensable to true moral progress. It would have been otherwise impossible to discern, which inclinations required restraint, and which stimulus. But if this great experience was then needed for morality in the future, it presented at the outset great dangers; for it increased the natural preponderance of the personal instincts. This tendency could only be resisted by a Discipline, arising naturally from the situation; nor would any Discipline have ever arisen, but for the complete subordination of the spiritual to the temporal authority. The only condition favourable for this was found in the free expansion of the system of conquest. During several centuries, a noble public activity prevailed over private life, and checked the tendency towards personal indulgence which marked the morality of antiquity. Although the zeal of Patriotism was, toward all without, nothing but National Egoism, amongst the citizens themselves it inspired some splendid examples of Devotion.

The increasing moral value of the three forms of Polytheism is shown in their estimate of women.

This estimate of the comparative moral influence of the three systems of Polytheism, coincides with the social position respectively assigned by them to the sex which best represents the Great Being.   The elevation of woman, which forms a measure of true civilisation, was with every other form of progress commenced by the original Theocracies.   This however hardly went beyond instituting the rudest form of Marriage ; from which the Conservative type of Polytheism never succeeded in freeing itself.   The inherent evils of polygamy are so obvious, that the wisdom of the priestly order would never have given it regular sanction, had it not been for sheer necessity.   It was made inevitable by other conditions, besides the animal passions of the male sex, always so difficult to restrain in the great and powerful.   The difficulty indeed was, to establish under any form whatever the institution of Marriage, and to oblige the man to maintain the woman.   Under the Theocratic system Wealth is so concentrated in large masses, that marriage could not have been established, without permitting, and even encouraging Polygamy.   But on the development of a military form of activity, a new need called for Monogamy, as alone being in harmony with that mode of life.   Besides Slavery offered to the sexual instinct a natural compensation for the legal restriction.   This second form of marriage remained as imperfect as possible with the Greeks, except the gradual perfecting of the rules relating to incest.   Their inferior military activity enabled them to manage their affairs, without confiding in women ; and their intellectual tastes gave them a disinclination for women's society.   The full development of ancient Monogamy was thus reserved for the Polytheism of Rome, where the honour paid to the Wife and the Mother was carried to its due limit. Private life accordingly became the habitual solace of the Roman after the labours of the camp, or the contests of the forum.   Women were necessarily invested with implicit confidence, during the long absence of their husbands ; and thus were required to preside over the moral training of the family, to which the task of the special tutor was considered subordinate.   The continual stimulus of a high form of public activity further impressed on both sexes a character of severity, which disposed both to set a high value on purity of life.

There are three successive stages of Polytheism; first Conservative, next Intellectual, and lastly Social. By these the main education of mankind was accomplished amongst our various Western ancestors. But notwithstanding the necessity for the two other forms, the first alone composed a true system, so as to comprise in its sphere the circle of human life. If Theologism had been destined to endure for ever, it would have been under this primitive form of Theocracy; although Fetichism still better marks the stability of the Absolute Religion. The Greek and the Roman forms of Polytheism, when compared with the Egyptian Theocracy, seem only long phases of transition, destined respectively to cultivate the intelligence, and the activity, when freed from an oppressive yoke. Their appearance sufficed to prove the wholly provisional nature of the Theological system ; for each lost its special character after having adequately fulfilled its peculiar task, and it died out with the achievement of that.

But the last phase brought antiquity really to the threshold of our Final State, intellectual and social. Under the influence of Greeks the Roman thinkers quickly freed themselves from Polytheistic Beliefs; and they even frequently reached a complete emancipation. Their practical life disposed them to feel the essential emptiness of the Metaphysical doctrines. They tended at once towards the Positive doctrine, based on the natural existence of the Order of the World, according to the theory of Aristotle, the first of philosophers, so far as the state of science allowed him to see it. In its social aspect, the efforts towards a reformation of life, were still more marked ; since they sprang from the necessities of the position. The existence of a warlike activity after a sufficient extension of the system of conquest left military energy with a purely defensive task, the object of which was to protect the rise of Industry, already springing into prominence. All the higher spirits began to foresee, and even to promote the final transformation of Theocracy, into the ultimate form Sociocracy ; under which each individual power should be devoted to the continual service of Humanity. This normal state of society was at first considered by the great minds, as being far nearer at hand than it could possibly be. They were thus led to resist the final stage of the transition, the Catholic Church, which they supposed could do nothing but retard the ultimate type.

A development directed by systematic care would no doubt now suffice to bring the various Polytheistic nations to Positivism, without passing through any Monotheistic stage. Since the Fetichists even would be disposed for this attempt to accelerate their progress, I shall hereafter explain the conditions and the course it would take, amongst the numerous races in a state similar to that of the Egyptians, Greeks, and Romans of old. But this fortunate opportunity was denied to the original evolution of mankind ; and thus nothing could prevent Theologism from passing through a protracted and final era of Monotheism.

This last phase of the Provisional Synthesis was in truth only really necessary on the social ground. For human intelligence would have been better directed by a system of Polytheism, if skilfully concentrated under a few deities, than by any sort of Monotheism. Indeed the Unity of Supernaturalism, even when modified as it was, by the sacred hierarchy of Catholicism, very inadequately represents the essential diversity presented as well by the external World, as by the constitution of our nature. Accordingly Monotheism never could entirely overcome the last protest made against it by the spirit of Polytheism, in the doctrine of Manicheeism, or the two principles. A really systematic Polytheism would certainly require more than such a dualism. It would not fulfil its function, either in logical method, or in scientific result, unless it admitted as many chief Deities, as there are Categories in the entire range of phenomena. True philosophers will one day have to modify the existing forms of Polytheism in this spirit, and peaceably substitute Positivism for it. And thus, under a competent guidance, the races of Asia and Oceania may be spared the long task of preparation, required to elaborate the civilisation of Europe.

To secure this result the only thing to be done would be to improve the method which Polytheism followed in its original concentration. Indeed the Unity of Theology effected by Monotheism, is only an example of that need for generalisation, which led to the substitution of gods for fetiches. The establishment of Monotheism was a mere extension of the subordinate doctrine of Polytheism, by which it sought to express the obvious regularity, which existed in all kinds of phenomena. For a special deity of the invariable had been created under the name of Destiny, possessed of a kind of paramount authority over the other gods. When the need of unity became supreme, what was done, was to make this superiority of Destiny more complete and more active ; and to reduce the ancient gods to the condition of mere ministers. If this natural course were regularly modified on system, Polytheism could easily be transformed into Positivism. It would only be necessary to divide the god of general Destiny, into as many separate Destinies, as a rational study exhibits to us in the physical, intellectual, and moral, world. This modification is quite in harmony with the spirit of Polytheism ; and it would enable Polytheists to dispense with the theoretic vagueness of Monotheism, which by a vain search after an Objective principle of Unity, has greatly retarded the construction of a final Synthesis. The supernatural wills would thus become immutable ; and would speedily be absorbed in the natural Laws, corresponding to these different Destinies.

Without pursuing this subject any further at present, I must point out that this course was impossible to the original evolution of Theologism. To pass through it requires an exact knowledge of the Universal Order, in those who are to direct this transition from Polytheism to Positivism. Monotheism was therefore at the outset indispensable to the progress of the intellect, though it ended by retarding it.

Mono-
THEISM, pp.
89-112.

Monotheism on the whole was an indispensable form of Theology.

We owe to Monotheism the popularisation of the third essential element of Logic, the art of combining ideas by appropriate Signs. As this art completes the permanent modes of the reasoning process it has assumed the part of representing the whole. The Logic of Signs makes us too often forget the Logic of Images, which is due to Polytheism, and above all the Logic of the Feelings, which is due to Fetichism. In spite of the credit it enjoys with the lettered, the first is by no means the most valuable of the three for the discovery of truth even in the abstract, and in fact is not the most effective for the propagation of truth. Its superiority is in Deduction, which Signs render more easy and rapid, at the risk however of confusion and verbiage. Images are more adapted for Induction, especially when inspired by feelings. Nevertheless as signs alone are capable of general adaptation, this quality must always give them a peculiar scientific importance. Positivism, whilst admitting their value, will always combine with Signs the two

Monotheism popularised the Logic of Signs.

other Logical methods, those of Images and Feelings, both still preferred by women and proletaries. That this method of Signs is due to Monotheism is undeniable notwithstanding the pretensions of Greek ontology. For when Unity of the divinity became the doctrine, it naturally led all minds towards general reflections, in which Images were impossible, and where Feelings could not supply their place, from want of clearness and precision. Signs thus became the sole habitual instrument of thought. The mind gradually came to employ them almost exclusively, and extended their use to all classes of subjects. Where their employment has become excessive, especially in the East, amongst people ill prepared for Monotheism, it has often produced, under the name of the *cabala*, a peculiar kind of intellectual extravagance, full of grave moral and social dangers. But these defects in no way affect the real value of the institution, nor the aptitude of Monotheism to cultivate it. Thus the rise, the maturity, and the decline, of the Preliminary Religion, respectively contributed the three main elements of true Logic, which have been duly united into a natural whole by the Final Religion. We see also that the popular use of the Logic of Signs must coincide with an equal extension in the deductive spirit. For the systematisation of Belief forced all to draw, from certain immutable principles, a variety of practical and even speculative consequences. Although this religious habit is common to all the Monotheistic populations, its chief usefulness is found in the West, where the division of the two powers led to constant discussions. The Religion of the Middle Age promoted Deduction by means of Signs, as that of antiquity promoted Induction by means of Images. In Logic as in Morality, the real Education of man was due to a long popular effort, in accordance with the general Belief, but without any direction from professors. It is only in our days that systematic influences can be brought to direct this spontaneous work of the people.

Moral value of Monotheism.

The principal purpose of the last phase of Theology is the Moral training of man.

Speculation and Action had been cultivated under Polytheism: Feeling was neglected.

Antiquity had duly cultivated first the Speculative, then the Active element in life. It had even established the natural superiority of the latter over the former. These two principles had been thoroughly implanted in all the nations fully incorporated in the Greco-Roman world. But it was far from sufficient to complete the training of the Western race ; since it did not include the Feelings, which are as much superior to the activity, as this is to the intelligence.   This, the natural centre of human Life, required therefore a third period of transition to be devoted to it.   Such was the final condition required to transform Theocracy into Sociocracy.

This last branch of Man's Education formed in the first place, a systematisation of general Morality, aiming at the ultimate substitution of Duties for Rights.   The proof of its power is to be seen in its ability to guide the great social revolution required by the condition of the West.   It accomplished the complete though gradual abolition of Slavery, a step in human Progress without which no decided advance could have been made.   When this work was effected the main elements of the final system could at once commence their decisive expansion, under the waning protection of the last provisional system.   In the great work of the Education of Man the Middle Age had a twofold mission : to reduce Morality to a system, and to give Freedom to the labourers.   This great social function required a final transformation of the Absolute Religion.   First spontaneous, then inspired, Religion next became revealed. *A systematic Morality was supplied by the Middle Age.*

The entire moral vigour of Roman Polytheism depended upon its political aim.   As soon as the military activity was exhausted, upon the completion of the work of incorporating the nations, it was seen how radically impotent the ancient creeds were to deal with that unparalleled corruption, which indolence and wealth had produced.   Theological morality could only be made systematic by recurring to a Supernatural Unity ; which was required to combine the religious doctrines, and to give sanction to the moral precepts.   Monotheism, the result of the whole cycle of previous Thought, was profoundly called for by the condition of society.   It was, in fact, the natural issue of the various forms of Polytheism ; since the extinction of the nationalities created the desire for a common Belief, to harmonise the general Brotherhood of Mankind. *Monotheism was essential to restore the condition of society.*

In order to accomplish its moral work, the last phase of Theology fell back upon the support of a Future Life, which had been only secondary in the earlier forms of Theology, when the divine agency was direct.   Recourse to a future life increased the sphere of positive reason.   For the Supernatural *The Monotheistic system concentrated its efforts on Future Life.*

Faith thus abandoned the present, as it already had surrendered the past when it gave up the doctrine of metempsychosis. The authority of the Priest concentrated itself solely on the Future; over which it established an undivided empire, the paramount importance of which no believer could gainsay.

And this required a basis of Revelation.

This institution naturally led to another doctrine, which must always present to us the chief feature of the last Provisional system. The Monotheistic belief being based on the criticism of Polytheism, had been obliged to authorise free rational discussion. At the same time that it employed this dangerous auxiliary, it needed means to free itself from the active solvent of the metaphysical spirit. To establish so arduous a compromise, they were brought to fall back on a Supernatural Revelation, without which these vague beliefs offered no consistency in theory, and certainly no influence over society. Monotheism could not, like Polytheism, content itself with confused and floating traditions. An artificial concentration so great as it was, required at least a religious Code, supposed to rest on a Divine authority.

And, in Catholicism, led to the separation of Spiritual from Temporal Power.

These conditions are common to all forms of Monotheism, which had a real historical existence. But in themselves they were not enough for the moral purpose of Western Monotheism. This great work must be attributed to an admirable social institution, the principal characteristic of true Catholicism, the separation of the Spiritual from the Temporal power, necessarily confounded as these had been, throughout the whole period of Antiquity. The moral weakness of Christianity, wherever this political condition is not adequately fulfilled, shows that the true value of Western Monotheism consists in its supplying the doctrinal foundation for this division. This is the chief reason whereby the Catholic phase of Religion became indispensable to human Progress.

This separation arose naturally from the moral condition of the Polytheistic world.

However imperfect this first separation of the two powers was, it was an obvious consequence of the general situation, when Greek Thought and Roman Activity became truly united. Monotheism had been a doctrine in the ancient world of mere philosophers; who, in spite of their visions of a rule of mind, maintained a position of bare speculation, amidst the resistance which they naturally met with from the Polytheistic system.

The gradual adoption of Monotheism, consequently, could only come about under a thorough sense of its moral superiority.

This alone could win for it general assent. Everyone began to feel, more and more, that the union of the two powers, indispensable as it was in times past for conquest, only gave a sanction in the end to unbridled depravity. It began to be understood, that the rules of Morality must not be left to be defended by those, to restrain whom they were most required. To make Morality effective, the Priesthood needed to have no authority but in the sphere of the intellect and the heart ; whilst within this, their proper sphere, they were entirely independent of political authority. Now, both these conditions were spontaneously fulfilled under the long official duration of Polytheism. At the same time the composite Roman Empire was evidently tending towards its dissolution, as a natural consequence of its vast extension. A purely Spiritual Power alone was now able to unite, by a common education, races too heterogeneous to endure any longer political concentration. Thus political tendencies concurred with intellectual conditions, and with moral wants, to suggest the spontaneous separation of the two forms of social authority. This separation of the Powers is at bottom the whole cause of the essential superiority, which the Western has over the Eastern form of Monotheism. The morality of Islam is not inferior in power to that of Catholicism, and its dogmas are less repulsive to the reason. The inferior social influence of Mahometanism is due therefore to the position of the Priests. In this military Theocracy, the Priesthood, always either the oppressor or the oppressed, as in antiquity, had no means of cultivating the supremacy of the Feelings over Thoughts and Acts. The inherent tendency of every Monotheism, even the Jewish, towards this moral education was always abortive, except in the West ; where the whole current of its intellectual and social history promoted this result. In order to reach habitually to those springs in the human heart, which give rise to human virtues and to vices, a Priesthood was required, such as could judge and give counsel to men in their conduct, without assuming to impose it on them by force. Now this state of things was a direct result of the nature of the situation in the West, even after the legal establishment of the new Faith. The rulers of the Polytheistic world no doubt adopted Catholicism from a sense of its moral superiority ; but they were as little disposed as before its triumph to yield it political authority.

It forms the key of the whole Doctrine and Polity of Catholicism.

This separation of the two powers was so closely connected with the social influence of Monotheism in the West, that the entire system of Revealed Faith was constructed with reference to it. We thus can understand how its true Founder, the incomparable St. Paul, was able, from the first rise of Christianity, to reduce to a system the doctrines and the institutions, which his successors extended in accordance with the needs of the case. An end, so distinct and so paramount as this was, modified in the minds of all, capable of comprehending its importance, the errors inherent in the Theological spirit. The succeeding volume will explain, how this noble purpose fully clears the Catholicism of the Middle Age, from the charges brought against it by the moderns. Even the least rational dogmas, from the historical point of view, deserve profound respect. Every true philosopher must see, how intimately they were connected with the moral object which this Provisional Religion had undertaken as its mission.

Moral value of doctrine of the Incarnation.

I will here only notice the dogma of the Divine Incarnation, which, with its necessary adjuncts, forms the only essential difference between the Western and the Eastern Revelations. This divergence in Theory answers in fact to the contrast in Practice, between the separation, and the confusion, of the two social authorities. The Musulman System retained, and even extended this concentration of both powers in one hand, as was required by a military Theocracy. It accordingly made the Revealed Faith as simple as possible, thereby avoiding any resistance from a Priesthood to the complete authority of the successors of the Prophet. But Catholicism would not have effected the separation of the two powers, had it not succeeded in giving the Priesthood a Supernatural Head, as the only way in which their social independence could be secured. The leaning of the greater part of the Kings towards Arianism shows, that in their way they felt the importance of this guarantee to the priests. Catholicism borrowed from Polytheism the hypothesis of an Incarnation; but it invested it with a far higher dogmatic authority, and especially with a nobler social character. A Divine Mediator pointed also indistinctly to the growing tendency in Humanity to find its highest providence within itself. The Human Type had furnished Fetichism with its general basis; though there it took no determined form, and retained only the moral character of man.

It assumed still further prominence under Polytheism, which left the imagination free to clothe the Governing Powers of the world with all the attributes of Human Nature idealised. Catholicism gave a new meaning to this tendency, and concentrated it on the Supreme Unity of the Godhead in which the two natures were combined, but not confounded. This development of the original theory of Incarnation could not but issue eventually, in the entire disappearance of the Fictitious Being; so soon as the Real Being had acquired sufficient majesty and power to take the place of its indispensable precursor.

Notwithstanding the separation of the two powers, strengthened as it was by all the doctrines and the institutions with which it was surrounded, the social influence of the Catholic system can only be explained by the fact, that it received constant support from the various practical arrangements, called out in the altered position of Western Europe. It is not Catholicism which produced the principal political changes that mark the Middle Age. It only reduced them to order, or invested them with a sanction when they agreed with its own nature. Catholicism itself would never have arisen without the pre-existing stimulus of these wants in society, which deeply altered the military life. War was then in the act of passing from Conquest to Defence: and pointed to a speedy rise of Peaceful Industry, which demanded a regeneration of Morality. In order to establish a system of conquest, Islamism concentrated, as far as possible, the two powers, although its great Founder was conscious of the importance of separating them. But Catholicism felt the need of dividing them, in order to establish a defensive system. All the essential characteristics of this new condition of society were in existence in fact before the foundation of Catholicism; and they even reacted on that potent genius, by which it was inspired. Although ordinarily attributed to the German invasions, I have shown that the necessary conditions appeared of themselves, when the Roman work of Conquest had been sufficiently accomplished. It has been already observed, as regards the change of Slavery into Serfdom, how it was promoted by the limitation of the slave-market to the area of the Empire. But the same thing is equally apparent as regards the other two conditions of Feudalism : first, the disintegration of the State, and next the graduated series of local authorities. Both these conditions

The new system of Defence seconded the movement.

coincided with the introduction of a system of Defence, by which all warlike energy was habitually localised.

And the Barbarian invaders adopted it.

The Invasions of the Barbarians, without being really indispensable to these different Social transformations, and though they could not have been avoided, served in general to strengthen, and certainly to develop still further the movement of society. In fact defensive activity was more visibly at work amongst the races with whom the system of Conquest never took root. The wandering tribes, who were as little capable of conquering as of being conquered, wished to pass at once into the agricultural state and occupy a country already under cultivation. Their exceptional expeditions aimed, not at domination, but at a settlement. These exhibited a tendency to the development of a military life, similar to that of Roman society; and they would have passed through it, had they ever adopted of their own accord a settled form of life. Their own form of Polytheism, which was obviously adapted to a life of war, was not congenial to their new position. They were then led to prefer the Religion, which they found established in the country they had adopted, and which alone suited the life that they sought. The only serious opposition to this could come from their priestly castes; but these had been rendered completely subordinate by the military chiefs, before Theocracy was established in these Nomad races. This explains their easy conversion to Catholicism, which often occurred even before the actual invasions. The incompleteness of their intellectual training was fortunately compensated by the strength of their social sympathies. Accordingly they readily adopted and speedily cultivated the customs, which were in accordance with their chosen condition. Their practical genius did much to correct the Asceticism and the Quietism, inherent in the Catholic doctrines; and their generous spirit of activity kept in check the egoism involved in the Christian faith. In their warlike disposition we can from the first detect a natural tendency towards a life of peace, so that each warrior was transformed into a mere director of agriculture. They thus quickly effected the decisive transformation of Slavery into Serfdom; and from this beginning gradually arose the complete emancipation of the working masses. The influences of Catholicism merely gave a sanction to the secular tendency towards industry. The same thing took place in regard to the

political disintegration and the Feudal subordination of the
Middle Age; both encouraged independence, as well as combination, amongst the knights of Feudalism. Both of these principles were equally valued by them, though the Catholic doctrine
did little to bring the two into working harmony together.

At the same time, as these races had passed beyond the
Roman phase of war, their new life was too pacific to satisfy
their activity, which was not absorbed by the employment it
had naturally found. The result was that military turbulence
which distinguishes the Feudal from the Roman mode of life,
where the national activity had absorbed all private contests.
But this difference, and it was one which the priesthood never
could overcome, still left Feudalism as the principal source of
the grand results of the Middle Age, and in regard to these the
influence of Catholicism has been greatly exaggerated. This is
clearly true of Chivalry, the social development whereof was
rather checked than promoted by the religious doctrine, which
was unable to appreciate its value. An institution of the kind
was so completely natural to the situation, and so completely
independent of the current belief, that it arose wherever the
same form of life prevailed; as we see amongst the Musulman
warriors of the time, and also amongst several Polytheists of
our own day. Catholicism had a larger part in the just emancipation of women. But its real and direct influence did no
more than cultivate purity, which is emphatically due to
Catholicism; without this the liberty of woman would have
speedily degenerated into an unbridled corruption, equally
fatal to both sexes. Tenderness, which after all is the great
feature of this admirable movement to raise women, and to
which purity itself was only the indispensable preliminary,
sprang solely from the spirit of Feudal life, and had to struggle
against the opposition of Catholicism.

It is impossible to do justice to the Middle Age, unless we
keep in view the simultaneous influence of the two heterogeneous elements, which were perforce combined in it. In
spite of the separation of the two powers, imperfect as that
was, the intellectual confusion, and the moral dangers, inherent
in Monotheism, necessarily prejudiced the social mission undertaken by the Catholic Priesthood. The priests would never
have succeeded in restoring harmony to the social state, had not
the state of society itself thrown up some practical forces, which

Feudalis gave its main social character to the Middle Age.

Medieval Life exhibits a strict com-bination of Catholicism and Feu-dalism.

naturally tended to regulate its action.   The Catholic discipline never could succeed in reaching anything but private life. Without the influence of Feudalism, it would have been profoundly injurious to public life.

Double system of Defence. (1) Against European nomads. (2) Against Mahometan conquest.

To explain the laws whereby the two elements of the Feudal world were combined, we must take into consideration the double system of defensive wars, which succeeded the regular establishment of Feudalism.   The success of the invasions would have tended to their perpetual renewal, if the first conquerors had not vigorously repressed subsequent irruptions.   But this long reflex effort of the new races shows us two phases, each distinct, and succeeding each other : the one is the case of the races who were, the other of those who were not, capable of being incorporated with the West.   In the first place it was necessary, by a wise mixture of concession and resistance, to restrain the Polytheistic tribes ; and to oblige them to become husbandmen, fixed on their own soil, however unfavourable it might be.   They were then permitted to attach themselves to the Western aggregate, on the simple terms of embracing Catholicism, which became the symbol of Western civilisation. But when the incorporation of the new races was complete, it found a great task for its united energies, one eminently qualified to give the new system strength as well as development, in the indispensable repression of the Musulman invasions.   The West could look for no compromise possible with a form of Monotheism, which aspired like Catholicism to universal ascendancy, and at the same time directed a system of conquest, analogous to that of Rome.   The net result of this unavoidable struggle was ultimately found to be, simply the sharing of the great Roman Empire between these two incompatible systems. When this territorial division had been duly established, the mutual pressure they exercised on each other must have given an impetus to the main social object of the two systems, by encouraging peaceful activity.   Thus the two great forms of Monotheism, neither of which could aspire to become universal, tended towards a speedy dissolution, for want of a great practical end.   Each in its way prepared the ground directly for the creation of the true System of Unity.   This alone could finally close that antagonism of the two, the continuance of which had abundantly shown how purely provisional had been the Theological and Military phase of human civilisation.

The Catholic-Feudal phase of transition will always deserve much attention and much gratitude of us, for having, better than any other system, founded the normal condition of Humanity, and for having directed the last preparatory stage required for its advent. The two forms of Polytheism, the Greek and the Roman, had brought about a presentiment of the Final form of Life, which naturally became more easy to understand, as it came more near to its fulfilment. These noble traditions, which were never lost by the true Chiefs of Society, especially the political Chiefs, continually inspired the whole Middle Age to organise as far as possible the system, of which Antiquity had caught a vision. Although efforts so premature could hardly meet with any durable success, they were as indispensable, as they were inevitable, if the outline was to be traced for the vast edifice, yet reserved for our age. In all essential respects the Middle Age really proposed the problem, which we have now to solve; and it even frequently indicated the general nature of the solution. The importance of these efforts will be felt, and their natural failure will be understood, when we reflect, that a great problem cannot really be propounded unless some kind of solution is at the same time suggested.

The Catholic-Feudal Period foreshadowed the final System of Society.

As regards the intelligence, I have already remarked on the power inherent in Monotheism, to cultivate the last general element of Logic. It will be enough now to add some notice of the peculiar tendency towards it, exhibited by Western Monotheism. By separating the two powers, and by systematising morality, it produced amongst the Catholic populations general habits of discussion and of meditation highly adapted to cultivate the Logic of Signs; for this was being constantly applied to the highest subjects of speculations. Besides a worship, which sanctioned the use of Images, and above all continually awakened the Sentiments, could not fail to foster, along with the other two, this third element of the thinking process, the Logic of Signs.

Developed the Logic of Signs.

Apart from its lofty practical mission, this intellectual effort of the West even found a sphere in theory, and that essentially popular, in the attempts common to Monotheism everywhere, to form a conception of the Order of the Universe. This grand generalisation contrasted with the speciality, and with the inconsistency, of the ancient Theological explanations. Although Catholicism, rightly absorbed as it was by its social duties,

Catholicism was originally favourable to the growth of Positive Thought.

H 2

neither could incorporate, nor ought it to have incorporated in its system, the intellectual movement of antiquity which gave birth to its own doctrine, still its scientific teaching during the Middle Age was one of admirable breadth. The subjection of Reason to Faith, with which it is so often reproached, was aimed only at the discouragement of premature speculations regarding the principles of morals. It thus concentrated intellectual effort upon Science, the only sphere which was really open to it, and one the pursuit of which was to form the basis of the whole subsequent construction of thought. Within these reasonable limits the Catholic system adopted the provisional doctrine as to the divine government of the material world, established by Aristotle to shelter positive study under the sanction of Theology (see Vol. III. ch. vi.). This strange combination of an absolute will in a Deity, with immutable laws in matter, was even adopted on authority in the great scholastic compromise as to the freedom of man's will, which closed the Middle Age ; when Catholicism, having accomplished its principal task, ceased to be really an active power. It could not have adopted the doctrine earlier, without utterly contradicting itself. In a word the Church was then only hostile to the Metaphysical spirit ; and we may now regret, that it did not still further succeed in preventing that phase from disturbing the growth of the Positive spirit, which was long under the special guardianship of Catholicism.

The moral aspect of the Doctrine of Nature and Grace.

The Theology of the Middle Ages had still more reason for excluding Ontology from the moral and social sphere, as the Catholic dogmas had already established the only principle which could guide the earliest systematic training of the moral and social world, at least for private life, the natural base of public life. The true author of the Theology, St. Paul, satisfactorily expressed the general principle by the constant antagonism between Nature and Grace ; and the doctrine was then as suitable for theory, as it was indispensable to practice. In the sphere of Practice, this principle pointed to the great struggle of human life ; in that of Theory, it opened the way for regular study of man's moral constitution. This was the only corrective proper to the essentially egoistic character of every form of Monotheism ; which makes it impossible to admit the natural existence of the purely benevolent affections, without preventing the creed from acquiring a form sufficiently systematic, and consequently debarring it from real influence. Whilst the visionary interests of men in a Life to come left it to Practical Morality to discipline their real interests in the Life on earth, Theoretic Morality was able to find indirectly a sanction for the higher sentiments, under the name of divine Inspirations. If Positivism is destined in both aspects far to surpass Catholicism, it is solely from the spirit of reality, which specially belongs to it. This reality enables us to get rid of the crude doctrine that man's soul is a uniform entity, and substitutes for it a sound cerebral theory; so opening to the scientific spirit that ancient domain of Grace, the last province of the celestial Regent, the Deity who prepares the way for Humanity. When Ontology sought in this ground to replace Theology, it succeeded, as usual, only in disorganising everything, without constructing anything; since it retained this vicious idea of the Unity of man's nature, whilst suppressing its proper corrective, the power of the benevolent instincts; and thus it brought out still more strongly, in all their nakedness, the Theoretical and Practical evils of this idea of the Soul as an entity.

With respect to theories of social life we can see that the Middle Age made a notable advance, although Catholicism could only deal with these questions empirically, that is, by the sole influence of its political doctrine, its principle of the separation of the two powers. Then arose the grand conception of Human Progress, which was to give birth to Sociology, when combined with the conception of Order which Aristotle in his Politics had systematised, as far as it was possible to treat social Order by itself. Had the spirit of those times admitted any considerable extension of rational positivity to the phenomena of society, a basis of experimental reasoning about society would have been discovered. For the three terms indispensable to the discovery of any kind of Progress were found in the mere comparison between the Monotheistic and the two Polytheistic systems, out of which combined Monotheism had arisen. The practical conviction of the superiority of the Romans to the Greeks, had shown to the latest thinkers of Antiquity an unquestionable Progress, in spite of their Theocratic prejudices which favoured the stationary, or even the retrograde spirit. A deeper and more general feeling raised the Middle Age above the Roman phase. At least the men of letters alone, whose influence was not great, disputed the popular conviction. When

The conception of Human Progress was indicated even in Feudalism.

this sense of the superiority of the Middle Age to the Roman was united to the belief, already general, in the superiority of the Roman to the Greek period, the proof of human Progress, at least on the moral and political side, was fairly established. The prevailing theory, however, failed to grasp these general facts; for Catholicism was led to disavow its origin in Greek and Roman civilisation.   To give strength to Revelation, which was necessary for its social object, it represented itself exclusively as the heir of the peculiar Monotheism, which had long distinguished a small province of Asia.   Nevertheless, although this artificial connection with Judaism, one as injurious to the Heart as it was to the Intellect, was theoretically paramount, it never prevented the thinkers during the Feudal period from duly honouring their social forefathers of antiquity.   Thus the notion of Progress began thenceforth to be dimly discerned, and that even in the life of Humanity as a whole; although the theory of Inspiration disturbed the influence which practical life would give it.   But these two influences, of doctrine and of practice, worked in thorough harmony in regard to private life; for in this the improvement was more complete and also more apparent.   During the whole of the Middle Age, the people of the West were continually animated with the noblest zeal for the improvement of the character, and even of the intellect, as a means for the elevation of human life.   The selfish end which the prevailing Theology gave to this tendency, would increase its energy, although it vitiated its purity.   Thus the notion of human Progress became thoroughly familiar to the people of the West.   In a lower degree it even existed amongst the Musulman race, in spite of the confusion of the two powers. Moral Progress, indeed, is inherent in the moral code of every kind of Monotheism, which always supposes a written type, to which each believer must more and more conform.   By this influence regularly and constantly exerted as it was, Monotheism, both in the East and the West, partly compensated for the disastrous failure of its theory to control the life of men in society.   The conception of Human Progress, when once firmly implanted in private life, would before long extend to public life, by virtue of the intimate connection between the two.

Catholicism secured especially a moral discipline by   All the intellectual features of the Catholic Synthesis were bound up with the moral system, which formed the main function of the independent Priesthood.   It was thus enabled to institute, even from the first, the earliest system of general reducing Subjective Life to system. education, the object of which was to guide human life in its entirety, supplying the want of an objective foundation by means of Revelation.. Morality was thus placed in that position of supreme importance, which belongs to it in the natural state of man. Although that morality was essentially personal, the priesthood wisely extended it to domestic life, and the wisdom of temporal rulers even applied it of their own accord to public life. By the agency of this moral system every relation of human life was emphatically improved. The chief human emotions were regularly subjected to an admirable system of discipline, the aim of which was to uproot on habit the smallest germs of corruption. This training of the heart was uniformly regarded as above that of the intellect ; and thus it introduced in a marked way a regular organisation of the Subjective Life, which, emanating from Fetichism, and developed by Polytheism, could find only in Monotheism its first systematic form. Even on its theoretic side, this course of education was a preparation for the ultimate form ; for it introduced, after its manner, into universal education the general history of Humanity.

However imperfect were these first efforts to systematise Practical wisdom in priesthood and people compensated for errors of creed. human Life, they deserve the greater admiration and gratitude, as the wisdom of the priesthood and the instinct of the public had continually to struggle with the intellectual vices and the moral dangers of the Doctrine they professed. Theology was only able to work out a system in its decline ; and then all it had to offer was the vague principle of a supernatural unity to give harmony to the intellect, and the unworthy motive of personal salvation, as a foundation of moral discipline. But so great was then the need of a universal reform of life, that any means were effectual to develop the tendencies then rife throughout the West. At its origin Theologism had been obliged to leave the instincts of human nature to their spontaneous impulse, in order to bring out what were their true tendencies. In its decline, on the contrary, it had to discipline them in order to determine their mutual relations, and thus to prepare for their ultimate systematisation. In both cases the natural disposition and good sense of man obviated the chief imperfections in the doctrines. Neither the moral impotence of Polytheism, nor the social feebleness of Monotheism, ever resulted in the practical evils which the theoretic errors of both might suggest. The pleasure which is given by the higher feelings is so great, that their tendency is to develop of themselves, when once awakened under the effect of the charm which is peculiar to them, whatever be the motive which originally awakens them; even although that motive be a personal one, and too often no other motive could stir their native dulness. Although devotion was inculcated in the name of an ineradicable selfishness, the habit of self-denial, and the cultivation of the life within, could not fail, whatever the ground, to produce deep-seated improvement, such as could be obtained in no other way. The moral unity which was thus worked out by Theologism in its decline furnished in the Middle Age the prototype of that, which now is presented by Positivism in its birth. To compensate for their vague character, the supernatural doctrines continued to give an undesigned consecration to the better instincts. If the collective body of imaginary Beings under Polytheism had served to represent Humanity provisionally, still more would this be the case, when under Monotheism they were condensed into one Being, whose more regular will answered better to the Order of the universe. But all these features of Catholicism hung on the independence of the priesthood; and they could not but cease, so soon as the priests began to lose the progressive character, which had made them independent.

Medieval society heralded that of Sociocracy.

This memorable period of transition is indeed best judged by its social tendencies, hampered as they were by the ruling doctrine. But this constant difficulty of its doctrine did not in fact prevent the Middle Age from preparing the way for the ultimate Sociocracy, either by tracing out its chief conditions, or by giving rise to its essential elements.

It accomplished three great social and national changes in Europe. (1) By the final abolition of Caste.

As regards the normal conditions of life, we owe to the Middle Age the sole systematic attempt made to abolish the system of Caste, which, however much modified by Military Polytheism, formed invariably the great substratum of the political organisation. Caste received a decisive blow from the celibacy of the clergy, which, by putting an end to the hereditary transmission of the highest office, heralded its abolition in all. The same tendency began to be shown in temporal government, in which also the regular succession was frequently modified by conditions of fitness throughout every grade of the feudal hierarchy. In the second place, general morality, being reduced to a system and made the special province of an independent body of clergy, led to the substitution of duties for rights, in spite of the innate proneness of Theology to set up authorities above all criticism.   The whole course of education and of discipline peculiar to the Middle Age tended to regulate real life, both private and public, in accordance with the prevailing doctrine.   This tendency was even regularly enforced by legislation, which everywhere sanctioned the deprivation of office, and even the confiscation of goods, to atone for, or repair a violation of duty.   Now, discipline such as this, and one always regulated by a public sense of the common interest, was a very different thing from that arbitrary action which was a consequence of the Theocratic origin of the ancient authorities. It indicated a direct and increasing tendency to transform Theocracy into Sociocracy.   This tendency became still more decided in international relations; where we see the new character assumed by the Western body of nations.   In place of the compulsory incorporation proper to Roman conquest, the Middle Age substituted a truly free association, based upon a community of Belief and of Education, with no other common authority but the Spiritual Power they acknowledged.   The settlement of the German races prepared the ground for this great political transformation.   It was completed upon the formation of the new corporate body in Europe under the indispensable condition of dictatorship wielded by the incomparable Charlemagne.   It was consolidated and developed during the Crusades; and it displayed its real character at the close of the Middle Age when, in spite of imperious tradition and powerful influences, the characteristic change was effected as to the centre of Western Europe.   This centre was irrevocably transferred from Rome to Paris; and it pointed to the fact that in place of the ancient Empire of the West, then only an empty title, there had succeeded a real Republic of the West.   The incorporation of the West in one, now carried on freely, would naturally gather round the central nation; whereas, when the Romans were accomplishing this work by force, it had gravitated towards one of the extremities.

These three political results of the Middle Age have left for ever traces that are ineradicable, however much discredited by our modern anarchy.   This is no less true of the natural harmony which the feudal system established between the principle

Marginal notes:

(2) By founding a sense of duty and of public opinion.

(3) By transferring the centre of the West from Rome to Paris.

It also gave its Chivalry, the social emancipation of Women, and the independence of the workmen.

of freedom and that of co-operation, of which spirit such noble illustration was given by Chivalry. But the most important influence of this admirable epoch of human history is, that it has left us as its legacy, at once the great social problem, and the essential elements of its ultimate solution. It emancipated women, and it formed the workmen.

The moral dignity of Women, culminating in the Worship of the Virgin.

The freedom of the loving sex within the home was commenced by the spirit of purity, which Catholicism enforced, and was completed by the spirit of tenderness peculiar to Feudalism : and by its agency the manners of the West were profoundly modified. It brought out the most characteristic and most spontaneous element of true moral power, and thus it indicated the final supremacy of general affection. Although the influence of woman in that age only took an organised form amongst the superior classes, it would be manifested most emphatically in the humbler families, where it would not be disfigured by wealth or rank. Although confined to the aristocratic classes, this new influence reacted during the Middle Age upon the whole sphere of human life. It even tended to modify the creed of the West, for it compelled Catholicism to give greater religious sanction to tenderness. Admirable efforts were then made to form the worship of Woman into a system, and it was the necessary forerunner to the adoration of Humanity. During the twelfth, the greatest century of the Middle Age, there arose out of these efforts a growing love for the Virgin, the most beautiful type which the Western scheme of Revelation could produce. This truly Human Mediatress was a better representative of the normal form of worship, than the Divine Mediator had ever been. The gradual triumph of her cult, which was spontaneous as well as systematic, was the more complete, as the higher minds bent themselves to clothe this ideal type with humanity, and resisted the zeal of the mystics, who aimed at transforming the woman into an immaculate divinity. The grandest invocations of Dante to the new goddess will henceforth serve for the adoration of Woman and of Humanity, especially in the characteristic triplet :—

> In te misericordia, in te pietate,
> In te magnificenza, in te s'aduna
> Quantunque in creatura è di bontate.
>
> ('Parad.,' c. xxxiii.)

The indepen dence of the Workmen

But this change in the social position of women is closely connected with that in the position of workmen, amongst whom the influence of women must be more complete, and even more pure, than anywhere else.   Thus the principal result of the Middle Age in all respects is the social independence of the workers, accomplished when the transformation of Slavery into Serfage had sufficiently prepared the ground for Industrial life under the wardship of Feudalism.

This immense revolution, as well by its practical consequences as by its influence on thought, directly advanced the entire West towards the ultimate state of Sociocracy.   It made pacific activity predominant, and so indicated the approaching maturity of the true Great Being.   The conception itself no longer con-tained elements of contradiction, since its different essential parts now began to tend towards an intimate union.   The necessary distinction between the employers and the workers was recognised immediately upon the entire abolition of serfdom, even before the close of the Middle Age.   This, the first germ of an industrial organisation, brought into view the want of a com-plete regeneration, in order to supply some proper substitute for the protection which serfdom had given to the population, who without it were in constant danger of material oppres-sion.   The necessity became greater, as the industrial chiefs, engrossed with schemes for their own elevation, aspired to succeed to the feudal authorities, and to rear a political system upon a basis of wealth.   At the same time the new spirit of practical activity directly tended to secure the general success of the Positive doctrine, by the fresh importance which it gave, at once to the conception of the Order of Nature, and to the need of improving it.   The progress made by the proletariat in Europe disposed men's minds to place true human happiness in the just cultivation of the benevolent feelings, whether in the family or in society, as being the feelings alone susceptible of universal use, and capable of taking the place of all others. In order to obtain for the lower classes this, the sole compen-sation possible for their material position, it would have been necessary that this noble end should have become the great aim in life of the powerful and the rich, and indeed the essential condition of their superior rank.   Now a morality such as this is incompatible with the visionary and egoistic character of even the purest Theologism.   It could be established only by the Positive Religion ; for none other could substitute the notion of relative duties for that of absolute

rights, and it did this by creating authorities uniformly open
to criticism.

But the
Middle Age
proposed,
and could
not solve,
the social
problem.

The preceding remarks show how the intermediate phase
of Catholic Feudalism prepared, and even traced out the normal
condition of Humanity. But if, what we have now to do is
simply to realise under all its essential aspects the programme
of the Middle Age, we must distinctly bear in mind, that when
realised, it involves a total change in the Political and Religious
system. The organisation of this great period never could answer
the fundamental problems, which yet it was its mission to propose once for all. Monotheism proved less durable than any
other form of the Provisional Religion, and it fell into spontaneous dissolution in the very act of extending its intellectual
and social empire. To close this summary estimate of Medieval
life, it is important to point out the unavoidable contradiction
between the principal characteristics of this, the last grand
phase of human Progress.

By its exag-
geration of
Feeling,
Catholic
Feudalism
was radi-
cally un-
stable.

When compared with the two preceding phases, this the
last stage in the transformation of Theocracy into Sociocracy
presented the same radical error : that is, it was only able to
deal with that side of Progress, which devolved to it, and it was
never able to combine with it the other elements, no less essential to its completeness. The civilisation of the Greeks sacrificed everything to the Intellect ; the Roman world gave undue
prominence to Activity. It its turn, the Catholic-Feudal
scheme pushed too far the natural ascendancy of Feeling, and
tended to set Feeling in antagonism with the speculative and
practical life, which it had to control. This exaggeration was
no less indispensable than it was inevitable ; for the task then
was, to bring into prominence the main element of human
nature, which had been fatally repressed by its subordinate
position. But this showed how unstable was the organisation
of the time, for it was ever exposed to the instinctive regrets,
felt by the most cultivated minds and the most energetic characters. Its incompetence became all the more glaring, because,
although its aim was the establishment of Unity in human life,
it was unable to combine the essential attributes of man's character.   Thus the full glory of Catholic Feudalism, which was
really confined to the twelfth century, in spite of its more
laborious preparation, endured a still shorter period than did
the other two phases of transformation. Monotheism, when it

continually claimed for itself an eternal supremacy, unconsciously exposed its natural instability; whilst Fetichism and Polytheism were too deeply rooted in human nature, ever to need this kind of reassurance.

No systematisation of human life can be permanent, whilst it is partial; and this is still more true as it concerns Feeling, than for Intelligence, or Activity. From the intimate connection between these three elements of our nature, every cultivation which is too exclusive ends in becoming contradictory. The weakness of the Catholic Synthesis, both theoretically and practically, could not but eventually destroy its moral power; for it placed it in antagonism to two movements which were equally inevitable and indispensable. Thus it came about, that the devouter spirits rejected that Future, which was the most favourable to the cultivation of Feeling, in order to preserve a Religion which was essentially based on egoism; at the same time the independent intellects disdained the most important kind of moral training, as apparently involved with an oppressive Theology. A system, such as this, could only acquire any high value through constant efforts by the spiritual authorities, to obviate the intellectual errors and the moral dangers of the dominant creed. Its utility was therefore at an end, when the priesthood lost at once their political independence, and their social morality.

It was placed in constant antagonism to Intellect and Activity.

The conditions fundamental to the Religion were no less liable to instability, than was its leading purpose. When we compare the rise of Monotheism with its reign, we see how, being the child of criticism, it was destined to perish by criticism, which it was as incapable of overcoming, as it was of avoiding. This attitude of contradiction was the direct result of the doctrine of Supernatural Unity, as was seen even in Islamism. But Catholicism would exaggerate the difficulty; because it separated the temporal from the spiritual authorities. Amongst all those intellects, continually employed in examining the consequences of the creed, some would necessarily be found to examine its principles. Now, the Creed of Monotheism was not fitted to conquer in the intellectual combat which it provoked. The most admirable of the Catholic institutions, the Mass, which condensed in one mystical rite, the Doctrine, the Discipline, and the Worship of the religion was so shocking to common sense, that it was always repulsive to over-speculative

Catholicism began with discussion, and perished under it.

minds, whilst it awoke distressing doubts even in the best hearts.

So Feu-
dalism had
encouraged
Industry,
but soon lost
its hold of it.

Nor did the social conditions of the Catholic-Feudal phase exhibit any superior stability. If the military activity of Antiquity was simply provisional, still more so must be that of the Middle Age, when defence had taken the place of conquest; and defence lost all its importance, so soon as the various invasions, general to Europe, were finally beaten back. In its social, as in its intellectual, effect, the better that this system accomplished its principal task, the nearer it drew to its decay. For it was not capable of directing the new form of activity, which it had called into existence. Industrial life became antagonistic to the Theological spirit; both in that it substituted natural laws for supernatural wills, and in that it drew men off from a future in heaven by the attraction of happiness on earth. Industrialism would have been able to have shown more consideration for the Feudal rule, if this had been transformed at an earlier date. But before the aristocracy had changed their military character, the industrial spirit had called out, throughout the West, practical leaders more capable of directing the altered form of existence and continually eager to change their civil eminence into a political rule.

And the
Separation
of the two
Powers was
quite pre-
carious.

Lastly the precarious nature of the Medieval organisation comes out forcibly, when we compare these two sorts of conditions, the intellectual and the social. Harmony between them, which depended on the separation of the two powers, was always doubtful; and it ended in irreparable contests when an object, common to both, no longer checked their inherent divergencies. This separation of the two authorities, notwithstanding the great part which it had in the Progress of the West, was then too premature to continue. It was the result merely of an involuntary balance of force between two powers, each of which aspired to an absolute command, whilst the general social condition continually made it impossible. Speaking in the name of an irresistible will, the priesthood could not confine themselves to counsel, except when insurmountable obstacles prevented them from commanding. The military rulers hardly accepted with a better grace their divided empire; and they aimed at concentration of command, as was required for warlike operations, even in defence. For this reason the normal separation of the two powers belongs exclusively to the Final system of Life. In that, the positive intellect and industrial activity work in unison to keep them separate ; for intellect and activity have there equally a relative character, and unity is maintained by both being subordinate to the Order of Nature. This division of authority, which would have been radically subversive in Antiquity, could not fail to be fatal in like manner to the Medieval organisation of society, although not till it had accomplished its essential purpose as an institution.

Thus the final stage of Absolute Religion found inevitable ruin in the natural consequences of its principal institution. Hitherto no system had fallen, except under the blows of those powers which were destined to succeed it. But the constitution of Catholic Feudalism was so little destined to endure, that it succumbed simply under the spontaneous antagonism of its own chief elements. The irrecoverable decline followed close upon its last important office, when the Musulman invasions had been sufficiently arrested by the Crusades. This, the concluding struggle of the two Monotheisms, proved to be as decisive a blow to the one as to the other. Catholicism especially could not but speedily feel the essential emptiness of its constant pretensions to universal dominion, a thing incompatible with any Absolute Religion, and exclusively reserved for the Relative Religion. At the same time its doctrine, for all that it was so laboriously constructed, so soon as the elaborate Creed of Christendom had lost its principal function, was directly challenged by the unavoidable contrast it presented to the simplicity of Islam. From the social point of view this, the great political achievement of the Middle Age, completed the decisive transformation in Western life. Military activity, already much reduced, lost its last general ground of superiority, and on every side Industrial life speedily assumed the foremost place. Finally, the irremediable partition of the old Roman Empire between two incompatible forms of Worship, led to a growing desire to seek, outside of any Theology, for the sole Faith which could unite in one all sections of the white race, and ultimately the entire human Family.

The Decline of the Middle Age dates from the close of the Crusades.

But this inevitable decline of Monotheism wholly differed from that of Polytheism, in that it was not at all counterbalanced by the gradual approach of a better system. It was only the Final Religion, which was the right successor of the last phase of the Preliminary Religion, and that by fulfilling

The break-up of Catholic Feudalism was necessarily followed by complete disorganisation.

better all the intellectual and social conditions. Now, the leading elements of the new life were not yet sufficiently mature, to permit even the idea that they were tending towards a new Organisation, more complete and more durable than that from which the West of Europe was so ardently and uniformly freeing itself. A most thoughtful philosophical examination, assisted by a sound theory of history, scarcely yet enables us to perceive this fundamental movement of Human Society, which could not but remain long unobserved. Neither the positive spirit nor industrial activity could show their true characters, so long as the Theological and Military organisation really held together. The utter confusion which succeeded its downfall was even indispensable to modern thought, in order to awaken its energies to the conception of a new universal System. Besides this, it was necessary that all the incentives to War should have been successively exhausted during a long anarchy in Europe, before the spontaneous assertion of industrial life could herald to the world the approaching Regeneration of man's practical existence.

REVOLU-
TION, pp.
112-116.
Material and intellectual development involved moral anarchy during the whole Revolutionary period.

Such are the natural causes of that unparalleled fatality, which caused the Middle Age to be succeeded by an immense Revolution in the West, one which only now is entering upon its termination in the central nation. Although the work of reconstruction has accompanied the critical movement with increasing energy, still the necessarily special character of the former and the naturally general character of the latter, fill with a negative tone the whole of the last five centuries. The vanguard of Humanity were then impelled to destroy a system which claimed to be universal, without any attempt to replace it, and whilst losing more and more all sense of general views. The aversion with which men then decried the Middle Age was blinder and more ungrateful, though less deep and less general, than that which the Middle Age had shown for Antiquity. In their eagerness to develop the intelligence and the activity which had not been duly cultivated by the Middle Age, the modern Europeans were naturally seized with a growing admiration for their Greek and Roman predecessors. Although this spontaneous return upon the past seemed to renew the chain of ages, the continuity of the race was interrupted by this fatal divorce from the Middle Age. The training of the moral nature, which had been so admirably commenced by that, was so far neglected in the Revival, as to portend the danger of an ultimate triumph of scientific materialism and industrial selfishness. A universal fury in particular was directed against the greatest work of man's wisdom, the separation by Catholicism of the two primary Authorities. Thus, whilst the West was pursuing with ardour material development and intellectual progress, it was more and more neglecting moral improvement, the essential foundation of any real social amelioration. The kind of intellect that was then in the ascendant was the one least calculated to submit to the just control of the heart, and it never ceased to protest against it. For the entire exhaustion of Theologism and for the time the immaturity of Positivism could only lead to the temporary ascendancy of Ontologism. The Metaphysical spirit, which was based on pride, and resulted in perpetual doubt, was the natural leader of this long insurrection of the intellect against the heart, although in truth its authority was rather nominal than real. Its essentially subversive character was concealed, so long as it was directed against an excess of Theologism; which its dissolving force did good service in reducing, without destroying its constructive power. Catholicism had however brought the supernatural philosophy to the simplest form compatible with the task it had undertaken in Europe; although Islamism showed how to reduce it still further, so soon as all sense of the social purpose of the doctrines had been lost. The sphere of reason was thus long delivered over to the metaphysical spirit, which was left free to develop the negative character that marked it, until natural philosophy was sufficiently extended to end the interregnum in thought.

In this profound mental and moral anarchy, society in the West was preserved from material dissolution by the spontaneous Dictatorship, which fell to the temporal power under various forms everywhere. It was the fruit of unavoidable conflicts with the spiritual power then in its decline aspiring to a pure Theocracy. This was the last important service which modern civilisation derived from the separation of the two powers. For, had it not been for the natural consequences of this separation, Europe would not have found any alternative between a degrading oppression and an entire dissolution of society. As it was, the temporal rulers, especially the monarchs, though in some cases it was the aristocracy, seized the chief power; and the confusion was thus confined to the inevitable

During this long dissolution, the temporal power alone preserved Order.

I

dissolution of the intellectual and moral system established in the Middle Age. So long as this lasting dictatorship was establishing its full empire, it unconsciously, and at times intentionally, favoured the laborious advance of the new elements of reconstruction. It only became hopelessly retrograde towards the end of the seventeenth century; when, having fully satisfied its political ambition, it began to see with alarm the essentially anarchic tendency of the movement, which it had till then promoted. This movement had become still more menacing, when, from being in the outset purely spontaneous, it ultimately assumed a systematic form. The growing influence of the Metaphysical spirit led the reformers to proclaim their principal critical doctrines, as being absolute dogmas, with which they pretended to regenerate the West. In spite therefore of the grave dangers, incident to its retrograde tendency, the new temporal Dictatorship continued to be the sole representative of Order, in the midst of populations more and more given over to anarchy. This perilous state of things could not but last, so long as the twofold construction of Positivism, gradually rising from the particular to the general, had not yet become complete enough and systematic enough, to establish directly the Final system.

And popular regrets constantly kept alive the spirit of the Middle Age.

This long struggle, however, never arrested the silent tendency of modern society towards a system, combining the moral qualities of the Middle Age with the intellectual and practical power of Greek and Roman antiquity. So long as the Catholic and Feudal system was undergoing a natural process of dissolution, all classes in the West joined without hesitation in a movement, of which no one saw the true character. This ceased to be the case, when the doctrine took a purely negative form, and presaged a final break with the system out of which modern society had arisen. There then ensued, during three centuries, deep-seated dissensions between all the elements in the West, in the very bosom of each nation, each class, and even each family. Some attached themselves to that principle of Order, which had become retrograde; others joined that principle of Progress, which was still anarchic; as nature, education, or circumstances, caused either party to feel more distinctly, the necessity of preserving the ancient system of discipline, or the necessity of developing the new powers of movement. In fact, these obstinate differences pointed everywhere to the decrepitude of a Religion, which could not protect its own institutions from ruin, as well as to the emptiness of a Philosophy, which aimed at destroying everything, without constructing anything. An increasing conflict such as this, wherein neither side could possibly obtain a complete success, made requisite a new system, capable of ultimately adapting Order to Progress, both of which are equally dear to modern nations. Beside that the habits of Catholic and Feudal life naturally subsisted in spite of serious modifications, the spread of the Positive spirit, and especially the extension of the Industrial life, did much to check the tendency to anarchy. Moreover antipathy to the Middle Age was only prevalent amongst those who had an active part in the revolutionary struggle, and especially amongst the literary class. The bulk of the people of the West could not absolutely forget this, the cradle of all modern civilisation. Women still looked back with regret towards the system, which had so nobly established their high social rank. During this long anarchy, as though they anticipated their true and ultimate function in society, women constituted, throughout the West of Europe, a moral providence, which alone has preserved us from totally losing the chief results, won for Progress by the Middle Age. In the same way, the proletariat never could forget that this great epoch had given them freedom; and they could not but resent the leaning of the literary class towards the Greco-Roman society, based on the slavery of the workers. They would come also to feel, with more and more pain, the total moral anarchy, the chief weight of which fell upon them, owing to the growing selfishness of their industrial leaders. This innate tendency of the two great moral powers of modern times, women and workmen, put a check at once on retrogression and on anarchy; though it left no less emphatic the necessity for systematic guarantees of Order. It seemed at least to show the need of a doctrine, which should adopt the whole sum of the past as the heritage of mankind; which should offer to the Middle Age the tribute of sanction, and to Antiquity the tribute of admiration.

The long duration of this stormy period of transition was caused by the time required for the twofold work of reconstruction. The only way to close this era of confusion for ever, was by raising the Positive movement to the same level of

The Positive movement required a long preparation of construction as well as of destruction.

I 2

generality which the Negative had obtained. In the sphere of practical life, it was essential that the industrial spirit should have advanced sufficiently to show in all its pacific activity the true Great Being, military struggles having finally ceased, and having become opposed to the manners of the West. In the intellectual sphere again, it was necessary that the positive spirit, long confined to the order of Material nature, should be extended to the world of Life ; so that it could adequately deal with the world of Society, and thus complete and coordinate its realm. The principle of Relativity, which had been immutably embodied in Cosmology by the doctrine of the movement of the Earth, was confirmed by the conceptions of Biology grouping the whole series of studies on Anatomy and Zoology. At the same time, the growing importance of the historical point of view prepared the way also for the coming and decisive transformation in Social speculation.

The work of preparation is now complete.

Henceforth all these conditions, intellectual as well as moral, are sufficiently fulfilled. They are the result of a special work of preparation, the course of which will be carefully examined in the next volume, and need not be treated in this. A peace of unexampled duration (1852) has thoroughly established the spontaneous extinction of the principle of War, and the manifest tendency of modern nations to form ultimately one vast family ; the object of whose practical activity is to cultivate the earth, in the constant service of Humanity. From the same scientific movement, which emancipated the intellect of the West, arose a Philosophy, at once comprehensive and bold, which effects the alliance of Order with Progress ; and which combines the future and the past by substituting ever the Relative for the Absolute. Its real character is sufficiently apparent from the double power, which enables it to appreciate the Middle Age, better than the most systematic reactionist, whilst it dispenses with Theology more completely than the boldest revolutionist.

Positivism will resume most successfully the work of Theology.

Thus, by the spontaneous cooperation of the two movements, the speculative and the active, the feelings and the thoughts of all in the West are steadily converging towards the true Religion. The great work of preparation is at length complete ; it is the only termination for unparalleled anarchy. Theology, as well as War, the ruling powers of the early education of mankind, have disappeared for ever from the more advanced portion of the race. The Affections and the Convictions have been combined in one general harmony; and both together point towards Humanity as their object. And thus the intelligence is directed, and the activity is ennobled, by both being subject to the influence of Feeling. Since the time of the primitive Fetichism, which, whilst it prepared everything, established nothing in human life, no system has attempted to deal with the entire sphere of our existence save that of the early Theocracies; and there it founded a harmony, which soon became hostile to development. Between this Provisional system and the final system of Sociocracy, the past history of mankind really presents only the natural succession of three necessary phases of transition—three partial evolutions, mental, practical, and moral, respectively under the influence of the three forms of Theology. The Polytheism of Greece, the Polytheism of Rome, and Catholicism, which might be called the Polytheism of the Middle Age, adequately fulfilled these three indispensable tasks of education, though each bestowed on its own sphere a cultivation far too exclusive. It is reserved for the Positive Religion to establish a conclusive harmony between them, one at once spontaneous and systematic. Based on an unassailable Doctrine, and furnished with a complete system of Worship, it establishes an organisation in which the intelligence, the activity, and the feeling will receive a far greater development than under the partial systems, intermediate between Theocracy and Sociocracy.

The Apostles of Humanity become therefore the real successors, at once of the Greek thinkers, the Roman chiefs, and the great men of the Middle Age. Conservatives as much as reformers, they accept all that the earlier methods contained in their programmes, and unite their various designs. For the temporary means then used, however, they substitute the definitive modes, which are best adapted to man's nature, under the constant guidance of a true conception of its wants. In particular they feel a profound veneration for the Middle Age, for its admirable attempt to institute the normal condition of man, the wise, though premature, separation between the moral power and the political authority. Their sense of gratitude is naturally carried on also to that pure Theocracy, the source of all social construction, and from which, intellectually speaking, Sociocracy differs only in its systematic knowledge of human

Positivism resumes in itself all the earlier phases of human society.

nature, in place of the early empirical conceptions. But the attitude which the Relative Religion assumes towards the Absolute Religion, which prepared the way for it, is seen to most advantage in the thorough respect it manifests for Fetichism.   Positivism will always gladly admit, that it has adopted from Fetichism the subjective method of thought, the only possible source of mental unity. Positivism does no more than transform into a wisely relative character, the purely absolute character, which the subjective method retained so long as it searched for causes, instead of laws.   The entire progress in speculation hitherto made by man consists in fact, on the one hand, in the proof of the impossibility of any Objective system of unity, and on the other hand, in the creation, out of the labours which this method promoted, of the scientific basis of a truer Subjective unity. If Positivism only differs intellectually from Fetichism, in ceasing to confound activity and life, the moral affinity between these two extreme terms of human civilisation is still more complete and direct.   Each, in its manner consecrates the universal supremacy of Feeling; and they are only distinguished morally, in that Positivism substitutes the adoration of products for that of materials.

The history of Religion is in fact the history of Man.

This picture of the intellectual and the social results of the past shows us in full the natural superiority of the Positive Religion, as well as its opportuneness in the present.   Nothing can better exhibit the reality, as well as the maturity, of the Great Being, so much as this complete sympathy between the most systematic and the most spontaneous of its various organs. The entire agreement between them solves the chief difficulty in theory, which consists in the explanation of the past, so as to deduce from it the future, and thus henceforward to build up our true Providence.   At the same time our moral preparation is likewise ended, since the continuity of man in ages completes the solidarity of man in races; and nothing now remains to check the natural ascendancy of the social feeling. It is in order thoroughly to establish conviction of these two ideas, that this long chapter has been devoted to the historical estimate of the civilisation of man, particularly as regards the phase the best adapted to characterise its nature and its tendency. The direct study of the positive theory of unity needed as its complement, a short study of the necessary preparation until it ended in that of its systematic establishment. Without really anticipating my third volume, this general sketch will much facilitate the historical examination of the movement, of which I have indicated the course and the spirit. Since Religion embraces the whole of our existence, the history of Religion should resume the entire history of human development. The Past, as a whole, may be summed up as a course of preparation for the Relative and Altruist Synthesis, by means of that Absolute and Egoist Synthesis, which alone could make its way at the first.

This historical theory supplements the doctrinal part of my subject; and I have now at sufficient length explained the general Theory of Religion; one which the rest of this treatise will be devoted to confirm and develop. According to the plan stated at the opening of the volume, I have now to proceed to analyse statically each of the essential parts of human life, by the constant direction afforded in this, the fundamental chapter of the volume.

CHAPTER II.

SOCIOLOGICAL INQUIRY INTO THE PROBLEM OF HUMAN LIFE; (AND
THEREIN,) THE POSITIVE THEORY OF MATERIAL PROPERTY.

Summary of preceding chapter.

THE preceding chapter as a whole showed the Unity of man to rest upon a constant alliance between Belief and Affection, in order to regulate Activity. Religion, by means of its source in Affection, establishes and maintains harmony within us; whilst, by its foundation of Reason, it completes and strengthens that harmony, making all subordinate to the world without us. These two fundamental conditions are necessarily combined in one in the final Synthesis, which refers both of them alike to the Great Being, who is the natural centre of man's entire life.

Study of separate social elements.

By thus constructing the Positive Theory of Religion, I have adequately reduced to system the most general conception of the Order of human society. On this its proper basis we must now treat directly of Social Statics—that is the application of these general notions to the two modes of our existence, domestic and political. The preceding chapter, being devoted to the elementary laws of the entire harmony of man, it would not have been proper there to treat explicitly of these separate constituent parts. We now however require a less abstract treatment, and must show the general Theory of Religion as applied distinctly to the family life, so as ultimately to extend it to the life of society.

In Social Statics private life may be treated separately.

These two forms of human life, the domestic and the political, are it is true strictly inseparable. Not only is the Family at once the source and the unit of Society; but, by a reaction less obvious though not less natural, domestic life is profoundly modified, and its growth is affected, by political life. Thus in the Dynamics of Sociology these two must never be separated, in order to bring out their necessary connection. It is quite otherwise in Social Statics; where, the subject being the general conditions, not the gradual progress, of human life, the

simpler cases must be considered before the more complex.
The type of the ultimate condition of Humanity, contained in
the latter portion of the preceding chapter and in the whole
of the General View, will have prepared the reader to regard
as its chief feature, the growing identification of private with
public life. But, for this very reason, the social laws of true
Religion will be best perceived in the domestic life ; for it is,
in truth, the universal perfection of the latter which is the
grand aim of all political existence.

At first sight it might appear, that the two did not admit
of any common religious principle. Domestic unity seems to
rest entirely on Affection ; Conviction is regarded as indispensable only to political unity. Further reflection, however, reduces this necessary contrast to a difference simply of the
degree which each of the two kinds of life allows to conditions
that are both equally indispensable. It is the nature of the
affections to become weaker, as their sphere is widened ; whilst,
by a natural compensation, the influence of the intellect is increased by the same ratio. This is why domestic union demands
more affection, and political union more conviction. Still, the
former can no more dispense with a certain community of
opinion, than the latter with an adequate agreement of sentiments. Times of anarchy, whether moral or mental, show only
too clearly this twofold necessity. In our days especially, the
deep shocks which family life throughout the West has more
and more to suffer, are much aggravated by difference in
opinion ; though it is true their chief source is in the relaxa-
tion of the bonds of affection. Conversely, the want of common
affection is alone sufficient to give rise to grave and constant
discord in the midst of political associations ; even where there
is a thorough conformity of opinions, based on a real agreement
of purpose. Hence, the principle of Religion is in all cases the
same ; it varies only according to the degree, in which each
essential element that composes it is separately developed.

The same religious theory applies to both.

This and the two succeeding chapters will therefore treat of
the application of this positive theory to the Family ; the remainder of the volume will be occupied with the direct consideration of Society. But, before studying the domestic
existence, Sociology must solve that which it explains the great
Problem of human Life. This will be the special object of the
present chapter.

*Arrange-
ment of mat-
ter in this
volume.*

In the preceding volume the Positive Theory of human nature was based on the conceptions of Biology as a whole. The chief problem of human life was thus shown to be the subordination of Egoism to Altruism, the relations of which have been exactly defined in the cerebral diagram (vol. i. p. 594). The whole of Social Science consists therefore in duly working out this problem; the essential principle being, the reaction of collective over individual life. This chapter is mainly intended to illustrate this relation in the whole extent of its consequences.

Let us, as a method of examination, suppose an imaginary case, in which human nature should be free to develop its emotional and intellectual force, without being compelled to make use of the powers of action. The actual preponderance of the latter order of cerebral functions is solely due to our material necessities. We can therefore conceive all necessity temporarily removed, where the situation was very favourable to supplying them, without supposing man to be free from the wants of his vegetative nature. It would be enough that the solid aliment was procured with as little effort as is the material of our liquid, or gaseous sustenance. In climates where the other physical wants are not great, certain instances of peculiar fertility closely approach the case supposed. It exists still more distinctly amongst the privileged classes; where an artificial situation frees them almost entirely from anxiety respecting these lower wants of our nature. Such would be, in the Final System, the natural condition of every one during the age of education. In this period, Humanity would undertake entirely to provide for its future servants, in order to promote their moral and mental training without obstacle. These two exceptional cases, the former a rare but permanent type, the latter common though destined to disappear, serve to show that the hypothesis in question has sufficient abstract reality to admit of special analysis; and without such a study, the social tendencies of feeling and intelligence would remain indistinct. Besides its utility in theory, the treatment of a hypothetical case will have considerable practical purpose, if it serves to exhibit the moral type proper for such situations. When poetry is regenerated, and has succeeded in duly idealising for all a natural existence free from all material necessities, it will furnish us with the true model of human conduct, the type towards which all, even the least prepared to attain it, ought constantly to tend. It will suffice here to use the hypothesis proposed simply for the purpose of ascertaining the true influence possessed by the active powers over human life ; and we shall infer what this is, in tracing the modifications that the original and abstract type will undergo, under the pressure of material necessities.

In the case assumed, the great Problem of human Life would be spontaneously solved, by the natural predilection, which would be felt for the unselfish system of existence. Although the personal instincts greatly predominate in the constitution of the brain, the paramount place they hold is chiefly due to the constant stimulus of physical wants. Were this removed, they would be easily restrained by forces arising from the varied contact of society. The natural course of human relations would dispose us all to cultivate the only instincts, which admit of a perfectly universal and almost boundless expansion. We should then find out that characteristic quality of the sympathetic feelings, that a great and continuous exercise of them would make up for their natural inferiority of force. The peculiar charm which they possess would soon place them above the selfish feelings, which, although more largely developed in the organ, would be neutralised by their habitual inertia. We can even conceive that, on the biological principles of inheritance, a few generations would succeed in modifying the cerebral organisation itself in a society so constituted, the volume of the organs of feeling becoming augmented or diminished by continual exercise or disuse.

Physical wants removed, Altruism would be universal.

We may now consider what would become of our intellectual life. We can see at once that practical speculations would be little cultivated, since they are chiefly due to our corporal wants. With this, true scientific training would lose its chief purpose, which is to direct industrial activity. The speculative instincts, which impel us to seek for the explanation of phenomena, are naturally much too weak to produce really sustained efforts. In a situation, where the environment gave them no strong practical impulse, either personal or social, they would soon weary of futile exertion, and would do little more than sketch out a few easy conceptions from the simplest analogies in nature. The human intelligence would then be free to follow its natural bent for artistic invention, a pursuit far more

Intellectual life would be concentrated in Art.

congenial to its nature than scientific, or even constructive labour.   The work of conception would be made distinctly subordinate to that of expression, the natural preponderance of which shows itself in so many ways, and results from its relation to man's social spirit.   Practically the main result of this apparent inversion of our actual condition would be to make the feelings the great object of the use of language, which now is devoted chiefly to express the thoughts called out by the external necessities around us, as these need to be modified by our collective activity.   Every strong emotion awakens in us a desire to express it ; and all experience shows us, how the very expressing it reacts on the feeling.   This reaction of expression is felt, even where the existence is one of solitude ; but it is much increased when language is carried out to its real purpose, that of interchange of ideas.   Now this gratification belongs chiefly to the instincts of sympathy, for no others can be adequately communicated, or shared by expression.   It is owing to this fortunate concurrence of qualities that Art really predominates both over Science and Industry, ever tending as it does to overcome the obstacles suggested by reason, in the hard necessities of the external world.   In the most miserable forms of existence, man exhibits unmistakably this tendency, the moment that he is relieved from the pressure of material want.   When the claims of nature have been satisfied, the degraded savage, the poor infant, and even the unhappy prisoner, like all sociable beings, turn their whole efforts to the direct expression of their better emotions.   The gratification which this expression produces increases with the sphere of the sympathies engaged.   Where these accumulated sympathies are successive in time, they augment the pleasure more even than where they are coexistent together.   Hence the incomparable charm inspired by the great poems of antiquity, the undoubted beauty of which is inseparably connected in our minds with the continued admiration they have awakened in so many successive generations.

Industry would consist in perfecting the means of Expression.

To complete the hypothesis, we have to consider the form of activity in the case supposed.   As our practical existence relates chiefly to our material wants, we can conceive how, in such a society, its intensity and even its character would be essentially modified.   But the activity of man would not be utterly extinguished by a condition, which is not found to affect so completely the many animals, that our providence artificially protects from these necessities. According to the first law of animal life, the active region of the brain, still more than the speculative region, tends continually to a direct exercise, quite apart from any external object. The only consequence is that its exercise becomes artistic, instead of being technical, without ceasing to be subordinate to the impulse of the affections. These do not, it is true, originate actions, properly so called, but merely manifestations; yet the same movements are needed for expression as for action. In a word, actions become games, which are not mere preparations for active life, but simple modes of exercise and expansion. This transformation would become particularly obvious in the case of the activity of the social body; which, being no longer absorbed by material undertakings, would give itself up to festivals, whereby to express and develop the common affections of the society. The artistic character would predominate in practical, as well as in speculative, life. We thus feel how much better Art is adapted to our nature than Science, or even Industry; for it has a more direct and purer relation to the emotions, which animate our lives. We should then have no Industry, save that of perfecting our special modes of Expression; and our only Science would be the 'Gay Science,' so artlessly preferred to any other in the knightly times of old.

An individual existence such as this would be attended by a similar collective existence, whether domestic or political; and it would be one, in which the instincts of Sympathy would gain an easy ascendancy. This would be marked by a more complete development of the family, and a less complete activity of the social life. The latter, indeed, is mainly stimulated to its intensity by the ever increasing need of the cooperation, requisite to meet our external necessities. But the immediate charm of the emotions of Sympathy becomes ever deeper, as the sphere of their action becomes more close. The highest of the benevolent instincts, simple Benevolence, though it be the least energetic of all, would still continue to inspire us directly with universal affection. At the same time, for want of any real common activity, it would be ordinarily engaged in communicating the domestic emotions; and these would find no antagonism springing up to mar their free expansion. In a word, social life, having no decided practical end, would, like

Collective action would take the form of national Festivals.

personal life, assume a character essentially esthetic.   But this artistic character of life would become more pure and more fixed, and would thus supply us with enjoyment, hard for us even to imagine, and which by its unfailing sweetness would unite profoundly in one the various families able to share in it duly.   The influence exercised of old amongst the different Greek tribes by the national Festivals, apart from any active bond of union, may serve to give us but a feeble notion of what these associations will grow to be.

And moral government would attain the highest importance.

In the condition we have supposed, classification of rank, based on personal merit, would at once supplant that which arises from material superiority, which is a mere consequence of our physical necessities.   Again the natural order which sets moral, above physical, and even intellectual, excellence would be better recognised, and less disputed.   Government there would be far more spiritual than temporal.   We may even assume, that the active and speculative sex would place itself in voluntary subordination to the affectionate sex, so soon as the excellence of woman had been abundantly manifested by a situation, where women had the freest scope for developing their nature.   The sweet reign of woman over life would be established all the easier, from the fact, that it would be confirmed by intellectual preeminence.   For the chief intellectual efforts of such a race would be in the direction of Art ; thus it would harmonise more often with those emotions, which women most value, and express most happily.

Progress would be direct from Fetichism to Positivism.

The successive phases, which such a society would assume, would exhibit a considerable modification of the law of the three states.   In particular, the intermediate stage would disappear almost entirely.   It would be impossible to dispense with the simplest phase, that of Fetichism ; nay, this would be ever found in a purer form, and would continue longer, for there would be no material activity to interrupt the natural preponderance of Feeling.   Still, I have no doubt whatever that the final result, in Positivism, would be made in such a world more rapid and more easy.   There is nothing inconsistent in this, if we reflect, that Theologism is properly, only a long transition, first Polytheistic then Monotheistic, from Fetichism to Positivism.   I have already remarked, that such an intermediate state is especially required by social conditions, which, in the case supposed, would cease to be influential.

Under the intellectual aspect alone, which would then be most important, Positivism could, as I have shown, succeed Fetichism directly, where the population was suitably prepared for a systematic modification. Now this would be the same, in that spontaneous evolution, which I have assumed for the case supposed. The simple belief, that Matter possesses a Will, would be prolonged by a situation, which did not stimulate the scientific spirit. On the other hand it would favour the passage to the notion of natural Laws, without that of Gods and Entities being seriously interposed. Although the intelligence would have lost the stimulus of those practical necessities, which have so greatly seconded the rise of the Positive spirit, its exercise alone would lead the mind ultimately to separate the Activity, natural to matter, from Vitality properly so called. And at bottom there is no difference in theory but this between Fetichism and Positivism, which would thus directly succeed to it. In the temporal sphere the reasoning would coincide with that for the spiritual sphere; for although the Industrial life would not be very much developed, the Military existence, which precedes it, would lose all its intense and permanent stimulus, in the absence of any material want. As there would thus be no habitual conflict of importance to disturb the free expansion of the sympathies, they would soon extend from the Family to Humanity, without being long arrested by Patriotism, the chief sphere of Theologism. This earlier development of the highest feeling would favour the similar concentration of the intellect, and directly tend to its cultivation.

The hypothesis assumed brings us therefore to the general conclusion, that the continued suppression of our material necessities would result in a more simple and more perfect type of humanity, and render its development more free and speedy. There is thus both a theoretical and a practical utility in this fiction; inasmuch as it brings out the essential quality of every animal nature, the constant subordination of the Activity and the Intelligence to Feeling. We may thus correct many dangerous illusions and many erroneous tendencies, which lead us so often to mistake the means for the end. *The hypothesis suggests an instructive type.*

Before closing the inquiry into the case assumed, it must be pointed out that it is necessarily an ideal one; it can be supported only by theory, and cannot be tested in practice. *But is wholly ideal, not actually found anywhere.*

The two actual cases, which were at first alluded to as the nearest approach to our hypothesis, are yet too distinct, to enable us to estimate the conditions by themselves.   For both the rich and the young are only relieved from the chief physical necessities by the special protection of society; which itself is paramount over them, and which with its imperious wants reacts greatly on their exceptional case.   At the same time we must not forget, how completely this sociological fiction accords with the conceptions of the poets as to the natural rise of civilisation. In fact, the Fetichist populations, where the conditions of life are very favourable, necessarily furnish the best concrete approximation of this abstract type.   Still, the constant modification imposed on such a type even there, from practical necessities, makes it a very imperfect and occasional mode of verification ; one which may assist the theoretic study, but can in no way supersede it.

Subjective, and ultimately Objective, Life in Positivism will realise it.

The Subjective Life, expanded and regulated by Positivism, will best realise this fundamental type of Humanity; for the conditions essential to it would be obtained, so soon as the physical world passes away of itself, and the moral world is brought out into full freedom.   In the last volume of this treatise I shall explain in detail this important development, which ultimately will become the chief privilege of true Religion.   But the same type would also belong to the Objective Life, the tendency of which is to approach gradually, by indirect and then direct steps, towards the Subjective Life.   Such will form the conclusion peculiar to this chapter as a whole ; which will now deal with actual existence, the better to estimate the necessary influence of the Activity which controls it.

Character of Personality incident to practical life.

We must first recognise the character of Personality, which is due to this predominance of practical life, the consequence of our human organisation.   Our recent inquiry assists us in determining that transformation of the sympathies, which is artificially induced by the progress of civilisation.   Thus only shall we see that the great triumph of Humanity consists in this, that its highest state of perfection, even in morality, is a result of that same external Fatality, which seems at first to condemn us to the coarsest egoism.

For, our practical wants are personal.

As the irresistible wants of nature, for which our activity must constantly provide, are personal, our practical life in the first instance can be no other than personal also.   Its influence is indeed at once positive and negative, exciting the selfish, whilst it represses the sympathetic instincts. Beside that the benevolent tendencies are not adapted to any such end, so long as it is individual, they are, moreover, naturally not sufficiently energetic to supply the requisite stimulus.

The same remark applies to the intellectual efforts which are required in order to act upon matter. They absorb the mind, and distract it from the sympathetic emotions; and they stimulate the personal instincts by fostering the sense of individual importance. Thus the activity, imposed on us by our physical wants, has a corrupting influence in the first place directly over the heart, and indirectly over the intellect. *And so, react prejudicially on the Intellect.*

This fatal influence, however, is only dominant, so long as the practical life is strictly individual, which in unfavourable conditions it may long continue to be. The moment that life assumes a social character, though it be only the life of the family, the habit of cooperation, simultaneous or successive, begins gradually to transform into a social mode the originally selfish character of labour. *Collective activity, on the other hand, improves the nature.*

This all-important change, the starting-point of our true Progress, can only be accounted for by two correlative laws respecting our material existence, to which attention has not yet been drawn. Properly amalgamated, they form the Positive theory of accumulation; without which all such progress from selfish to unselfish toil would be impossible. Accordingly, the admirable native instinct, which everywhere guides the institution of language, gives the name of *capital* to every permanent aggregate of material products; and thus indicates its fundamental importance to the sum of human existence. *Positive Theory of Capital.*

Of these two economic laws, one may be called subjective, the other objective; for the former concerns Man; the latter concerns the World without. They consist of these two truths: first, each individual can produce more than he consumes; secondly, products can be preserved for a longer time, than is necessary to reproduce them. It is clear that this quality belongs only to physical products. For, since intellectual productions are not consumed by being used, but only by our own indifference, the same difficulties do not meet their continued accumulation. Accordingly, the wealth of the intellect is created sooner than any other; and it serves as the *The two essential economic laws* starting-point for all, although all soon react mutually on each other.

This elementary position is so far from being recognised, that although this, the first of economic truths, may be said to prove itself, it has been frequently denied by the metaphysical spirit of modern times.   It has been extravagantly argued, that every generation of man necessarily consumes all that it produces, in forgetfulness of the fact, that the material progress of the species would be utterly impossible upon this preposterous assumption.

This Metaphysical misconception will serve, by contrast with the Positive law, to show its reality and importance.   But it can be proved directly, even as regards the first attempts of labour.   With many species of animals, whose efforts are confined to the collection and preservation of useful substances, where no labour is bestowed on any preparation, the power to accumulate, beyond the personal necessity of the individual, and even of the family, is undeniable, and that, however small the activity of the animal.   With us, whose labour consists in a greater or less adaptation of the substance, the conditions of manufacture often diminish the amount of accumulation, although the results of our labour are rendered more valuable and more lasting.   Still, even in that case, we may see, down to the rudest savages, that each head of a family can produce far more than what is needed for his own subsistence and that of those who belong to him.   The real amount of the excess has never been fairly examined, or the number of the families which one labourer can ordinarily maintain.   We ought, however, to ascertain this natural proportion, and the statical and even dynamical laws of its variation, in order to determine the normal proportion of the agricultural, to the rest of the active part of society.   This question, however simple, has been considered only by a class of mind, which obscures all questions that it touches; and this accounts for the indistinctness in which the subject is involved.   We may, however, assume as an average, that, under all conditions which are not very unfavourable, the labour of every agricultural family can support at least one other, as numerous as itself, if not two or three.   This is however the only instance, in which the first economic law is open to dispute; since the production of food is that industry, where the excess capable of accumulation, is naturally less abundant than in the other branches of labour. In all the mechanical and chemical arts, relating to shelter and clothing, each worker can easily supply the real, and even the artificial, wants of many other individuals. I shall elsewhere show, as one of the essential bases of the industrial hierarchy, the law, that human industry is concentrated, in proportion as its object is elevated under a higher training. It is, however, sufficient here to recognise generally the reality of our first economic law. It is the sole foundation of our capacity really to live, not merely for self, but for others, be what it may the true motive of the exertion to labour.

The second material condition of social life obviously pre-supposes the first, though it by no means follows from it. Its truth is less liable to be denied by sophistical reasoners, since it concerns the external world, the earliest field of all positive notions. It would not be difficult to imagine a condition of the earth's system, which would expose all our productions to destruction in less time than would be needed to replace them. If we admit this hypothesis for a moment, we can see that all civilisation becomes at once impossible. But the most un-favourable physical circumstances, to which we are exposed, are far removed from any so terrible a fatality, even as regards those agricultural productions which are the least capable of being preserved. The moist heat of the forests of Guiana, where meat becomes putrid in a few hours, may be overcome by our remedial devices, so far as to render these pestilential districts actually habitable, before they have been rendered healthy by human skill. In most circumstances a few simple precautions, soon discovered by the lowest savages, suffice for the preservation of nearly all articles of food, as the case of besieged cities has often proved for cereal provisions. This second economic law becomes, like the former, more distinct, as industry becomes more elevated in design, and more concen-trated in execution. In the arts relating to housing, the law may be verified by historic examples, and the same is often the case in the arts concerning clothing.

Having ascertained these two elementary conditions of labour, we shall see, that by their joint operation the accumu-lation of temporal wealth is possible. Even were the excess produced much less, and capable of preservation for a much shorter period, than ordinary instances would show, still, the

Second law: products can be preserved longer than period re-quired to re-place them.

The two laws together ge-nerate accu-mulation of Capital.

fact, that this surplus exists and can be maintained beyond the time requisite for reproduction, makes the formation of material commodities possible. Directly they are formed, they increase with each generation both of the family and the state, especially when the fundamental institution of Money allows us to exchange at will the less durable productions, for such as descend to our posterity.

Theory of transmission of Capital.

Such is the first essential basis of all real civilisation. Nature imposes on us an irresistible necessity of a continual activity to maintain material existence. And our highest powers are subordinate to this. Although the constitution of our cerebral natures, To live for others, is undoubtedly the grandest of human attributes, it would be rendered abortive by this indispensable condition of human life, unless we were able to accumulate and then to transmit the materials it finds requisite. Now, any sort of accumulation requires an appropriation of the consumable products concerned; certainly collectively, and indeed individually. But before we consider the immense social reaction of this institution on the intelligence and the feelings, in proportion as the originally egoist activity was gradually transformed into social activity, we must first deal with the Positive theory of transmission of Capital. For the whole civic value of accumulations, so obtained, is due to the possibility of transmitting the products.

Origin of Wealth.

Actual labour, that is to say, our real and effective action upon the world without, forms necessarily the starting-point whether spontaneous or systematic, of all material riches, public or private. For, before we can make use of them, all natural products require some artificial operation, though it be only the collecting them on their soil and transporting them to their destination. But, on the other hand, material riches have no great importance, especially as regards society, except under a concentration superior to any which can result from the mere accumulation of the successive productions of a single labourer. Hence capital is never very largely increased, until by some means of transmission the wealth obtained by several workers is collected in the hands of a single possessor ; who then provides for its proper distribution, after duly seeing to its preservation.

Transmission of Wealth.

Our material possessions may change hands either freely or compulsorily. In the former case transmission is either gratuitous or interested.   In like manner, the second case may be either violent or legal.   These are in fact the four modes in which material products may be transmitted.   Admitting as these must only of individual use, they require appropriation, ultimately to individuals, as the wants they supply are also individual.   Now in every form of civilisation above the lowest, transmission has a greater influence on the formation of useful capital, than direct production; so that it deserves an equally inviolable respect from society for the natural laws which control it.

Placed in the order of their dignity and in the inverse order of their influence, the four chief modes of transmission form the following series, which corresponds also with the historic order of their introduction.   They are Gift, Exchange, Inheritance, and Conquest.   Of these modes the two middle terms alone are very usual with modern populations, and are the best adapted to the form of industry which prevails amongst them. But the two extremes have had a larger part in the original formation of great capitals.   Although the last must finally fall into total disuse, it will never be so with Gift; notwithstanding that with our industrial selfishness we are wont to overlook its importance as well as its moral beauty.   The social value of the concentration of wealth is so unmistakable to all whose minds are not blinded by envy or cupidity, that from the most ancient times instinct led many races to heap wealth on their worthy leaders.   When developed and concentrated by religious veneration, this eminently social tendency became in the old Theocracies the great source of the immense fortunes which we too often ascribe to conquest.   Amongst the Polytheists of Oceania many tribes show us admirable instances of the real power which this institution may exert.   When reduced by Positivism to a system, it will supply the final society, as I shall ultimately show, with one of the best temporal supports of the action of the spiritual power, so as to make riches more useful as well as more respected.   The most ancient and the most noble of all the modes of transmitting products will do more to effect the reorganisation of industry, than the empty metaphysics of our gross economy can easily conceive.

Be this as it may, the mode in which products are transmitted can only affect the rapidity and the permanence of the accumulations obtained.   Without taking into account any

The economic uses of Gift in the Past and in the Future.

Mental and moral value of Wealth.

special mode of the primitive formation of capital, I shall proceed to consider the great reaction exercised over the whole of human nature, on its personal as well as its social side, merely by the continuous existence of these great reservoirs of power. Supposing them even to result from conquest, stores of food possess a great mental and moral value. To estimate this rightly will do not a little to check the anarchic tendencies to discuss the origin of riches, when the object is to consider their employment.

Analysis of Capital.

I cannot now examine any further the Positive theory of accumulations, as arising from the natural excess of production over consumption. But every reader, who during the metaphysical period of his life, paid special attention to the pretended science of the economists, will at once see the light which is thrown upon the formation of great capitals, by resolving the process into three successive phases : Production, Preservation, and Transmission. We learn from this that the last two operations are indispensable to the social result, and thereby deserve equal respect with the first ; though this alone is taken into account in the anarchy of our present habit of thought. Nevertheless whatever may be the importance which succeeding thinkers may give to this idea, I must not forget that it forms but an incident in a great question of Social Statics. To state it alone may serve to show the utter emptiness of all speculations on the material existence of Humanity, when separated from the rest of the conclusions of Social Science. For the theory just sketched is only useful now to define the true normal action of the Activity on Feeling and Intelligence, and consequently its profound influence over the whole social system, at once in its domestic and in its political aspect.

Effect of Capital on Egoism.

We have already seen that, but for the accumulation of products, either simultaneously or successively, the wants of nature would give the whole range of human life a thorough character of Selfishness. It remains to show, how the institution of Capital tends to transform this ; so as ultimately to permit the universal ascendancy of Altruism.

Capital is essential to any Division of Labour.

This grand transformation is due to the fact that each worker ceases to direct his chief activity to the satisfaction of his personal wants, and finds for it some social or at least some domestic object. In fact he only creates wealth in order to transmit it to others. Now amongst the four natural modes of transmitting products, the two latter may be regarded as really included in the two former. For Inheritance is only a modification of Gift, law or custom supplying the place of the formal will of the testator. In the same way, Conquest is essentially a form of Exchange, the vanquished yielding his liberty in consideration of life. This relation, it is true, by no means effaces the actual distinction between them ; but it enables us for our purpose to regard the transmission of products, as though it were really voluntary. Thus understood, the institution of Capital forms the necessary basis of the Division of Labour; which, in the dawn of true science, was considered by the incomparable Aristotle to be the great practical characteristic of social union. In order to allow each worker to devote himself to the exclusive production of one of the various indispensable materials of human life, the other necessary productions must first be independently accumulated; so as to allow the simultaneous satisfaction of all the personal wants, by means of gift or of exchange. A closer examination, therefore, shows that it is the formation of Capital which is the true source of the great moral and mental results, which the greatest of philosophers attributed to the Distribution of industrial tasks. This indispensable qualification of his theory would be much confirmed by the view which I have advanced, that normally capital may be analysed into provisions and instruments. Not to interfere with the general and abstract spirit which Social Statics require, it will be better to put aside this important distinction as not applying to the earlier ages of society, where materials are collected rather with a view to support the workers, than as a means of assisting their labours. Nevertheless we must from the first remember, that, in any advanced civilisation, each labourer is more dependent on his fellows for the instruments he uses, than for the provisions he consumes.

We thus see how the formation of Capital, as it permits the natural division of human labour, leads each industrious citizen to work at his craft in the main for others. A further influence on the character of labour is this, that it must be considered as essentially voluntary ; for compulsory labour can give little permanent result. In truth, even when the labourer ceases to be a slave, it is but rarely that he rises to the abiding sense of his true social rank, and insists for long in looking on his business as the mere source of personal gain. But this, the earliest

It causes all labour to be for others.

morality of industry, the result of servitude prolonged by
modern anarchy, forms in the general progress of the species
only a transitory phase, and even through this the natural state
can be distinctly traced.   Since every worker does in reality
labour for others, this truth must be ultimately recognised, so
soon as Positivism has succeeded in establishing in society an
exact conception of the real fact.   The familiar adoption of this
truth will be supported in its influence over the sympathies, by
the simultaneous growth of new religious convictions as to the
natural existence of the purely benevolent instincts.   For a
religion which admitted of no really disinterested affection would
naturally confirm the selfish spirit of industry, itself just freed
from serfdom, and long developed under an inadequate concentration of moveable capital.

And that, be-
fore this cha-
racter of
labour is re-
cognised.

In estimating the great influence upon morality of the
transformation of labour, due to the accumulation of products, we must in Social Statics look on man as if he already
possessed the full sense of his real dignity.   It will be the province
of the Dynamics of Sociology to consider the inevitable obstacles which so long retarded the growth of this belief.   Its full
adoption is reserved for the modern regeneration of society, and
it will form one of its chief characteristics.   In Statics the element of time must be abstracted, in dealing with politics as
with mechanics, so as to grasp more thoroughly the true tendency
of each combination, without reference to the period of its completion.   The use of this important rule of logic may be here
justified by the fact, that changes in the methods of industry
have led to great spontaneous modifications in the whole cerebral system of man under all civil, and even all religious, forms
of society.   To confine the influence of the benevolent instincts
to the periods, when their existence was recognised in theory,
would be no less absurd than to make the laws of gravitation
commence at the time of Galileo.   Long before it was recognised
by real science and sanctioned by true religion, the natural activity of our instincts of sympathy gradually modified our moral
nature, in proportion as the actual situation became more favourable to affection.   Even during the slavery of antiquity, industrial life showed this inherent tendency ; it was much developed
under the practice of serfdom, and still more largely since by
the enfranchisement of the labourer, in spite of the egoistic
influences produced by the anarchy of modern life.

If the altruistic instincts did not exist in us, as Theology supposes, the mutual services which this activity of industry calls out, would certainly not be able to create them. Were this dismal hypothesis a true one, the reciprocal assistance of man to man would never become gratuitous; and the only moral influence which this aid would have, would be to develop a constant prudence of self-interest. But the actual constitution of our cerebral system shows that the contrary is true, little recognised though it be, and even though the benevolent feelings were less developed naturally than they are. So long as the germs are there, their natural capacity for almost infinite development by social relations necessarily supplies them with continuous life in every situation fit for awakening them, whether that truth be perceived or neglected. Now no stimulus is equal in power to that which results from constant exercise, even though it springs from interested motives in the first instance. The deep moral power of this Theological discipline of the Middle Age may be similarly explained, and the obstacles it met are essentially the same. Although the doctrine recognised nothing but boundless egoism, the habit of sacrifice and good works involuntarily awakened the sympathies inherent in the human character in Christian or Musulman alike. Another general example, which gives a decisive corroboration to this view, may be seen in the moral influence of military life. The life of war, according to our cerebral system, would appear, more completely than any other form of existence, to be surrendered to the various personal instincts. Nevertheless, since it can only develop by the continual union of those who share it, this single condition is enough to produce admirable instances of devotion; indeed in the infancy of humanity warlike life became very rightly the great practical school of the social virtues. Hence, if both the theological and military systems show how valuable a moral effect may result from good actions suggested by interested motives, may not industrial life have the same quality in even greater degree? The great and universal obstacle to the fuller development of this quality in industry arises at present from the want of system in all peaceful activity; so that, as it is too commonly practised, it does not fill the labourer with a sense of his social value. This blot in our ill-regulated social life may it is true much affect the sympathetic power of industrial effort, but it can never destroy the

In Statics we rightly assume the altruistic character of labour.

power of moral improvement inherent in a type of existence, in which each of us each day renders undoubted services to each other. When the Final society of humanity shall have reduced labour to regular order, in the same way as the Preliminary society regularly organised conquest, the tendency now latent in labour will develop higher social qualities than ever previously, since the relation between public and private life will be more unalloyed and also more direct. This certainty warrants us in Social Statics in insisting on the influence which will eventually prevail, as being a real though little recognised force; whilst it will be for Social Dynamics to consider the mode and the period in which its actual ascendancy will be felt.

Egoism instigates conduct which reacts on the sympathies.

As in the course of the volume I shall have constantly to rely on the reaction over the sympathies, indirectly caused by conduct originating in self, I will here give the general principle. It follows directly from the Cerebral Theory laid down at the end of the preceding volume.

Correspondence between social and personal instincts.

In the first place we must remember the special relation which naturally exists between each of the three social instincts and some one of the seven personal instincts; so that by its superior energy the latter serves to counteract the original feebleness of the former. The most personal of all our instincts, that of self-preservation, that to which from its ordinary preponderance the generic term *cupidity* has been specially appropriated, is frequently able to awaken much attachment, and even veneration; when experience has shown how valuable even to individual success are social relations. The same tendency equally belongs to the two instincts which aim at perfection, that of destruction or that of construction, which ordinarily second the instinct of preservation. I shall devote the ensuing chapter specially to consider the happy faculty which the sexual instinct has of stimulating each of the three social instincts. The maternal instinct obviously admits, though in a less degree, of the same constant influence. The higher personal instincts, pride and vanity, are not easily reconciled with attachment, and they tend almost to exclude veneration; but they often do much to cultivate goodness towards beings of all kinds who accept of protection.

The social instincts usually require the personal impulsion.

The egoistic and the altruistic regions of the brain by means of their mutual relations, strengthened by habit, together direct the ordinary action of man and animals, the higher energy of

the former supplying the natural feebleness of the second.   The
sympathetic instincts are rarely sufficiently strong to produce
directly any very decisive action.   Thus the motive of nearly
every sustained course of activity arises almost invariably from
some personal instinct.   Even where the object is strictly
social, it is impossible wholly to avoid this fatal consequence of
our cerebral imperfection.   Still the ordinary results are much
less vicious than such a necessity might lead us to expect.
For, directly the personal instincts have really placed us in a
position to follow the social instincts, the irresistible charm of
the latter enables them at once to regulate a course of conduct,
which they would never have had the strength to originate.
In the General View I examined the most distinctive case of
this admirable moral reaction in sketching the true theory of
the conjugal union.   Public life, even in the midst of our
modern anarchy, shows us often the same effect on the sympathies, arising in the first instance from pride or vanity.
Although political power is almost always acquired under the
stimulus of these two personal instincts, usually assisted even
by cupidity in its strict sense, it still produces an excellent
transformation of the moral nature when it lasts long enough
to bring out prominently the social usefulness of the power so
obtained.   Sociology thus deals with the great Cerebral Problem presented for solution by Biology, and secures the victory
of Altruism over Egoism by the indirect assistance even of the
most purely personal of the instincts.

We thus learn that the reaction upon the sympathies which
we have just attributed to industrial life, and which is developed
by the agency of capital, may be reduced to a great natural
law, common to all the higher animals.   And so the activity,
which our material necessities force upon us, is not so corrupting
as its direct tendency would indicate.   The happy effect it has
over the moral nature forms the chief result of that providence,
spontaneous at first and then more and more systematic, which
the true Great Being never ceases to exert over our destinies.
Regenerated thus through the agency of earlier accumulations,
practical life may form a valuable stimulus to our highest
instincts.   Affection is then capable of a far greater expansion
than under the social condition, which at the beginning of the
chapter was suggested as an ideal type of humanity.   Were
mutual affection relieved of every active care, it would soon

Ultimately industry calls out the highest affection.

assume a quietist character not at all favourable to its development. In our actual condition to love is to wish good, and consequently to do good. Energetic love therefore supposes some wants in another to be satisfied. Provided the satisfaction can be continuously attained, the efforts required to obtain it are more stimulating to the sympathies, than if the conditions were over-favourable. In the imaginary life free from wants which I lately assumed, I represented the expression of the affections as the sole source of the influence on the brain. But the power of expression, even in such a case, must always be far inferior to that of effective action, which moreover is easily combined with free expansion of the feeling. The habitual practice of good deeds will always remain the great instrument for cultivating the benevolent feelings, even though it originate in personal motives. No emotional influence can ever produce so strong an influence over the affections. We know how much better expression awakens the feelings, when it makes use of the language which action itself spontaneously suggests.

Material progress will be the instrument of moral progress.

It would be useless to add anything to confirm this theory of labour, for everything in modern existence strengthens it day by day; and that in spite of the increasing anarchy, under which industrial activity has hitherto developed. We may at once conclude, that when the education of mankind is further advanced, material progress, so far from opposing moral improvement, will be found to be its great support.

Intellectual effect of capital.

The same reasoning applies still more to the effect of Capital on intellectual development.

Practical wants originate real science.

Were it not for the irresistible impulse continually given to them by our physical wants, our highest mental faculties would remain essentially dwarfed. There would be, as I have just shown, no real scope for any but the esthetic powers, which would be directly engaged in the ideal expression of our better sentiments. Instead of efforts to conceive an external world, on which we should not be compelled to act, we should content ourselves with some vague theories, which might serve to satisfy a curiosity, easily contented and almost puerile, and which would be quickly exhausted by any prolonged fatigue. It is in the main for the purpose of modifying the order of nature that we need a knowledge of real laws. Thus the positive spirit, mainly characterised by rational precision, originates in practical conceptions. But this would never have

given it in the abstract sufficient generality, if the activity of
man had always remained quite personal, for want of the requisite accumulation of products.   It is therefore to the
gradual formation of Capital that we owe our real intellectual
growth.   In the first place, it enables individuals to apply
themselves specially to intellectual life, by liberating them
from material labour ; in the second place, it gives the intellect
a vast object by opening to its collective efforts great and
distant results.   Where these conditions do not exist, practical
life is an obstacle to scientific cultivation ; for it confines our
discoveries in nature to the purely empirical laws, which are as
incoherent as they are special.   Hence the powerful impulse
to speculation which is given by our material necessities, is due
to the formation of large masses of Capital ; and thus an activity, which is originally intended to the service of the individual, is made use of for the species.   Capital thus combines
the labours of generations; and with its aid the true philosophical spirit gradually constructs that general notion of the
order of nature, which, long confined to the first laws of mathematics, eventually comprehends all spheres of thought, even
that of the moral and social world.   But our feeble intelligence,
which is far more esthetic than scientific, would never persevere
in so difficult a study, unless some material fatality existed
constantly compelling us to modify the economy of the world ;
and, in order to foresee its chief results, to know its laws.   This
it is which makes us at last reject for ever all *à priori* theories,
whether Theological or Metaphysical, as being found illusory
and worthless.   The great readiness with which they are formed
would constantly recommend them to us, did not our practical
necessities show us their emptiness, and their utter incapacity
to furnish us with real prevision.   This is the only way in
which the human mind can learn to place its true intellectual
power in a complete submission to the order of nature, whilst
reserving to our practical skill the duty of improving it to the
utmost of our strength.

Although in appearance we are, in so doing, exclusively
pursuing material progress, we are necessarily tending to the
true perfection of the intellect, which is to transform our brains
into a faithful mirror of the world which controls us.   Some
of our modes of scientific prevision, especially in astronomy,
realise this high state of perfection, when the abstract elabo-

And perfect
correspon-
dence grows
up between
man's brain
and the
world.

ration of calculations within the human brain duly prepared by training, comes to results identical with those of direct observation of the phenomena around us. Such harmony between the subjective and the objective may be easily explained, as a consequence of the natural law, by which we are forced to draw from without the original materials of our mental creations. This admirable combination of fact and thought, as difficult as it is important, becomes certainly one of the chief general results of human wisdom; nor could it be established until after immense preparation stretching over twenty-five centuries, and rising from the simplest to the most complex facts. We thus obtain order in our conceptions, even in our most spontaneous productions. In fact, the real laws of our moral and mental nature belong essentially to this system of positive sciences, between which they furnish the chief connecting links. The special study of these forms the natural basis of the highest of the arts, that which concerns our moral perfection, but for which all other progress would be illusory.

It stimulates Poetry and Art.

Next, scientific conceptions, which originate with our material wants, proceed to influence most deeply esthetic expression, itself naturally independent of the order of nature. For a better knowledge of man and of society must much improve the sublime art which is employed in bringing out our highest emotions in order to regulate our ruling motives. Thus industrial activity, forced on us by our physical wants, not only compels us to construct the sciences, but also to perfect poetry and morals; although it seems to turn us from them so long as it is imperfectly cultivated. It is impossible to measure the true share of our material needs in the creation of our esthetic triumphs. Some partial indication of their general influence may be traced in the fact of the imperfection of primitive art in those populations which are most thoroughly exempted from all severe practical labour.

Influence of industry on morality.

The influence exerted by industrial life over morality can still less be denied, especially when we consider the scientific development which it involves. Since we cannot usefully modify the secondary laws of the external world except by constant submission to its primary laws, this habit of subordination has, amongst the moderns, given rise to a valuable discipline rising from acts to feelings. We begin by learning first the laws of nature which are the most easily grasped and the least capable of modification; and we are thus trained to obedience more easily and more emphatically. The habit of submission, the beginning of moral discipline, rises in cases which are beyond our will, and gradually extends to those which are within it, so soon as its beautiful influence over the character is thoroughly felt.

We thus learn how our material necessities tend gradually to regulate, not merely our activity but our intelligence, and even our sentiments. Positivism gives a systematic form to this natural subordination of humanity to the world, and exhibits it as a part of the great law of the encyclopædic series of the sciences, by virtue of which the more complex and the nobler order of laws is always governed by the more simple and more material. At the same time, it gives a sanction to this submission as the general groundwork of human improvement, which requires this immutable type to give it regularity and stability. But whilst we offer blessings to the fatality which becomes the chief source of our real greatness, we must refer all the benefits we receive from it to the active providence, first spontaneous and then systematic, by means of which the true Great Being renders more and more salutary a bondage once found so oppressive. This transformation of life, the chief triumph of our species, rests necessarily on the gradual substitution of the social for the personal character in the whole of our practical existence; the instrument by which it is effected being the steady concentration of Capital.

Positivism elevates it as the natural state of man.

I have now explained the fundamental influence exerted by our material activity over our intellectual and our moral nature. I proceed to show its direct operation on society in the aggregate, in its domestic and also its political form. But as this forms the subject of the rest of this volume it need only be summarily treated, so far as it connects with the main theory of this chapter.

Our practical necessities would, in almost every case, stifle our best domestic faculties, if our activity, for want of accumulated wealth, always retained a personal object. To live for others, which hereafter must become the ruling feature of the largest aggregates of human society, would not then be found, even in the family; where age and sex would never attain to their proper influence over life. The oppression of women, the slavery of children, and the desertion of the old, would prevent any

Effect of capital on domestic life.

influence from the domestic affections extending so as to act for our moral improvement. But material necessities exercise a very different influence, directly previous accumulations relieve the individual from the need of providing exclusively for his sole existence. On the other hand, the obligation of constant labour comes in to strengthen and to develop the domestic affections; which supplied the first motives to produce more than the individual required. Man thus began to recognise, and to be proud of the duty of supporting woman; and marriage begins to assume its highest function, the mutual perfecting of the sexes. The constant action and reaction of the one spouse upon the other, the principal source of happiness and of morality, remains almost dormant, so long as woman is compelled to labour in the field, and cannot adequately exhibit her true nature. At the same time children, being freed from the necessity of providing for themselves, become susceptible of a real education, which fosters the growth of their better feelings. Thus too the old, whom the misery of early states of existence condemns to a terrible destiny, begin to acquire a position of authority and dignity, and can bring their experience to the common service. All the domestic ties, which would be left vague and desultory had we no real physical wants, are mainly consolidated by the obligation of continual labour, provided that there be accumulations of subsistence to enable each relation of life to manifest its natural character.

Domestic life leads to wider associations.

Thus in the primary association of the family this influence which arises from our necessities modifies our natural feelings, the true spring of our ordinary conduct. It is in this narrow but close circle of relations alone, that labour in the first instance teaches us the duty and the pleasure of living for others. In the larger associations of human society the same paramount influence operates, though in a different manner. It tends however to the same general result, by forming elements for the combination of different families.

It presents the germs of political bodies.

The mere government of the family exhibits, as I shall shortly explain, all the essential germs of the true political association. We find distinctly the temporal rule in the authority of the active head, whose labour maintains the entire family. The spiritual power is represented by the moral influence of women and by the intellectual superiority of the old. At the same time these two elements can only be properly shown in general society, in which the various human powers belong not merely to distinct persons, but to different families.

At the opening of this chapter I showed how, in the absence of material necessities, the political association would be completely dissolved. I proceed to show directly, how these necessities concur in the establishment of the principal forces in society, though only when the formation of capital makes command and obedience at once possible.

Direct effect of capital on society.

Although individual eminence, be it physical, intellectual, or still more moral, forms the starting point of all temporal authority, superiority becomes permanent and complete only in those families which are capable of supporting others, by means of an adequate accumulation of capital. This material condition alone can dispose those who fill a dependent position to a habit of submission, a feeling which is soon ennobled by veneration. At the same time, the ruling families then satisfy their instincts for power, and this is gradually softened by goodness, when protection is duly appreciated on both sides. Then the happiness of living for others, long confined to the domestic circle, admits of an almost infinite extension, and that without losing its reality so long as superiors and inferiors are wisely sensible of their mutual dependence. If, on the other hand, all were absorbed by their personal wants, none would have either the leisure or the capacity to take the lead of the rest ; and our higher instincts would remain dormant, in spite of the cultivation they received in the home.

Without capital there could be no ruling families.

This change of condition, from that of pressure to one of ease, is still more requisite for moral government. It rests immediately on personal worth, which can only be fully developed in families relieved from material labour by the providence of preceding generations. Without this means of sustenance our speculative powers would lose at once their vigour and their object. On the one hand, the most capable minds would be engulfed in petty cares. And on the other hand collective undertakings would remain on a small scale, so that the mass of the labourers would never learn the permanent value of a class specially devoted to speculation. Thus the practical activity required by our material wants furnishes not only the motive which instigates us to cultivate the reason, but also the order of men devoted to its pursuit.

Nor any speculative class.

Activity is indeed the basis of religion.

The result then of the foregoing reflections is, that to all government, whether of the State or of the Family, just as to the constitution of the brain, a most salutary influence is imparted by the organic necessities of our physical nature. An inevitable destiny, which at first sight seems to confine us in every way, ultimately proves to be the essential condition of all our greatness. Without it our real life, both personal and social, would have neither distinct guidance nor useful object, both of which are required to develop and to regulate our powers. In a word, the Activity which governs our whole existence becomes the necessary basis of the Religion which is to control it. Thus, in accordance with the most general law of the order of nature, our highest attributes are made dependent on our lowest wants. But we must not forget the effect of human art, whilst admitting the power of nature; we ought to recognise that this fundamental change of our existence is due to the gradual concentration of material wealth, by which alone we establish a sense of real solidarity throughout all the generations of mankind.

The normal type realises the best side of the imaginary type.

A careful consideration thus brings us to the conviction, that the real type towards which Humanity is tending is in no way inferior to the imaginary type which I suggested, a freedom from all physical wants. The only superiority of the latter is in its supposed spontaneity. This makes it the more fit to indicate the general direction of the progress of man in the gradual development of his best qualities. But the highest type, both moral and mental, whether individual or collective, is reached better under the pressure of material wants, than would be the case were we relieved from them. The only difference is, that this normal state becomes more difficult to create, and consequently far more gradual.

The true theory of human Activity, reconciles the Principle with the End of life.

Thus the great problem of our life, the ascendancy of Altruism over Egoism, is capable of a true solution, towards which all our aims are tending, whilst the realisation of it, though never destined to be complete, forms the best measure of our constant progress. When I stated this problem in its biological aspect at the close of the preceding volume, I showed it to be, according to my cerebral theory, the gradual subordination of the personal instincts to the united strength of the sympathetic and intellectual powers. The main difficulty of the task, stated in its simplest aspect, consists in duly combining two adjoining organs, that of universal affection and that of the constructive intelligence, both placed at the top of their respective regions of the brain. The same view has been worked out in Sociology throughout the opening chapter which forms the key of this volume. The substance of Religion was there shown to consist in a continual alliance between Affection and Belief as the guide of Activity. Now, the present chapter completes this crucial demonstration, by showing that the object sought by this union is the best guarantee of its completeness and its permanence. Till this has been ascertained, the general solution must necessarily appear remote, owing to the apparent contradiction between the Principle and the End of human life. In' fact no religion, not even Polytheism, succeeded in effectually regulating the Activity, which Positivism alone consecrates and systematises directly. The notion of human unity would thus be incomplete without this complement, the importance of which requires a special chapter to be devoted to the Problem of active life.

Activity, even material activity, is so far from being incompatible with Affection and Belief, that it is the main foundation of harmony between these two elements of Religion. Although personal in the first instance, Activity gives to man's energies an external aim, which becomes gradually more and more social, whilst the very pursuit tends to strengthen the sense of fellowship in the human race, no less than the conception of the order of nature. It has its rise in our purely animal, though our most energetic, wants; but it increases in dignity continually, by virtue of the entire agreement which reigns between all the sources of human improvement. Since the most important of all natural laws makes the social subordinate to the vital, order, and the latter to the material order, the same classification holds good for the progress of each of these; for progress is in fact only its special form of development as modified by man. Thus material progress, long by an inevitable necessity the exclusive object of man's care, furnishes him with the basis on which he is eventually able to build all higher improvement, physical, intellectual, and ultimately moral. But there is, besides this normal course of progress, the direct influence of the lowest form of activity over the highest qualities of our nature, so soon as sufficient accumulation of

Material Progress is the source of all Progress.

capital has taken place to transform its originally self-interested character.

Transition is
necessarily
slow.
It forms no part of Social Statics to estimate the time required for this great transformation of life. This will be properly considered under the Dynamics of Society. At the same time it will be right to indicate the general principle, the same which marks the whole of this volume, and which was applied in the first chapter to its highest example. We shall find it in the practice of regarding the normal condition of man as prepared by a long education, during which the ultimate condition of sociability is disguised under a primitive form of individualism. We shall see this more clearly, if we look on the early stages as engaged in developing, the final society alone as capable of harmonising, the powers of man. This great distinction, further drawn out throughout this work, should make us feel most lenient towards the past, a period of trial, in which the only thing that could regulate the human capacities, was their own condition of activity and their mutual antagonism. Their spontaneous development, disorderly as at first it proved, must in that stage have run its natural course, or it would have been crushed under a premature discipline. In the final state, on the other hand, the complete systematisation of all the powers of man already developed is the chief object of all forethought, whether speculative or practical. It is the bad use of them which then forms our great danger. Besides, the natural laws they obey have been discovered after this great course of experience, and enable us to reduce their discipline to system. Now, putting aside any question of time, it may be taken as a statical truth that human activity could only assume its true character, after gradually passing through the entire scale of human organisation, rising from the lowest wants to the noblest instincts. For it is only through the growth of the character and the intellect that any other improvement can be disciplined. Our practical existence must therefore retain its personal character, until the modern regeneration of life is actually accomplished, and thus shall give it its true social character. This conclusion will be strengthened when we come to consider the admirable, though premature, attempt of the Middle Age to reduce to order forces which were still imperfectly developed.

Reaction of
the Family.
This at once brings us to another inquiry, one which displays

a new side of the great Preparation of the race.   The continued tendency of our practical life to strengthen the grosser instincts, which are themselves so much the more energetic, had been so long in operation, that the ultimate regeneration of life would have been impossible, had not another influence spontaneously arisen to cultivate the finer qualities.   This duty during the entire era of training was nobly filled by the family affections. It is the object of the ensuing chapter to treat of these at large.

CHAPTER III.

POSITIVE THEORY OF THE FAMILY.

The theory of the Family has hitherto been left to reactionary schools.

THE universal divergence of opinions in modern times on the subject of the Family shows all the importance and the difficulty of forming a truly Positive theory of this fundamental institution. In spite of the great step which the Middle Age made towards the definitive state of domestic existence, all reasoning on the subject has been far in arrear of our practical notions, and has retained almost everywhere the thoroughly anarchical spirit which it had in antiquity. With the exception of the incomparable Aristotle, who alone rose above any serious misconception, the Greek philosophers totally misunderstood the true character of the Family and its natural relations with society. Modern thinkers, again, though in a more favourable situation, proved no less unable to rise from the Metaphysical to the really Social point of view, and contented themselves with repeating, whilst even within the influences of Catholicism, the same subversive fallacies, as the type of the system of the future. It is only since the formation of more rational thought in morals and politics, which the upheaval of the revolutionary principles has favoured, that theory has begun, on this great question, to approach more nearly to practical good sense. But this most necessary step remains the exclusive work of that admirable but reactionary school, which at the opening of the century, so completely exposed the emptiness in social matters of the negative metaphysics of the 18th century. The striking reflections, with which the illustrious Bonald upheld the superiority of the Egyptian, and still more of the Roman, conception of Family over that of the Greeks, have never yet had justice done them by the body of the thinkers of progress. On the contrary, all the modern notions of the Family are as deeply tainted as the ancient were by ideas destructive of the true character of the Home. Our intellectual situation is in fact so

critical, that on the most fundamental and apparently the most
easy of all ideas, the principles of Order are left to the cham-
pionship of mere reactionaries, who can give it no real effect;
whilst, on the other hand, all the efforts of the progressive party
are anarchical, and consequently barren of result. This opposition is only reconciled by Positivism, which proclaims itself the
heir at once of the several schools of De Maistre and Condorcet.
My earliest sociological writings, reprinted in the last volume
of this work, attacked systematically the revolutionary and
metaphysical doctrines with more vigour than do any of the
Theological schools, and that in the name of the most advanced
progress. Though specially concerned with political, they
necessarily embraced implicitly the domestic questions. The
Family formed the subject of an important section in my chief
Philosophical work, wherein I elaborated my earlier sketch.
At the same time it is only here that the true theory of·the
Family, based on an exact knowledge of human nature, could
lead the way to a final reconstruction of the institution, as
suggested in my oral discourses.

It will however be well on historical grounds to consider the
origin of these misconceptions, for they will point out, roughly
but forcibly, the last phase which the institution of the Family
must assume as the basis of any true Regeneration of Society.
The question is full of difficulties, and there was one grave
error in the best ideas of the retrograde school, that of regarding the institution as not liable to change, whereas it is continually advancing towards a type which it is never destined to
reach. This in Sociology is the ordinary fault of simply Statical theories, without Dynamical motive or purpose. But this
defect, which was almost unavoidable in Aristotle's day, ought
never to recur in our times, when the' reality of progress has
been obvious ever since the Middle Age. The error has been
simply due to the incapacity of the thinkers, who pretended
to maintain an Absolute philosophy, at a time when the Relative philosophy only could secure social reorganisation. However dogmatic their decisions, the pretended fixity of the Institution of Family was repugnant to modern reason, which, seeing
real though slight traces of improvement made in earlier times,
had a vague faith in its future advancement. Whilst the true
law of these modifications of the great institution was unknown,
observation of them could only exercise an anarchic influence,

*Mainly, for
want of a
true theory
of Progress.*

by seeming to authorise all the arbitrary hypotheses, which a blind desire of progress could suggest. The formation however of a true Science of Society takes away any danger, which speculation on subjects so delicate might cause to the healthy action of our modern life. All the sophisms in question may be completely met by Positive proofs. It will be easy to unite all that is needed for improvement with the conditions of permanence, in accordance with the essential spirit of the new Philosophy. We shall see how the great modifications, through which the Human Family as an institution must pass, will appear to be the natural result and proper complement of those, which it experienced in the long education of the race. Far from ever tending to any dissolution of the Family in Society, the result of the change will be only to make stronger and more comprehensive the spirit of Family, in accordance with the true conception of human nature. We are to consider here the Statical aspect of the institution, i.e. the type towards which it constantly tends. The succeeding volume, which deals with its Dynamical aspect, or its progress, will more specifically treat of its modifications and history. But it will be borne in mind in this, as in succeeding chapters, that the special laws of this change are only a new form of the great principle, which of the two great constituent elements of Positive Sociology—Order and Progress —makes the second the result and consequence of the first, according to the maxim :—*Progress is the development of Order.*

Double aspect of the Family.

The true theory of the human Family may be treated from two aspects, differing essentially but both natural, the one being the moral, the other the political. Both of these intimately correspond, and each of them is adapted best to fulfil certain important uses.

Families, not individuals, are the units of society.

Under both of these aspects we shall regard the Family as the direct constituent of Society, that is to say, as the simplest and most spontaneous form of association. To analyse society into individuals, strictly so called, as the anarchical schools insist, would be no less unreasonable than immoral and would tend rather to dissolve, than to explain, our social life, for the theory only holds good when association ends. It would be in Sociological reasoning an error as great, as in Biological reasoning it would be, to analyse the body chemically into ultimate molecules, which have no separate existence during life. It is but too true, that when the social system is very deeply affected, the decomposition penetrates in some degree even to the domestic unit, as is but too visible in our own time. But, although this is the most serious of all the anarchic symptoms of modern society, there are not wanting signs, on the one hand of a general desire to maintain as far as possible the old domestic relations, and, on the other, of a natural tendency towards the formation of new families, at once more stable and more homogeneous. These morbid instances confirm the primary axiom of the Statics of Sociology—that human society is composed of families, and not of individuals. According to a principle of general philosophy laid down in my Positive Philosophy, a system can only be formed out of units similar to itself and differing only in magnitude. A *society* therefore can no more be decomposed into *individuals*, than a geometric surface can be resolved into lines, or a line into points. The simplest association, that is the family, sometimes reduced to its original couple, constitutes the true unit of society. From it flow the more composite groups, such as classes and cities, which form, as I shall subsequently explain, the counterpart of animal tissues and organs in the organisation of the Great Being. However, this mode of conceiving the family is valuable chiefly in the rise of the Positive Religion, when the idea and sentiment of Humanity has not yet grown sufficiently familiar. So soon as the New Education shall have brought home alike to the minds and hearts of the races of the West the moral and intellectual principle of the Final Religion, the union between families will be felt to be so close, that it will require an habitual effort to consider them apart, even abstractedly. Instead of defining human society as formed of Families, the contrary will be usual, and it will be the practice to regard families as the smallest societies capable of spontaneous endurance. For, if political life rests primarily on domestic, the latter must depend on the former for the principal source of its perfection, and for the best guarantee of its maintenance. The ideas of Family and of Society can only be temporarily separated, during the great period of training peculiar to our race. In the ultimate organisation of life they will only represent two unequal, but connected, phases of the same life; and in real science they will be treated separately, only so far as to understand better the general laws of the collective organism by studying them at first in their least complication. This mutual combination of families forms in fact the chief character of our true domestic life.   In order to find families without societies we must go down to the animals: but then the family is no longer a permanent institution, and only subsists in reality during the education of the offspring. When it exists beyond this period, we observe a constant tendency to the formation of associations more and more extensive ; and this tendency has amongst the truly sociable races no limit, till it is checked by the ascendancy of Humanity, as I have already shown in the chapter on Biology.   Thus, in the human order, the only complete type of the universal órder, it is as impossible to have families without society, as society without families.   The continuous development of the true Great Being more and more makes political and domestic life identical, as must result from the growing connection of private and public life.   But, by reason even of this close relation, the natural laws of every human association should be scientifically explained with reference first to the lowest degree ; although the superior degree alone will be sufficiently characteristic to reveal those laws in the early stages of positive thought.

Moral and political sides of the Family.

In accordance with this general rule, which is strictly applicable to all possible aspects of the human family, we must be careful to study the Family as the element of society from both these sides.   It must be regarded, at once as the spontaneous source of our moral education, and as the natural basis of all political organisation.   Under the first aspect, each family now in being is maturing the future society ; under the second, the existing society is increased by a new family.   All the domestic ties really belong to both of these forms of the family ; but they are not introduced alike spontaneously, and the order of their succession is not identical.   I prefer therefore now to discuss them separately, and to treat them together in a subsequent place, as stated in the General View.   From want of due care in separating these two phases, the best thinkers who have hitherto considered the human family, have left it as a theory somewhat confused, for they have not distinctly separated the human, from the various forms of the animal Family.

The definitive type of which is reserved for Vol. IV.

The method of treatment here employed applies equally well to the primitive, as to the definitive system, of the Family ; for it is the characteristic feature of Social Statics, that the two are essentially in unison, the final state being only the complete development of the original.   The sketch here given will therefore do much to facilitate the special treatment of the question in the fourth volume, where the Family will be considered in its full maturity, though it is right that the leading features of it should be stated here.

The moral value of the Domestic life consists in its being the only natural medium, through which mere Personal life is gradually enlarged into a truly Social life. This, its spontaneous work, is due to the general law laid down in the preceding chapter as drawn from my theory of the Brain, as to the special relations of the Egoistic instincts, and the Altruistic inclinations. In truth, the superior force of the domestic affections does not arise simply from the fact of their sphere being narrower than that of the social affections strictly so-called. It must be referred also to the fact, that their nature is less pure, by reason of an inevitable admixture of personal feeling. The sexual and the maternal instincts, which alone are peculiar to the Family, are in themselves hardly less egoistic than the mere instinct of self-preservation, aided by the two instincts of improvement : and their character is still more personal than that of the two instincts of ambition. But they awaken special relations, eminently adapted to bring out all the social feelings : hence their peculiar moral value, for which nothing can be a substitute. Thus it is through their very imperfections that the domestic affections become the only natural medium between Egoism and Altruism ; and thereby we obtain the essential basis of a real solution of the great human problem. At this point the true perfection of these sentiments is undoubtedly found in their becoming more and more social, and less and less personal, without at all losing their intensity. Such is in fact the necessary meaning of the constant variations they exhibit in the gradual growth of Humanity, as will be shown in the History of human progress in my next volume. It will suffice, if at the close of this chapter we trace the Statical principle of the tendency, which arises from the growing reaction of Society over the Family.

Having thus determined the general character of the moral influence exercised by the domestic affections, I proceed to exhibit its operation under each of the natural phases of this life.

In the human family the gradual education of the social feeling commences of itself under the necessary relations formed at our birth. From them we get first our notion of the

MORAL AS-
PECT OF THE
FAMILY, pp.
155–160.

The Family
forms the
transition
from Egoism
to Altruism.

Phases of
Domestic
Life.

Involuntary
Family Re-
lations.

continuity of past generations, secondly that of the solidarity of the living generations.

1. Filial Relation.

We experience the yoke of the Past, before the Present has begun to affect us :—a thought which should check the subversive ideas of those, with whom sociability is a thing only of simultaneous existences, and who still ignore the inevitable empire exerted by preceding generations. In this first phase of the moral training the mixture of egoism and altruism is very obvious. The submission of the infant is not one of choice, and thus cultivates at first only the instinct of self-preservation. But the continuous relations which the child thereby contracts soon awaken, and gradually form, a superior instinct, equally natural, though less vigorous. Filial respect then begins to give dignity to an obedience which was long involuntary, and completes the first elementary step towards true morality, I mean the disposition to love our superiors. Once introduced under the irresistible influence of the most personal of all our wants, the habit of respect abides with us, and increases by its own charm, in proportion as the services we receive from others become better appreciated by us ; nay it even survives any objective protection. From the narrow limits in which it arose, the sentiment gradually extends to the widest influences of the same kind ; until it comprehends not only all our ancestors properly speaking, but the whole of our predecessors of every degree, and at last includes the Great Being itself.

2. Fraternal Relation.

This foundation of our whole moral training in the Filial sentiment is soon, in the normal case, expanded by another movement of sympathy, which has special reference to the solidarity of the race. The Fraternal relation next stimulates in us the simple feeling of attachment, free from any sense of protection or competition, especially when difference of sex more effectually removes any notion of rivalry. But the very excellence of this sentiment is a fresh example of the law just stated as to the superior intensity of the altruistic instincts when in combination with egoistic. Brotherly affection, when freest from any sense of inequality, is usually the least powerful. We thus see how frivolous are the complaints, which in the anarchy of modern times are made against the ancient system of inequality of rights amongst the brothers of a household. Far from being during the best period of the Middle Age an ordinary source of discord amongst brothers, it naturally tended to increase their mutual cooperation. In the first place, it strengthened attachment by awakening respect in the inferiors, and benevolence in superiors. Secondly it called in on both sides personal feelings to support the social affections. On all grounds, the final system of domestic life must be more like the practice empirically instituted in the times of chivalry, than the anarchic system of absolute equality introduced since the Revolution. Be this as it may, certain it is that the fraternal relation is the last of the involuntary series of the social emotions ; it forms that one of the domestic affections which is most fitted to extension without ; and furnishes everywhere the spontaneous type of Universal Affection, or Fraternity.

To these two phases of our moral education, which are made for us, the Family supplies two other kinds of relation, which, from our creating them for ourselves, are closer and more important. They act inversely to the two preceding; for they begin by developing the sense of Solidarity, and come later to suggest that of the Continuity of the race. *Voluntary Family Relations.*

The first and the principal of these last ties consists in the conjugal union, the most powerful of all the domestic affections. Its superiority is too well understood, even amidst the anarchy around us, to require any other special notice than a better analysis, based on the true conception of human nature, one which disposes of every disturbing sophism for ever. The excellence of this relation results from this: it is the only one that brings out at once the three social instincts, attachment, veneration, and love, which are only separately cultivated in the other domestic relations, and even there are not individually so well developed, as in a true marriage. More tender than the fraternal affection, the marriage union awakens a veneration, more pure and more vigorous than filial respect, and a goodness, more active and more devoted than the protection of the parent. This threefold and combined instinct, continually augmented by the natural reaction between organs connected and adjoining, becomes necessarily more defined, as marriage tends to fulfil its essential conditions. *3. Conjugal Relation.*

Ever since the decisive institution of the practice of Monogamy, it has been more and more felt that the active and the affective sex, each without laying aside its proper qualities, must unite in a bond, at once exclusive and indissoluble, *Theory of Marriage.*

one surviving even death. Whilst time tends to weaken all
the other domestic ties, it cements more closely, in the typical
case, the only union which is able to produce complete personal
identification, the constant object of all our sympathies. In
the second place, the superior force of the conjugal affection
follows from its natural connection with the most powerful of
the egoistic instincts, next to that of direct self-preservation.
There is no finer instance of the law of the power of the self-
interested motives to awaken the benevolent inclinations connected with them; for nowhere else do we find these two
kinds of instinct in such profound union. But the inadequate
theories of human nature, which have prevailed up to the
final solution of Positivism, still much exaggerate this reaction; and they have even led to a view of the most fundamental of all human institutions, which indeed is no less
irrational than immoral. The purest Theological systems,
be they Mussulman or even Christian, continue to regard
Marriage as exclusively relating to the propagation of the
species; and they find in celibacy the sole form of moral
perfection. This twofold mistake comes of a false theory of
human nature, which assumes that the disinterested affections
are foreign to our nature, and consequently independent of
any real law, obeying only the arbitrary will of an imaginary
power. This error has been directly examined in the General
View, and is incidentally refuted in the entire course of this
work. It will however find more special notice, when, in the
concluding volume, I come to consider the mature form of the
Domestic constitution. It is unnecessary to pursue the subject
here any further than simply to state, that the sexual instinct,
however indispensable in ordinary cases, especially with the
male, only prepares the way for true conjugal affection; and this
it would be wholly unable to create without a direct sentiment.
The animal passion only produces relations, which frequently
lead the man to do full justice to the woman. But, when the
feeling of attachment is thus created, it subsists and grows by
reason of its native charm, quite apart from any coarser stimulant, in accordance with the general law governing all cerebral
reaction. It even becomes stronger and more constant, when
the conjugal relation is maintained habitually pure, although
in this case the original sexual feeling is not extinguished,
at least in the man; but affection is upheld by some material

support. In my fourth volume I shall show how this, the highest state of the conjugal union, will imply in the final system due regulations respecting the procreation of the human species. Hitherto, whilst increase in the animal races is wisely regulated, this has been left in man to blind passion. But, without in ordinary cases suppressing the pleasures of sense, it will be enough to make the true object of Marriage, the mutual perfecting of the two sexes, as the Positive Religion ordains, by the light of a true cerebral theory. Thus viewed, conjugal attachment tends to develop the feelings both of veneration and of goodness; since each sex finds itself at once the protecting and protected, by the admirable combination of the superiority in affectionateness of the one, and the preeminence in activity of the other.

Our moral development is completed in Family life by another class of affections, weaker and less voluntary than the preceding, but specially connected with the most universal of the three instincts of sympathy—Benevolence. In the character of sons, we learn to *venerate* our superiors; as brothers, to feel *attachment* to our equals. But it is the paternal relation which directly teaches us to *love* our inferiors. True goodness always supposes a sort of protection; which, without being incompatible with the Filial and Fraternal relations, does not form one of their essential elements. In Marriage, as yet it belongs only to the man, and the Positive system alone can make it habitually reciprocal and common to both, by bringing out into better light the true office of the wife. But, even under the Positive system, the Paternal feeling will retain its natural power of developing, better than any other feeling, the widest of all the social sentiments : that which urges us directly to satisfy the wants of our kind. The protection, which this relation involves, has a charm and an intensity, such as can nowhere else exist ; for it is independent of any return to detract from its purity. However, this noble feeling is naturally too weak in the dominant sex, with whom it ought to be even stronger, at least in the existing phase of the Family, where the duty of protection belongs exclusively to the father. Still more, the want of choice in this relation, as it is, hinders the full exercise of a providence which properly prefers a voluntary devotion. These serious deficiencies are usually compensated by the concurrent aid of various personal instincts. The paternal is

4. Paternal Relation.

ordinarily the least pure of all the domestic feelings. Pride and vanity have no small part in it; and even mere avarice is not an uncommon alloy in it. In no other relation is the law more marked : that selfish motives tend to strengthen benevolent inclinations. Still, the Paternal relation forms the indispensable complement of our moral training under the growth of the domestic influences. Without it the fundamental sentiment of the Continuity of the race would fail to be duly cultivated ; for it is the only one of these relations, which extends to the Future the common bond in the first instance felt towards the Past. Thus, the two extreme terms of the domestic life dispose us, the one to respect our predecessors, the other to provide for our successors. The superior complication of the affectionate influences, which produce the true Paternal feeling, makes it easier to modify the general result. Therefore, it is this one of the domestic connections, which has undergone the most constant varieties of type ; and these I shall estimate in my next volume, as seen in their progress towards constant improvement. This, in the Positive system, will consist chiefly in Paternity being rendered, at once less factitious and more voluntary, by increasing the influence of the mother, and by encouraging the practice of adoption.

POLITICAL ASPECT OF THE FAMILY, pp. 160-181.

These are the essential phases in their natural series, through which the domestic life acts upon the human heart by spontaneously freeing it of its original and personal, and preparing it for its ultimate and social, character. No other course of training can so effectually assist this natural development. The moral side of the Family having been now treated, its political characteristics will next occupy us. We have to ascertain that form of the institution, which is best adapted to these results upon the affections. The functions and the feelings being thus brought into connection, the proper correlation of the first would finally express that of the second. The preceding theory of the Family will therefore form the moral basis of that, which will ultimately form the true theory of the family—the political conception of it. The rest of this chapter will deal with it from this point of view. The point of view under which it has hitherto been considered is indispensable, but it will only be directly applicable for such of the social speculations as regard education. For any other purpose, the political rather than the moral notion of the Family will be kept in view throughout this work, as being at once more complete and more systematic. The domestic relations will be found always classed in the ratio of their growing comprehensiveness, and in the inverse ratio of their decreasing energy. This is in accordance with the fundamental principle common to every Positive classification. On the other hand, the moral point of view of the Family, which follows the succession of ages, does not give any series quite homogeneous. If we take the two groups of family relations, first the involuntary, and then the voluntary, we get the four types in the following order :—filial, fraternal, conjugal, and paternal. Now in passing from one to the other, our law of increasing comprehension and decreasing energy is only conformed to within each group ; that is to say, when we pass from the filial to the fraternal, or from the conjugal to the paternal. But when we attempt to proceed from the fraternal to the conjugal we reverse the law ; for we pass to a narrower and yet a more powerful relation. Hence a sense of incongruity in our series. Whereas, if we study the Family as being the true social unit, the voluntary relations must come before the involuntary, and the series of domestic relations becomes homogeneous. At the same time it is also completed by an indispensable term, that of the household, which at first would not be properly understood. This direct study of the domestic life is of more importance, as it leads to that of the political constitution properly so called, from the fundamental identity which is found naturally between the two kinds of society. In fact the human Family is nothing but our smallest society ; and the entire species, on the other hand, is only the largest of families.

Every true family, even amongst the animals, begins with the mated pair, and frequently is not extended beyond. For polygamy does not really effect more than a mixture of different families, instead of one family. Besides, this indefinite condition is only permanent amongst such of the sociable animals as are found with the sexual instinct strongly developed, and the force of attachment weak. In our race it forms a stage of transition of greater or less duration, during which the excessive concentration of riches, especially under the Theocratic system, leads to the support of several females being concentrated on a single male. There is no need now to refute directly the unfounded impression, that climate was the determining cause of the monogamic, or polygamic, form of the

Monogamy, the basis of the Family.

domestic union. No true combination can be anything but binary; less even in the moral, than in the physical world. In Social Statics therefore, where the normal condition alone is considered, without reference to the initiatory stages of preparation, we must have regard solely to monogamy, as the necessary basis of any domestic union.

Conjugal union is a type of true Religion.

In this, the fundamental stage of the human Family, the natural laws which govern all associations are capable of easy verification ; for the extreme simplicity of the case does not admit of any misconception becoming permanent, however much any such may have stood in the way of the discovery of the laws. In no other case can we so distinctly see the necessity for every permanent union to be based on all the three essential phases of cerebral life—Feeling, Intelligence, and Activity. For a union resting on Affection, however complete, suffers the deepest change, and is frequently broken up, for want of a common Faith, to give strength to the mutual love. Even when the harmony of the affections is strengthened by identity of opinion, there is needed a certain habit of cooperation between the two forms of activity, to enable the union to resist effectually the various shocks it may meet from without or from within. Thus, Marriage, the best type of association, shows clearly all the essential elements of Religion ; for it is a combination between Love and Faith, the end being the gradual amelioration of moral life, controlled by law but capable of improvement. This simple case of the domestic union, being one in which Positive demonstration has so clear a superiority over Metaphysical conjecture, cannot fail to throw light on the true spirit of civil order. When harmony between conviction and action is seen to be indispensable in the most intimate of all unions, can it be ignored in the case of associations more complex and less natural, where every perturbation that arises is of still more serious consequence ?

Like every association it implies government.

Beside this conclusive evidence that all associations should rest on a combination of the three regions of the brain, the Positive theory of Marriage is a striking example of the first axiom of sound politics : Society can no more exist without a Government, than Government can exist without a Society. The most unhesitating levellers do not ordinarily carry their dangerous theories so far as to apply them to the conjugal union. In it they feel their fancied equality to be wholly out of place. Between two beings in truth, even if united by strong mutual regard, no harmony can exist, unless one commands and the other obeys. The greatest of philosophers, when twenty-two centuries ago he drew the first outlines of the true theory of human society, said with that wonderful delicacy of his, for which he does not receive due credit :—' The principal strength of woman consists in overcoming the difficulty of obedience.' Such in fact is the nature of subordination in marriage, that it becomes indispensable to the sacred end which Positive Religion assigns to marriage. It is in order more fully to work out her superiority in the moral sphere, that woman should gratefully accept the just rule of man in the practical. Whenever she rejects it in any degree, woman's true character, far from becoming nobler, becomes deeply degraded ; for the scope, at once given to pride or vanity, checks the constant exercise of the feelings which are the distinctive marks of the female character. This fatal effect on the affections is even caused by independence simply resulting from wealth or rank. But it shows itself in a more marked manner, when the revolt of the woman involves her in a life of labour ; efforts whereby she blindly destroys her highest dignity in attempting to found upon force that ascendancy which can only be obtained through affection.

This view of the moral purpose of the conjugal union dissipates all the other difficulties which the institution of marriage can present for our solution. Next to the constant necessity for a government, in order to maintain any association, the domestic union most clearly exemplifies the essential elements of all human authority, which have been so slowly developed in political society. Even the state in which women are slaves does not altogether exclude some recognition of the natural division of the two powers, spoken of as the spiritual and temporal, the former moderating the necessary authority of the latter. But it is only a complete state of Monogamy, which fully brings out the influence through mutual affection of the counselling, over the ruling, member of the pair : an influence, without which marriage would fail to effect its essential function —the mutual improvement of the sexes. From Monogamy too flow the two great characteristics of the true marriage association, as explained in my General View : the freedom of woman from all material labour, and her general superintendence

And illustrates the division of Spiritual and Temporal power.

of home education. In the next volume, this, the Statical view, will be supported by the Dynamical sketch of its actual progress in history; and then we shall trace in the natural varieties of marriage a constant tendency towards the fulfilment of this normal type. And thus, the Positive account of the marriage union establishes at once not only the fundamental axiom : that there can exist no Society without Government ; but also the maxim which is but its complement : that every Government supposes a Religion, to consecrate and to regulate command on one side, and obedience on the other. To reduce to a system the elemental order on which the social organism is based, it will be found that we are only laying down, in the most simple and obvious case, the Positive ideas, which with due extension will serve for the entire field of political sciences. Inversely this truth is useful, for we learn how the sanctity of marriage appears yet more strongly from the fact, that the sophistry, with which it has been attacked, is but another phase of the current of many anarchical doctrines.

After this view of the marriage union, as the bond of the Family, a sketch still more brief must apply this view to the parental relation and duties, then to those which unite the Family and Society.

Parental relation. It will be simpler to consider the Parental and the Filial relation together; or rather to confine the inquiry chiefly to the former, which alone is of importance in our political inquiry. The Filial relation is, from a political point of view, almost passive ; and only requires special examination as forming part of the moral theory of the Family ; and this has already been adequately treated. It should however be remarked, that its place is after that of the Parental relation in the series of the domestic relations, starting with Marriage, on the principle of decreasing energy, and increasing generality of the corresponding affections ; for Veneration is a sentiment less energetic than Benevolence.

Its reaction on Marriage. Its condition, true Monogamy. The Parental relation consolidates and develops the domestic society, based as it is on the conjugal union. Although the Family can adequately effect its great social purpose, when not extended beyond the original pair ; it is yet certain that the production of offspring, besides its own importance, gives strength and force to the family union. A common end, equally dear to both parents, gives warmth to

their mutual affection, and is perpetually at hand, to prevent
or to moderate, any difficulties which arise from incompatibility
of opinion, or it may be, of humour. This precious influence,
however, can only be realised in Monogamy. In any other
state, the Filial relation is seriously weakened, both as regards
the parents and the children, from want of the requisite concentration of the affections. Monogamy also brings out a still
stronger motive for the rule of perpetual Widowhood; which as
shown in the General View is a duty in Positive Religion fundamental to marriage; and for this pure monogamy is essential.
All persons of sense in the West have long seen with regret the
unhappy position to which a second marriage almost invariably
condemns the children of the first. Thus strict Indissolubility
in the Conjugal union is not more necessary for marriage in
itself, than it is to give to the Parental and Filial relations that
stability, which is essential to their fulfilling any high moral,
or even any true political use.

The Parental sentiment, being less energetic than the Con- *Its influence on the moral nature of parent and child.*
jugal, has been more exposed to the sophistical attacks of every
form of moral and mental anarchy. The community of children
was always more easily admitted into the utopias of the Metaphysical schools, than the community of women. Still, the
authority of the Father will always furnish the best type of
supremacy of any kind. The mutual reaction of Benevolence
and Veneration, in moderating both obedience and command,
can have no more natural and complete example. But this
second constituent of the domestic system is at once more
susceptible of modification and perfection than the Marriage
relation itself; inasmuch as it is based on a still wider circuit
of affections. Its natural character can be understood only by
reference to the great social purpose it will fulfil, when that,
which in every early form of civilisation is exclusively devoted
to the Family, shall be extended to embrace Humanity itself.
This subject will hereafter occupy us, in treating of the necessary relations between the domestic, and the strictly political,
method of rule. However the moral theory of the Family
indicates the general mode, in which the Parental authority
reaches its full development; the great end being to cultivate
the sacred influence exerted by such authority over the feelings
of the child and the parent respectively. The first step towards
a sounder system will be a better division of power between the

Father and the Mother, according to the true nature of the two sexes. If the child must continue to owe to the one parent its material support, it is especially from the other parent that it must receive the rudiments of its education, intellectual as well as moral; at least this must be until the completion of the entire home training, as was explained in the General View.

Limits of the care of the Parent for the child's material interest.

In the same manner, a check must be placed on the blind and unthinking anxiety which parents exhibit for the temporal success of their children. The spirit is as active now, at least amongst the richer classes, as it ever could be, when the social functions were essentially hereditary. Men are still induced, by an unreasonable affection for their offspring, to transmit to them a position similar to that which they themselves have possessed. But as soon as the moral importance of the entire Home life and the rightful subordination of the Family to the Society are thoroughly and universally recognised, the natural limits of the temporal protection which parents owe to their children become unmistakably plain. When they have received their earlier education the reasonable course would be, for the children to obtain from their parents, whatever may be the fortunes these possess, no further support than what is indispensable for their honourably entering on the career they have chosen. Any further bounty to any great extent, such as to make the children independent of labour, is, speaking generally, a real abuse of wealth ; for wealth is always tacitly entrusted by society to its holder for a social purpose ; nor ought it to be perverted from its proper use by personal predilections. In the second place, whilst the natural anxiety of parents for their children's welfare needs to be made both more enlightened and more moderate, its field of operation may very well be extended,

Revival of practice of Adoption.

by a better use of the great institution of Adoption. The final system of Humanity will give a new meaning to this valuable instrument of social improvement. When it was spontaneously called into existence in the earlier forms of civilisation, its value was effectually checked by Caste : a system, which though essentially effete, exercises some bad influences even now over modern society. In dealing, in the fourth volume of this work, with the mode, in which Positivism proposes to regulate the continuation of the species, we shall see how the system of Adoption will enable many married pairs to know the gratification felt by parents; extending it to pairs, who were worthy of being parents, but that their marriage has been, voluntarily, or otherwise, unfruitful. Without some such interchange, those pairs who have offspring would find themselves frequently overcharged with children. But the chief value of adoption as an institution is this. On the moral side, it heightens the affection which arises between the protecting and the protected, when the relation is the result of a fortunate choice. On the political side, adoption facilitates the wise transmission of social functions as is shown in a later passage. This remark is only introduced here to show, how much inferior to its normal type the Parental, or second part of the Domestic system still is, and to show also what is the general character of its final form.

There is one other natural element of the family, the Fraternal relation. This, when the primitive and incestuous confusion of families is properly overcome, is the sole direct link between the Family and Society. The animal races are usually found to grow less prolific, as they rise in the Scale of Life. Thus our race would be the least numerous of all, were it not possessed of the wisdom to counteract by artificial means the natural disadvantages of its position. In spite of the lesser fertility of the human as compared with the lower animal races, it is plain that its continuance and its increase are due to the fact of there being several children in a family. Since the average duration of human life may be taken as about the double of the age, at which the best productive union usually takes place, each pair ought to produce in the typical case at least one child of either sex. But besides that this number would leave the population simply stationary, it would not suffice to counterbalance the frequent cases of those who left no offspring, and also the mortality of early life. The natural arrangement therefore would be for each marriage to produce three children of the two sexes; and it is usual in statistics to count five heads to each household. This number suffices, especially in our modern civilisation, to maintain the population at its level, and even slowly to increase it; and this is confirmed by a valuable observation, which meets the dangerous theories of population put forward by a famous school of economists.

The Fraternal relation therefore has in it nothing accidental; and we have only here to give a brief outline of this

Fraternal relation. Normal limit of the Family.

part of the domestic system in its normal form.   Its moral importance has been sufficiently treated above.

All jealousy being removed by the free power of disposition in the Parent over his property,

Having less energy in itself than the rest, the Fraternal sentiment, more than any other of the family sentiments, has suffered from various disturbing causes.   It has never been subject to any real discipline except during the Middle Age; and then only with the higher classes.   The form which it then took, the paramount superiority of the eldest son, was designed to give permanence to the power of the great families.   Nor was this custom in truth so injurious to the growth in moral force of the true Fraternal feeling, as the anarchical doctrine of equality between the brothers, by which it has been for a time succeeded.   Still, we see at once how even then much less scope was given to the · Fraternal, than either to the Conjugal, or the Paternal relation, in that training of the affections which is the grand task of the Family,   We have had as yet no example of the beauty and power, which the Brotherly instinct is ultimately capable of developing; and this we shall not see realised, until the Positive Religion has in a better future, throughout the West, elevated our Domestic life to be the natural base of our Political life.   The monstrous hatreds between brothers in many a tale of antiquity will remind us of the perversion which the brotherly instincts suffered from the hereditary succession to offices.   The same result appears in a lower degree when the succession of the eldest is simply to the inheritance of wealth.   The system of the future, however, which makes every Family minister to Society, will free the authority of the father from every restriction arising out of mere domestic selfishness.   The father will have entire liberty of leaving by will the property which he has acquired by his own efforts, or has received and preserved, to any one to whom he pleases, without reference to his own family, though under full responsibility to opinion for the right exercise of this privilege.   The sons, therefore, having no ground for coveting the parent's estate, as they have long renounced any claim to his offices, there will be nothing to check the course of their mutual affection.   It will receive fresh strength from the adoption of the law of perpetual Widowhood, the complement of Monogamy, which will add the sense of veneration for the same parents on both sides, and give the feeling of brotherhood a perfect stability.   There will be again

a lively sense of union impressed on the brothers of a family, And the brothers
by the joint protection which they will owe to their sisters, being bound to support
when the exclusion of the daughters from succession to their their sisters,
father is made the rule. These remarks on the constitution of
the Family, the working out of which is reserved for the fourth
volume, have their use here in showing us, how far the Fraternal
relations are yet from their full maturity. They also show
how in the Positive system the moral education as a whole
turns to good account such of the domestic affections as bring
families together, apart from the benefits arising from adoption. The way in which the ancient world instinctively took Brotherly affection
the bond between brothers of one house as the type of the will develop the spirit of
greater bond between the members of one society, suggests a general Fraternity.
striking picture of the moral spirit which will animate our
descendants, so soon as the life of the race is directed by
system, and not given over to chance.

To treat the Family in its complete phase, there is yet The domestic relation :
another branch of it to be added—the *domestic*, or that of Master Master and Servant.
and Servant—one which is almost forgotten as a part of it in
the anarchy of modern life. How important and how natural
is this relation may be gathered from the common practice of
language ; for we apply all the names for the Household to the
Family, the simplest form of human association. Even under
the ancient Slavery, the word *Family*, which properly implies
the slaves as well as the children of the house, indicates the
manner in which the two were regarded in connection ; the
children as the higher, and the slaves as the lower, of the subjects of the common Chief. Since the entire abolition of slavery,
the domestic system, in spite of increasing moral confusion, has
had in itself a tendency to form a subordinate order of personal
relations between the master and the servant ; such as might
come to create a very close bond of union between rich and
poor. Thoroughly reorganised as it will be in the future,
this tie will be most valuable in aiding the maturity of the
social sentiment in its fullness. It will be a fresh means of
kindling, on the one hand the sense of Veneration, on the
other that of Benevolence, by means of the moral tone which it
will impart to the obedience of the servant and to the rule of
the master. The sense of regard between these two, though less
the result of nature, and less tender, than the sense of regard
between brothers, is yet freer and broader than that ; and thus

The domestic relation is the link between the Family and Society.

it is admirably adapted to be the last natural link, between the ties of Family and our relations to Society. It is but from hasty conclusions, drawn simply from our modern life, that we are so apt to suppose the condition of service to be confined to a very narrow class. A deeper study will give it a far higher meaning; and will show that the affection, which it inspires, may exist in various phases throughout almost the whole range of society. In the Middle Age, the greatest natures felt themselves honoured by fulfilling domestic offices, if only it were for

As in Chivalry.

chiefs of sufficient eminence in dignity. In fact such service formed a very important part of the education of the Knight, even though the squire were bound to obey a woman. Upon the rise of the Industrial form of life out of the feudal system, a custom was introduced, which was a real phase of domestic life, the system of apprenticeship, the ordinary mode

General Apprenticeship a part of education.

of training for the modern workman. It will be one of the tasks of Positive society to reduce this elementary institution to method; and to make it capable of extension to all classes. It will form, in the moral education of each of us, a state of transition between the age of those relations of the family which are made for us by nature, and those relations of family which we select for ourselves. The social value of it is this, that it trains us up as fit to command by first accustoming us to obey. We shall see in the last volume the mode in which the manners of the final organisation will give dignity to this form of life. Nor will it cease to be noble, even in cases in which service is prolonged through life, indications of which state of things we may perceive in those populations, who have been preserved from the hardness of Protestantism and from the selfishness of Industrialism.

Counterpart of the Domestic relations in Society.

When we add this supplemental class of the domestic relations, that of Service, we are led to feel the need of calling in the whole range of the personal relations in society, outside the family, in order to give to our moral conception of the family its full expansion. Each of the five affections which have been treated, the paternal, the conjugal, the fraternal, the filial, and the domestic, corresponds in truth with an analogous sentiment beyond the family, less vigorous than itself, it is true, but capable of producing a similar effect on the nature. For example, the master, or the protector, the friend, and the disciple, shadow forth something of the character of the father, the husband or the

brother, and the son.　The Final Organisation will thus endow
with fresh vitality these ordinary relations of life.　It will bind
the private life of each individual to his public life, by a series
of intermediate ties, forming a gradual transition from our home
associations to our social duties.

The Positive conception of the Family, thus treated as a
whole, explains the importance which in the opening of this
chapter we attached to the close connection between the two
essential aspects of family life, the moral and the political.　It
shows us, moreover, how thoroughly the social constitution of
the Family is dependent on its moral purpose; for it is on the
moral ground alone, that all the great characteristics we have as
yet mentioned have been based.　The reciprocal influence, however, of the organisation, on the object, of the Family must not
be overlooked; for without it there is no security for efficiency.
Its right constitution is the special bond between the domestic
and the political system.　The great subject of the Family
would therefore be very inadequately treated, if after analysing
the Family in itself, we did not go on to consider its general
bearings on Society.　The Political organisation in every society
is strictly dependent, it is true, upon the domestic; but the
changes which progress invariably introduces into the domestic
system, can be understood only by reference to slow modifications in the political.　Were this grand reacting influence overlooked by us here, our conception of the family would fail to
have that Relative character, which best distinguishes it from
the Absolute conceptions that have marked all schools of Metaphysical philosophers.

Reaction of Society over the Family.

But before entering on this final view of the subject, it may
be useful to condense in one general idea the whole of our views
which precede.　The key to our conceptions of the Family is
this: its part is to cultivate to the highest point the influence
of Woman over Man.

The Family means: the influence of Woman over Man.

The essentially selfish character of those active instincts,
which go to the maintenance of human life, as we saw in the last
chapter, would be most imperfectly purified in us, without
the gentle and continuous influence over the affections of the
loving sex.　First as Mother, presently as Sister, above all as
Wife, lastly as Daughter, nay as Servant, in a lower degree repeating these four sides of home life, the mission of Woman is
to save Man from the corruption, to which he is exposed in his

She purifies, through Af-fection, the Activity of Man.

life of action and of thought. The greater strength of her
affections naturally marks her out for this essential duty; but
Society, as it progresses, will give it an even higher place in the
economy of life, by relieving the loving sex from every anxiety
which can interrupt the force of those affections, be it in action
or in speculation. This is the real end of the Domestic life;
and such the character of the phases of its gradual completeness.
In each of these natural forms, the influence of woman shows
itself in the ascendant, owing to the greater tendency of her
nature towards moral improvement. In all ways, even phy-
sically, we are far more the sons of our mothers, than of our
fathers; beyond all brothers is a true sister precious; the love
of the wife is usually even deeper than that of the husband;
the devotion of the daughter is above that of the son. It
would be a waste of words to enlarge on the superior zeal of
the woman in all domestic service. In any way in which
we view it, Woman is the real centre of the Family. And
although this, her true place, has been but imperfectly manifested in the preliminary stages of human society, the truth
has asserted itself with enough distinctness, to foreshadow
what it will be in the future. Thus the Positive theory of the
Family consists in making systematic that influence which
the Affection of Woman by its very nature exerts over the
Activity of Man.

Point of con-
tact between
Domestic
and Political
life.

With this principle we are now in a position to pass on
directly to the connection of the Domestic existence with the
Political. Both are essential to that real solution of the problem presented to us by human life, the constant subordination
of Egoism to Altruism.

To trans-
form Egoism
into Altru-
ism, a moral,
as much as
an intellec-
tual influ-
ence is
needed.

The only possible control over that continuous activity,
which is the condition of man's life, is supplied at first merely
by the personal instincts; and these are closely bound up with
the organs relating to those material wants, such as it is the
part of the activity to satisfy. It was shown in the chapter
preceding, how the combined energies of the race tend to pass
into a spirit of sympathy between man and his fellows, as the
progress of society works itself out. Yet withal, the mere
necessity of providing for man's wants, of itself has hardly
power enough to bring about so great a modification of the
active powers, as to withdraw them from the control of those
personal instincts which first called them forth. In addition to

this stimulus of the material world without, we need something
to awaken the unselfish instincts within us ; that their lower
energy may be counterbalanced by their more habitual exercise.
This influence within the nature itself is of a compound kind,
the one moral the other intellectual; distinct, but capable of
combination. The moral side of the influence consists in the
self-expansion of our benevolent affections; without which there
could be no elevation of the nature. The intellectual side of
the influence is found in a due recognition of the Order of
Nature, to which man is subject, and of the limits within which
it can be modified by man.

These two sources of influence receive each a special stimulus
from the two principal forms of social life, the domestic and
the political. The life within the family has a deep effect on
the whole moral nature. It supplies it with relations, so close
and so varied, that they foster in turn all the feelings of
sympathy, and fill us with a deep sense of its peculiar charm.
A series of ties, first those which are formed for us, then those
which we select, dispose our nature to become one as it were
with the only beings whom any of us can ever truly know.
They, to whom this opportunity of seeing into the secret hearts
of those about us is denied, may often doubt that it is possible ;
but that it is actually realised by many of us must be clear to
anyone who reflects calmly on the difficulties and the circumstances which surround it. A cold and critical temper is far
from being the best guide to enable us to judge the true
character of natures, so complex as those of man. They who
reproach love with so often being blind, forget that hatred is
always blind ; and with results far more fatal. The truth is,
on the contrary, that were it not that we habitually see those
who belong to us through the eyes of affection, we should
never do full justice to their best qualities. And, again, it is
just this habitual sense of mutual love which makes those
qualities shine out with a strength, such as nothing but this
close intimacy could produce. We need not always accept the
judgments which the wife, the mother, or the son, may form of
those dear to them ; but we must remember that they are
drawn from sources of knowledge, to which the eye of a
stranger has no access. Thus the life within the Home, the
great end of which is to foster the affections and sympathies,
gives us the most difficult and the most precious of all the

The Family supplies the moral influence and moral knowledge.

subjects of knowledge, the knowledge of human nature. The knowledge which the Home can give us is naturally practical and not theoretical ; but there is nowhere else that we can find it in sources of equal purity. To give this knowledge a scientific character, all that is needed is a due conception of that which is in a stricter sense social life. This latter method of training, however, has hitherto been impossible, until the Preliminary stages of civilisation had been at length completed. It is therefore from the experience of the family that we really have imbibed all the ideas, incoherent it may be, but real, to which the race have hitherto attained respecting the moral, and even the intellectual nature of man. Woman is the great natural medium, through whom these precious truths are transmitted from generation to generation ; as it was she, by whom they were originally taught to men. And it is in her within the bosom of the family, that we shall ever find our best guide to a knowledge, without which speculations about society would have but little solid base. Thus the life of the Family, with Woman as its central figure to bring out to each of us its direct meanings, has a further office beyond that of fostering sympathies which would never come to maturity elsewhere. So this, its principal part, is as constantly accompanied by an intellectual training, such as we could acquire from no other source. Thus we get that entire harmony in the twofold action of the influences, which tend, as we showed above, to transform the nature of man's continuous activity from a personal into a social form. The practical life of the City teaches us by the insight of experience, the natural laws of our material life ; whilst the sympathetic life of the Family reveals to us the workings of that moral life, which is for ever acting upon the material. Such is the double course of instruction concentrated around the Home ; where the Father and the Mother direct, the one the Intellectual, the other the moral side ; whilst the scientific combination of the two is the final work of the whole course of our mental preparation.

Society the intellectual influence and knowledge.

Precious as beyond doubt is the training which the mind receives within the Family, the intelligence requires for its characteristic expansion an ampler and less intimate society. Life in the Home belongs by its nature to the sentiments. In knowledge of moral truths, it suggests the germs ; but they can only assume a complete form, by contact with the more general relations of social life. The emotions, which the family calls forth, are in reality too keen and too constant to give free play to the esthetic faculties : and, indeed, these only appear to good effect, when they seek to give expression to affections other than those of blood. So Political life, the moving principle of which is continual activity, becomes the true source of our intellectual development, theoretical or practical. This is its true function, so that we often regard the progress of the intelligence and that of the social system as identical. There can be no doubt that political life also enlarges the sphere of the feelings ; but only so far as it opens to them new channels, not by altering their character. Of the three instincts of sympathy which the Positive theory attributes to human nature, Veneration, Attachment, and Benevolence, no one belongs exclusively to public life. All develop their true vitality within the Family. It is only after this primary training of the Home, that Society can give them a higher form ; and they would have little real stability but for such a foundation to rest on. It appears, however, that Political life has yet another quality, more marked even than its intellectual office : and that is its own special power of awakening the collective forces, which react so profoundly on the whole range of human life. But when we come to examine the laws which govern these forces, we shall see that their real origin is an intellectual one ; because it is from common opinions alone, that we get unity in the controlling forces of our active life. The result is, that Feeling corresponds naturally with the Domestic, Intelligence with the Political side of life ; though each of these forms of our existence in turn calls forth indirectly the qualities which belong to the other. The Family permits the Sympathies to thrive, by a series of ties never interrupted, and at first involuntary. Society calls into play the full powers of the Mind ; in order to give direction to that which specially distinguishes society, the progress of mutual cooperation. The one gradually inclines us to an habitual standard of generous feeling ; the other disposes the mind to more and more broadness of thought. In this way, Private life and Public life combine their work in a twofold part towards that radical transformation of the nature, which is the fixed object of all human Progress. The suggestions of the affections first, and then the influence of ideas, combine in clothing with an ever growing spirit of sympathy the naturally personal character of the ruling instinct for action.

It will add to our understanding of this combined action of the affections and of the intelligence, if we regard each of these as centred in its appropriate organ. The centre of the moral unity is Woman ; and she always remains its chief representative. The mental centre of unity, however, as relating to a course of training far more complex, long remains with no distinct organ of its own. But whilst treating the Statics of Society, in which we look to the normal condition and not to the period of its fulfilment, we must regard the second element of social regeneration, as having, like the former, its own particular seat. Its real centre, in truth, is the Priesthood, whatever may be its actual origin or constitution. As soon as the conception of the Universal Order has taken sufficient hold on the mind, whether in a theological or a scientific form, so as to give a direction to human activity, it soon assigns recognised duties to a distinct class or caste, round which the whole spiritual influence groups itself. A body of such a kind performs in the political organism a function essentially the same as that, which woman exercises in the domestic system. It tends to inspire with intelligence, as woman inspires with sentiment, the material forces which are developed by the mere circumstances of practical life.

These two essential elements of the regeneration of man require themselves a long and difficult course of training, one that is the great end of our entire education as a race. Neither the affectionate sex, nor the speculative class, have yet adequately attained their true character or their due social rank. Yet withal, the parts which they have to fill have long been very clear, and the spontaneous indications of them are perceptible in the early stages of our history. Each of these spiritualising influences has its own path of progress to pursue, but their common end will more and more bring them into harmony ; although the combination of the two is not in so advanced a stage, as is the growth of each separately.

This comparison between the Family and Society in the abstract shows that Home life and Public life have for their normal form the same Statical conditions ; and we may expect to find the same Dynamical course in their progress, apart from differences of degree. The Home exists, we may say in a word,

to give system to the influence of Woman over Man. So we
may say that Society exists to direct the action of the Intellectual
over the Material power.   The simultaneous training of these
two elements of human regeneration is the great object of our
early phases of social life; the natural combination of the two
is the essential base of our ultimate social state.

Thus presented, the organism of society is seen to be in
entire conformity with the organism of the individual, as follows
from the subordination of the one to the other.   In the social
existence, domestic as well as political, as in the existence of
the individual, Feeling and Intelligence combine to regulate
the Activity.   In whatever way we regard them, the elementary
conditions are the same, and in like manner the combinations
are analogous.

Homologies of Social and Individual harmony.

This brings us to the original conception underlying our
entire Social Theory, as worked out in the first chapter of this
volume.   Harmony between two elements, whether in the
Individual or in the Race, makes up the real Religious condition, one that is of complete Unity.   The true theory of the
Family and the rational theory of Society are thus, logically
deduced from the Positive theory of Religion.   I first placed
the true Synthesis in the combination of Love with Belief; and
I now find in the Affectionate sex and in the Speculative class
the kindred elements of all human Order.   Conversely, this result brings out and verifies the soundness and the fruitfulness
of the original theory of Religion.

Positive Re- ligion corre- sponds with both.

These general principles respecting the natural connection
between the domestic and the political system must be followed,
in order to complete the study of the Statical conditions of the
Family, by some notice of the way in which Society reacts upon
it ; for without this, the modifications which time and place
import would be inexplicable.

Modes of Reaction by Society on Family.

This general influence is brought about by two distinct
causes : the principal one, which is involuntary and even hitherto
usually overlooked ; the other, the secondary, which being more
or less voluntary was the only one of which account was taken,
and that but imperfectly.   The first consists in the changes
which the domestic system undergoes in the gradual enlargement of the activity, the master instinct of man's life.   The
second consists in the institutions, which have been introduced
to bring the modifications of the Family into correspondence

1. Sponta- neous, by changes of social ac- tivity.

2. Artificial, by direct change of in- stitutions.

with those of Society. This, be it remembered, takes no account of opinions which have directed or led up to these changes, without acting on them directly. Although these two influences have in general acted only on the higher classes, they have at length penetrated the entire social body, owing to the natural tendency, whether voluntary or compulsory, to make changes adopted by the chiefs of society general throughout the whole.

Mischiefs incident to family life.

To see the general direction of this double power, by virtue of which Society is constantly modifying the Family, we must now turn to the inherent imperfections inseparable from all domestic life; such as we trust our wisdom is destined hereafter to improve and correct.

1. May be perverted to foment Egoism.

In the first place, as I have shown above, the affections which the Family calls forth are not in any case entirely without alloy. They have always more or less marked an element of the instincts of Self; and indeed it is from this they derive their peculiar energy. It is in fact just this union of these Personal and Social instincts which forms the characteristic feature of the influence of the Family, and whereby it becomes the only possible mode of passing from mere Individualism into true Sociability. If, on the one hand, domestic life is that which prepares us best to feel the charm of Living for others, on the other hand it places us in the situation that best enables each of us to abuse this power over others. It may therefore develop either Egoism or Altruism, according to the turn which it receives; and this may explain, though it does not justify, the contradictory estimates which philosophers have always passed on the institution itself. In fact, the decisive bias which the influence of the Family takes is necessarily determined in most cases by the greater influence which Society continually exerts over the families that compose it. This is the reason that, notwithstanding unreasonable criticism to the contrary, the life within the family habitually develops our sympathies, which are the only instincts not repressed by the contact of society. Such is the way in which the Family is invariably brought to perfection by Society. For Society continually acts in purifying the leading characteristic of Family ; and more and more prepares it for the great part which it has to play in the moral world.

2. May create an

Beside this too frequent source of degeneracy, the development of Egoism in place of Altruism, the life within the aggregate
selfishness. Family has another source of very serious imperfection, one that is the great topic of anarchical rhetoric. It is true that in forming a very close unity, it has a tendency to give that unity very undue prominence. It seems therefore that even where family life does not stimulate the individual instincts in the strict sense, it cannot avoid arousing a sort of aggregate selfishness almost equally dangerous, as well as very liable to become a mere veil of personal selfishness. But without disguising the danger, we must point out that this is merely an evil which besets more or less every partial association. Till now, we have never known any society, which in the true sense of the word is general, that is, which embraces the whole human race. All the smaller groups of men have at first a tendency to engage in mutual hostility, which becomes more serious as the group grows stronger within. The sophists who attack the Family, with their usual inconsistency, forget that the institution of Country is open to the same charges as that of Family; though no one disputes the healthy moral influence of Patriotism. In the Positive theory of human nature, we see clearly how we must before everything arouse the instincts of Sympathy from their original torpor, whatever may be the danger of these potent instincts afterwards receiving an obnoxious bias. We may be sure that the ultimate growth of the benevolent inclinations to their maturity will in time eliminate this original source of evil, as soon as the conditions become favourable to such a result. Now, this follows of necessity from the pressure which Society incessantly exerts over the Family, to give it a more general purpose. If nothing but the idea of Country could lead us up to that of Humanity, in spite of the spirit of ferocity it once kindled in men, will not the life of the Family, which has of itself a moral power more vigorous and more continuous, guide us to the purely Social sentiment, though it be through a stage of collective Egoism?

Society therefore, under the latter as under the former These evils
are steadily
corrected by
the action of
Society. aspect, tends more and more to correct the principal imperfections of the institution of the Family, and to give fresh efficiency to it in its special sphere. The influence of society operates simultaneously in the two ways stated above. It belongs to the Dynamics of social science to consider them in their successive stages. But the Statics of social science may mark

out their natural source. We thus see that the gradual progress of practical life has deeply modified the institution of the
Family.   This reaction is not merely perceptible in the case of
the great change of society, that in which the activity takes a
form purely industrial, instead of being essentially military ;
and this has been the great source of the improvement of the
Family by Society.   But a similar effect, in a lower degree,
can be seen in all the modifications, through which history shows
us that the warlike life has passed.   In the Dynamics of the social
science, I shall show how the original establishment of Monogamy
in the West and its perfection in the Middle Age, had their origin,
the first in the rise of military activity, succeeding to the stag-
nation of the Theocratic era, the second in the transforming of
Conquest into Defence.   As to the lesser influence which Society
consciously exerts over the Family, so far as it modifies the institution, this is so manifest that it has hitherto been exaggerated in
the most unfortunate manner.   It has even been exercised when
the collective activity had a very pronounced character, and
promoted institutions the aim of which was to bring the
domestic system more into harmony with its own.   It manifests itself in a more special way, whenever the political constitution gives sufficient independence to a Priesthood.   We then
see at work regular efforts to bring the Family to perfection,
though on a thoroughly wrong theory, first in the ancient
Theocracies, and then in the triumph of Monotheism.

In a regene-
rated Society
this action
will be far
higher.

The last volume will be the proper place to exhibit directly
the Family in its complete and regenerated type, one which is
the necessary consequence of all its preceding phases.   But this
volume on Statics must determine the common tendency of
these successive variations, and will thus enable us to form
some general conception of the complete type, though without
fixing the time or the mode in which this will come about.
We can here regard it as the result of the combination of the
two influences considered above, the second of which, the
deliberate influence of Society, will be no longer subordinate,
and will serve to regulate the spontaneous changes of the
Family on system.   The new form of human life, in the
Future, which will give an undisputed sway to the activity of
Peace, will put an end to the antagonism that the state of
War created between the benevolent instincts awakened in the
Family, and the bloodthirsty passions familiar to Society.   On

the other hand, it will develop the family life in that immense portion of society, the People, who are the best fitted to enjoy it, and to whom it has as yet been forbidden to know this, the sole moral equivalent for their material poverty. In a life such as this the Family becomes the manifest base of Society; and reciprocally political life is that of which the special function is to strengthen and perfect family life. But, whilst Woman receives her due place of ascendancy, the Priesthood will also obtain its legitimate influence, by the force of the only religion which takes into account the whole of human nature, collective as well as individual. A theory truly scientific will be its constant guide in its systematic action over the moral improvement of man. It will show how this moral perfection depends both in the Society and in the Family on those benevolent instincts of mankind, the existence of which was ignored and even denied by earlier systems of Faith. This is the only mode of ending that terrible alternative before which our most conscientious thinkers hesitate; on the one hand, the complete dissolution of society in its domestic, as in its political form, by abandoning society to chance; on the other hand, the open acceptance of the splendid visions offered by many social utopias, however crude and impracticable be their schemes.

This conclusion, as the summary of this chapter, brings out the universal force of the principle with which this work opened: every partial systematisation requires the general synthesis as its condition. I first adopted it in the range of science exclusively, and I then extended it to the necessary connection existing between the coordination of the intellectual world and the reorganisation of the social world. Finally we see that domestic life and political life can only be regenerated the one by the other. This conviction, which the position of the West will more and more develop, will exhibit at once, the immense difficulty of the Synthesis our times require, and the qualities of heart and mind required for its gradual accomplishment.

Here, as elsewhere, no partial reorganisation of thought is possible.

CHAPTER IV.

THE POSITIVE THEORY OF HUMAN LANGUAGE.

NATURE OF
LANGUAGE,
pp. 182–190.
Place of lan-
guage in
this volume.

THE nature and the object of this chapter will best appear from the statement of its bearing on the two preceding chapters, of which it is the complement, and the two succeeding chapters, to which it is the introduction. The relation it holds to both of these constitutes it a middle term between the first and the last chapters in this volume ; and it may even serve as a direct link between them. The true Theory of Language on one side is intimately bound up in that of the Unity of the race, the subject of the first chapter, and also on the other in that of the natural Variations of the Order of society, the subject of the last chapter. The former of these inquiries will occupy the opening part of this chapter ; the latter its conclusion. Between the two will come the Theory of Language in itself ; which I shall treat, first in its nature, then in its object, and lastly in its history.

Domestic
Order only
completed
by Political
Order.

Before showing the connection of the present chapter with the two which precede it, I shall begin by showing their connection with each other. A comparison of their conclusions will exhibit this. In the first the study of the personal activity, which is the ruling principle of man's material life, shows us that its ultimate form is one essentially unselfish. We have seen how, for this indispensable change, a long and difficult education was needed ; one which, without being able to give direct discipline to our forces, had power to develop them, under the impulse derived from their originally personal strength. Then, passing on to the study of those relations of the affections, which must bring about this regeneration, I showed that life in the Family can ultimately fulfil this great mission. Still, I showed at the same time that its moral value is long limited to the Family itself, the universal power of which it tends to develop. During the whole continuance of the education of the race, the principal end of the Domestic Order is gradually to form the Political Order. It is from this latter finally, that the critical influence originates, whereby the family affections are raised up to their high social office, and prevented from degenerating into collective selfishness.

From this point of view Sociology regards the fundamental institution of Language as the chief continuous instrument of this reaction of the Political over Domestic life. The real and inner constitution of Humanity is thus completed by a third element, one which binds the various social unities together, whilst Property gives consistency to the Material existence, and the Family opens to it a full Moral life. *Language the instrument of this reaction.*

In accordance with this general principle, the present chapter unites the two which precede with the two which follow. This threefold basis of human life tends to the permanent formation of true Religion, the chief object of the opening chapter. In the first place, the institution of Property decides the essential *object* of Religion, by permitting free action to those continuous energies which it has to discipline. Next, the Family furnishes Religion, by its *source* in Affection, with that moral power which this discipline requires. Lastly, Language provides Religion with the general *instrument*, by means of which the regulating Faith is formed, transmitted, and applied : that Faith itself springing out of the development of the intelligence, under the conditions imposed on it by the Order of the External World. *Language is the medium by which Belief operates.*

It is with Religion that Language must be directly compared ; since both spontaneously relate to human life in its totality. They both alike arise out of the very functions which it is their object to regulate. They are created moreover in similar ways ; for both have two natural sources of origin : the one moral, which directs ; the other intellectual, which assists, completes, and develops the work. In a word Language, like Religion, is inspired by the Heart, and created by the Intelligence. It is thus associated first with the Family and then with Society : the first, the basis of the expansion of the Affections, the second that of the progress of the Mind. Its first function being to communicate emotions, Language, like Religion, has most natural affinity with the sympathetic instincts which alone are capable of complete transmission. The working out of the intellectual construction, indeed, is subordinate in *Language comparable with Religion.*

both to the moral inspiration, be it either to express affections which we feel, or to satisfy wants which we experience.

It arises from Feeling, and is perfected by Thought.

It was shown in the second chapter of this volume, how the chief consistency of Religion is derived from that very activity which it has to discipline. This characteristic reaction is yet more evident and more direct in Language. Its practical growth always corresponds to our continuous wants. Its extension by theory is also due to the same source; that is, it is called upon to formulate the ideas which have to regulate the activity. We must not however forget that this twofold necessity would not be enough to inspire in us the institution of Language, if it did not take its rise spontaneously in the Affections, and were then extended to the Activity, and finally to Speculation. The errors of philosophy have entirely inverted this order, in giving exclusive attention to the influence of the intellect. This is to commit, in the case of Language, the same mistake which was made towards that of which it is the type, Society itself; namely, to exaggerate without reason the function of reflection, and to neglect that of the spontaneous instincts.

Language is transformed by, and along with, Society.

We must here draw attention to the felicitous harmony which exists between the institution of Language, and the radical transformation undergone by the Activity. In fact Language, like Religion, has its bearing at once on the life of the individual and on that of the society. But it is from the latter that it derives, even more than does Religion, its main function and its natural source. The direct relations of Language are all with social life; and properly speaking, it has never relation to individual life, except through the close connection between these two. This great institution therefore naturally conforms to the transformation, through which man's active existence is destined to pass; and it testifies by sure signs to the unselfish character of that existence, even in the midst of the empire of Egoism over society. Thus too, at the close of this chapter, we shall find that the great perfection of which Language is capable will be seen only in the Positive state; when the whole of man's permanent activity will take the collective form, by an habitual cultivation of the active instincts of Benevolence.

Language is: the expression of social unity.

Following out these general truths, we may sum up the great analogy between Language and Religion, by this formula:

that Language is the expression of that essential unity which Religion creates. Failing to seize this, the only point of view which is really universal, philosophers both of the Theological and of the Metaphysical schools, have hitherto missed the profoundly social character of this institution. It is so essentially relative to the social, and not to the individual, side of man, that mere personal impressions have never obtained any adequate expression; as is seen in the constant difficulty which the sick experience in expressing their sensations. To give the lowest degree of completeness to Language, the influence of men in association must always be presupposed; and indeed the cooperation of successive generations is quite as indispensable as that of contemporary individuals. The greatest efforts of the most systematic genius would always fail to construct by themselves any real language. And thus this, the most social of all institutions, places in hopeless contradiction those retrograde philosophers, who are bent on limiting their science to the individual point of view. Indeed, the very sophisms by which they blaspheme Humanity itself, could not be uttered at all, but for a system of expressions, which are the work of long generations of men cooperating together.

From this general principle the special theory of Language may be deduced. We must deal first with its essential attributes in order, then with the corresponding parts of its constitution.

The inquiry must first be confined with more scientific precision than it could be in the preparatory schools of Philosophy, which never distinguished properly between the study of language in Sociology and the analysis of its conditions in Biology. This confusion accounts for the fatal contradictions which followed upon the strange theory, that animals were not endowed with language, and that failed to see the chief features which mark off the language of animals from that of men. *Biological basis of Language.*

To end at once this metaphysical confusion, we must go back to the definition of Signs, of which Language in all its forms consists. A *sign*, properly speaking, is the result of a certain constant connection, whether voluntary or involuntary, between a movement and a sensation. From this connection arise the facts: first, that every movement reproduces objectively a particular sensation; and next, that the reaction of this sensation upon the brain becomes the subjective substitute of the *Language consists of signs: i.e. the connections of movements with sensations.*

original movement.   Thus, the brain transmits without its various impressions within, by means of this mutual relation of the two systems of nerves sensory and motor connected with it.   Besides this, the communication follows the same course in fact, whether the nervous apparatus of motion set in relation with the apparatus of sensation during the act of communication belong to one individual, or to two distinct persons.

A sign is the constant link between an objective impulse and a subjective impression.

Hobbes with great ingenuity compares the use which men make of Signs to the influence exercised over our life by the constant relations of Order, simultaneous or consecutive, presented by two phenomena.   We know how these relations when observed assist us, in the power they give of foreseeing a phenomenon by means of its correlation; so that one becomes to us the *sign* of the other.   This luminous analogy need not be pursued, but it will serve at least to remind us, how completely the true function of Language illustrates the cardinal principle of the Positive Philosophy : the universal subordination of the Subjective to the Objective.   It is only by this union of the world Within and that Without, that we can give our Spiritual world that cohesion and uniformity, which are the natural attributes of the Material world; qualities which belong to the material world from its greater simplicity, according to the law of the increasing complexity of phenomena in their ascending Scale.   It is precisely in giving this fixity that the great force of language consists ; which it secures by connecting Man with the external World.   The same holds true even in purely artificial relations.   For, besides that true Signs are never arbitrary, the mere existence of this relation between a phenomenon and a symbol suffices to connect Man and the World ; and we have no need to inquire, how the relation in question was originally brought about.   Still I should be slow to approve the extreme extension, which the more vague school of thinkers have often attributed to the words, *language, sign,* &c. ; so that they would regard the whole Order of Nature as forming a sort of natural language, which each element of the universe explains in equivalent terms.   Putting aside such irrational exaggerations, which can do nothing but confuse a solid theory of Language, we may content ourselves by giving a systematic form to ordinary language, and confine the word *sign* to express the constant link connecting an objective influence with a subjective impression.   This definition only differs from that which I have suggested

above, by being more abstract and more precise, as will appear
if we compare the two.   Every movement which recalls a sensation, is essentially objective ; and that even when the organism
in 'which it originates is the same as that which is addressed by
the sign.

The Biological theory of Language was sufficiently treated
in the last chapter of the first volume ; and it will therefore
only be necessary to refer the reader to that (vol. i. pp. 513,
582.)   It is only essential to repeat the chief distinction : that
between the involuntary form of language to which the lower
animals are confined, and the voluntary form to which all the
superior animals rise, as soon as they reach that type of organisation in which the complete separation of the sexes appears.
In the former cases, definite acts become the necessary signs of
the feelings which actuate the animal, or of the purposes which
it forms.   This language, which should be exclusively called the
language of action, is spontaneously understood by all living
beings similarly organised.   But it can be thoroughly comprehended also by all the higher animals, by virtue of that common groundwork of organisation which makes all living nature
one ; the various grades of which are due only to the perfecting, or to the developing, of these general attributes.   Still,
whatever the importance of this first form of language, it can
only be considered as the natural basis of the second form, the
sole object of this chapter.

As to voluntary language, this is always artificial, even with
animals, who all modify, just as we do, the institution in
its first form.   For they know how to change, in accordance
with their wants, without or within, the ordinary connection
between movement and sensation, the combination of which
produces the signs.   The formation of these signs however can
never become an arbitrary matter ; or it would lose its chief purpose, for it would fail to mark even any personal sense of
relation between two things, and far more completely would it
fail in communicating such relation either to the family or to
mankind.   The Positive theory of the Brain shows, how these
voluntary signs acquire the requisite fixity from their originally
arising out of involuntary signs ; and then they are gradually
decomposed and simplified, without ceasing to be intelligible.
We are thus irresistibly led to feel the natural bond between
the true Sociological theory of language, and the simple Bio-

*Language of
action is
common to
the lower
animals.*

*Voluntary
language is
a social insti-
tution,
formed upon
the basis of
the involun-
tary lan-
guage.*

logical theory.   In fact voluntary Signs are always true social institutions; for their. original purpose was always that of mutual communication.   If they have a further use in the perfecting of the individual existence, and in particular of mental power, this indirect property, which is almost wholly confined to the human race, would never have sufficed for the formation of Signs.   The ancient Philosophy, it is true, gave this individual character of language an undue importance; but this was from the want of a true social point of view.   Beside that this voluntary language is the only form of language, which need directly interest us; it is the only kind of language which admits of any real progress, according to the gradual complexity and extension of society.   If it seem peculiar to Man, this is only due to our higher capacity for social union.

Language is not confined to Man, but is best studied in Man.

All true naturalists, and especially Georges Leroy, have besides recognised the fact that this kind of language, which is voluntary and capable of progress, is developed in the other higher animals.   Each race forms its own natural language, according to its organisation and its circumstances; a language such as is always in practice understood by the higher races, and indeed by the lower within the same order of the vital scale.   This language gradually reaches its perfection by the successive influences which are brought to bear on it, first from emotions within, and then from circumstances without, thus deciding its form.   If it seem to us not to advance in the animals, that is from want of a sufficiently careful study.   Under all circumstances it is invariably subordinate to the corresponding social state; and consequently it is subject to the same natural limits as society, and to the same artificial hindrances.   Now, I have shown in the first volume of this work (p. 498) the irresistible fatality which prevents any race but our own from reaching its full social expansion.   The natural progress of the other races of animals towards a type of social existence is speedily checked by the ascendancy of man.   The same result necessarily follows for the languages of other races.   In each of them there has now been almost always attained, by many of them there was long since attained, the utmost advance of language possible under the conditions limiting their existence.   The superiority of man, however, forms ordinarily the most powerful of these obstacles.   But we can see, if we suppose that paramount influence absent or even suspended, that a distinct state of progress would be visible in these animal races sufficient to disprove the assumption, that the languages and the societies which they form are not capable of any advance. Everything therefore unites to show that the true theory of language is one which is based on Social and not on Biological science; although it properly originates in purely physiological elements. The theory must therefore be framed on the study of the human type in particular, which, to say nothing of its far higher interest, alone, as in every study of the cerebral faculties, illustrates the laws of the subject.

From this point of view, more than from any other, the Positive system furnishes the only means of penetrating to the true nature of animals. But we must not forget that the relation between these two orders of scientific study was inverted for a long time. Without the convincing light thrown on the study of the human mind by the study of animals, we should never have got rid of the empty speculations of metaphysicians on human language, which they insisted on regarding in an absolute manner, and in its most complex forms; unless indeed they were searching for some supernatural origin for it. All these insoluble questions take a new form or disappear altogether, as soon as we cease to study man apart from the other races of which he is the master. But apart from this great service to commence with, the comparisons furnished to us by the study of animals, are of immense importance in guiding us to the Positive theory of human language; as this is the only means of tracing it to its proper biological origin. The voluntary signs necessarily have their root in the involuntary. And the study of the involuntary signs is at first carried out best in the lowest animal orders, where these are found free from any external complications.

But the involuntary base of language is best studied in lower animals.

This affords a good instance of the general tendency of Sociology finally to absorb Biology, as I have shown must be done in all the higher questions relating to Life. For of these two sciences, which are properly inseparable, the simpler must always limit its labour to prepare the way for the more complex; and to that it must look for the only satisfactory solution of the chief vital problems. When the Positive theory of human Language is sufficiently formed, it will soon give a fruitful impulse to the sum of all that philology has as yet accomplished of valuable, though empirical, research. Now

But human language ultimately explains the animal languages.

the full importance of the notions thus obtained will not be duly brought out, until we see their power of throwing light on the inferior languages of animals.   Thus only can Philology acquire its really encyclopedic character by ultimate incorporation with true universal Science.   But this line of thought will only be dominant in the last volume of this treatise.   Here it remains only to build the Sociological theory of language on its Biological basis ; and thence to trace the gradual growth and formation of voluntary signs out of their origin in the involuntary signs.

ANALYSIS OF LANGUAGE, pp. 190-198.
Three possible languages.
1. Of scent.

All artificial signs are originally derived, even in man, from mere voluntary imitation of different natural signs, which are involuntary and produced by the physical conditions of life.   This spontaneous origin of Signs alone can explain how they should be formed, and why they should be understood.   The movements which form them must in the ordinary way, in order to signify without impressions felt within, be addressed to senses which are capable of being affected from a distance.   This brings us to recognise three kinds of language, respectively concerning smell, sight, and hearing.   The first of these senses is however too imperfectly developed in man to occasion any true system of signs.   Nor could races, endowed with this faculty more abundantly than man, ever form any such language, for want of convenient access to the elementary odours, which must be sought for usually from without.   It is only when communication through other channels is cut off, that, in cases of urgency, recourse is sometimes had to the sense of scent.   In such cases man has been found to supply by his intellectual superiority, the lower power of his olfactory sense.   Very ingenious artifices have been made use of, by which this faculty has been employed to convey even the simple tones of sentiment, when this method of correspondence has been attempted by two beings of high power of sympathy.   The language of flowers, which is still in use in the East, is addressed not only to the eye, as is usually supposed, but also and specially to the sense of odour. However, if this system of communicating by signs is mentioned here, it is only to show us by contrast, the essential condition of every real language, that is to say, the ready reproduction at will of its natural elements, by movements originally connected with the passions expressed.

Only practical lan-

In accordance with this obvious principle, the cerebral

organ of language can only employ two systems of external guages:
2. Sight.
3. Hearing.
signs; the one addressed to the sense of sight, the other to that
of hearing. Each of them has its own special advantages, which
with the higher animals causes the use of both together The Language is
derived from
mimic, or
musical, in-
stinct.
peculiar force with which they can give expression to the most
powerful emotions produces a certain spontaneous rudiment of
the esthetic power; and it gives rise to the two fundamental
arts: the mimic, and the musical; each distinct in its origin,
though easily used in combination. From these two spontaneous sources all our artificial signs follow, as interchange
of feelings under the increasing expansion of the social relations
gradually loses its force, and passes into interchange of thoughts,
in the manner shown in the General View. This gradual alteration, with the highly civilised populations, leads at length to
a total reversal of the natural order; and the assumption prevails, that Art is derived from Language, instead of the contrary. But all that we know of the animal kingdom at once
refutes so mistaken a view, for throughout we find gestures and
cries more commonly used in communicating feelings, rather
than ideas, and even more than in planning schemes. The same
truth is evident in man, when social life is limited to the domestic relations or to loose political connections. As activity
gains in importance, and the consequence is the enlargement of
the social influences, the intellectual side of human language,
theoretical or practical, slowly overpowers our perception of
the emotional, and accordingly of the esthetic side also. Still
this is the invariable source of language; and the traces of it
are never lost. In fact, the close connection between the three
parts of the cerebral life makes it impossible to transmit
thoughts, or to concert action, without also communicating the
feelings which inspire them. Nor is the impulse of feeling,
whether personal or social, indispensable only to Contemplation
and Meditation, to direct their course, or to sustain their energy.
For the same cerebral law holds good in the ultimate intellectual function, that of Expression. This also must be regarded
as inspired and kept in action by one of the feelings, even when
it is used, as we might suppose, as a simple vehicle for scientific
or technical exposition. We see this better when we reflect,
how such a mental function requires more than others, muscular
exertion; and for this the nervous centres have to be specially
stimulated by the reaction of feeling.

At the first dawn of progress, whether in the individual or in the society, Gesture is established long before the rise of Music, as we see in most animals. Beside the advantages special to signs addressed to the eye, the spontaneous adoption of them follows from the fact, that the movements which produce them are at once more readily repeated, and more closely connected with the corresponding affections. At the same time, the evanescent character of mimic expression speedily leads to a radical modification in the fundamental art; in order to fix its essential results, although it diminishes their esthetic power. Thus the first phase of the art of imitation gradually falls into disuse, after giving sufficient impulse to the two chief arts of form, first Sculpture and then Painting. The mode of language which is addressed to the eye, draws its main elements from these two arts, and especially from the latter. But its indirect origin from the original imitative instinct may always be seen by those who study it on Positive methods. If the art of Writing springs originally from an actual picture, every picture was originally intended to record some expressive attitude.

To pass to the second great source of language, it is easy to see the way in which Musical expression early acquires, and more and more develops, a superiority over the Mimic expression, at first in exclusive use. Although sounds are imitated with less ease than forms, and are not so closely associated with our chief feelings, yet their greater independence of time and place renders sounds better fitted for near communication, in all races sufficiently advanced to produce them at will. Accordingly animals themselves use this form of language freely, even so low down in the scale as those without vocal apparatus properly so-called; and we see this in many of the insect tribe. But this invaluable organ, the larynx, which seems at first sight to be adapted only to the vegetative life, furnishes the higher animals with the best means of enlarging their mental and moral life; for it raises the communication between man and man to such a point of perfection, that the finest shades of thought can be transmitted by it. The birds, it is true, show us every day wonderful instances of the superior facilities enjoyed by this mode of transmitting feeling. But since it is less spontaneous in its origin, the motive force of society is even more essential to bring it to maturity, than is the case with mimic expression.

To assume that the sounds which the different animals utter

have made no advance, would be as unphilosophical as to suppose that human speech had been always what it is now.   As
we showed in the preceding volume (vol. i. p. 502), every animal
race is really a Great Being more or less abortive, owing to
development arrested chiefly under the overpowering weight of
Man.   If we apply this dominant law to the question before us,
we shall find that the utterances of all sorts of animals really
arise, like those of man, from the combined efforts of the race,
and are gradually brought to perfection in a long course of
effort by successive generations and the living members of each
generation working together.   The limits placed upon this
development are caused by the numerous obstacles, especially
those of which man is the cause, which stunt the progress of all
the animal races.   Thus the social point of view must hold so
important a place in the Positive theory of Language, particularly oral, that it must be the basis of any explanation of the
language of animals.

ances are so-
cial, even in
the animals.

We may further see the ultimate superiority that Vocal expression at length obtains over Mimic, by noticing two qualities
which the former enjoys, the one statical, the other dynamical;
though to neither of these is justice usually done.   The first
consists in the close dependence of the organs of expression on the
Brain, in which the chief nerves concerned in speech have their
origin.   No other part of the muscular system is so closely connected with the nervous centre.   The vocal organs are thus
anatomically the best fitted to express our emotions and our
thoughts, however delicate.   None of the higher races could
find much difficulty in manifesting these faculties of expression,
which are spontaneously suggested by our natural cries of joy or
pain.   In the next place we may call to mind what was shown
in the volume preceding (vol. i. p. 563), the great advantage
possessed by Oral expression compared with Mimic, in that it
admits of a real monologue, that is, the speaker can address
himself.   This quality, with the others mentioned, has caused
the almost exclusive adoption of this system of Signs by all the
higher animals; so that in fact, the other modes of communication are only called *language* by a metaphysical extension of
the term.   We see in a word, how this facility tends to increase
the importance we attach to a mode of expression which can
be practised readily by each for himself in private.   This is
indeed an ample compensation for the fact, that the mode of

Oral lan-
guage ab-
sorbs all
other.

expression by the Voice is not so spontaneous at first, as that of expression by Gesture.

Visual lan-
guage be-
comes a
mere auxi-
liary, but it
reacts on the
oral.

Thus it is that with all the human races, the language addressed to the Eye, which at first was in use, ends by being a mere auxiliary of the language of the Ear, as is the case with the greater part of the higher races of animals. Such would be the normal state of the system of expression best adapted to a phase of life, in which the affection always controls the intelligence; and where, accordingly, the Signs which are best adapted to the mind yield place to those which correspond best with the heart. But, besides this continuous assistance, the language of the Eye has from the first exercised over that of the Ear an influence which, if less obvious, is deeper: one which has a great share in determining the final form of human language, as it furnishes the best distinguishing feature of language.

Language of
Sound. Its
decomposi-
tion.

In proportion as the progress of civilisation developed the intelligence, theoretical or practical, and reduced the part which at first belonged to the feelings, the Eye, the sense which specially ministered to the intelligence, gradually modified the Language of the Ear, of that sense in closer relation with the sentiments. This inevitable influence of written language made the primitive oral language more analytic and less esthetic, so as to enable it to express ideas relating to the external world and our constant action upon it. The same principle has done much also to extend the original domain of Art, though at the same time it diminished its energy. In fact, language in its purely musical form could not possibly extend to that great field of expression which includes *images*, properly so called; for images are all originally connected with impressions derived solely from the sight. The language of vocal sounds is in fact of so synthetic a nature, that until it is decomposed in the way of which the language of sight admits, the fixer sensations which this latter can express cannot be given. Observation in short must be supplied by imagination. There is no inherent impossibility in expressing forms by sounds, so long as the notation, even when artificial, is sufficiently habitual. It is of every day's experience, with children and even with animals, how easily this relation may be formed. The primitive language is greatly enriched by the intelligence without losing its esthetic character, in spite of the inevitable weakening of its musical power. The imagination strictly so called draws also a new force from the same source, since it obtains an almost continuous exercise, in perfect conformity to its nature. For the impressions felt by the Eye, only furnish the highly complex function of imagination with elements; but they do nothing to assist the brain in its composite task. It is well known on the contrary that, in all matters of art, and indeed even of science, the imagination is never so active as when the eyes are shut. Thus, musical art, when sufficiently modified, is more favourable to the expansion of the imagination than is the art of imitation.

The first great modification due to the growing influence of Signs addressed to the Eye rather than to the Ear, is in the decomposition of the primitive music into two distinct branches, which are soon entirely separated, although their affinity remains marked. Whilst the more emotional part of the first art of sound retains its original name of *Music*, the more intellectual part receives the name of *Poetry*. But the etymology of the word *music* is enough, without the various kinds of evidence furnished by the history of ancient times, to show what was the true character of the original form of this art, when Poetry was long only a part of Music. When Poetry became independent of Music, it was with the special purpose of increasing the influence of the Priesthood, who were the great authors of this separation. Poetry now in fact received a consecration from Religion ; and music properly so called became subordinate to Theocratic Poetry. This change more and more commended itself for public adoption, as the growth of the intelligence, theoretic and practical, led men to the necessity of a less synthetic language ; one in which ideas and purposes might receive more adequate expression. Notwithstanding the consequent loss of esthetic power, Art acquired far more in range than it lost in intensity. By virtue of this wider scope, Poetry soon became everywhere the first of all the fine arts; amongst which Music, though capable of more expression, holds only the second rank ; itself standing at the head of the special arts, all subordinate to the general art of Poetry. Such is the historical explanation of the final arrangement of the Arts in a series, which was shown as a principle in the General View. This separation between Poetry and Music, and the inversion of their original order, are the chief features which distinguish true human Language from the language of all the other animals. The similar inversion between the

[side note: Decomposition of art of sound into Music and Poetry, the latter taking precedence.]

primitive Music and the original Mimic art is not in truth special to our race. Most of the higher animals attain to it in the same way that we do. But none of the animal races succeed in reaching that more delicate form of analysis, which marks the stage in which the mere language of Poetry is distinct from the language of Music. This latter is the form of language, beyond which natures of a lower order of intelligence never rise.

Decomposition of verbal language into Poetry and Prose.

With still better reason, we may regard as proper to Humanity, the fresh modification which, under the growing force of the same motives, leads to a further differentiation in the language of Poetry, and gives it a form better adapted for use, though even less powerful in expression. From this second great change the actual form of human language results. And the use of *prose* properly so called, the origin of which is suggested by the name, for the first time gives full scope for all the purposes, active and speculative, of which language is capable. The new wants both in thought and action which increasing civilisation involves, require this separation of the two forms of language into Poetry and Prose. With all civilised populations it goes back as far as the epochs anterior to direct recorded history, as I shall show in the succeeding volume on the progress of society. As to the influence of Language on the affections, in the form of Prose it obtains fresh resources and even increased purity; although its artistic power is less, when the actual language of poetry differs very distinctly from language in ordinary use.

History of special modes of language, as Algebra, is deferred.

These are the three great changes by which the normal type of Language is gradually formed. To the expression of Gesture, with which man started, succeeded that of Music; the expression by Poetry to that of Music; and lastly Prose took the place of Poetry. Each of these essential changes in the natural order evidently had reference to general communication, the grand purpose of this elementary institution. But it was no less indispensable for the growth of the most important kind of special progress; the advance of the intelligence, practical or theoretical, in its task of guiding the activity, the dominant element of human existence. There is no necessity to give any detailed account of the special modes of language which arose out of a still further and analogous differentiation of ordinary language, intended to meet certain scientific requirements.

The most remarkable of these is the language of Algebra, on which subject it may suffice to refer to what was said in the former work on Positive Philosophy. It would be a subject of high philosophic interest to show how the gradual formation of this language of Algebra fell of its own accord into the same course as that which I have been tracing for Language generally. But this must be reserved for the special study of the philosophy of Mathematics, in the Subjective Synthesis, which I propose to follow the present work upon the philosophy of Society. In this place I must limit the inquiry to those systems of Signs, which are sufficiently general to affect directly the essential character of human Progress.

This leads me to fill up the preceding remarks by pointing out another philological institution, which uniformly resulted from a further indirect reaction of visual upon audible language. I have already shown how the original art of Gesture produces the two principal arts of form, in order to fix its chief modes of expression. The same want is felt in the language of the Ear also, which is naturally even more evanescent. But the system of Audible Signs has not, like that of Gestures, the means within itself of correcting this great defect; nor can it evolve a special art adapted to remedy it. It is therefore forced, in spite of the superior place which is its due, to borrow this indispensable instrument for fixing its signs from visual language. Thus visible Signs have indirectly a place in the institution of Language as a whole. When the mimic art gave birth to that of painting, or even at first to that of mere carving, the natural aid it gave to language was effected by drawings or reliefs intended to preserve the meaning of the chief symbols used. The result was the first form of Writing, which consisted of a complete system of visible signs, representing the Vocal Signs, and which by taking their place when needed, effected their purpose in the main. The special name which this form of writing retains, the Hieroglyphic, will always record the sacerdotal character of its origin and object. In the early Theocracies it formed the only intellectual bond between successive generations. But the populations that succeeded in really freeing themselves from a government of Priests, which soon became oppressive, contrived to effect the same object of transmitting thoughts by means of an institution, not so spontaneous, but

Origin of Art of Writing.

Visible Signs substituted for Vocal Signs.

1. Hieroglyphic.

capable of dispensing with the constant use of a double language. This new want became more obvious since the preservation of Hieroglyphic writing required a special Caste, whose yoke was burdensome to the people. Such were the constant influences which, outside the Theocracies properly so called, led to the completion of the institution of language by the fortunate yet recondite discovery of Alphabetic or Syllabic Writing. It is too obvious to need comment that this final achievement, without which no intellectual continuity would be possible, is that one of the gifts of expression that is most peculiarly confined to Man. No society amongst the animal tribes could possibly reach the stage, in which this crucial discovery in thought is secured. But to moderate any mistaken sense of pride in this peculiarity of man, it is just to remember that the impossibility which prevents the higher animals from doing the same thing is a consequence chiefly, that they cannot overcome the bar imposed by the ascendancy of man on their social advance. But for this fatality, the cerebral organ of language is sufficiently developed in several animal races to give the most favoured of them some such social instrument as Writing. Be this as it may, no other race, but Man, has reached this last perfection of Language; one in which its two early forms, the Mimic and the Pictorial, are closely combined.

Such are the mutual relations of the essential elements of human Language, when we have analysed its very complex nature. It must be borne in mind that our inquiry is dealing with Language, only so far as it is common to all times and places. When I conclude this difficult theory, I shall have to point out, how impossible it was to accomplish it, until Sociology had become a science; without which neither the principle nor the true character of Language could have been determined. Apart from some happy suggestions on special points, it is not more than a century since all thinkers, who ventured to hazard anything on this great topic, ended by having recourse, more or less openly, to Theological sources of argument. Henceforth, I trust, the Positive spirit will be in a position to deal directly with the domain of philology in all its extent; for it is one intimately connected with the general reconstruction of philosophy. And that, without waiting for any special treatise in order to develop the notions just propounded.

2. Alphabetic.

Theory of Language only possible as a branch of Sociology.

I have now to continue and work out systematically the PERSONAL OBJECTS OF LANGUAGE, pp. 199–212. scientific theory of human language, by explaining from the point of view above stated, the chief ends which Language serves in our real existence, individual and collective. In this second inquiry we shall, as in the former, give to Language its full philosophical meaning, that is, according to the true In Language we must include all forms of Artistic Expression. definition of it, the whole of those agencies which enable us to convey to those without the various impressions we have within. This system of expression forms in fact an indivisible whole, in which the most used and yet the least expressive part, Language in its special sense, cannot be really separated either philosophically or historically, from that part specially known as Art. Art, it is true, that is in its widest sense including not only its common basis, Poetry, but also its four essential branches, Music, Painting, Sculpture, and even Architecture, forms the necessary complement of Language to give utterance to all our deepest impressions. Besides, Art constitutes the only portion of Language which is really universal, that is to say, understood by the whole human race, and in different degrees, by all the superior animals. Lastly, this, the most emphatic portion of Language, furnishes the true source of the most usual portion. To separate these two forms of Language would be therefore both arbitrary and irrational, at least when we reduce Art to its two principal elements, Song and Drawing, the exercise of which will become as general as the use of the mother tongue, so soon as the education of mankind shall have been placed on its true footing.

There is no better proof of the inherent incapacity of meta- Language though needing individual organs, is essentially a social faculty. physicians to attain to sound philosophical ideas than the vain attempts they have made to find an individual origin for an institution so thoroughly social as Language. It is melancholy to see how much these metaphysical sophisms captivated a mind so excellent as that of Hobbes. Contrary to all evidence he holds that the use of Signs to aid thought was practised first by individuals, before signs passed into use in communications between persons. When we first trace the influence of Language on our individual life, we must see at once how impossible it is for us to return to this fantastic notion, which the Positive Philosophy finally discards. At the same time we recognise as a general law, that all the functions of the true Great Being, notwithstanding that they belong to a collective existence, require individual organs for their actual realisation. Now, of one of such modes of realisation I am about to treat, so far as it is effected by the initial institution of Language.

Language, one of the five intellectual functions of the Brain.

Before undertaking directly to trace its relations to the three essential elements of our cerebral existence, we must determine the proper office of Language in the Logical system generally. For on that depends the whole of its s rious influence not only on our speculative, but also on our active, nay even our emotional life. According to my Theory of the human Brain (vol. i. p. 543), Language forms in fact one of the five intellectual functions, although more than the other four, it is subject to the influence of Feeling. Thus its reaction on Feeling in turn, however powerful, is essentially determined by its mental character ; and this must be in the first instance examined.

Logical character of Language.

The preceding volume has laid down the Positive theory of human Logic, that is to say, the use in combination of Feelings, Images, and Signs, to facilitate Observation, and above all Reflection. In the first chapter of the present volume, I have already traced the historical evolution of these three general elements during the three principal phases of the Education of the race under Theological systems. We thus know how Fetichism, Polytheism, and Monotheism, respectively developed in all the advanced races, first the Logic of Feeling, then that of Images, and lastly that of Signs. These three successive evolutions were the result therefore of use alone, at once general and continuous, without any special or dogmatic rules. From these three stages through which it gradually passed, the complete and final form of human Logic has resulted : now that the Positive Philosophy has established a definitive concert between all the necessary elements. This explanation enables us now to conceive the true Logical character of Language, and to get rid of all the metaphysical exaggerations, which introduced confusion into every inquiry conducted on that method.

Relation to the Logic of Signs.

Comparison with,

It will suffice to give in a general way, a plain comparison of this last Logical element, the most artificial of all, with each of the two preceding.

1. Logic of Feeling.

We ought to regard as more certain than either of the other two, the Logic of Feeling, that is, the art of assisting the combination of ideas by resorting to the connection between the corresponding emotions. No artificial method can possibly

be so efficient as this instinctive one; for from it in reality
spring all the great inspirations of the intelligence, notwithstanding the unthinking contempt it meets from the majority
of modern philosophers. Its efficiency rests indirectly on the
cerebral law, that the Emotional organs are more energetic than
the Intellectual. But this primitive form of Logic has
naturally two serious drawbacks, first that it is not entirely
under control of the will, and then that its materials are not
capable of great precision. We are not capable of reproducing,
exactly as we wish it, the Emotions which are the fittest to
stimulate our various Thoughts. Besides this, since our conceptions are necessarily far more multiform than our feelings,
the correspondence between them cannot become very accurately
defined.

These two detects are at once remedied, when the Logic of
Images becomes sufficiently developed to be an habitual assistance to that of Feeling. In fact the reproduction of Images
is much more under control than that of the Feelings, and
besides it admits a far higher degree of complexity. It is
therefore much easier for us to associate each notion with an
Image than with a Feeling; and thus we can better promote
the natural combination of Thoughts. In fact this amounts to
calling in the apparatus by which we observe to aid that by
which we think. But although the former is more active than
the latter, it is less active than the apparatus of feeling. Hence,
this second Logic, that of Images, though more available and
more precise than that of Feeling, has less power. Besides,
Images are very far from being reproduced or multiplied, at all
in the measure of our wants, especially our intellectual wants.

2. Logic o Images.

Hence comes the Logical Function of Language, that
is to say, it completes, as far as possible, our general means
of mental combination by converting into a practical instrument those impressions which are the most entirely under
control, as well as the most varied. Signs are far from possessing that close and natural correspondence with Thoughts
which Feelings, and even Images have. But when the association between Signs and Thoughts has been sufficiently confirmed by mature exercise, the facility with which we can
reproduce and multiply Signs is such as to render the work of
speculation both more rapid as well as more exact. Nevertheless this, the proper use of Signs, ought never to be conceived

The Logical value of Lan-guage: it completes the Logic of Feeling and of Images by that of Signs.

of apart from the general theory of Expression. This was the irrational course of all the Ontological schools, except during the Middle Age ; for, looking only to the artificial mode of Logic, they utterly overlooked the two natural modes of Logic, that of Images and that of Feelings. We may disregard these pretentious authorities, the effect of which would be to reduce the reasoning faculty of man to mere Language ; for the immutable laws of our nature have invariably given to the instrument of Feelings and of Images, a higher logical value than to that of Signs. The great use of the third form of Logic consists in fact in its assisting the second, just as this assists the first form of Logic ; so that Signs facilitate the combination of Images, as Images aid the association of Feelings. However the union of Signs with Thoughts may become direct ; and indeed it must often do so, in abstract ideas. There indeed we establish an artificial connection between the world within and that without. But this immediate relation of the two is one much less stable than the relation based on the spontaneous help of Images and Feelings. We ought therefore to look on our logical instrument taken in its highest form, and it is as yet almost in its germ, as consisting in the happy combination of these three general processes : that each Word should recall as far as possible an Image, and each Image a Feeling. We shall then have called in the Order of nature without, to complete the work of our development within ; for we shall thus connect our Emotions, which are essentially subjective, with Signs, which are principally objective, the instrument being Images, objective in their origin, and subjective in their seat. We thus see how false and narrow are the ideas of those who have pretended to analyse Logic ; inasmuch as they have turned all their attention to the most voluntary, but the least powerful, of the three essential modes of combining ideas.

Reaction of Language on Cerebral System.

Now that we have determined the direct office of Language within, we can better trace the indirect reaction of this great institution upon all the sides of our cerebral life.

Expression reacts on Feeling, and on Thought, but not directly on Character.

This inquiry need concern only two distinct influences : one over the Affections, the other over the Intelligence. For Language has no direct influence on the three practical functions, except to obtain the muscular action which it needs. For this, Energy to put it in motion, Caution to keep it continuous, and Persistence to follow it to the end are always indispensable.

No one of the other four organs of the Mind has any direct association with the three organs of the Character, in the strict sense. But, with the exception of this constant relation, and it is a normal element of real expression, the cerebral organ of Language only modifies the Active region of the Brain by the intervention of the Affective region, as in general the whole Speculative region does also. If signs can often exalt or moderate Courage, Prudence, or Perseverance, it is only through their action, direct or indirect, upon the Feelings. We must therefore here limit the cerebral influence of Expression, first to the Affections and then to Conceptions. These two relations besides must be considered in a manner thoroughly general ; nor must any attempt be made to connect them specifically with any particular propensity, or any of the various faculties. But after having sufficiently seized the spirit of this theory, the competent reader will be able to supply all that may be wanted to clear up these subordinate points, which it would be out of place to follow out here.

In studying both sides we must steadily keep in view the Social purpose, the special mark of Language, the communication from man to man of Feelings and Thoughts. The simply individual point of view is so far from fitting this great subject, that it prevented the metaphysicians from properly appreciating even the influence of Language on the intellect, though their attention was solely given to this. *Both must be looked at from the Social side.*

To apply this principle first to the influence of Language on the affections, it is easy to explain, by means of the first law of animal life, the profound reaction of Expression over Feelings. It is indeed an instance of the general law of *exercise* throughout the whole vital series. Our inclinations urge us to express our emotions, even in solitary life, just as they urge us to act in order to satisfy them. The gestures which combine in forming expression, at least in its imitative form, are essentially the same as those which are used in action. Besides, we express our feelings, for the most part in order better to satisfy them, by procuring the assistance of our fellows. If, therefore, on every ground Expression be the result of Feeling, it must tend in its turn to develop and strengthen Feeling. This strict action and reaction, which universally apply to all the affections, belong in particular to the sympathetic instincts. For as they find free vent they produce around us in others new *Emotions are strengthened by Expression.*

emotions adapted to stimulate us in the best way; and the process of alternate reaction is continued almost indefinitely. At the same time Expression never forms the most powerful means of awakening Affection, for this is always strengthened far more by the Action which Affection suggests. But, next after *practice*, properly so called, Language becomes certainly the best general stimulus to Feeling. All the preliminary orms of religion, and especially Catholicism, understood profoundly though in an unsystematic way, this precious faculty of our nature, when in order to perfect the moral culture they resorted to the regular exercise of Prayer. The Final Religion will on system turn this faculty to far higher use, and will give a direct expansion to the sympathetic instincts in the Subjective Life, as will be specially explained in my last volume.

The more fully, the more the expression is complete, as in Writing.

The influence which Language by its nature has upon Feeling becomes in the case of every emotion, but especially any benevolent emotion, both more lively as well as more deep, according as the expression is more complete and more vigorous. The various degrees of this influence may be very clearly seen by comparing the three general forms of communication between man and man: Gesture, Speech, and Writing. When the former is used alone, its influence on the actor himself is less than either of the others, however great its influence on the person addressed. Expression by the voice, especially when freely accompanied with the appropriate gestures and attitudes, has a far higher moral effect; and this has been recognised at all times in religious prayer. But expression in writing, in spite of its being carried on in silence and solitude, affects the agent far more keenly, when it results from a spontaneous act. The mental effort involved becomes a new source wherefrom to kindle the affections, provided that it does not absorb the intelligence. Besides writing alone admits of all the fulness and precision that expression requires. Thus the letters of two lovers are usually, if they deserve the name, more tender even than their conversation. The reaction of Expression on Feeling is therefore always to be measured by its own cerebral force. But its moral influence extends even to the case in which language is entirely passive, that is to say when we employ formulas borrowed from other sources. Although the forms of prayer contained in religious books cannot often precisely suit the true situation of each believer, still the well directed use of these forms, does not fail to exert a very healthy influence on the spirit. It is however less than would be the case, if the believer had composed his own particular effusion, either at the time of uttering it, or, it might be, long previously. We may say the same for those passages from the great poets, which we find of great service in putting our spontaneous utterances into the most perfect form. In this case too the excellence of the expression is increased by the remembrance of all the sympathies these very words have awakened in those who have gone before us. Nevertheless, however superior in the way of art, these passive effusions which we repeat never reach the same degree of influence that our smallest original expressions have; they are never so appropriate to the occasion, nor so spontaneous.

In this general theory of the influence of Language on Feeling, it has been assumed that Language is confined to its most usual form, that of Signs properly so called. But its moral influence becomes still more marked, although following always the same laws, when expression rises to the dignity of art; when it combines with the artificial Signs an apt use of the external Images, which naturally arise from forms or sounds. The superior power of such a language gives it a very decisive influence on the feelings, even when not strictly original and spontaneous. This power even compensates not unfrequently for a total absence of spontaneity, and even imperfect suitability to the occasion, as we constantly see in the influence of religious ceremonies and works of art over spectators, who stand aloof from any part in them. Advantage is too often taken of this tendency for the purpose of stimulating artificial emotions, by the use of formulas and compositions addressed to feelings still dormant. When I come to treat of moral training, I shall take great care to bring out carefully the practical importance of the normal rule, that Expression must always be kept subordinate to Affection. But, whilst Expression must never anticipate Feeling, it may be used, though with very great moderation, to give a fitting encouragement to the flow of the higher sentiments at the moment of formation. If this stimulus be premature, the most powerful artistic impressions will leave behind them little but memories; and these will have no influence on the feelings, until the cerebral organ of language itself reproduces them at some fitting time. Until this is effected, Expression coming before Feeling often leads

Artistic expression has an even stronger effect on emotion.

to the serious danger of preparing the way for an affectation, whereby true emotion becomes ever afterwards impossible. It is not even sufficient for the expression to relate to an actual feeling. It must also have as its constant object a real communication, either individual or collective ; but this may be equally subjective, or objective. If the presence of the adored object without us were regarded as indispensable to the moral effect of our effusions, we should be unable to account for the influence on the brain of religious prayers.

Intellectual
effect of
Language.

Now that we have sufficiently determined the influence of Language upon the affections, it remains to consider its action upon the intelligence. If we regard language as expressing conceptions rather than feelings, it will suffice to distinguish two orders of thoughts, the one Esthetic, the other Scientific. There exists, doubtless, a third class of conceptions, those which are ordinarily called Technical : that is to say, ideas relating neither to the emotions of our hearts within, nor to the notions we form from the world without, but merely to our power to modify by action the environment around us. At the same time, I propose here to put aside the natural distinction, which I have already so frequently used, and which will be needed in the rest of this treatise, that between the Technical and the Scientific class of ideas. For the influence of Language on the Brain must be essentially the same for the whole of our ideas concerning the external world, whether we think with a view to immediate action, or not. The only intellectual distinction we need here take into account is that of the subjective or the objective nature of the conceptions to be conveyed. Any general subdivision of objective ideas into scientific and technical, would lead us into digressions, which I would rather leave to the reader. They require no new principle : merely a sufficient amount of attention to the differences already drawn out in my theory of the Brain (vol. i. p. 540), between the two kinds of Contemplation, and also the two kinds of Meditation.

Artistic
effect.

The normal influence of Language upon artistic construction forms a natural mode of transition from its moral to its scientific value. In fact the compositions of art, though in the full sense intellectual, have no use but to recall in a finer way our own feelings. This is the reason that the artistic power of Language mainly arises from its direct influence on the affec-

tions awakened.   Accordingly, to follow out the esthetic effect
of language would lead only to an unnecessary repetition of
principles already stated.   The influence of Language upon
Art does, however, possess another essential element, the only
one I need specially deal with.

It consists in the capacity Language has of assisting the *Language promotes the combination of artistic images.*
spontaneous combination of the mental Images which constitute
the true domain of Art.   This aid to thought may result in the
first instance from the artificial Signs of which ordinary language is composed, so soon as use has previously connected them
with the forms and the sounds to be suggested to our minds.   I
have already explained the power of words to kindle our deepest feelings by a very natural quality in them which must often
have appeared supernatural in the long infancy of human reason.   We can understand how, *à fortiori*, words suggest images
even more easily;   for the higher degree of resemblance
between words and images involves a closer connection.   If the
inner life, so carefully cultivated in the Middle Age, were not
now deplorably neglected, the daily exercise of meditation
would enable everyone to feel for himself how the least word
can awaken some image, whether of sympathy or veneration,
little as the word itself may seem akin to it.   Now the realisation of Art consists on the one hand, in the happy combination
of mental images, duly clothed with beauty;   and on the other
hand, in the vigorous communication of these inner images, by
a corresponding system of outward images, furnished by sounds
or forms.   Under each of these two essential aspects, the
operation may be much promoted by the use of Signs, equally
adapted to represent the inner or the outward kinds of Images;
for signs, like images, are drawn from without, but are employed within us;   they are objective in their source, and subjective in their seat.   But after duly accounting for the artistic
influence of Language in the strict sense of the word, no difficulty will be found in extending the same explanation to
Language in its most expressive form, that in which it becomes *Still more so does general Expression in Art.*
Art proper.   For the outward Images, which are at the service
of the musician or the painter, must evidently serve, even
better than purely artificial Signs, to combine and translate the
inward Images shaped by the emotions.   When the reformed
Education of the Future shall have rendered the arts of sing-
ing and of drawing as familiar to all as speech or writing,

everyone will make constant use of the precious assistance that these arts will afford for all artistic compositions, public or private. These intimate laws of our cerebral constitution are now only practically known to a small number of poets and artists, sufficiently well trained to apply one art to the con-

Effect on Worship and Prayer.

tinual perfecting of another. But Positive Religion, when it shall give universal prevalence to the Encylopædic system of Education, will soon bring about a sense of the reality and importance of this connection between the Arts, one of such direct interest to the entire sphere of human Worship. Then every intellect will be capable of original art, at least so far as to compose its own prayers ; and all must feel how valuable is this interchange of resources between the arts of expression ; for we shall all find its use in perfecting our performance of the daily duty of Prayer.

Effect of Language on speculative powers.

Now that we have established the great use of Language in aiding the most powerful of our cerebral functions, and the constructions best adapted to our intelligence, it remains to show its even higher importance in the least spontaneous, and the most abstract of our mental operations. Its part in scientific conceptions was regarded with a most mistaken spirit of exaggeration, under the reign of Metaphysics. Thinkers, who were themselves almost invariably given up to vague and floating ideas, owed what these had of apparent fixity chiefly to Signs. Besides that they profoundly misconceived the direct combination of real notions, they entirely neglected the reaction of the Feelings over the reasoning powers, and even that of Images. Their whole attention therefore was concentrated on Signs, the least powerful of the three general aids to reflection ; and they attached far too great importance to the adaptability which is the great quality of Signs. Although scientific studies have often given a partial confutation of these metaphysical aberrations, the positive spirit in philosophy had not acquired views sufficiently general to construct a better theory, until the foundation of Sociology had established the only point of view in agreement with the true theory. For, it is only when we refer language to its social purpose, that we can duly estimate its principal theoretic importance.

Speculation has two stages, as it is, or is not, communicable.

We must, in fact, distinguish in every scientific construction, two natural phases : one simply preparatory, in which conceptions are not capable of communication ; the other in which they are communicable, and which alone is final. We attribute too great a part to Signs in the former operation, and not enough in the second.

Whilst ideas, inductive or deductive, are in the first process of formation, the principal logical office belongs directly to the feelings, which guide and sustain the effort of the mind, calling in images so as to make its work more precise and more rapid. Signs have only a subordinate part, that of giving greater fixity to the elements and the results of each abstract speculation ; and these are seriously exposed to be modified or effaced without such help. The whole science of calculation offers us from its primary steps, admirable examples of this precious faculty. Indeed abstract numeration would become impossible to us beyond the number three, as it is with the animals, if the power of giving names did not enable us to preserve and distinguish the different groups of units. But this indisputable usefulness of Signs with respect to the simplest notions very much diminishes as subjects become complicated. Outside the sphere of mathematics, Language really only assists this first phase of meditation, in so far as it furnishes, according to the happy expression of Hobbes, some *notes* to mark out the course freely chosen by the intelligence. Properly applied here and there, they give increased precision to the conditions and the products of this provisional construction of the mind, before it would bear any formal statement in argument.

Whilst conception is in formation, Language only suggests notes.

It is altogether different when the mental action tends directly to communication, which is the proper object of all mental action. Communication is the only decisive proof that any conception is matured. Not only does it verify the fact that the conception is real, preserving us from mistaking the subjective for the objective ; but it effectually makes out that the conception has acquired due precision and consistence. Even when we are forming ideas merely for our own personal use, we ought to look on all those which we are unable to communicate as hardly sufficiently worked out. For, though they are not essentially chimerical, the test that we cannot impart them, should alone suffice to set them down as vague, confused, and floating. Now, the language which immediately aids in communication must be of great use also in that elaboration of thought which makes communication possible. Its office is no

But expression is the test of maturity of conception.

longer confined to furnishing mere scattered notes, as in the
first sketch of the idea. Its function is to effect a continuous
train of exposition which develops and clears itself at the same
time that meditation goes on ; and thus the spontaneous flow
of conception becomes difficult to distinguish from the formal
expression which assists it.

Especially
the most ma-
ture form of
Expression,
Writing. This logical value of Language is shown in the two general
modes of communicating ideas, the first in Words, the second
in Writing. The first, the least perfect and the more easy,
forms only, with a true thinker, a preliminary trial, public or
private, whether his conceptions are mature. Even when successful, oral expression can never be adequate ; for the rapid
manner in which it is uttered and comprehended forbids the
requisite depth of examination. But whilst speech can enable
us to judge of the reality and the opportuneness of the work
submitted to attention, it shows very plainly the efforts further
required to give the clearness, precision, and coherence which
are needed, if the result is to have completeness and permanence. This final state of excellence can only be obtained by
written exposition.

All great
conception
needs the
complete-
ness of writ-
ing. Not only does Writing, and Writing alone, by preserving the
ideas which are formed, enable them to be critically considered,
apart from any oratorical effect. Besides, the clearness and
continuity which are proper to Writing lead us, as it is gradually
and silently worked out, to the last degree of precision and of
consistency of which human thought is capable. It is impossible to reach this point when one is confined to oral communication even in public. All great conceptions after being
sufficiently prepared by meditation, have reached perfection
only under the pen, in the way of full written exposition.
Accordingly, in writing, the part which language has in
thought becomes more inseparable from the simple mental
effort ; and it justifies the celebrated aphorism of Buffon
(that the style is the man), a saying that should not have been
limited to artistic grace of composition. It is in writing
especially that we can often observe the cerebral phenomenon,
mentioned in the preceding volume, that of expression preceding thought, without affecting their parallelism. The organ
of Language, more active at that moment than the apparatus
of Meditation, leads the way for the time in the immediate
sentence, guided by the effect of those which preceded. It

thus furnishes expressions, which may be premature; but which will presently be perfectly apt to the argument. This phenomenon, besides confirming directly that the organ of expression has a separate existence, shows also how deeply it coöperates in the intellectual labour of written composition.

In this summary analysis of the scientific office of Language, I have had chiefly in view the use of words and notations; as more fit for the elaboration of abstract thought. But for scientific as for esthetic uses, we must recur to the precept already explained, of invariably regarding Language in its entirety, that is to say, in its intimate connection with Art. This, the esthetic part of the complete system of human expression, as it is at once more concrete and less analytic, is not so well adapted to scientific dissertation, as it is to artistic composition. Still even in science it can fulfil a part, very much more apt and more effective, than our very imperfect scientific canons would lead us to suppose. In the 'Positive Philosophy' I have already pointed out, how well fitted the artistic spirit is to give completeness to our scientific theories, by bringing out that free range which all positive conceptions must have by virtue of their relative character. Moreover, as I showed in the 'General View,' the Education of the Future will have to prepare the way for the Logic of Science by the Logic of Art. These two considerations naturally lead us to dwell on the more special and continuous office which Art has to perform for Science, I mean its title to be the natural complement of Language, so far as it can directly aid the two essential parts of scientific elaboration. When the problem of man's cerebral powers is no longer broken up in details, as is now done by our specialists, the importance of thus making Art the instrument of Science will be seen in common use, and will present nothing anomalous. It will be obvious to all, that our intellectual culture ought to have the synthetic character demanded by that entire unity we find in the system of organs peculiar to the Intellect.

Science needs the combined resources of Expression, artistic and literary.

The aid of Art will be specially useful to Scientific Thought in that stage which precedes the work of exposition, and which is less adapted to the use of artificial signs. In this phase our speculative conceptions are more general and less exact, and are thus more easily open to the influence of Poetry, and even to that of Images, whether musical or graphic. The same aid may be extended to the first and most abstract conceptions; but

Aid of Art in Scientific thought and exposition.

it is best fitted to the very highest, as being those which are the most closely akin to our nature, according to the General Law of increasing generality and decreasing intensity. Even during the second stage of Meditation, that in which our speculations pass from Conception to the process of Communication, not excepting that written exposition which completes the full maturity of reflection, Art may still be able to give direct help to Science, though it be in a lower degree. These ultimate Conceptions are then reduced to a condition more exact and less synthetic it is true, but still one which by reason of its greater vividness, allows artistic representation by Images to supplement the Logical value of artificial Signs. If our academical pedantry despises the aid of the Arts in the formation of Ideas, a race of thinkers hereafter, better trained in Music and Drawing, will know the true value of both. The Arts supply Language with resources it never can dispense with, even in abstract reasoning. The Positive Theory of human nature, by thus insisting on the regular use of Art as an aid to Reflection, apart from its reaction upon Feeling, shows the high importance of calling into play all the resources which can contribute to the difficult task of systematic thought.

Such are the normal relations which the institution of human Language bears to the various sides of our cerebral life. These general indications will be fully developed in the sixth chapter of this volume, on the general scheme of Social Life. The following volume will exhibit the same points with increasing distinctness; for it will trace the gradual Evolution of the race in its entirety. And lastly, the fourth volume will follow out in detail, and will apply the same principles, so as to show the final condition of this great institution of Language. The foregoing suggestions will, however, suffice for the abstract point of view, which we have here to keep in view in order to found the true theory of Language.

SOCIAL FUNCTION OF LANGUAGE, pp. 212-218.

In order to complete this theory, I have only to extend it to collective life, the only possible source of Progress. But no very long examination of this the social side and the proper function of Language will be necessary. We required a very careful explanation of the reasons, why an institution solely devoted to mutual intercourse nevertheless should exert a profound influence over the chief individual functions. This difficult question had been so narrowed and even obscured by the older philosophy, that to reduce it to positive methods, required several intricate discussions. There will be no occasion for any such elaborate argument in treating a question so well defined as that of direct Communication, first for domestic, then for political purposes; the only difficulties attending this discussion being such as arise from the impossibility of getting the right point of view.

Viewed in its social aspect, the institution of Language may lastly be compared to that of Property, the Positive Theory of which was expounded in the second chapter of this volume. For Language fulfils for the spiritual life of Humanity an indispensable office, analogous to that which Property fulfils for its material life. Having first rendered help in the acquisition of all human knowledge, theoretical or practical, and then having promoted the development of Art, Language enshrines as it were this double form of intellectual wealth, and transmits it to new cooperators. An essential difference, however, between these two conservative institutions is due to the different modes in which the stores of Language and those of Property are preserved. The products needed for our personal wants, being necessarily destroyed in the act of use, are by the institution of Property entrusted to the keeping of individual holders; and their usefulness to society is even increased by judicious concentration of them in particular hands. On the other hand, Language forms a kind of wealth, which all can make use of at once without causing any diminution of the store, and which thus admits a complete community of enjoyment; for all, freely participating in the general treasure, unconsciously aid in its preservation. Notwithstanding this essential difference, the two kinds of Accumulation, Language and Property, are exposed to a similar abuse: due in both cases to the wish to enjoy without producing. The holders of material Wealth are apt to constitute themselves the sole judges of the way in which it should be employed; and they too often take this to be nothing but their personal enjoyment. In the same way, those who have contributed nothing to the intellectual wealth of Language, set up claims to distinction in the use of it; and thereby excuse themselves from all real social service. This tendency to become the mere pensioners of society, is both easier and commoner than the claims of the idle rich, and it is certainly not less injurious; because the collective nature of the

Language is the spiritual analogue of Property; but unlike Property, it admits of no individual appropriation.

resources of Language makes it more marked. Language, which the Great Being vouchsafes as a free gift to all its servants for the communication and perfection of Feelings and Thoughts, too often serves only to give form to unreal emotions, and yet more often to disguise the want of native ideas.

In determining the social importance of Language, the main idea which I wish to keep in view is the profoundly Collective character of its structure, a point to which Positivism alone has fully done justice. Practical sense was not able to correct the learned errors introduced into this question by a Philosophy, which could not look beyond the individual. In the absence of a really Positive theory of Language, a singular respect still continues to be paid to men, who pretend to teach us dogmatically an Art which really comes from a common effort of the race : one superior, perhaps, but akin to that shown by other animal races. Though the pretensions of the professors of Grammar are even more absurd than those of the professors of Logic, the former have not yet been so completely found out as the latter have been. The barbarous and ill-chosen terms that Grammarians use in their systems ought long ago to have shown how ridiculous are their claims to be arbiters of Speech.

By the institution of Language the true Great Being is perpetually revealing to us its existence, whilst educating us in the knowledge of the universal Order which reigns around and over us. This Order is profoundly impressed upon the actual structure of all our Signs ; for their value depends entirely on their fixity, a thing which would be impossible, but for permanence in the system of nature. The objective side of every word points to the external Order of which it is the expression ; whilst the subjective side of every word assumes an Order of ideas within ; and these the word itself strengthens, by renewing the relations of our system of ideas to the system without. By following out the luminous suggestion of Hobbes (p. 186) on the theory of Signs, the Positive Philosophy conceives of the voluntary relations which form Signs, merely as an extension of the involuntary relations, by which the external world is ruled. Thus Language takes a really sacred character, becoming a part of Religion itself, by directly contributing to the Unity of Man, both individual and collective, and that by artificial means. The mere existence of Language is a standing reminder to us of the Great Being, which is the author, the maintainer, and the fosterer of Language, watching its growth with a constant care, such as no personal force could ever equal. Since philosophy first raised itself to the truly universal point of view, we can at once perceive how false is the position of those who deny Humanity. The worshipper, Christian or Musulman, when he thanks his god for the benefits which he really receives from the Human Providence, is forced to offer up his anti-social prayers in language, itself the perpetual creation of the Supreme Being whose existence he ignores. So too the Communist and the Socialist who obstinately shut their eyes to the Continuity of mankind, cannot preach their wild schemes of reform, except in formulas built up by the united efforts of preceding generations.

This collective character of Language is so strongly marked that it is developed even better by public than by private life.

At the same time Language always originates in the Family, as is shown by its formation being more a work of the affections than of the intellect. But it does not attain to any high development in the domestic sphere, especially with regard to artificial signs, or speech, which has long been the dominant element of Language. Races in which families are united only for temporary expeditions, for war or the chase, have only a limited vocabulary. Although domestic life especially cultivates the esthetic side of Language, I have already remarked that the fine arts attain their full growth only in social life. Gesture, the primitive form of Language, is a sufficient, and even a better mode of expressing feelings between beings who are in such close accord, that they would rather choose this, the most synthetic form of Signs to communicate one with the other. On the other hand, their ideas, whether relating to action or to speculation, are transmitted rather by mere imitation than by teaching properly so called: Example takes the place of Instruction. We have fallen into a very obvious misconception, but one which will no longer be endured, when, observing how much the Family contributes to the transmission of language from man to man, we regard it as the author of Language. This office, which naturally belongs to the Mother, is in reality a social duty, performed by the agents of the Spiritual Power within the Home. There is also another impediment to the full growth of Language in the Primitive Family, in that the

Language originates in the Family, but can only develop in Society.

degrading oppression of women, in such societies keeps down the sex which has the most power of developing the institution.

Gradual development of Language in Society.

The real advance of Language is therefore possible only in Society properly so called ; and it is accomplished only as the social relations grow wider and more complicated. This is true of the imitative side of human Language ; but it is still more applicable to the purely artificial Signs, the employment of which is constantly becoming more extended in general use, as it is in the speculative and practical efforts of the human mind. Speech is enriched with new terms, when thought, for scientific or technical purposes, expounds the Order of nature, or prepares the way for its improvement. The structure of Language too is a matter of gradual development, as the relations of society tend to improve, in the evolution and transformation of the collective activities of man. My volume on the Philosophy of History will show many an instance of this close union between Language and Social Progress : nor need I here add more upon this subject.

Priests and Poets have developed Language, but the community founded it.

If any particular social class were entitled to claim for itself the chief part in the creation of human Language, it would certainly be the Priesthood. For it is the Priesthood who use Language in the way best fitted to develop as well as to fix it, when they carry out a systematic education, such as no imitative mode of communication would be adequate to convey. On the collapse or decay of Theocracies, Poets succeed to Priests in this important function, in right of which they have created so many pretentious fancies respecting the origin of languag . Pure Philosophers, much less mere *savants*, have not the smallest claims to be considered as the authors of Language, with the exception of a few academic terms, for the most part clumsy in construction. Even the two classes of men, Priests and Poets, who have the best title to be looked on as the founders of Language, have in reality done nothing but contribute, in the degree of their own needs, to the development of an institution which has always sprung up naturally, by an instinct common to the race. The teaching of the Priest, and the creations of the Poet, obviously suppose the existence of Language ; for they could no more themselves originate Language, than they could originate Society, which it is the habit also to attribute to their efforts. It is from this popular instinct that all human languages derive their admirable consistency; for at the same time it preserves their uniformity, and promotes their development. That form of language, which is at once the most systematic, and least extended, the hieroglyphic symbolism of Algebra, has been slowly worked out by the labour of generations, and has consequently sprung from the interchange of ideas. It is beyond the powers of any single mathematical genius.

We thus find that the Public has an indispensable and substantial part, in all human composition, whether scientific or artistic, although special classes so unreasonably claim the exclusive credit of its creation. This instinctive power of the race need in no way surprise us, when we remember how closely the institution of Language is bound up with our Cerebral system. It is easier to learn than to invent; yet the extreme ease with which languages are acquired from the tenderest age, so long as they are not presented to us in a scholastic form, points to the instinctive nature of the origin of Speech. The essential laws of Language are indeed much better observed by children, as they are by the people, than they are by the great majority of Philosophers, and certainly by the majority of Grammarians. Besides our languages, notwithstanding the high degree of complexity which they have now reached, are for many purposes understood by the most sociable races of animals when trained with sufficient care.

Language is an instinctive faculty, as we see in children, and even animals understand it.

Mankind collectively, therefore, is the true author of Language, and its true guardian. A just repugnance to needless innovation will always preserve that sense of propriety which accounts for the slow growth of our phraseology. We see how apt new phrases are, when we follow their etymology, for they have sprung from wants long experienced. The very ambiguities of Language, which academic pride attributes to the slender vocabularies of the people, bear witness often to profound analogies, not seldom happily seized by the common instinct of mankind many centuries before the learning of philosophers has been able to perceive them. In my work on Positive Philosophy I have already pointed out the most striking instance, the two senses of the word *necessary*, the double meaning of which had never been explained until the Positive Philosophy was enabled to do so (Pos. Phil. vol. iv. ch. 49). I might also illustrate this remark by many other admirable phrases of double meaning: such as, *just, order, property, humanity, people,* &c.

Etymology shows us the popular and spontaneous nature of Language.

The senses of the word *Positive* which I have already traced
(Pos. Pol. vol. i. p. 45) will enable the reader to continue this
thought for himself.

Language,
by its com-
mon sense
often checks
the errors of
Philosophy
and Science.

Lastly, the same human Providence that creates and preserves Language, uses it to correct as far as possible, the aberrations of the speculative intellect, which has hitherto been so
strikingly inferior to the practical instinct of man. The wildest
dreamers, when forced to make themselves intelligible to the
public, have to begin by becoming intelligible to themselves.
The true universal Logic, so deeply impressed upon every language in general use, detects and checks the wanderings of
fanciful Philosophy, and also those of idle Science. The language of mankind has only to find expression for ideas and not
to systematise them; and hence it naturally gives its sanction
to established truths however opposed they may be to the prejudices of speculation. For instance, whilst Philosophy in its
Theological, as much as in its Metaphysical form, denied the
instinctive existence of the benevolent emotions, Poetry, more
truly inspired with the common wisdom of all, idealised these
affections in some of its noblest creations.

PROGRESS
OF LAN-
GUAGE, pp.
218-220.

Having thus shown the social nature of Language as an
institution, I shall close this chapter by a study of the laws of
its progress. But in doing this, I am bound, even more than
in the other subjects of this volume, to content myself with a
general principle. The development of Language as a special
branch of human evolution is even less adapted to a detached
study than any other branch of that evolution, inasmuch as it is
so closely bound up with the general movement as a whole.

As in all other cases, we must attend to the principle of
following out the true object of the institution under consideration, for this object is always plainly to be detected from the
earliest stage of every real product of civilisation. We cannot
in fact find any better example of this grand rule of Social
Philosophy, for in Language the object of the institution is
singularly well marked. The mistakes of Metaphysicians about
the progress and final form of Language were all due to their
obstinately adhering to the individual point of view in dealing
with a question, which above all others required to be considered
from the social point of view.

Unity is the
ultimate
form of

As the common instrument of all forms of communication
between men, Language is obliged to follow the same laws of

change as these forms. Its advance therefore depends upon Language as of Religion. that of human society, for which I have already laid down the general laws of progress. Like civilisation as a whole, Language has first to encounter a long preparatory stage, during which it is quite sectional; until at last it acquires its full character of universality, as the social relations gain strength and completeness. Thus *unity* forms the ultimate state of Language, as certainly as it forms that of Civilisation and of Religion, of both of which Language constitutes so essential an element. For when opinions and manners have grown more or less into conformity, the languages by which men systematically communicate their thoughts and their feelings will not constitute for ever a source of division in the race. That Metaphysical Philosophy, which was wont to treat Language only as the general source of individual Logic, was not likely to conceive the ultimate unity of many tongues.

In its origin within the Family, as with other animal races, Its development follows that of the social groups. the Language of Man presents at first as many varieties as the families which use it; yet it does not lose the type common to the species. In this stage the development of language is as limited as the area of its use. When society commences, it permits at the outset but small groups, which however closely united within, are surrounded by hostility without; for the beliefs of Theology and the activity of War only associate certain families in tribes by detaching them from all others. A belief in fictions, like a purpose of destruction, can never lead to union amongst mankind as a whole. Now language can only follow the same course as that consensus of opinions and of manners which it presupposes, and which it continues. Accident alone, and this would not be lasting, could push the area of any language beyond that of the particular phase of civilisation out of which it arose. If it exceeded the area of the temporal union, it would not exceed that of the spiritual. Even then its natural tendency would be, to unite the respective populations. In the midst of the most sanguinary contests, man has always shown an involuntary repugnance to kill his enemy, if he asked for quarter in the mother tongue of the victor. These considerations I shall leave to be more properly explained and verified in my succeeding volume on the Philosophy of History.

I shall also reserve for the fourth volume of this work my

We may look
to a Univer-
sal Lan-
guage upon
the realisa-
tion of Uni-
versal
Unity.
view of that ultimate unity, which I hold to be the inevitable
destiny of human Language. Though the utopias of a universal
language conceived by the Absolute and Individualist Philosophy
were merely fanciful, the continual recurrence to them during
the last three centuries, and that even by men eminent in
thought, foreshadows, like so many dreams of the kind, a near
attainment of that end. It was no doubt futile to hope for a
universal language, whilst creeds remained divergent, and
habits of war survived. On the other hand, we should commit
the same mistake, if we looked forward to the races of mankind
united by the bonds of the Positive Faith, and by peaceful
industry, yet for ever speaking or writing different tongues.
The date of such an ultimate agreement can be foreseen even
less than its form. Still, whilst leaving both points for the
fourth volume of this work, I have thought right to complete
the Statical study of language, by indicating from its general
nature, the ultimate Unity into which it is destined to pass.

Language,
like Reli-
gion, will
unite the
Order of
Man and the
Order of Na-
ture.
In conclusion, I would recall the comparison with which
this chapter opened between Language and Religion. But
that which then appeared a simple analogy, now assumes the
character of an intimate connection, by reason of their common
tendency to promote the Unity of Man. Apart from the inevitable stages of transition, topics to be treated in the next two
volumes, we can frame an ideal picture of the modes in which
Women and Priests, the two great organs of the future Spiritual
Power, will each in their way extend the sphere of Religion
and of Language. With the first utterances of infancy woman
will reveal to the child that eternal Mother of all who gradually
constructed all forms of speech. On the other hand the Priesthood, whilst explaining the growth of the Universal Language,
which will then be familiar to all, will be enabled to reveal the
presence of that immutable Order, at once within and without
Man's life, an Order of which Language is but a general means
of perfecting. In this twofold work of education Language
will be directly fulfilling its sacred mission, that of giving
greater harmony to the Soul within, by making it more in
unison with the World without. And thus the generations
that are to come will grow in love and in respect for that Order
created by Man, whence all such blessings directly issue, and
no less for that Order of Nature around us, the necessary basis
of all human effort.

CHAPTER V.

THE POSITIVE THEORY OF THE SOCIAL ORGANISM.

THE three preceding chapters taken together now furnish us with sufficient material for the abstract study of Social Order, the essential elements of which have each been separately considered.   These elements in fact properly answer to the three essential divisions of our cerebral life, Activity, Feeling, and Intelligence.   To each of these, one of these preliminary chapters has been devoted; and it will serve to show the character and general conditions of each, as seen in the simplest and most spontaneous form of human society.   The second chapter dealt with that Industrial Activity, on which all human Order depends; and it expounded the real theory of individual Property, an institution necessary for the development of that industrial Activity.   The third chapter, on the Family, treated of the expansion of the Social Sentiment, both in the Continuity of generations, and the Solidarity of contemporaries; and I showed that in the family life alone can the social instinct find any solid basis for growth.   The fourth chapter examined the general system of Communication, moral as well as intellectual, on which the entire evolution of the human understanding is based, whether artistic, scientific, or technical.   Thus, Religion embracing the totality of our life, the subject of the first chapter will stand towards these three subjects in the following order: first, the relations which Religion has to regulate, secondly, the feelings to which it appeals, thirdly, the instrument of language which forms the foundation of its teaching.   From the social point of view, the order of these three subjects, Property, Family, and Language, coincides with our natural growth from the personal instincts to the highest social feeling by the intermediate education of domestic duty.

In rising now from the domestic order to the political order,

Relation of the three foregoing chapters to the initial chapter on Religion.

Social Statics have only to put together doctrines necessarily
formed out of the materials already prepared. We have determined for the real unit of society, the Family, its practical
end Industry, and its moral constitution ; and we have further
examined in the laws of Language, the means by which each
family communicates to óthers its feelings and its thoughts.
Taken together, these furnish Social Statics with the needful
basis for the direct study of social life in its more complex form.
This is reached, when families become grouped to their full
extension of number and duration in time.   The twofold difficulty consequent upon this increased complication in establishing
the abstract Theory of Human Order, is fortunately compensated
by an increased breadth of the laws in question.   In proportion
as societies increase in extent and in permanence the connection
between their various units becomes more close, whilst their
points of difference insensibly disappear. Although in Sociology
the theory of the Domestic Order should precede that of the
Political Order, it is the former which presents the greatest
scientific difficulties, and which is exposed to the greatest
practical risk of error.   The same thing would be seen, if the
Positive study of the Social Order were carried out with as
much detail into the simply Individual Order.   As concerns
the individual, Philosophy must content itself with determining
the governing truths.   The study of the individual is in truth
more complex than any other study ; for the influences which
affect individuals are more diverse and more numerous, whilst
their effects are far less uniform.   Hence in the first chapter
of this volume, I determined to place moral science as the
seventh and last stage in the classification of the sciences.   It
supplies the last step in the scale of increasing complexity and
speciality.   Thus if the wider relations of the study upon which
we now enter, that of the Social Organism as a whole, call for
greater efforts of abstraction, on the other hand we shall find,
that the laws of Social Order are seen in it with more regularity
than the laws of the special elements treated in the three preceding chapters.

The concluding portion of Social Statics will be devoted
first to the general conditions of the social organism, and next
to the essential laws of its life.   If the latter would seem to
belong rather to Social Dynamics, this only relates to modifications of place and of time.   The vital functions which belong

to it in all places, and in all times, form the principal part of Social Statics, and this will be reserved for the sixth chapter, the present chapter being devoted to an analysis of the Social Organism. Having determined its parts we have now but to study in the abstract the laws under which they are combined.

I therefore proceed to the Positive theory of the various social forces, for without this all Sociological reasoning would be incomplete.

POSITIVE THEORY OF THE SOCIAL FORCES, pp. 223-235.

Every true social force, is the product of a cooperation, on a larger or smaller scale, concentrated in some individual organ. This cooperation may be subjective or objective; it is almost always both at the same time, in proportions varying with the degree that time or space enters into the subject. The only form of force truly individual is physical force in its strictest sense; and even then it is only individual, when it makes no use of weapons, for these suppose some kind of co-operation, either in the past or the present. Now force of this kind is easily overcome by the smallest combination of others. As to intellectual force, vanity itself has to admit, how much it owes to predecessors and contemporaries. Besides, by itself, it is unable to generate any real force such as can issue in immediate act. The efficiency of intellectual power is always indirect, and requires voluntary assent, either on the part of any who yield to its influence, or at least in those who form that public opinion which induces them to yield. The influence itself tends to promote cooperation, but cannot dispense with it. We must say the same thing of moral power, properly so called; its influence is deeper but not more direct; it depends entirely on cooperation.

All social force results from co-operation,

But whilst insisting on the necessity of Cooperation as the basis of every social force, we must not forget the second half of the preceding definition, the need of an individual representative. Although all social functions are essentially collective, their exercise always requires a person as their organ, more or less conscious. Cooperation, which was not so concentrated, would remain perfectly sterile; indeed, until it has an organ, the cooperation is only seeming. For it means the grouping of several individuals for a greater or less period of time, around one pre-eminent individuality. When this influence from the centre anticipates the readiness of the parts towards combination, Cooperation is systematic, for it results from the action

Concentrated in a personal organ.

of the chief over the followers. The cooperation is spontaneous on the other hand, when the tendency to combine shows itself before a common centre is found. But in the latter case, hitherto the more common, the cooperation, and consequently the force, does not really arise until the concentration is complete.

Double character of every human association.

This essential condition of concentration in a person, is the point in which the Positive theory of the social forces differs so strikingly from the various Metaphysical theories. The vague, and therefore subversive ideas, which still prevail respecting political power, spring in truth from forgetfulness of the need of condensation in a person, as the leading feature of all social cooperation. In its ordinary form, this first principle gives rise to the cardinal axiom : Society without a government is no less impossible, than a Government without Society. In the smallest as in the largest associations, the Positive theory of a polity never leaves sight of these two correlative ideas, without which theories would lead us astray, and Society would end in anarchy. The constant presence of both in combination points to the double character of the true Human Organism, that it is collective in its nature and individual in its functions, each of its individual elements being naturally independent.

All force is centralised cooperation.

Since in Sociology, every force results from a Centralised Cooperation, the Statical Theory of these forces is mainly concerned with determining the general laws of this cooperation.

All social force is at once material, intellectual, and moral.

The first principle is that a true social combination must take in all the essential sides of every human life, however unequally these may share in it ; for such is the tendency of personality to preponderate that the cooperation will be either sterile or precarious, if any one of the principal cerebral regions is left out. The neglected instinct will either embarrass or dissolve the combination. In Sociology therefore, we must treat every real force as being at once, material, intellectual, and moral ; that is to say, at the same time as concerned with Action, Speculation, and Affection. These three essential elements, however, may be very unequally distributed, and the leading element alone gives its name to the combination, though we must never forget the inevitable presence of the others. At the same time, both moral and intellectual influences have a place in the composition of forces supposed to be the most strictly material, except in the mere case of superiority of muscular force. The latter case need hardly be considered in such a race as man; for even in the earliest stages of civilisation, it is held in check by the higher influences. In the converse case, moral and intellectual influence would both be incapable of founding any real force, if they could not obtain the requisite amount of material support.

Before studying the combination of these three essential elements of all social power, we must decompose each into the two principles which belong to it. Without this analysis, we shall not get at a knowledge, either of the elements themselves, or of the mode in which they are combined. *Analysis of these three elements.*

Material power, for instance, is made up of two constituents, Numbers and Riches. Each of these may produce a force capable of imposing conduct without deciding the will. Numbers may be the more irresistible of the two; but as a ruling power it is not always so oppressive as Wealth. For the union which its rule implies renders it very sensitive to moral impressions. Wealth, on the other hand, which admits of extreme concentration in individual hands, soon acquires a personal character; its power often then becomes tyrannical, for it has the control over those costly products which are constantly in request to sustain life. In the truly normal condition these two sources of Power are closely combined; for Numbers have either produced Wealth, or consent to be controlled by it. But the two have such very different tendencies towards extension or concentration, and their interests so often conflict, that these two kinds of material force may well be regarded as distinct. Wherever a real intellectual and moral power exists, it is enabled by means of this very difference between Numbers and Wealth to bring both into general harmony. On the other hand, in times of spiritual anarchy, the opposition between Wealth and Numbers becomes more marked, and seriously endangers material order at the very moment when it is most needed to restore the ruptures in society. Lastly, the two kinds of material power have different affinities for the other two kinds of social force, for Numbers are most accessible to Moral influence, whilst Wealth is most ready to admit Intellectual influence. *1. Material power is composed of Numbers and of Wealth.*

Material force, beside that it is of principal importance as the primary basis of Social Order, is the only form of power which it is at all difficult to resolve into its component parts, as not immediately evident from general principles. The other two social forces may be analysed directly by the aid of my theory of the Brain.

2. Intellectual power, of Conception and Expression.

As to intellectual force, it is quite enough if we separate it into Conception and Expression. Although the latter implies the former, Conception would have no result if it never issued in Expression. The normal condition requires their intimate union, like the combination of Riches with Numbers. But unfortunately it is quite as easy to separate them. For the talent of Expression is more common and is more easily trained than the talent of Conception; so that the faculty of statement is often found in those who can themselves produce nothing, and who use it only to exhibit borrowed thoughts. At the same time, true thinkers are usually sufficiently capable of exposition, whether oral or written; so as to make their thoughts intelligible to others. The supposed instances of thinkers without the power of expression are really only cases of incomplete reflection; and if they cannot impart their ideas, it is because they have a loose hold on them themselves. It is one of the great services of sound intellectual training to bring out the superiority of the thinkers over the talkers or the writers. In periods of great change their places are too often usurped; and those who have thoughts of value to proclaim, are often borne down by the easy popularity of men who only put old ideas in some new shape. Humanity is not long the loser by this neglect of thinkers who are worthy organs of its life; but the honour that belongs to them is too often delayed until death has given them a subjective existence.

Numbers and Expression are direct forces, Wealth and Conception indirect forces.

If we compare the two parts of material force with the two parts of intellectual force, we see a contrast between the direct influence of Numbers and of Expression, and the indirect influence of Wealth and of Conception. In both cases it is this indirect force which gives the main element of real power, at least so long as social order is not greatly disturbed. When the two forces, material and intellectual are combined, we also see a marked affinity between the two direct modes of each pair, and also between the two indirect modes of each pair. Thus Expression is naturally akin to Numbers, whilst Conception is akin to Wealth; because the two former rather tend towards expansion of force, whilst the two latter tend towards concentration of force. And in both cases we find that true discipline requires due subordination of the direct influence to the indirect influence.

The third element of social force, the Moral, may also be 3. Moral power is composed of Command and Obedience. resolved into the two spheres of command and obedience. Here, as in the last case, my theory of the Brain will enable us to decompose moral influence into its two natural forms, the Heart and the Character. The Character, as in immediate relation with Execution, often obtains the upper hand, like Expression and Numbers. In truth it is the Character, much more than the Heart, which gives moral ascendancy, at any rate during objective life. But the subjective existence soon redresses this temporary superiority, and brings out the normal harmony between them. As the social state becomes more regular, the Heart prevails over the Character, as being the source of the impulses, although the character alone determines results. In the second chapter of this volume, we traced out the natural law that the motive of action is usually the result of cooperation between Egoistic and Altruistic instincts, the latter acquiring an ultimate ascendancy. The true discipline of Moral force therefore, like that of Material and Intellectual force, involves the right subordination of the direct to the indirect form of power.

Moral force however, presents this grand difference from the These correspond with Character and Heart. other two : that it concerns directly the working of all social force ; whilst the other two simply supply the bases. There is accordingly a contrast between its two modes of influence which is not found in the others. The more direct form of Moral power, the Character, being more active than the indirect form, or the Heart, contributes more specially to the formation of social force ; whilst the maintenance and control of social force, on the contrary, depend on the indirect form, the Heart. In a word, the Character prompts us to command, the Heart to obey. During the earlier stages of human progress, when the problem was rather how to develop, than how to discipline the human forces, the Character acquired a natural ascendancy, and the spirit which disposes to submission was little honoured. But the Final Order of society will more and more show the true dignity of obedience ; for now the problem is to bring the existing forces into discipline, and this must be done by giving the ascendancy to the Heart. And the Positive theory of human nature prepares us for this work ; for it places the centre of cerebral unity in the Affections.

Each of the three essential elements of every social force, Combination of all as we see by this analysis, is exposed to peculiar dangers; since each of them results from a combination between two principles more or less opposed. This also shows how impossible it is to found any real force with one of the three elements. It is the cooperation of the three, which prevents or remedies the aberration of any one in particular. Man is no less prone to revolt than he is to submission. In order that obedience may become sure and permanent, the nature of man as a whole must be duly under control; if any one leading instinct escapes from the influence, it may withdraw all the others. Men will recognise separately material force, intellectual superiority, and moral authority, but they will not frankly yield to any of them, until they are all harmoniously united. This is the reason why the division between the Temporal and Spiritual Powers, the essential basis of the Final Order of Humanity, was incompatible with early stages of civilisation, where every means of social control had to be united to overcome the natural lawlessness of primitive man.

In Sociology however, we must note three forms of force, each bearing the name of that element which has the largest part in it. The difference is very pronounced in the political sphere; and it may be seen even in the domestic sphere, at least where the Family is fully constituted. That is to say, the active Head of the family, the Grandsire, and the Wife, are the centres respectively of material power, of intellectual sagacity, and of moral influence. But the habitual predominance of the first, or material power, shows how unequally apportioned are the three social forces; since their activity is in inverse proportion to their dignity. The great movement of human progress is for ever diminishing this disproportion; but it can never efface it. For this reason, even in the ultimate ideal of man, I have regarded the rule of the social world as necessarily belonging to material power; whilst intellectual and moral power can be nothing but moderating influences.

This essential distinction is quite in accordance with the true theory of man's nature, when we regard the Human Organism as a whole, without giving exclusive attention to its cerebral centre. The greater importance of material force is a consequence of the greater activity of the vegetative life in the organism, where the material wants, which never cease, irresistibly determine the ordinary course of our existence. When these are supplied by the collective labours of society, their effect upon our lives becomes higher without ceasing to be preponderant. But our moral and intellectual growth, instead of being checked by this predominance of the material wants is, as I have shown in the second chapter of this volume, actually elevated by it.

In the Theological or Metaphysical stages of Philosophy, and especially under Monotheism, there was no adequate allowance for this preponderant activity in material life. In spite of the facts it was overlooked in all social theories. At the same time the condition of slavery, and after that of neglect, in which the labouring population was plunged, led social philosophers to forget the vast part played by material wants.

This was neglected by Theologism.

Our modern conceptions must rise to the level of our moral standard, and we must invest material labour with a philosophical importance demanded by its social value. The prejudices of his day are the only excuse for Aristotle in excluding labour from his admirable encyclopædia of science. Modern Sociology cannot do the like. It was for this reason that no true synthesis of human life was possible until the advent of the Positive Philosophy, which alone had sufficient reality to give material labour its real place in the drama of Man's life. The necessity for this gives a fresh harmony to our social construction, and is far from increasing its difficulties. It is only thus that the system of human nature is duly coordinated with the system of external nature. There would be between the two an impassable gulf, were it not that the daily need of acting upon the external World is the guiding motive of our individual life. The doctrine of the old Theology, that labour was a consequence of the divine curse on man, was as irrational, as it was immoral; and it exhibited an utter incapacity to guide either Philosophy or Society. The Positive Religion at length makes material activity the essential condition of Unity, whether in the individual or in the race.

Positive Religion, however, makes material activity the basis of unity.

In reality, the social law of the natural supremacy of the practical power, becomes a mere application of the most general law of the Order of Nature. In my Classification of the Sciences, which is at once objective and subjective, I have already shown that the higher elements are always dependent upon the lower. This follows from the universal principle that decrease in generality implies increase in complexity. To the Positivist

In accordance with the law of dependence of the higher on the lower order.

therefore, the preponderance of material force in society is far from being a distressing anomaly. It is just as natural as the dependence of social on organic Order, of organic on inorganic Order. When our emotions are at length in harmony with our convictions, we shall learn to offer blessings to this destiny of our lives, as a prime source of our intellectual development, and of our moral improvement.

Material force, whether in the form of Numbers or of Wealth, is never independent of Intellectual and Moral influence.

The ascendancy of material force, the primary basis of all social Order, gives rise to an error, natural in itself and much increased by pride, especially in the absence of any doctrine capable of explaining the true economy of human life. In fact the special organs of this Practical Power come to regard it as independent both of Intellectual, and of Moral Power. The assumption is aggravated by the fact, that it is as common with those who submit, as with those who exercise control. The Positive Religion however introduces sounder habits of thought and of feeling, by insisting on the real facts of daily life. When material force is the direct product of Numbers, it calls out voluntary combinations, which cannot exist, or even begin, without a sufficient convergence of opinions and of feelings. In periods of anarchy this unity is least apparent, and we see how unstable are the various practical forces, when the least disturbance arises in the intellectual and moral bases of power. When material power rests solely upon Wealth, the same consequences arise. For experience shows too often how greatly the existence and the use of riches depend on the control of the prevailing ideas, and on the sentiment of the time. How shallow and ignoble are those economic theories, which represent material life as independent of any mental or moral influence. A change in opinion, such as the Musulman's abstinence from wine, would, in such a country as France, profoundly modify industrial life, both public and private.

This Intellectual and Moral influence will increase, whilst Power becomes itself more specially Material.

However little the great and the rich in their pride may think it, Material Power is largely created and sustained by the direct and indirect influence of Intelligence as well as Feeling. These contribute to it in so close a degree, that their relative shares can hardly be distinguished. At the same time the course of human Progress exhibits a law which, to avoid misconception, I will state at once. The part which Intelligence and Sentiment indirectly contribute to Material Power increases with the progress of civilisation ; whilst the direct part which they contribute diminishes. That is to say, as the Social Forces gradually pass into more special organs, the possessors of Material Power find themselves less and less the masters of intellectual and moral power. At the same time their proper position as temporal chiefs is secured to them, owing to the greater readiness in public opinion and in habits to accept authority, as increasing civilisation shows the public utility of thus concentrating Power. The respect which the people show for rank or wealth is far from being usually so servile, as satirists in ancient, and still more in modern, times pretend. In my chapter upon Property, I pointed out (p. 133) a universal tendency in men, from the earliest stages of history, to found great fortunes by free gift. The character of sanctity attributed to particular families does not account for this tendency, but was rather the mode of its expression proper to the provisional Religion. When the social use of every human force is directly taught by the final Religion, the true power of riches will be as much increased as the proper duties of riches ; for their right employment and value will be better understood. Positivism thinks more of regulating the employment of power, than of discussing its origin ; and thus the worthy possessors of wealth will be more popular and more respected, although we reduce to its due place the personal merit which the acquisition of wealth alone merits. Instead of losing by being treated, morally speaking, as public functionaries, the directors of Capital will gain a freedom and a rank, far higher than any they could possess amidst the blind passion for wealth as an exclusive possession of the individual.

The Social Organism, therefore, is a single whole just as, and even more than, the individual Organism ; where we know how much material functions, in spite of their governing the rest, have constant need of the cerebral functions. The instance of Wealth is the only one, where the intimate alliance between the three elements of social power can be misconceived. Literary vanity is perhaps a source of more evil than the insolence of wealth ; but it rarely leads men to suppose that intellectual power can altogether dispense with material support. The weakness of men of letters for temporal power would rather imply that they are conscious of the real weakness of that form of skill of which they are so vain.

The three Social Forces are closely combined.

Still, Intellectual Force is, after Material Force, the most

Next to Material Power, Intellectual exerts the largest social influence.

important of all the social influences. Intellectual superiority indeed, has greater actual effect than Moral superiority, inasmuch as it comes closer to our more urgent needs. No doubt, Mental Power, even more than Material Power, is helpless without a sufficient amount of moral support, but for which its insight would not inspire confidence. But although Intellect without Morality cannot acquire any real social ascendancy, the past presents too many examples of great mental eminence united to singular poverty of Heart and even of Character. These abnormal types however have at times obtained a very well-deserved influence, where circumstances neutralised the defects of their natures. The instinct of the public is sounder than the judgment of pedantic moralists, and allows for the difficulties presented by the order of nature, and by the discovery of the practical ways of acting on it. Real services of thinkers in these two spheres are rewarded by the respect and gratitude of mankind, however serious the moral defects by which they are accompanied. Their services are at once capable of public use ; whilst moral greatness, in itself rarer and more valuable, is at first only seen within a sphere more or less domestic, except in the case of certain eminent rulers. The Heart in its turn sanctions this honour shown to Intellect, when it is paid on grounds of public good, the end to which the Heart is ever working.

In the Final state, opinion will reverse this order, and will respect first, Moral, then Intellectual, and lastly Material Power.

We must, however, herein distinguish carefully between the ultimate form of morality and the preparatory stages of civilisation. In these the question was more important, how to develop, than how to judge, the various powers of man, and consequently intellectual eminence was more valued than moral, the special part of which is to control the rest. When this work of discipline is regularly begun, the instinct of public opinion changes its tone. It is then felt that the right employment of the human powers should be the main care, all danger of these real forces being extinguished having long past. At the same time, a better knowledge of human nature brings out the indirect, yet higher, power of those feelings by which our lives are unconsciously governed, Thought and Action being but the ministers of Affection. At length we see, how the training of the sympathetic instincts is the great source of true happiness, public as well as private. The Positive Scale of human progress is thus complete, and public opinion tends to correct the order of importance originally given to the three natural elements of social power.

This change in the degree of honour, however, implies no change in the relative place held by each kind of Power. As having a usefulness wider and more direct, Material Force will continue to prevail over Intellectual Force, as Intellectual will prevail over Moral Force; although the latter, apart from its greater rarity, more deeply affects our destinies as a whole. Moral greatness, as I shall show in the fourth volume, can find its true place only in the Subjective Life; for there the material necessities no longer exist to render practical and speculative services indispensable to man. During the Objective Life, the ultimate ascendancy of Moral Power is foreshadowed by the social respect that is paid to the Affective Sex, the principal organ of Moral Power. But the late period at which Humanity has recognised the true value of Feeling, will show that in degree of real power it is necessarily placed after Activity, and even after Intelligence.

But this is only from the moral point of view, and in the Subjective Life. In real power, Material Force must always be paramount in authority.

In this classification of the three great elementary Forces of the Social Organism, we have a new instance of the general principle of classification so often applied. Decrease in generality and intensity, corresponding to increase of complexity and dignity, is very marked in the passage from Material to Intellectual Power, and from the latter to Moral Power. Thus the Positive Synthesis coordinates our social opinions and our philosophical conceptions, giving consistence to the former, and practical value to the latter. My general law of Classification just mentioned, had originally a merely Subjective purpose, as a logical instrument for the true coordination of thought; but I have invariably pointed out, that it had also a necessary correspondence with the Objective Order of phenomena. It has now been applied to the classification of real existences and their various properties. The 'Positive Philosophy' gave several illustrations of this principle; and in this work they are far more numerous and marked, and it may be applied to the collective Organism of man.

The order, in fact, corresponds to the general law that, decrease in generality and intensity corresponds to increase in complexity and dignity.

Again, this fundamental arrangement of the social forces is to be recognised in the growth of the individual, which in successive periods reproduces the movement of social progress as revealed by history. In childhood we perceive, and long overestimate, the ascendancy of Material Force; experience then

Individual life recognises the same series in the Social Forces, beginning with Material, and ending with Moral.

proves to us the reality of Intellectual Power; and it is only in our maturity that we are convinced of the worth of Moral greatness. It is true that the Education of the future, will hasten the recognition of all three forms of power, and also diminish the effect of personal differences; but thoughtful minds will never have any difficulty in tracing the necessary course through which Humanity must pass. Nor will Language fail to bear witness to the same fact; for it reserves the word *force* for material power, and applies it only with qualifications or by metaphor to the two modifying influences, intellectual and moral power.

Force, in Sociology, answers to Tissue in Biology.

This classification of the social forces really sums up the abstract theory of the collective Organism. It takes the same place that the doctrine of the elementary tissues holds in the study of individual organisation. In both we have first, a primary tissue, the seat of the life of nutrition; in Biology, it is the cellular tissue, in Sociology, material force. We have next, in the Individual, as in the Social Organism, two orders of tissue, of lower energy but of higher dignity, the one passive, the other active, their respective functions being rightly to understand and fitly to modify the environment. All thinkers able to follow it out will see in this analogy a new proof of the soundness of my Statical Theory, both of the individual and of Society.

It is an extension of Aristotle's theory, that society results from combination of effort and distribution of function.

Force, either dispersed or concentrated, is indeed the natural basis of the Social Organism: Intelligence, artistic or scientific, modifies it in conformity to its environment; whilst the Heart, in its masculine or feminine form, inspires that Organism with suitable springs of action. Thus the Positive Theory of the Social Organism may be drawn deductively from the grand principle, laid down twenty-two centuries ago, by the true founder of provisional Sociology, which explained Order apart from Progress. The incomparable Aristotle laid down the true principle of every collective organism, when he described it as the distribution of functions, and the combination of labour. Strangely enough, our modern economists claim the discovery of this luminous conception, whilst narrowing it, with metaphysical empiricism, to a mere law of industry. The first of philosophers repudiated this particular application of the theory. In its original form, he gave it the wide extension required for its systematic use. But the theory could only establish the true doctrine of Order, when there was a conception of the entire course of human Progress to point out the nature and the right classification of the Social Forces. A complete philosophy of history was an essential condition. Having this at length we are able to complete the theory prepared by the genius of Aristotle.

At the same time, before proceeding with this subject, I shall complete this systematic sketch of Social Organisation, by tracing the relation borne by our conception of the collective Organism to that of its Environment. To combine this pair of ideas, the being and the environment, is indispensable in Biology, and is so in far higher degree in Sociology ; not merely that we may understand the *life*, but also to fill up our notion of the *structure* of the organism. *Relation of Collective Organism with its Environment, pp. 235–239.*

The abstract study of the Organism had first to be treated apart from that of the Environment. This is a rule even in Biology of that Subjective method, whereby alone true system is possible. Modern science has been forced into the contrary practice ; and the provisional method still keeps its hold upon our minds, in theory as in practice, exaggerating the influence of the external world, as in the case of climate. Still, even if it has been abused, we must never forget to give its due importance to the second special term of every organic conception, I mean the conditions with which it is environed. This is the only direct mode of connecting the general study of living Nature, individual or collective, with that of lifeless Nature. *Influence of environment must never be neglected.*

Sociology is at once connected with Cosmology, when, as throughout this work, we conceive the human Being fulfilling his destiny upon this human Planet ; the celestial and terrestrial constitution of which necessarily determines Man's. This compulsory union of the human race in their world forms the first universal and perpetual bond between the families of man ; for if they were free to quit their dwelling-place on earth, they would speedily forget the connecting ties of sympathy, and would be perpetually dispersing themselves to seek a new habitation. Yet such a bond is far from a sufficient basis to explain the social union, even were the Great Being completely formed and settled over the entire surface of our planet. We must go farther into detail, in order to explain those smaller societies which are long the natural germs of the great human Family that is to be. We shall get this special point of view *Restriction of Man to this Planet concentrates the race ; local settlement forms tribes and nations.*

spontaneously, if we follow out to its proper limit the rule just expressed as to the primary classification of the Social Forces.

The environment is the base of every society.

Thus the moral order of every human society is necessarily based upon the intellectual organisation, and this is based upon the material constitution. Now the material order would have no natural base, if we conceived it apart from its environment or special conditions. These conditions it has to modify as a means of supplying our vegetative wants; but to modify them it must duly submit itself to their limits. This standing necessity thus becomes indirectly the base of every organisation of society, not only in the race as a whole, but also in every population capable of separate existence.

The smallest family implies property and local appropriation of soil.

No doubt every association is formed from within, and not from without. But even the smallest society is dependent on the reaction of the external world upon its internal life; and this reaction is as indispensable as it is inevitable. Even domestic life, where the motive of affection has the best opportunity for gaining the ascendant, is dominated by its material conditions. In the first place, a family implies property in the food and implements needed for its daily wants. It requires next its own ground either for hunting or fishing, if not for pasture or agriculture. Now these links with the world without are not only necessary for its life, but they are most useful to its unity; for any discord which arises is forced to give way before the imperious call for discipline and cooperation imposed by external difficulties. Again, when families become tribes or nations, the same necessity for adapting life to meet external wants remains active, and exists in a more extended form. Man becomes with civilisation more capable of dealing with the external world, as having more complete possession of his powers. But our collective life as a society is none the less dependent on our material conditions. It is true that they grow easier to endure, when we learn better and better how to modify them, instead of surrendering ourselves tamely to their weight.

Property in the soil is anterior to agricultural settlement.

In my volume on History, I shall point to a common error, that which would find an origin for the institution of Property in the soil in the definite settlement into agricultural life. Every family must have its local reservation; and the same must be true on a larger scale of any tribe. In both cases Property long retains a collective character; special appropriation being but temporary; and hence its existence has been overlooked. But the wars, which result from these undefined forms of Property, may serve to convince us how intense is the feeling of appropriation in early tribes; for nothing less could give rise to such struggles.

The point, however, is not important in Social Statics, where we are concerned with the type and not with the history of human life. The nomad state is quite natural to man; it admits of far more intellectual and social life, and is continued longer, than in our settled societies we are apt to suppose. Property in the soil in its perfect form is established later than lawyers or even philosophers imagine; but it is always and everywhere the ultimate basis of human society. And in the Statics of Sociology we have to consider the ultimate type, leaving to the Dynamics of the science the study of the phases through which it is attained. *Statically considered, it is the base of society.*

We shall better comprehend the relations of the Social Organism with its Environment, if we revert to the theory with which this chapter opened as to its connection with the three that precede. Each of these chapters treated one of the three great elements of society, corresponding to the three great elements of our cerebral constitution. The Social Organism embraces them all. We have to regard every Family as being through Language connected with the race, and through territorial Property as connected with our planet. Thus the institution of Country completes the essential life of every society, domestic or political, by drawing attention to the dependence of the Organism on its Environment. Even before settled societies are formed, this want of a local seat is imperfectly supplied. The Tent, the Car, or the Ship, are to the nomad family a sort of moveable Country, connecting the Family or the Horde with its material base, as with us the gypsy in his van. We everywhere see man struggling to give his unstable existence a surer hold, by attaching it to some more stable substance. And he finds this in many a basis which is not absolutely fixed, though it is much more fixed than man. We are all familiar with the revolutions of our planet, and with the movement through space of the solar system little as it is determined; but this does not destroy the sense of security which we feel towards the Earth, as our solid and fixed abode. *Man needs a stable base for his life. He finds this in Country, however limited in area.*

The institution of the Fatherland fulfils its great part, when

The sense of local fixity will be largely developed.

it lays the foundation for that material force which I have shown to be the base of all Social Order. Power and Wealth only command our real confidence and even only attain their full authority, when, by possession of the soil, they are connected with the external Order of nature, and gain from its consistence a new title. The desire of possessing Property in the soil is one which is far from being about to disappear, as some suppose; on the contrary, it is most natural, and will gain a fresh influence by being common to all families alike. In the fourth volume I shall show how, in accordance with past history, through the possession at least of his own home, every citizen will be able to enjoy the inestimable boon of property in immoveables. This specific appropriation of particular localities will offer no obstacle to the full current of social cooperation, but will tend to increase it; as every separate home will give further solidity to the human Family, just as every dialect will enrich human Language.

Influence on economy of life of territorial property,

The Fatherland again, beside this direct effect on the material basis of social Order, indirectly modifies in settled societies the entire Economy of life, both of individuals and of society.

On thought,

The bonds which unite man with the soil will serve to check the intellectual pride which needs to be reminded how much the Subjective depends upon the Objective. We thus feel completely and closely, how essentially fixed is the Order of Nature, and how subordinate is our power of modification. Even Language, and consequently Art, is improved, by drawing closer the ties between Man and the World on one side, and Man and Humanity on the other.

And on morality.

In the moral sphere, this connection with the soil gives fresh force and stability to our higher affections. The very word *Fatherland*, and the use of the word *House* for family, testify to the close bond between the possession of the soil and domestic life. It stimulates our sense of Solidarity, or membership of a body. And as to our sense of Continuity with the Past, we can hardly conceive its existence at all without a local basis for our traditions to take root. Such is the double effect it has upon the Heart; but it also fosters in the Character the qualities of perseverance and prudence. If it seem to check the spirit of enterprise, it undoubtedly elevates our spirit of resignation and real nobility of character, by giving us at once independence and mutual confidence. And it prepares us to seek for our true guarantee against arbitrary wills in a wise submission to external necessity.

So marked is the political influence of territorial property that in place of insisting on it, there might be more need to combat the exaggerations respecting it, into which our Physiocrats fell in the last century. But the reader will hardly need to be told that, though the soil is an indispensable instrument for the creation of Wealth, it is certainly not the true source of it; for all temporal power, we have seen, comes from human life as a whole. In the succeeding volume we shall see how essential is territorial property to the entire course of human activity, not only for the Industrial life, on which we are entering, but for the Military life, through which we have passed. The ' Positive Philosophy' gave many illustrations of the importance of settled societies in developing the ancient system of Conquest.

Political influence of territorial property.

We have thus the whole of human life, both in the family and in the national group, associated with its earthly habitation, thus completing the Statical Theory already stated for Property, Family, and Language. Having analysed the Social Forces into the three forms, Material, Intellectual, and Moral, I had only to connect them, as I have just done, with the general laws of External Nature, which ever govern them.

The whole of the Social Forces are thus connected with Nature.

We have thus established a true correspondence between the Statical Analysis of the Social Organism in Sociology, and that of the Individual Organism in Biology. But this analogy must not be pushed too far; for the former is capable of being resolved into its component parts, whilst the latter is not. The elements of Social life are not destroyed by being separated : those of individual life are. And thus, if we insisted on an exact similarity between the two, we should get fanciful comparisons instead of useful suggestions. Biology has hitherto been the guide and preparation for Sociology; but, as shown in the first volume (p. 473), Sociology will in the future be rather the type for the ultimate systematisation of Biology. Throughout philosophy the direct study of the true Great Being, the only being which attains to its perfect development, will form the groundwork of our knowledge of the smaller organisms, and that for purposes of Science as well as of Logic. The Subjective Method, the sole source of any real Synthesis, implies this passage from the higher to the lower study. And

Relation of Social with Individual Organism, pp. 239–242. The Social is always superior to the Biologic treatment.

this is the principle of all true classification, which ought to follow the order, of which society exhibits the universal type, that is to say, the higher organisation determines the lower. The public and private life of the individual is, as it has ever been, subordinate to the social Organism of which he is a part. And this is the point of view from which we must conceive the relations of every other unit to its system, whether in thought or in expression, whether in the real or in the ideal world.

Analogies of Biology and Sociology.

There is therefore no justification in trying to find servile analogies in analysing the Social and the Individual Organism, imperfect as our conception of the latter is in the hands of our academic specialists. At the same time there is a real correspondence in the main analyses of the two sciences. If we take the best ascertained points in Biology, we may decompose structure anatomically into *elements*, *tissues*, and *organs*. We have the same things in the Social Organism; and may even use the same names. I have already shown how in society the three forms of Social Power correspond to the *tissue*, the most marked and most important constituent of all. As to the *element*, this is supplied by the Family, which is more completely the germ of society than the cell or the fibre is of the body. We have only to find in Sociology what it is that corresponds with the *organ* in Biology.

Family, Authority, City, correspond to *element*, *tissue*, *organ*.

This may readily be found by following out what has already been said as to the relation of the Organism with its Environment. The Fatherland establishes a relation between the soil and social order; and thus the *organs* of the Great Being can only be *cities*, the root of the word being the nucleus of the term *civilisation*. Cities are, in truth, themselves beings; so organically complete that, as each is capable of separate life, it instinctively aspires to become the centre of the vast organism of Humanity. In this tendency the Social organ differs radically from the organ in Biology, which has no such separate completeness. Nor can our analysis of society be carried further than this notion of *organs*, or we shall be led into fanciful or passing distinctions. The smallest *city* contains all the *elements* and *tissues*, required for the life of the Great Being, in the Families, and in the Classes or Castes, within it. The greatest human associations always began really in a mere town, which gradually incorporated others by its attraction or by arms. The eternal instance of this truth is the great name of Rome.

Between the City, uniting man and his dwelling-place, and the full development of the Great Being around a fitting centre, a number of intermediate forms of association may be found, under the general name of *States*. But all these forms, differing only in extent and in permanence, may be neglected as undefined. In Social Statics, we must keep in view the existence of Humanity in its completeness, however distant may be its actual advent; and we may therefore rest in that form of association which has a complete and distinct career of its own. When Property, Family and Language, have found a suitable territory, and have reached the point at which they combine any given population under the same, at least the same spiritual, government, there a possible nucleus of the Great Being has been formed. Such a community, or city, be it ultimately large or small, is a true *organ* of Humanity. When the Supreme Being has its full development, we shall see how these essential organs will be combined into *apparatus*, such as we have in Biology. But to attempt this now would be premature as well as useless; and we see how indistinct and arbitrary are all the definitions of the intermediate states, such as are called provinces, nations, &c.

All intermediate associations are *States*.

Nevertheless, we shall not run any risk of forcing our analogies, if we extend to the analysis of society the other two anatomical conceptions of Biology. Besides cells, tissues, and organs, every individual organism gives us a more elaborate degree of vital structure which we call *apparatus*. There is, further, now recognised an intermediate form of organisation between tissues and organs, which is called *system*. Statical Biology therefore gives us five stages of organic life: cell, tissue, system, organ, apparatus. We may find five similar stages in Sociology, though all are not essential. They will however serve to combine the different nuclei of the Great Being, whilst these remain various and separate as they long must be. Although the advent of Humanity in its entirety is yet distant, it has long been familiar to the loftier spirits and minds. As was stated in the first chapter of this volume (p. 87), the greater statesmen long dreamed of a universal Family of Man, so soon as the Roman Empire was complete. But this idea gained force and extent, when the separation of the Spiritual community from the Temporal society in the Middle Ages pointed out the natural mode of the ultimate unity of Man. When the Catholic

Social analogues of *apparatus* and *system* in Biology

bond of union was destroyed, the various relations, industrial, scientific, and artistic, continued to keep all minds in the West fixed on the hope of a complete assimilation of the human race. Until this hope has found its satisfaction, we may properly think of the different groups, out of which the Great Being is to arise, in such a way as will point to their ultimate combination. Thus, the *cities* which form the social *organs* may be imagined as grouped into *nations,* so as to correspond with the *apparatus* of Biology. We may further go on to group the social *tissues,* that is the *classes,* so as to correspond with the *systems* in Anatomy. It will serve to give precision to our ideas of the common functions of these tissues in the organ. We thus get, in Sociology as in Biology, the five statical types arranged in both sciences in an analogous series. In the ultimate realisation of Humanity these two provisional terms of *apparatus* and *system* will not be needed to carry on an exact parallelism, so far as regards the Social Organism. The notions they express will be modified in a way I need not dwell upon here. We may notice their existence, without attaching too much importance to them in the general analysis of Society.

Sociology. mainly concerned with three orders Families, Classes, Cities.

Whatever use may ultimately be made of the five divisions, I shall confine my attention in this work on Sociology to the three modes of analysing social life, the same three which will prove of the main importance in Biology. And I shall treat the Social Organism as definitely composed of the Families which are the true elements or cells, next of the Classes or Castes which are its proper tissues, and lastly of the Cities and Communes which are its real organs.

THEORY OF SOCIAL ORGANISATION, pp 242-272.

This conception, which has a scientific as well as a logical value, enables us by the light of the reasoning above to determine the Positive Theory of Social Order, by means of the great principle of Aristotle previously alluded to (p. 234).

This principle, in fact, lays down as the two general conditions, Independence and Cooperation, the task of any collective organisation being to establish due relations between the two.

1. Distribution of function, the test of political society.

On the one hand, without separation of function, there would be no true association between a number of families; they would only form an agglomeration, even in a settled community. Distribution of function is the point which marks off the political society, the basis of which is Cooperation, from the domestic union, the basis of which is Sympathy. This is a striking proof of the utterly anarchical character of the modern Revolutionary Theories, which end by exalting mere individualism, for they bring all down to a common level.

We thus get the essential character of the Great Organism as made up of beings capable of separate life, but joining more or less voluntarily in a common end. The classes formed by the various combinations of the three elements of every social force differ from each other; but their respective functions are only completely called out by an increasing diversity of occupation.

This, the source of the differences and even of the inequalities between men, is also the chief agent in the gradual extension of the Great Being, until this reaches the natural limits of its abode on the planet. Directly that a settled society brings out the social importance of this fundamental principle, the Distribution of Functions, fresh fields are at once opened for the growth of the spirit of Solidarity with contemporaries, and of Continuity with our predecessors. A valuable reaction upon the moral nature follows along with it, owing to the stimulus it affords to the instinct of general Benevolence. Each family, when confined to a labour which directly produces only what will satisfy a small portion of its own wants, is forced to recognise the importance of other families to itself as well as its own usefulness to them. When the Feelings and the Thoughts are brought into harmonious relations with such a position, human existence at once develops its true nature ' To live for others.'

On the other hand, the noble part played by this Distribution of Functions would be abortive, unless it were completed by a Combination of Efforts, either spontaneous or disciplined. Nay, the division of occupation is very apt to give rise to serious struggles, intensifying as it does differences in habit, opinion, and propensity, between different families. The desire for Cooperation, which cannot be separated from the desire for Independence, must also be regularly satisfied; it finds satisfaction in that primary social institution, founded to secure joint action. A power to amalgamate men is the more needed that the combative and self-regarding instincts are more energetic than those which prompt us to union. This is the part of that cohesive force in society, everywhere called *government*, the business of which is at once to combine and to direct. The admirable conception of Aristotle respecting the Distribution of Functions and the

Its social effects.

2. Combination of efforts.

Combination of Effort happily correlates the two necessary elements of every political idea, Society and Government.

Its moral and social results.

It must also be remembered, that by reason of the Distribution of Functions, every human life has its double side : the one special, the other general. Every family has first duly to fulfil the common task assigned to it by the Great Organism, of which it is a member. But to do so, it needs constantly to rest upon the sense of that general Harmony, towards which it contributes its note. Now, every true citizen is thus penetrated with a sense of Order ; and he grows earnest to cause it to be respected by others. The same disposition, moreover, fosters the growth of the three social Instincts within each man, particularly the widest of these instincts, General Benevolence. Such is the compound process which disposes men to submit to Government ; so soon as a suitable governing Power succeeds in availing itself of the disposition ready to its hand.

Origin of Government.

This last condition of Order, a Governing Power, springs spontaneously out of the inequalities between men, upon the separation of social functions. The cerebral organisation of our nature, if in part it disposes us to Obedience, stimulates men also to assume Command. My classification of the faculties (*see* vol. i. p. 540) will at once suggest to a careful reader, which of our instincts contribute to obedience, directly or indirectly, and which to command. The desire for command is almost always stronger than the willingness to obey ; though the latter has been much underrated in our anarchical age. But the vicious tendency to command is more injurious to private happiness than to public order. For this vulgar form of ambition leads to nothing, without striking qualities of intellect and still more of character. Even then, it rarely attains great success unless duly supported from without, especially by a favourable position of affairs which is seldom within our own control. Hence far more families are made miserable by this idle passion than are gratified by it. Unless duly trained, it often issues in a moral disease ; one that the materialism of our day is slow to recognise.

The spirit of command, on the other hand, becomes a true benefaction to society, where families have been disciplined, educated, and so placed as to have the means and the responsibility of exercising power rightly. Power such as this forms in the heart of every society a government of a kind, and it only continues so long as it fills its double part of control and direction. It implies a general acceptance of its rule, avowed or understood; and this is not given so blindly or so slavishly, as many are wont to think. Men who ignore the existence of unselfish instincts naturally attribute obedience to fear, which is not true even of the animals; and they have gone so far as to make a virtue of revolt, which usually springs from a powerful individuality. Declamation from of old has attacked the so-called Despotism of the East; but the real cause of unreasonable submission is too often the difficulty of finding a better government: the force of habit or the proneness to reverence has but little to do with it.

These metaphysical ideas about the vices of submission have given a kind of sanction to the thirst for power, which the ambitious represent to be devotion to the public good. Our sympathetic instincts are, alas! too weak to sustain us in the great and prolonged efforts needed for ambition of the useful order. And if men's egoism did not create more active incentive to exertion, societies would often find it difficult to obtain a government, or to replace it when lost. Such a danger is averted by the very defects in man's nature; for the wisdom of mankind from of old has turned what is a chronic malady in some, into a mode of securing a general good. How it is thus converted we may see by the light of the law stated in the second chapter of this volume (p. 128) on the connection between the selfish and sympathetic instincts. For successful ambition usually enlarges into a sense of public duty; at least in natures which are not utterly evil or incapable of improvement. *Social effect of ambition.*

It is fortunate then that the ambition of some families supplies all the rest with that government which they need to control and direct the forces generated by the Distribution of functions. These governing persons usually even deserve the respect they receive; and they ultimately often justify the general readiness to accept them as models.

How, and how naturally, such a power arises, we may best see, by looking not to the general function whereby all citizens conspire to maintain and complete the State, but to the different special functions of the citizens. This general function of all citizens is not at first sufficiently defined to have an organ at all. The particular functions of each citizen being clearly marked, throws up in each group a special government of its *Government of societies arises out of the directing force of smaller groups.*

own, which controls and directs it on a small scale, as occasion arises. This is the germ of the wider government of society, which is the product of the smaller combinations when their common ends are duly made general. Military activity, the only one fully organised at present, has a direct tendency to form lasting combinations; for it can gain no success without union.

As the school of government was in ancient times War, so in modern times it is Industry.

The ultimate form of life, the Industrial, has also the same political value, though its action is long restricted to private life. When undisturbed it throws up its permanent chiefs, men whose importance is continually on the increase, as we may see in history in the succeeding volume. As the ancient world had in War its school of discipline and of government, the modern world finds these in Industry. The habit of regarding all citizens as public functionaries, so as to determine their duties, has more than a purpose of social morality. It is just as necessary for theory, to explain the origin of political government. Thus government springs from agreement between the natural chiefs of the various types of Industry, who gather round their best representative. The habits of command and of obedience already formed in Industry have only to extend to public spheres, to found a power in the State capable of controlling the divergencies, and regulating the convergencies, of the individuals within it.

Government rests on force, as Hobbes saw.

Thus the principle of Cooperation, the basis of political society, calls out the Government required for its maintenance and growth. It is a power essentially material, arising as it does from rank or wealth. It is important to note that social order can have no other direct base. The famous maxim of Hobbes, that government is the natural result of force, is the principal step which till now the Positive theory of power made since Aristotle. It is true that in the Middle Age the admirable discovery of the division of the Temporal and Spiritual powers had been made: but the occasion was in its favour, and it was due to feeling rather than reason; nor had it ever been regularly justified on principle before my own early essays (*see* Appendix, vol. iv.). What caused the bitterness that Hobbes' view encountered was the metaphysical nature of its origin, and the want of distinction between the statical and the historical character of government. Had his critics been more wise or less angry, this should only have shown them the merit of this great law, of which the Positive Philosophy alone saw the importance.

As was shown above, force is essential as the basis of every human society. We have only to suppose it absent, as happens in times of anarchy. Those who are so indignant with Hobbes' principle would be rather perplexed, if they were told that political government must be based on weakness, if it be not based on force. But this would be the real consequence of their theories, if we follow out the analysis of the three constituents of social force. For, through want of a real Material Force, the basis of power would have to be found in the Intellect or the Heart, and they are far too feeble for such a purpose. Their sole business is to modify an already existing system of control, and till Material Force has succeeded in forming this, neither the Intellect nor the Heart can have much effect on society. Whenever force as a fundamental base for politics is absent, they will seek as far as they can to restore it, without attempting to supply its place. Social science would remain for ever in the cloud-land of metaphysics, if we hesitated to adopt the principle of Force as the basis of Government. Combining this doctrine with that of Aristotle, that society consists in the Combination of efforts and the Distribution of functions, we get the axioms of a sound political philosophy.

We get the same result by tracing the Positive Theory of human nature, as explained in the first volume. We have previously shown how much more vigorous are the instincts of command than those of obedience. The first can only meet satisfaction in certain families, and thus the rest are urged to a state of chronic revolt against all and any control. The whole history of the past is an illustration of this, notwithstanding the spirit of submission inculcated by the long ages of theological and military discipline. The tendency towards insurrection would be fatal to humanity, and distract all progress, unless a vigorous use of material force were always at hand to restrain it. Our own stormy times show us the need of this check, and we often see it broken down, now that the mental and moral discipline of the past are discredited. Nowadays everyone must command, and as everyone has a possible chance of commanding, he is generally only disposed to obey force, and is seldom ready to yield to reason or to affection. The consequence is a wretched state of degradation, found in the very men who fiercely declaim against the so-called servility of our ancestors.

But Force requires further powers, as its complement.

But though force is the indispensable foundation of every organisation of society, we must remember that by itself it is wholly insufficient. Force always requires a double complement in the intellect and the heart, and further a proper controlling influence, to make it the durable base of political authority.

1. Intellectual.

Material order being secured, a proper organ is at once ready to take the general direction of the social combination. The government of the society is only an extension of the special government of each smaller group ; and these lower forms of authority are wanting in the breadth of view required for this purpose. At least, capacity of the kind would be very exceptional, and would only succeed in primitive forms of society. The point of view required for governing a State in all its relations, so that its authority should be felt and respected by all, implies an intellectual training as to the past and future of civilisation, which is rarely to be met with in the average heads of private undertakings. It was rare enough, even in old times, that military ability was found to imply political skill, and it would be hopeless to expect it in mere industrial ability, which is necessarily special even in vast modern works. Thus governing power requires its intellectual complement to enable it to fulfil its duty of simply maintaining order ; and certainly it needs it for that of directing movement.

2. Moral.

In the second place, moral weight is no less indispensable to Government, to secure it that respect, without which it cannot govern, or even exist. And we must remember that political power always results directly or indirectly from a cooperation voluntary or involuntary, active or passive ; and this may always be withdrawn the moment the desire for union is weakened. Thus without the aid of any spirit of insurrection, Power which is always suspected and always envied, is liable even in stable states to be overturned, when it reaches a given point of unpopularity. However natural may be its authority, a moral sanction for Government is just as indispensable as an intellectual guidance.

3. Social control.

After the moral and intellectual supports of Power, we come to that which it is so difficult for society to supply for it, and yet without which it cannot be permanent, a regulating influence. All force is liable to abuse ; especially is this true of that political or material force, which on the mental and moral side is so meagrely qualified for rule. The truth is, that every power from the first tends to find its own regulating influence by exercise, according as it is accepted by the public which it affects. And in this unconscious way power always found its own means of regulating itself, during the early ages, when the development of man's capacities was of more importance than the discipline of them. The authorities of former times, Military or Theological, were too absolute in their nature to admit of any really systematic discipline. This belongs only to the last phase of the transitional epoch, which prepares the way for the final system ; and it is but a foreshadowing of that, as I showed in the historical sketch which closed the first chapter of this volume. But the Social Organism, it is clear, will be in a most imperfect condition, so long as the Political Power, which is to control the various activities of the State, is itself without any check to control its dangerous tendencies. The abuse of a kind of force, which is itself the product of personal ascendancy, may do more than check the progress of society. In an organism so complex and so extensive, the abuse of power might menace it with actual destruction.

Close study, therefore, shows us that there are three things necessary for all political power, besides its basis of material Force : an Intellectual guidance, a Moral sanction, and lastly a Social control. Without all three, political order will never be stable, even with all the support it receives from the domestic order. It may be in a distant future that this social control will ever be fully supplied ; but in Social Statics we must neglect all questions of time, and conceive the organism of society in its fulness. We must complete our ideal at any rate, although such a picture has hardly begun to be a reality. Social Dynamics will explain this slow advent, and will show us in history, even in the distant past, the germs of this institution ready to make themselves felt. *Political power needs all three, besides its basis in Force.*

In truth the only mode of meeting this want of a regulating influence for political power, is in establishing a broader and higher society, which may embrace the political society, just as that did the domestic. This is the mission of true Religion. By the complexity of its nature the collective organism of Humanity possesses in a high degree the power which the indi- *The regulating power is, Religion.*

vidual organism has only in its rudimentary form, the power of acquiring new, and even essential organs. To create such an organ is in fact the main task to be overcome by the Great Being, one which it has only once really to perform in the whole of its long and difficult course of development. But once accomplished it is adequate to enable that Being to fulfil all that its true nature and actual circumstances demand.

Three de-
grees of
Society.

Man's cerebral system, alike endowed with powers of Feeling, of Action, and of Intelligence, disposes him to three kinds of association, according as each of these three powers takes the lead. We thus get three successive orders of human society, diminishing in intensity of union and increasing in extension of area. Each of these becomes naturally the unit of the succeed- ing order of society. They are the Family, the City, and the Church. The latter does not appear distinct till long after the two former are complete; but in Social Statics we must from the first consider it as an essential element of man's life, leaving it to Social Dynamics to explain in detail the reasons for its late appearance in history.

1. The Family. 2. The City. 3. The Church.

First there arises spontaneously the most complete, but the smallest of all societies, the Family, based on common sympathy and directed by affection. The Family forms the unit of the political society, which is larger but less close; and which has for its principle the aggregate Activity of the members, and for its government the material Force called out by such activity. The City or the State is again the unit of the religious society, the Church; the widest and least complete of all, which is based on common belief, and governed by Faith.

Character of Church society.

The Church accordingly unites in a free union the Cities, in the same manner as each City spontaneously unites various Families; first grouping them in classes according to their functions in the society. It forms the most general bond of the great organism, the universal character of which it alone can represent, by virtue of the reality and the completeness in its doctrine, and this is found in the Positive Religion. Another of its peculiar advantages is the entire separation of the Church from the State. This, the essential condition of the real work of the Church, was attempted by the admirable efforts of Catholicism in the Middle Age. Premature as this attempt was, religious society has been so completely severed from the political society, that with the advanced races of man the old union of

the two is impossible. Positivism now returns to the undertaking with a suitable doctrine and favourable conditions, so
as to be in a position at last to found the true universal Church.
Its social work must at first be confined to the populations of
the West and their offshoots ; but its creed is so complete and
so real, that it is equally fit to be extended to all parts of the
planet.

Whilst the great human organism was without any spiritual
unity, the need of binding together the various states which
made up the whole, gave extravagant d:.iensions to political
societies. The foundation of a universal Church will enable the
gradual reduction of these huge and temporary agglomerations of
men to that natural limit, where the State can exist without
tyranny. I have, for this reason, treated mere Cities, along with
the tracts of country which voluntarily adhere to them, as the
immediate organs of the Great Being. These may seem narrow
dimensions for the political society ; but posterity will admit,
that a doctrine which aspires to endure as long as Humanity
itself, is not to be bound down to all the notions familiar to our
time of transition. No combination of men can be durable, if
it is not really voluntary ; and in considering the normal form
of the State, we must get rid of all artificial and violent bonds
of union, and retain only those which are spontaneous and free.
Long experience has proved that the City, in its full completeness and extent of surrounding country, is the largest body
politic which can exist without becoming oppressive. To extend
the range of material force beyond this, its natural limit, would
require violent and arbitrary procedures, the effect of which is
always uncertain. But besides this, the Positive Faith, with
its calm grasp over human life as a whole, will be sufficient to
unite the various Cities in the moral communion of the Church,
without requiring the help of the State to supplement the task
with its mere material unity.

Political aggregate is properly, the City.

Thus the final creation of a religious society whereby the
great organism is completed, fulfils all the three wants of the
political society. The intellectual guidance, the moral sanction,
and the Social regulation which government requires to modify
its material nature, are all supplied by a Church, when it has
gained a distinct existence of its own. For, as to the first, the
Positive creed, since it embraces the activity as much as the
intelligence and the sentiment, can always supply general truths,

The Church supplies all that the State needs for guidance.

important in the ordering of societies, and even important in the conduct of private undertakings. Again, this Faith gives a distinct moral authority to any of the practical powers which deserve it. This it does by its capacity to unite the present, first with the past, then with the future. And thus the Temporal authorities receive a real social consecration, being connected with the entire life of the Great Being, and thus becoming its true material servants.

Germs of this intellectual and moral guidance in old societies.

Intellectual and moral guidance of some kind as duties of any religious society are so essential to the existence of a government, that in one way or other they will always be found. Though they cannot be completely systematised except under the Positive creed, they had a very distinct part in the long provisional period of Theologism. Before the Great Being was known, and when no one could speak in its name, the imaginary Powers which represented it to the infancy of Humanity, undertook both to consecrate and to direct the organs of government. And, though these Powers had only fictitious existence, they were not without effect ; for the imagination clothed them to an adequate degree with a mental as well as a moral authority. The grand obstacle to their utility was one which continued to be insurmountable during the greater part of the whole Theological system. This was the confusion of the State and the Church : in the Theocracies, this meant the domination of the State by the priests ; in the Military epochs, the domination of the Church by the statesmen. It was, however, the intellectual side of the old religions which suffered chiefly by this double confusion ; and even their intellectual value was not quite neutralised. The moral sanction, on the other hand, which government gained was increased by the union of Church and State to a point where it often became oppression.

But social control requires an independent Church.

It is far otherwise with the third and true political function of Religion, the formation of a real government of society, able to repress or to remedy the evils to which all governments are prone. This function cannot be filled indirectly. In its nature it implies that the Church is not only distinct from, but independent of, the State. This separation between Church and State is only possible, or is only permanent, when the religious society is more extensive than the political society, and tends to become truly universal. And so, we see how the chief political usefulness of Religion follows as a direct consequence of its grandest social object, tne purpose of uniting all men. In fact, the higher generality which the Church acquires, fits it, in every State where it is recognised, at once to check and to direct the Government, though without ever overstepping the limits of advice. For the different material powers thus recognise the influence of a power, wider although less intense than themselves, but of higher intellectual and moral resources; one which, though always confined to the intellect and the heart, is capable of great practical services.

The Priesthood therefore completes political government, by supplying it with a constant regulating power, whenever the priesthood is so far distinct from the government, that it can as little dominate it, as be itself dominated. Either of these two conditions would deprive it of any such power; for temporal power would fatally corrupt the Priesthood, whilst unnatural dependence on the State would degrade it. The true balance is very difficult to maintain, and it was impossible under the old systems; for Theology was always urging religious authorities, as Militarism was always urging the political, to acquire an absolute empire. The admirable attempt made in the Middle Age, only shows how impossible this was; for the great and noble efforts persisted in through ages to establish the true equilibrium between the Church and the State, only succeeded for at most a century; and then soon broke down without recall. It is only when Religion has become Positive, and when Military life has been replaced by Industrial, that the true separation between the two comes about of itself, and endures without effort, in one complete harmony of society. It concerns not our subject of Social Statics, whether this end be near or distant. Suffice it that this ultimate result is in full accord with the true nature of the Social Organism; and that without this it cannot fulfil its mission, or even reach its maturity. *Influence of the Church on the State.*

Such is the influence of the Religious on the Political society, in the perfecting and ordering of political Government. But the Religious society has its influence also on the Domestic society, the unit out of which the other two are formed. The Family again, though as a society less imperfectly constituted than the State, since it rests on a higher principle, has in a lesser degree its kindred evils, such as the Church alone can prevent or correct. It is true that the political society, or the State, reacts in a useful way upon the domestic society, or the Family. *On the Family.*

But this casual influence is not enough ; for it cannot touch the true source of domestic oppression, the unlimited power of the head of the family. Antiquity always respected this arbitrary principle, for it could not modify it without danger to the Family, the elementary basis of the State. The truth is, that the domestic society can only be properly disciplined by an authority, purely intellectual and moral ; training the will, but not enforcing acts. This second function of the Priesthood, therefore, requires, like the first, complete separation from government. Hence it could not begin until the Catholic system of the Middle Age was established ; and of this it forms the great achievement. In the narrower sphere of the Family, the Priesthood can exert, without hindrance, an influence which is both closer and purer ; one which the influence of women instinctively seconds. However this influence over the Family, like the influence over the State, was impossible without social independence ; and this Theology possessed only temporarily. When independence was gone, the Catholic priesthood was as impotent to regulate the Family, as it was the State. Both alike fell into a condition of increasing disorder, intellectual as well as moral ; until, in our time, all the bonds of society seem giving way. In the sphere of the home, as in that of politics, the Positive Religion is the only one which can found a power to give order to society ; with a title to give sanction, as well as counsel.

It corrects the abuses and errors of both.

These are the two indirect purposes, whereby the widest and highest of the three kinds of human society preserves and completes the other two. The religious society, which is the direct organ of the widest extension in the present, an extension to be limited only in the Future by the planet itself, has also the special attribute of full continuity with the Past. The Family as well as the City feebly represent in their smaller degree both the Past and the Future ; but the Church alone can train within us the true feeling for the destiny of man in its grandeur, conceived both in space and in time. It has moreover a further part in modifying the State and the Family. And by tracing this out we may better understand how the normal establishment of a Church will complete the natural constitution of the Social Organism. We may go on to conceive the Priesthood, in the spirit of beneficent Revolution, constantly correcting morally the order of classes within the State, and of individuals

within the Family.   It is this striking power it has of systematically redressing the natural inequalities of external life, in a
way that seems almost subversive, which in the Statical point of
view distinguishes the Church from the Family and the City.

When the Priesthood is adequately separated from the State, *Rectifying social classi-fication.*
they form, when compared, a fundamental Classification of
Society, which we will consider at length, as it is more general
than any other classification, and gives us the essential principle of every order of human arrangement.   Once grasped in
this crucial example, it will be easily followed in minor cases.
Thus the social influence of Religion consists in supplying a
constant rectification of the material classification which arises
in society, a constant effort to bring it to the loftier type.

We must properly distinguish three social powers, respec- *Constitution of the Spiri-tual Power.*
tively based on the three necessary elements of collective force,
in spontaneous relation with the three essential sides of our
cerebral nature.   Of these three, the Material is vested in the
great and wealthy, the Intellectual in the wise and in priests,
the Moral in women; the three representing a basis of Force,
Reason, and Affection.   The first, the power of which is direct
and emphatic, springing from continuous and irresistible wants,
cannot be mistaken, and needs no further explanation.   Not so
with the other two, the intellectual and the moral forces.
These are combined both in the State and in the Family, and
form one single power; this, under the name of *spiritual*, has
as its part to modify the material power.   Nevertheless the
religious society, which is both vaster and more complete than
either the civil or the domestic society, will have to retain the
threefold division of the human authorities, just as we see it in
the rudimentary forms of association.

The power of the Priesthood is no doubt essentially intel- *Its intellec-tual and moral attri-butes.*
lectual.   It rests always upon special knowledge of the order of
Man and of Nature, even when this order is supposed to be
governed by imaginary beings.   The general economy of the
world necessarily determines every human existence, both individual and collective; imposing upon each the grand conditions
of its life, and admitting of modification, only in secondary cases.
This order is indispensable alike to teach us resignation, and to
stimulate our activity; and it invests with a high authority that
class which specially dedicates itself to study it, so soon as the
gradual division of labour enables such a class to be formed.

Thus the Priesthood deals with civic life, by its daily instruction in physical science, and it deals with domestic life through its constant inculcation of the moral law : both physical and moral spheres it combines by means of those intellectual laws, which are the proper domain of the spiritual order.   If it ever declines from this threefold intellectual superiority, it soon loses all its social influence.   But, though intellectual eminence is the basis of its real power, this is insufficient without a moral power to complete it.   Whether to advise, to sanction, or above all to direct, the Priesthood needs a certain greatness of character, without which force of intellect will not receive the confidence it ought to inspire.   For this reason intellectual power must never be separated from moral power, if it is really to act upon the domain of material force.

Comparison of the Spiritual Power with that of Women.

In truth the highest powers of the Heart belong not to the Priesthood : these are the privilege of Women.   Qualities of this kind, which are so powerful in the Family, in the City do not give rise to a power sufficiently marked.   They do their work indeed wholly in the home life of the affectionate sex, and they are not strong enough to give to public life what it needs for Counsel, Consecration, and Discipline. Brilliant exceptions apart, and these will always be extremely rare, the moment that woman leaves the sanctuary of the home, she necessarily loses her greatest strength, which is more bound up with the Heart than with Intellect or Character.   That unalloyed spring of feeling, which is her true greatness, not only shrinks from all material rule, as does also the true Priesthood ; but it does not aspire to the consulting and teaching office of the religious power.   Hence woman cannot without forfeiting her proper nature acquire the knowledge of real life, public and private, which is indispensable to the spiritual power.   Her true civic influence is only an indirect continuation of her home influence, fostering everywhere the higher inspirations.   The loving Sex, therefore, in spite of its beauty of feeling, which every Priesthood worthy of its name will ever duly respect, can never enter into any competition of social influence with the contemplative Class.   This will always be the only systematic organ of the Power which controls society.   The Priesthood however must reach a moral standard such that it can speak to Man in the name of Woman.   Then the mother, the sister, the wife, the daughter contribute their precious aid within

the home. On the other hand, the natural influence of the
affectionate Sex within the Family forms within it a true
Spiritual Power ; which the Priesthood sanctions and completes,
by investing it with a systematic form, as we shall explain in the
next chapter. We have thus, ultimately, two principal powers
civil or domestic, one of which orders acts, whilst the other
modifies the will. At the same time, that there are three forms
of power is suggested by the double character of the Spiritual
Power, which regulates the Material. In the State, it adds a
moral weight to its intellectual authority; in the Family, it
strengthens the heart with the help of the head.

Material and Spiritual power were always distinct, even
when they were centred in the same organs, as during the
greater part of early civilisation. It might have been seen in
the continual succession to power, first of the Priests, and then
of the Warriors, according to conditions of time and place ; and
observers of old would have perceived it, had social science
been sufficiently advanced. But ever since the religious society
became in the Middle Age, as it will always remain, far wider
than the political Society, the separation of the two forces is an
idea familiar to the Western world, which modern sophistry
will never expel. To be finally recognised it needs only the
systematic sanction which it receives from Positivism. This
could not be given it from any other source, for want of an adequate knowledge of Man's nature, individual or collective.

Material and Spiritual Power, always distinct.

We must fully recognise that it may be useful long to retain
hereafter for the two elementary powers of Society the names
which they received in the memorable Mediæval period, when
they were first distinguished. But we may contrast their historic titles with the more scientific terms which our philosophy
will give them ; and we may take the opportunity of here re-
viewing their various contrasts, and of showing that which will
ultimately prevail.

Historical origin of terms. Temporal and Spiritual Power.

Two of these contrasts are suggested by the absence of true
correspondence between the ordinary names of the two social
forces. For, when we call the one *Spiritual,* the word suggests
to us that the other is material. This expresses the true nature
of the powers in their full breadth and reality. On the other
hand, when we call the second power the *Temporal,* the term
again points to the perpetuity of the first. Now, this second
contrast is as significant as the first. When the old mystical

The terms are not strictly contrasted.

sense of eternity is interpreted by Positivism as a relative perpetuity, it exactly marks the most profound of all the points of contrast between the two social powers. In fact, the Civil power can be the organ merely of Solidarity, or the union of contemporaries. The present is its world; it speaks with no authority as to the past, which it little understands; nor as to the future, which it cannot properly foresee. Its position is so little intellectual, that it would be but blindly groping its way, if the Spiritual power did not help it with the only clue to escape from its empirical situation. For, on the one hand, practical measures, dealing with the present, must start from the past and work towards the future; or they would be wanting in the first case in a basis, in the second case in an end. On the other hand, the Religious power, as the great organ of Continuity, alone represents the two boundless periods which precede and succeed the world of to-day, the proper sphere of Political action. The true Priesthood, whose privilege it is to speak in the name of the Past, the subject of their constant study, and of the Future, the object of their continual aspirations, is empowered to bestow a peculiar and potent consecration on every practical authority, civic or domestic. Thus the want of strict relation between the two terms, Spiritual and Temporal, usually used in contrast, points at once to the true nature of each, and to their respective provinces.

Among many points of contrast between these two Powers, the most characteristic of all is that between their natural tendencies: the one Theoretical; the other Practical. This will be the ground from which the terms for them in ordinary use will be drawn in the future, when the systematic view of society has gained due acceptance. The division between Speculation and Action, in fact, comprehends the two points of difference mentioned above. Furthermore, it has the great advantage of marking, for every phase of human life, both public and private, a contrast which is usually taken into account only in the highest social functions. When every occupation duly fulfilled is looked upon as morally a civic office, the distinctions between the man of theory and the man of practice, down to the smallest arts, answer to the distinctions of Spiritual and Temporal power. When in the Middle Age a power grew up which advised without commanding, it was only the extension to the general and most difficult of all arts, that of governing society,

Marginal notes:

Contrast between:
1. Spiritual and Material.
2. Perpetual and Temporal Powers.

3. Principal contrast, between Theory and Practice.

of the fundamental distinction between Theory and Practice long established in simple cases. The influence of Morality over Politics is the true. if unnoticed source of the larger and more systematic spirit, which marks modern speculation upon human society. Thus the terms, Theoretical and Practical, best express the spirit of dualism in the two coordinate social forces, and the necessity for extending it to every part of the Organism of mankind.

The two differences which follow are suggested by the one above. The first thus suggested is that between the General and the Special. As the preceding volume showed (p. 351), true Theory is always General, whilst sound Practice is always Special; for every man in thought should grasp substantially the whole sphere of conception ; but it is impossible that in action any man should aim at the whole range of execution. The specialism, which is the ambition of those who call themselves theoricians, is on scientific as well as on social grounds a monstrosity ; it is only possible in the confusion of our times, and it is the leading obstacle to a regeneration of modern society. The mutual dependence between every element which goes to make the economy of the physical, intellectual, and moral worlds is so complete, both in thought and in reality, that to study them separately, either in Science or in Logic, would be utterly irrational. No part of this Universal Order can be properly understood without the rest. Real life needs them all in their entirety ; and thus only can it attain any sure guidance. Whereas Specialists can only give men of practice mere information; and even this cannot ordinarily be trusted. Without generality of view, and this cannot be attained apart from a complete grasp on all sides of Nature, speculative abstraction is only mental weakness ; one which can as little serve the public, as it can give happiness to the individual. What practical men require for their special undertakings in dealing with the economy of nature is systematic study in this sense of the universal order of things. Theory and Practice are thus closely associated, the spirit of generality and the spirit of detail being duly allied ; for both are indispensable that human wisdom may accomplish its work. Thus the Spiritual power fulfils the first function assigned to it above, that of filling up the gaps which Civil society, spontaneously dealing only with facts, of necessity leaves unsupplied.

4. Contrast between the general and the special.

Spiritual power the most general of the Arts.

Apart from the natural contrast between Speculation and Action, that between Generality and Speciality marks an essential difference between the two social forces in respect to active life. Sound Philosophy like true poetry, is not simply a speculative faculty. Poetry, by virtue of its real and healthy effect on life is called, and most justly and specially is called, an *art*; and Philosophy deserves a similar recognition of its practical services to life. These two sister Arts never should be separated; and in the true Religion they are united, so as together to equip the Priesthood for the most important and difficult of all arts, the art of training the will by conviction and persuasion. But whilst the action of Art and the influence of Science are equally necessary for the art of Morals, the value of both in combination must be completed by recurring to the known relations between the Soul and the Body. The nervous connection between the vegetative organs of the body and the affective portion of the brain is such, that sometimes the only way of acting upon the moral instincts is by first treating these bodily organs. Again, bodily health can often be restored only by establishing cerebral repose. In short, Art is as truly indivisible as human nature. All forms of Art must be profoundly harmonised by the true Priesthood; without this they would never rise to the level of their great social mission. We must not look on the Spiritual power as simply contemplative. Its privilege is to furnish the special arts with scientific principles, by means of its higher knowledge of the laws of Nature; and it is also master, and it alone, of the general Art which all the special arts imply: the art whose subject matter is no one of man's labours; but Man himself.

The subject of this general Art is : Man.

To practise any industry a man must be by habit, healthy, honest, energetic, and intelligent. The art, which aims at maintaining or making the man such, ought to be studied by all classes. But these rules, of universal usefulness, are peculiarly the property of the only order of men who can teach them on system. In this matter, Civil government is only the ally of the Priesthood, bringing its material force to bear indirectly on men's will, where certain acts have been enjoined or forbidden. Thus, the improvement of the External World demands a number of special industries, as distinct and as independent as the classes of laws which concern their subjects. But the direct improvement of Man, the author of all these

arts, is itself a kind of general industry; which in spite of its
vastness cannot be divided, and which is the proper office of the
true Priesthood. The special arts all depend on Cosmology, or
the sciences which concern Nature; the general art depends on
Sociology, if we include in it as an introduction the science of
Biology. This then is the basis of the ultimate distinction
which will exist between the two powers; the one relating to
Nature, the other to Society. The intelligent economist Dunoyer recognised this truth, without formally proclaiming it;
when at the close of his honourable labours he laid down the
famous distinction between the two kinds of industry: that regarding the World, and that regarding Man. And the same
reasoning points to the moral conditions of the Spiritual power
no less than to its intellectual requirements. The true priest
who dedicates his life to purify the wills of men, must keep his
own spirit in that tone, from which only great things can flow
in practical or speculative life. The first experience of his
power to guide others must be made in his power to guide
himself; for in no other way will others trust his skill.

After this distinction between the generality of the Spiritual
power and the essentially special character of the Temporal
power, we may complete the fundamental contrast between them
by a difference directly connected with the preceding. That is,
the local sphere of the one is universal, of the other always partial. The Priesthood whose Art is general, the only one everywhere indispensable, may and ought to extend its work to all
corners of the planet, when its doctrines are sufficiently real and
complete to become universally prevalent. On the contrary,
Material power, whose duty it is to direct special and local
operations, cannot without oppression rule more than a given
territory, and that one much smaller than we now suppose.
The ties of interest which these partial operations establish between different regions of the world, do not need to be, and do
not admit of being, centralised formally. Wisdom, not Force,
ought to preside over those practical institutions which are
needful to bring these constant civic relations into due uniformity. The same holds good of the temporary enterprises undertaken by several governments in concert. The Emperor of
the West was during the Middle Age a disturbing element, the
casual remnant of an earlier system, one which tended only to
impair the harmony of the Catholic world. We shall trace this

5. Spiritual
Power is
worldwide;
Temporal
Power, local.

in the next volume.   Instead of growing larger, as the great
society of man increases, Political governments ought on the
contrary to be much reduced, for the very reason that Religion
everywhere establishes a voluntary uniformity of manners and
of opinions.   In fixing the natural limits of States in the last
volume, I shall show that they need not ultimately exceed that
of cities along with the country tract which freely adheres to
them.   This last difference between the Priesthood and the
Stat :, that between their spheres of local extension, in the full
maturity of the social organism will be the most striking con-
tra .: between them, and that in a higher degree than in the
Middle Age.

We have now found five points of contrast all in close connection, and which signally display the fundamental separation
of the two grand social powers.   Each of the five characters
points to the independence of the Priesthood, in order that it
may advise, consecrate, and direct the authorities which deal
with practical life : being itself the great organ of universal
Solidarity between men, and especially of the Continuity of
successive ages.   At the same time, all these reasons concur to
show the necessity, on mental as well as on moral grounds, for
debarring the Priesthood from temporal power, and consequently
from wealth.   In order that it may foster and preserve the
generality of Thought and the generosity of Feeling which are
required for its social work, it must be thoroughly relieved from
all care about details.   Command of any kind is fatal to the
Priestly functions in two ways ; first, the attention to practical
details disturbs the breadth of view they need, whilst the employment of force instead of reason and affection corrupts the
feeling.   We have a noble illustration of this in the incom-

parable Aristotle ; who in a time when the two powers were
completely confounded, kept himself always free from the
dreams as to a government of the wise which attracted so many
sophists.   Since the separation effected in the Middle Age,
even anarchy can hardly be the excuse of the thinkers, who
under a vulgar ambition so completely mistook the first duties
of their superior intelligence and aspired to public power.

Descartes and Leibnitz shrank from any such degradation ; and
it is mournful to see Bacon fall a victim to ambition, whose intellect can be cleared only at the expense of his character.   The
good sense of the public will second the efforts of governments

to defeat the pretensions of so-called thinkers to assume political power. In accordance with Positive principles, the aspirations of theoricians for temporal power, will be looked on as clear proof of mediocrity of mind, no less than of weakness of character.

At the same time, we must not exaggerate the necessary separation of the two kinds of power, as if it were the result of our cerebral constitution, instead of being, as it is, a useful rule of human experience. Different as Theory and Practice are, the only reason why they cannot be simultaneously combined by the same person, is that the habits of intelligence and character they call into use are not properly compatible. The theoretic intellect, it is true, naturally prefers deductive reasoning; the practical prefers inductive. And, according to our cerebral theory, there is a natural difference in the higher personal instincts which answer to them; since vanity, or the love of applause, is more marked in the man of speculation, and pride, or the love of power, in the man of action. But these differences, not resting on distinction in character or sympathies, are much too weak to constitute real divisions between natures. Education can usually modify natural disposition to either side; so that whether a man belong to theory or practice mainly depends on the habits in which his life is cast.

Difference between Theory and Practice is one of habit rather than constitution.

Though the two kinds of life are radically incompatible, the separation between them is merely an artificial arrangement, and is not an arbitrary distribution. The theoricians will be infinitely fewer than the practicians, not exceeding one in ten thousand of the human race in the normal condition. On the other hand, their duties are far more difficult; for if they have the same general education as the rest, it will have to be completed by a laborious course of study of their own. Besides, mediocrity is less admissible in theoretic than in other functions. True theoricians ought always to be men of superior intelligence and feeling, designated for the Priesthood by these qualities. But eminent practicians would have made very capable priests, if they had ever had a career in life which inclined them to the office. And in like manner, men of theoretic ability may reasonably think they could have succeeded in practical life, had they ever had the requisite experience of affairs. This is some excuse, though not a justification, for the empty ambition of temporal power, which so often afflicts men

Naturally, the two careers may be interchanged.

conscious of an intellectual and perhaps of a moral superiority to the ordinary political leaders. The fine life of the great Cervantes is a good illustration of the ease with which the higher speculative intellects might become eminent in action, had they with good cause changed their careers to practice. His practical gifts of heart, head, and character during the energetic years of his early life seem to show that in fortunate circumstances he might have made a statesman of the first class. On the other hand, Cæsar, Charlemagne, and Frederick might have become great in speculation, if their lives had been from early years so shaped. The distinction is in the habit of life, not in mental constitution. And in the final system, where the normal age of the Priesthood will be late, we may see the careers not infrequently changed; and men of action will transform themselves into men of speculation, both having received a common education.

Cervantes,

Cæsar, Charlemagne, Frederick.

The pride of science is too ready to undervalue practical genius, which often tests power of mind better than speculation. Practical men sometimes increase their intellectual labour by preferring the tedious method of induction to the more direct method of deduction. Ideas formed on an inductive method may be less general and consequently less consistent; but they are often more near to truth as well as more useful. Practical and theoretic reasoning require very equal mental force, unless in such cases as that of the abstract labours of the rare men of genius who have advanced the human destinies.

Practical genius requires no less power than speculative.

Not only would it be pedantry to suppose any absolute division between the Theoretic and the Practical intellect; but it would be fatal to any true Classification of Society. This great arrangement of human life is only an extension of the fundamental principle of all division. The principle itself admits of a long series of gradual modifications. Now, we get this quality in the theory just laid down on the essential division of the two social powers; and thence we point out the type and the source of all human classification.

The best mode of getting at the true division will be to choose, among the five characteristics just mentioned, the distinction based on the higher generality of the Theoretic power. It will be sufficient to recognise the relative nature of this quality, naturally admitting various degrees. Other social di-

Higher Generality in the Theoretic Power is the main source of social classification.

visions will follow from the principal one as their functions become more special.

However, we must first recognise that the theoretic order admits of no classes within it. The only divisions within it are personal, due to native ability or acquired knowledge. Any fixed distribution of the different spheres of labour is out of keeping with the synthetic character of the Priestly office, which must maintain with scrupulous care its character of generality. It is because the true spirit of breadth is thus cultivated by the leading class that each of the active orders can devote themselves to their special labours, without losing sight of the universal harmony, which is sufficiently represented by others. The system of specialism, which since the fall of the pure Theocracies has more and more marked abstract study, was only fit to build up one by one the stones of the vast foundation of objective fact, on which the ultimate Synthesis of man is to rest. Were it to be permanent, it would lead to intellectual anarchy, and to the dissolution of society. My work on Positive Philosophy showed the importance of recalling science to its original function, as in the maxim : *Know thyself*, completing it thus, *Know thyself, that thou mayst improve thyself*. This formula will express the study of the general Order of the universe and its Modifications. We must even give up, as I showed in the General View (p. 249), the division which I adopted in my form r work between the scientific and the esthetic genius. They were only separated when the Theocratic system began ○ decline. That grand comprehensiveness, the spontaneous tendency of those epochs, will be reconstructed on system by the wisdom of the ages to come. The new moral Power will even be more complete and more simple ; for it will free itself from any tendency to command, which beside its injury to the character, constantly narrowed the breadth of ideas, by imposing anxiety over pressing details.

And the grand cha-racteristic of the Priest-hood.

Apart therefore from the essential separation between the Theoretic and the Practical power, the classification of society consists in due subordination of the grades of the Temporal power, according to their special functions. These may be determined by the same law of decreasing generality with increasing dependence which in my early philosophical writings (*see* Appendix, vol. iv.) led me to the Classification of the Sciences. The various social ranks are all classed according to

The prin-ciple of generality determines the classi-fication of the Tem-poral Power also.

this principle, and are minor illustrations of the law which marks the Speculative class from the Active mass.

Strikingly illustrated in military organisation.

Gradual diminution in the generality of view belonging to each office is very strikingly shown in the only form of collective activity which hitherto has been thoroughly organised. Military duties fall so naturally into a series depending on this principle of subdivision, that they have given the titles usually borne by authorities everywhere. Thus, even in war, every superior is to his inferiors something like a spiritual chief; that is to say, he is concerned with the general rather than the particular view, and has to do rather with reflection than with acts.

And applicable to the hierarchy of Industry.

In industry, where from the nature of the case the diversity of function is much greater, the differences of rank are still quite in confusion, and do not appear open to the same principle. But it is really just as applicable, as I shall show at the close of this treatise, both in the final state, and in the course of history. I will only here point to the two leading divisions, which in due combination complete the great classification of society. The basis of it all is the universal separation of employers and workmen. Now, the latter as compared with the former, obviously show decreasing generality of view with increasing independence. The same principle runs through the division into four great orders of the industrial chiefs : Bankers, Merchants, Manufacturers, Agriculturists, the numbers of whom increase as we descend the scale.

Ultimately, also, to the whole social system.

The relations of practical life are in so rude and unorganised a state, that we can hardly perceive their final order : but even as they are, its normal conditions are patent. Our ultimate state will exhibit a classification of society more distinct than any we know in all sides of human life. From the High Priest of Humanity down to the humblest labourer, society will show the same principle at work distributing ranks : generality of view decreasing as independence of life increases. Thus the law of Human Order will be but an extension of the law of Universal Order, where the higher phenomena are in constant dependence on the lower.

Final harmony and cohesion of the social system.

When, in a regenerated system of education, men are more disposed to recognise this connection between the two laws, the order of the social world will seem not more arbitrary, though it be more capable of improvement, than the order of the external world. Again, the spirit of unity, whereby the classifica-

tion of the social world becomes strictly homogeneous, will incline individuals to submit to greater respect for it.   Each
rank commands that below it, by virtue of a title exactly similar
to that which the second holds over its own subordinates.   Revolt therefore is always an act of inconsistency.   We need not
enlarge on the tendency of this common feeling to give cohesion
to the body politic.   In their attacks on the Popes, the princes
of our modern times indirectly aroused an insurrectionary
temper in their own people.

In spite of all, the organisation of society must ever remain Moral equ
valent for
personal
exposed to a disturbing influence which, since caste was finally injustice in
discredited, has been one of the chief cares of every Priesthood social ar-
rangement
conscious of a social mission.   The natural law of the classification of society relates only to the order of duties, and not the
distribution of duties to individuals.   The assignment of duty
to persons, not going according to birth, is often felt to be arbitrary, and is often justly complained of.   Functions requiring
high powers of generalisation often fall to very ordinary intellects.   And the same thing occurs with respect to qualities of
feeling and character.   The gradual perfecting of the human
order will diminish these abuses of society ; but they will always
demand constant care from the Spiritual Power, whose business
it is to regulate all social relations.   Its main remedy will be
to cultivate in all a mixture of resignation and dignity ; so as
to take the bitterness from social inequalities which are inherent
in society, and to make up for humbleness of position by surrounding personal merit with respect.

Even with the vast improvement which will result from the It is impos-
sible to hope
selection of a successor in the various social functions, it will for complete
social ad-
be impossible ever to arrive at precise correspondence between justments.
function and agent, so great is the independence of the human
elements of the collective being—Humanity.   It would be to
disturb, not to perfect, the order of society, did we not care
mainly for the employment of the various powers in society,
and much more than for their origin, or the person who
possesses them.   We are very little able to distribute these
powers aright, knowing so little as we do the laws involved in
them.   We do not see therein, it is true, the capricious Deity
to whom even Dante assigned them, but we fail to comprehend
the subtle causation which decides the possession for each of us
of natural or acquired advantages.   All we can do is to see how

real it is, and how powerless we are to modify the laws by which success is attained, at all in the degree required by perfect social harmony.

Strict equity in social distribution is unattainable.

Practical success in all its forms, Industrial or Military, depends on causes utterly beyond our powers of prevision, though prudence may be able to turn the conditions of it to account. Speculative success is less liable to these accidental influences; but is yet not wholly free from them. Amongst those influences which we can comprehend and know to affect each individual life, the greater part are withdrawn from our interference. Though the future of civilisation may find means to transplant many citizens to more suitable countries, this resource is available only for the few. The mass of men can no more choose their abode than they can their age. It remains for the fortunate to compassionate and help their less fortunate brethren. There is often as great inequality in the proportions, under which physical, intellectual, and moral qualities are found in the world. The utmost that we can do to improve them is to affect the conditions of their natural development; and this wholesome form of Equality will be one of the striking results of an education common to all.

True merit, and real happiness, depend on right conduct in that state of life, to which Nature and Man have carried each of us.

After all that we may do to establish correspondence between the character of each social office, and the capacity of those who fill it, we shall always find a great imperfection. Even if we resolved on putting everyone in his just place, we should be prevented by the short span of life in the flesh; for we should never have examined the claims of each person in time to change him to his rightful post. Nor must we forget that the bulk of social duties may be fulfilled without any great natural aptitude, provided this is made up by suitable experience, for which there is no real substitute. Since the man however well qualified to be a capable organ of any function in society, always needs a special apprenticeship in it, we ought to respect all positive possession, be it of power, or of wealth; and to recognise how much this undisturbed enjoyment of the personal title to it enhances its value to society. As to natural faculties, we ought even less to feel pride in them than in the acquired advantages of position, for the natural are more beyond our control than the rest. Our true merit, like our real happiness, depends on the right use of those powers, which the dispensation of man or of nature may have entrusted to our keeping. By this rational teaching of the truth, the Spiritual Power will labour to fill individuals and classes with a sense of dignified submission to the necessary inequalities of society, inequalities which in so complex an organism may involve severe abuse.

With all this habit of accepting social inequalities, complaints would often break out, unless the feeling at the bottom of them were not from time to time duly gratified under the general guidance of the Priesthood. This they do by virtue of that faculty of Judgment, which is the great characteristic of the Spiritual power, and whence it makes good its title to advise, to sanction, and to discipline. Their powers of Judgment, naturally beginning with the office, will be ultimately extended to the individuals who fill it. The Priesthood will no doubt do its utmost to keep within limits that change of persons in all positions in society which, if left unchecked, would soon lead to greater evils than the abuses which it professed to remove. But it will also create and maintain as a contrast to this objective order of rank arising .from positive power, a subjective order of merit based on personal esteem, and formed after thorough appreciation of individual characteristics. This second classification by order of merit is visionary, and would be pernicious, if adopted in any but in sacred functions; but by the contrast it exhibits to the classification in the world, it may suggest useful modifications in life; and at least may recompense those who suffer by inevitable inequality.

The judgment of the Priesthood will redress social inequalities.

The direct and exclusive ability of the Spiritual Power to fulfil this task is one that we cannot dispute. It is the happiest mode in which it can execute its special duty in the vast system of man's .cooperative existence, the duty of giving a general direction to the particular office of each member of society. The convergence to a common end of disparate human acts and lives, by means of which the great Organism of Humanity is maintained and perfected, is the point of view for the Priesthood to occupy in their abstract classification of individuals: Honour should be awarded to each according to his particular ability to serve Humanity. Their own position in society inclines them to bring forward, as prominently as possible, this order of merit, by contrast to the order of power required by the concrete classification of practical duties. This order of merit too will be the dominant one in the eternity beyond the life of sensation, when the Priesthood systematically enforces the commemoration

Especially in subjective Life.

of man's life. The ancients often would extend to the dead the vicious classification which had prevailed in life, but the Middle Age attempted to redress this injustice ; and, without attacking society, drew attention to the actual mistakes of which it was full. But the task is one fit only for the Positive Religion, which alone has the means of passing a just judgment on social merit. In dealing with the subjective life beyond the grave, it is relieved from considering either the material accidents which give prominence to external circumstances, or small personal qualities. When sound principles of human classification have been made thus familiar in the subjective life, they will not be confined to the dead ; but public opinion would desire to extend them to the living, if the Priesthood did not anticipate the wish.

This judgment of persons is the supreme task of the Priesthood[1]

The supreme duty of the Priesthood sums up all others, and is the most difficult of all, as it demands the most exact discrimination. In fulfilling it all advantages of position must be put aside, as well as all advantages of education; for the latter is as much the result of accident as the former, and not more the result of merit. Nor must the dead and the living be judged solely by the products of their visible lives ; for these will vary by accidents of time and place often too strong for the personal agent. It is a threefold husk of circumstance, through which the Priest must pierce, if his judgment is to discriminate truly the value of the man within. So great is the difficulty of this that it is impossible, unless the Priest can take in the entire life of the individual. Few are the characters which are so marked as to be duly weighed until their career is ended. And herein is a new proof how impossible it is to replace the concrete order of the World by the abstract order of Merit. This priestly function is of all others that one which is most liable to dangerous abuse, unless invariably exercised with sagacity and probity. It calls for a most delicate application of universal truths, and the utmost impartiality in the society which resorts to it. Of all the functions of the great Organism, it is the one which suffers most in times of confusion. It is to a true philosopher one of the saddest of spectacles, to see how not merely power but reputation are the prize of the lowest natures ; whilst the higher are forgotten or repressed for want of any spiritual discipline.

When the Priesthood is capable of fulfilling this task of

judging all characters it will have attained its true office, the For it, the highest faculties and training are required. hardest to found and to complete. The function of Judgment unites in itself all the attributes of Spiritual power, and displays, better than any other, the moral and intellectual resources required by the highest organ of Humanity. The complete social independence of the Priesthood and their unreserved renunciation of all Political power are thus equally indispensable to their true mission. It requires also, that they be profoundly imbued with the synthetic spirit, strengthened and developed by a comprehensive education in the collective sciences, and preserving the natural alliance between Science, Art, and Industry. The devotion of the intelligence to the continued service of the social feelings is thus made the grand duty of a class, whose part it is to complete and to direct the great Organism ; a class who would only plunge it in convulsion, were this dominant principle of morality broken down.

Before quitting this subject, and before concluding this chapter, there remains to be cleared up a great difficulty, as to the fundamental principle of the Positive classification of society. I mean the apparent contradiction between two similar uses of the general law of Classification.

At the beginning of this chapter I propounded the Objective and subjective generality. Positive theory of the social Forces, as the foundation of my Statical doctrine ; and I treated the three elements, material, intellectual, and moral, as being classed according to their decreasing generality. On the other hand, we have just shown that the Spiritual Power is to be reckoned as the most general of all the apparatus of the social system. The contradiction between these two views appears direct, and indeed insurmountable. However, with a proper explanation, it will strengthen the principle of classification, and throw fresh light upon its value.

This is not the only instance where an explanation of the Apparent inconsistencies of classification. kind is required. In the Positive Philosophy an example was mentioned, though not very precisely, in the industrial classification (vol. vi. p. 499). In the General View (vol. i. p. 234), a more marked example is given, in the seeming opposition between the Esthetic and the Scientific series. The case before us is the best marked of all, and almost shows a want of consistency in the very foundation of the social theory in question. An explanation of all together, will be quite in place here ; nor will it interfere with any other independent solution of a difficulty to which attention is now drawn for the first time.

The solution of these.
The answer to the question lies in the distinction between two kinds of generality, the objective and the subjective; that is to say, between external phenomena and our conceptions. Thus the series of the sciences whereby thirty years ago (*see* App. vol. iv.) I succeeded in establishing the true law of general classification, contains in its most complex term a principle which objectively is the least general, and subjectively the most general. Social phenomena are certainly the least universal of all; and yet our ideas respecting them are the most general of all our ideas, since they are perpetually present to all our thoughts. So during the long infancy of the human reason, whether in the individual or in the race, the truths as to society are thought to be more easy of attainment than the laws of astronomy. The other domains of nature show the same contrast in less degree. As their complexity increases, subjective generality increases, and objective generality decreases. For the more complex order being always based on the more simple, our notions of the latter are formed out of detached groups of our notions of the former. Were our scientific education more rational, and our objective studies preceded by a subjective introduction, we should readily see the connection. And it is very apparent in the great and lasting sense of pain, with all its intellectual and moral evils : when the ordinary school training with its antiquated methods tears us from Social studies to force us violently into Mathematics.

Spiritual Power highest only in subjective generality.
Thus every system of Positive classification presents a continuous decrease of generality, whether we proceed from the simple to the composite, or the contrary. Only, the generality relates in the first case to things and beings, in the second to thoughts. Objective generality is marked by independence; subjective generality by dignity. Thus throughout the entire scale, there is a sort of compensation between independence and dignity, in every step of the series. We have a decisive example in the case which introduced this explanation; without which my philosophy would fail to fulfil its promise, and would even lead to error. The Spiritual power surpasses all others in subjective generality and in social dignity; on the other hand, Material power is the more general objectively and the most independent. Material force therefore forms the essential base of the political construction, spiritual power being the apex.

To complete this chapter, I have only to treat the historical course in which the great Organism has to pass to its full maturity, hitherto considered apart from all questions of progress. This is an essential complement of my Statical theory, but it will be sufficient if it be briefly touched on. Having stated the principle, the illustrations of it may be left to the succeeding volume on history or social dynamics. HISTORICAL SKETCH OF SOCIAL FORCES, pp. 273–275.

The same theory of the social forces which applies to their normal and complete state will equally explain the course followed by the collective Organism in its development. Taking the three elements, material, intellectual, and moral, which make up every human Force, the perfect system is attained when the two latter are closely associated in restraining the violence of the first. When the second, or intellectual, is combined with the first, and the third is neglected, we have the conditions of the earlier stages of history ; but even then the moral Force is indirectly exerting its influence. *1. First stage, predominance of Material and Intellectual Force.*

Of this primitive combination between the two first forms of Force, we have two different modes, the Theocratic and the Military types ; according as the intellectual masters the material Force, or as it becomes its servant. Both are equally, though in different ways, indispensable to the main work of the early regimen, the vigorous development of the different attributes of man, without regard to their ultimate discipline. *In twofold form, The cratic, or Military.*

It is impossible to regulate powers which do not exist ; unless like the metaphysicians we think to create what we only define. Besides any premature systematisation would be wanting in base as well as in object, for want of a sufficient power in the moral element which ought to inspire it. And further, it would check the development of real forces. Seeing the immense difficulty which the formation of the great societies of mankind presented, as did the establishment of the spirit of discipline which alone can make them permanent, it is fortunate that our natural instinct is towards strength rather than control. In the first chapter of this volume, I pointed out how unjust are the complaints of Christianity against the supposed immorality of Polytheism ; for the various human powers needed a full scope for their growth before they could be reduced to order. And the same holds good of all the other aspects of the Social Organism. *A necessary stage.*

2. Second stage, union of Intellect and Feeling.

On the other hand, this primitive regimen is necessarily temporary, for it is out of harmony with the laws of human nature, individual or collective. If the growth of our powers occupies our earliest attention, our latest is claimed for their discipline; for it is the source of our happiness, public or private. But in the normal state, the Intelligence must pass over to be the servant of the Heart, instead of remaining in its alliance with Might. Under the guidance of the Heart it can devote the resources which a long experience has given it to form the systematic discipline best suited to man's nature as a whole. This new work is more in harmony with its ambition, for the Heart is a master far pleasanter than Force; its commands are nobler and less imperious.

Though the intellect long regretted the days of its supremacy under the Theocracies, it recognised at last how passing a phase this was, and even how degrading its results. From the Middle Age downwards, before the doctrine or the situation were favourable to it, all the grander spirits showed us the Intelligence aspiring towards its great part, that of disciplining Material Force, without encroachment on the one hand, or weakness on the other. This admirable attempt could not be otherwise than abortive; and then it entered on its old dream of a Reign of Intellect, the folly of which for want of a sound theory of human nature was not apparent. But in its vain efforts to gain the mastery anew over Material power, it succeeded only in throwing it into confusion, tearing up the indispensable stays of the structure, and sacrificing the fruits of the preceding ages. Its helplessness and its regrets now warn the right-minded, and they will soon teach the wrong-headed, that the common unity aimed at in the Middle Age must be sought again on truer bases, at once intellectual and social. The object of the present chapter has been to exhibit this normal condition of Unity, in all the main features of its structure. The work of the succeeding chapter will be to show the mode in which this organic whole proceeds in active existence.

The abstract theory of Social Forces, on which the preceding chapter is built, is still further of use to explain the Subjective order which succeeds to the Objective order. By its means we may conceive three systems of human life, according as the dominant principle is Force, the Intellect, or the Heart. The first presides over the indispensable education of the race, giving free play to all our activities. When these have reached a point where they are capable of discipline, the second system gives them their objective organisation. But this normal condition, ever limited to modify the dominion which rude necessity assures to Force, fails to satisfy our legitimate desires, as they constantly aim at making the Heart supreme. This great end is the mark of the third system, which belongs only to our subjective life, to be treated specially in the last volume.

CHAPTER VI.

POSITIVE THEORY OF SOCIAL EXISTENCE, SYSTEMATISED BY THE PRIESTHOOD.

INTRODUC-
TORY
SKETCH,
pp. 276–289.

Scope of this
chapter.

At first sight it might be thought that the subject of this chapter is either contained in the Statical theory which has just been elaborated, or else belongs properly to the Dynamical questions to be treated in the succeeding volume. A clear notion of the purport of this chapter will be secured when this doubt has been duly removed ; and we shall arrive at this by means of a definition of great importance.

Use of the
term *exist-*
ence : the ac-
tive energy
apart from
change.

For every living being, we need to introduce, between the kindred ideas of organisation and of life, an intermediate term, one at present vaguely conceived, and for which we must reserve the special name of *existence*. It may be applied to all real substances, in order to express their proper and continuous form of active energy. In Biology, it corresponds with the fixed side of every system of vital phenomena : the *life* of every being consisting of the series of modifications to which its *existence* is subject. This general distinction becomes more and more marked, as we reach organisms of greater complexity and more easily modified. Its chief use is in Sociology, where it has held its ground under an indirect form, ever since Aristotle founded the theory of Order, without any notion of laws of Progress, which were left for modern thought. Whilst science regarded human societies as immovable, the term *life* could not be properly applied to them, for it implies a series of changes always terminating in death. The word is only in place, when the idea of constant Progress is established. The general term, *existence*, was therefore more apt to express the essential active side of the Great Organism. Now this is the point of view of the present volume, where the laws of structure of the Collective Being of Humanity are a necessary preliminary only to the study of its primary functions. In Social Statics, the notions of Organisation and Activity must never be separated. But that form of activity alone, which is common to all places and times, is properly included in *existence*. The changes arising from these two causes, to which we give the name of *life*, are the proper sphere of Social Dynamics.

In the inorganic world, the activity of any system tends to destroy its structure; and this holds good even in Mechanics. In living beings, on the contrary, Structure and Activity are bound up with each other within the due limits of intensity and duration peculiar to each case. Their structure is only developed, and indeed is only preserved, by the appropriate degree of activity. The extent and the complexity of the one correspond to those of the other, as we rise through the scale of beings. Thus their most complete union is reached only in the organism of collective Humanity. When we regard the Activity only as tending to preserve the Structure, its study belongs to Social Statics. When we regard it as the source of Development, it belongs to Dynamics. The present chapter is thus a necessary transition between the preceding chapter and the volume to follow. After tracing the *structure* of the Collective Being, I proceed to the laws of its *existence*, as a prelude to the laws of its *life*. The Statical study would be wanting in completeness, and the Dynamical would be wanting in due preparation, unless this link were introduced; and it will prove to be neither a repetition of the former, nor an anticipation of the latter. *Correspondence of Structure and Activity.*

The better to explain this intermediate doctrine, I proceed to show further relations between the leading notions contained in the preceding chapter on the three concurrent modes of human association. As we have seen, every man belongs at once through feeling to a particular Family, by the activity to some City, by the intellect to a Church. Whilst engaged on the mere study of Structure, there was no need to examine which of these three simultaneous forms of society was the most important. But for a full study of Existence, we must begin by establishing the natural order of their rank. This is then the time to decide the abstract question of importance between the Domestic, the Civil or Political, and the Religious Society. *Of the three modes of association, Family, City, Church,*

This question will be solved by resorting to our fundamental theory of human nature, whereby cerebral existence is made *The City is the chief,* dependent on corporal existence, and thus the Activity prevails over the Intellect, and even over Feeling. Thus it is the City, the essential organ of active cooperation, with which man is chiefly concerned; though we must constantly conceive of the City, as prepared by the Family, and completed by the Church. Although political society is necessarily composed of many domestic associations, the former alone determines the sum of the existence proper to each of the latter, since the general distribution of human labours everywhere decides men's respective occupations. This fact, unmistakeable in the first traces of civilisation, grows more marked as Solidarity and Continuity are extended. Besides, the general instinct confirms this view, since man is ordinarily regarded as *citizen*.

In spite of the Catholic Church.

This first point decided, there would seem to be left no doubt as to the second branch of the preceding question. For if Feeling admits its dependence on Activity, must not the Intellect do the like? However the Theocratic system, where the intellect had an exceptional supremacy, gave rise to a serious misconception. This was, it is true, corrected in the Military societies, in which the State obtained a distinct preponderance, even when the Church was wider in extent than the State, as it was in Greece. But in the Middle Age, the confusion reappeared with more gravity, owing to the mystical character of the Monotheistic Synthesis, particularly in the West. That, the final form of the provisional religion, strove to snatch the individual from the solid realm of civil existence, in order to plunge him arbitrarily into a vague religious existence, where even the claims of Family were forgotten. Our emancipation from Theology has hardly yet been carried to the point of closing this struggle between the believer, be he Christian or Musulman, and the citizen. Now, however, but for the negative character peculiar to modern thought, no doubt would remain as to the relative importance of the Intellectual, and the Political, Society.

In Positivism, the Church is the complement of the State,

The Positive Religion, by virtue of its complete reality, gives the undoubted supremacy in rank to the State; though it is the only Religion which assures to the Church its proper character of universality. In accordance with the principles stated in the preceding chapter on the three forms of human association, the Religious society is specially destined to strengthen and develop the Civil society, as the Civil does the

Domestic society. The greater extent of the Religious society
is no real ground for its supremacy where that greater extent
is counterbalanced by great difference in general character.
Thus the State, when it does not exceed its natural limits
of size, naturally prevails over the Family. In such case the
necessary ascendancy of the Activity is perfectly compatible
with the due expansion of Feeling ; and a true and healthy
unity is definitively established. On the contrary, any harmony
would be momentary and even illusory, if based on the supremacy of the Church over the State ; for the Church answers to
that part of man's nature which has the least capacity for
command. Directly the intellect ceases to devote itself to the
continual service of the Activity and the Feeling, it instinctively
tends to indefinite extravagancies ; which would soon destroy
even the degree of association which it can admit. The apparent
positivity of such idle speculations offers but a slight check
upon these aberrations.

Thus, the Religious society must devote its special characteristic of universality to complete the Political society, by
uniting the different cities, on the principle of their common
and constant dependence on Humanity. But the superior extension of the Church is no reason that it should hold itself
out as a better representative of the true Great Being than
States or Families. The greater extent in space of the Church,
always so slight in comparison with extension in time, is no
ground in itself for any right to represent a Being, who is best
imaged by the fulfilment of every social duty. Humanity
may often be better represented by a single Family, than by
a vast association which corresponds with only one of its essential aspects.

In spite of the greater extent of the Church.

Positivism renewing the great Religious work which failed
in the Middle Age, closely associates with it the essential
supremacy of Civic existence, a happy feature of the Roman
system. The true separation between Church and State, far
from altering this natural supremacy of the State, will on the
contrary much strengthen it, by permitting the reduction of
each political society to the normal limits, within which its
utmost force is developed. The faulty and confused notions
now prevalent on this head are due to metaphysical prejudices
about the supremacy of the intellect, and to the impotent disdain
shown by Monotheism for an existence of reality. Positive

The City, the middle type of asso- ciation, is the centre of collective life ; the Family being the preparation for it, the Church the completion of it.

Religion on the other hand brings at length into final harmony sound theory and practical wisdom; for it groups the social science as a whole round the Civic, or middle type of society. The State, the necessary centre, thus represents the natural rule of the activity; the smaller society the Family, and the larger the Church, supply respectively the indispensable training of the heart, and the true intellectual complement. This is the ultimate type of unity, through which we can proceed to the abstract study of social existence; the mission of the Church being ever to organise the Family and the City.

This was empirically attempted by all the early Religions, in spite of defective doctrine.

This, its true work, far from being at all unfavourable to the due growth of Religion, will greatly strengthen and develop it; for it forms a direct bond between the religious and the other two types of human society. Theologism, by reason of its chimerical and absolute nature, was never able to apply itself rightly to this twofold task of social organisation. But so truly is it the main business of Religion, that we constantly find the Priesthood labouring to effect it, as they certainly did in the grand periods of the early Theocracies. We find them, accordingly, forced by their own good sense, and this was but the expression of the universal instinct of the time, to counteract the radical faults of their own doctrines, doctrines really alien to the form of existence they were called on to control. The marks of Positivism, on the contrary, are its reality and its comprehensiveness; qualities which directly fit it for this noble mission. For it establishes a true harmony between the suggestions of practice and the teaching of theory; instead of calling on practice painfully to supply the defects of theory. However, whilst we see herein a new proof of the superiority of our system, we must be filled with respectful admiration for the wisdom of a Priesthood, which knew so well how to turn to good account its most defective creed.

For instance, the Church took the social, not the logical, view of Pre-destination.

In the normal state, Religion, the sum of all the conceptions formed by the Great Being, is of necessity something above and beyond any Priesthood; and none will ever succeed in maintaining itself quite at the high level of its difficult mission. The contrary was true, whatever our prejudices against priestcraft, during the greater part of the preparatory stage, even under the Theocracies; and certainly it was so under Catholicism, at least until the Priesthood became retrograde. Their fine intelligence drew a happy result out of the almost limitless mysticism of the creed which they had to apply ; and perpetually turned it to the service of the great social end ever in view.   A striking example in point is found in the great controversy on Predestination, which arose about the middle of the mediæval period.   In logic, the party who favoured the pre-determined Damnation of the wicked were more consistent than those, who confined themselves to the Election of the just ; for Predestination strictly involved both. But the moral and social evils of the former view of Damnation were so obvious, that this heresy only originated or flourished by a weak subservience to blind logic.   The stronger intellects, whilst supporting the orthodox view, which confined Predestination to the Election of the just, must have seen in the incident how inevitable and how near was the break up of a creed, which could neither restrain criticism, nor satisfy it.   Cases of the same kind will often be mentioned in the third volume, where we shall treat of the social influence of the great dogmas of Western Catholicism.   The same tendency too will be even more apparent in the ancient systems of Theocracy, during their long period of social power.   In them, the good sense of the Priests had not only to counteract the defects of their Theological creeds, but also to decline the tempting opportunities for exercising political power offered by the system.

Whatever the theoretic superiority of Positivism, it should not incline us to undervalue the social services of Religion in the Past ; for Religious government existed long before it could effect its proper work.   In essence, its great task has never been altogether neglected ; at least since the establishment of Theocracies, even in their fetichist form.   Humanity indeed is incapable of creating any one of the capital institutions of society.   In the rudest types of social existence, the essential germ will be found extant ; for human nature is at bottom homogeneous, and its advance is nothing but a gradual development.   Positivism would be no true Religion, unless it were ready to take up the inheritance of Theologism and even of Fetichism, in every aspect its natural predecessors.   It undertakes only to systematise the ultimate form of human life, which is itself the spontaneous issue of the entire course of civilisation.   The Priests of Positivism would be unworthy of their office, if, misled by the anarchic spirit of modern thought, they failed in lively veneration for the truly grand natures of the

Society has never been without the germ of Religious Government.

illustrious Priests of old, pure types of intellectual and moral greatness.

In any case, in Social Statics, where questions of movement are excluded, the abstract theory of Social Existence must be conceived under the social conditions best fitted to sustain it. The final stage will however only call for treatment here in its essential economy, that is, in those features which are common to all times and all places, and are inseparable from human society as such. The third volume of the work will give special examples of these features, tracing their early rudiments, and following out their gradual development. The fourth volume will then be devoted to exhibiting these same elements in their full maturity. Such is the organic unity of the three essential parts of this great sociological scheme, the whole of which is founded on the theory of human Unity contained in the first chapter of this volume.

We are now in a position to define exactly the substance of this chapter on the Social Existence, as being in effect the necessary conclusion and the natural complement of the preceding chapter on the Social Organism. That chapter, taking the Family as the true element of society, carried on the abstract theory of the collective organism, as far as the distinct rise of religious society, the highest degree of human association. The Organisation of the composite being thus established, we can proceed to show its general type of Existence. This will be best studied in the adult stage, and we shall thus avoid all unnecessary complications in this, the most arduous of scientific studies. This method of reasoning is amply justified by the constant practice adopted in Biological science, both in its dynamic and in its statical side. It would be singular if we neglected precautions adopted in speculations of far inferior complexity. I am quite aware that the apparent novelty of this course may occasion for a time serious difficulties to my readers, so few of whom can have had the training that I have insisted on in the entire Scale of the Sciences. I ask of them this : to judge this volume, the principal foundation of the entire work, only after a second reading, when they have mastered the treatise as a whole. All conscientious students are in the habit of thus proceeding in the lower sciences ; and it is not too much to ask that the same good sense should guide the study of the highest. Criticism without this obvious precaution is unworthy of consideration. But, if it be followed, I feel confident that the two volumes to come will answer most of those difficulties which will no doubt arise on the first reading of this, where I am obliged to employ an unusual amount of abstract reasoning.

That the establishment of Religious society should mark the full maturity of the Collective Organism, it must be clearly distinct from the Political society, and its nature requires a far wider extension. This condition may be detected latent in most of the ancient Theocracies, and then in Greece; but it has in these an appearance of accident, which continues up to the Middle Age. Even then the difference between Religious and Political society is very marked only in the West, where the Priesthood and the Government were essentially separate. This was never effected by the Musulman Monotheism, in spite of the differences in the populations which it embraced in its sway, without uniting them. For Social Statics it is enough if we can cite a single case in History of the separation of Church and State, in order to exhibit the type of the general condition in the abstract. This reliance upon scientific logic is more appropriate in Sociology, in that, any dangers resulting from it will be detected by the preliminary theory of human nature, to which all speculations in the social science must be brought for guidance and correction.

Religious Government is established so soon as it is distinct from Political.

The separation, therefore, of the two powers, Spiritual and Temporal, marks the full maturity of the Social Organism; for, without it, the Organism is too incomplete for us to trace its general existence. It is, in fact, this feature which alone really distinguishes the human society from the highest of the animal societies. These often exhibit a domestic existence, having real analogies with our own, and sometimes the rudiments of a true civil existence, one even permanent and able to develop further but for man's exclusive ascendancy. But no animal society sufficiently combines sociability with intelligence, so as ever to form a religious association, in which mere community of thought unites groups wider in extent than those which result from common sympathies or common labours. We may here repeat to the self-assertion of Man what was said in the first volume (p. 502) about our too hasty judgment of the lower animal natures. We often mistake what is a mere arrest of development, mainly caused by obstacles from without,

Organised Religion the mark of mature human society.

for a real organic incapacity. This may well be the cause of the absence of organised religion in all other animal races; inasmuch as in ours Religious life is attained only after a long period of social existence; and from this the other races are debarred. Family, and even Property, at least in its collective form, precede and prepare for Religion regarded under its social aspect. As to the intellectual source of Religion, it differs little from similar ideas to which animal intelligences attain, at least up to the point where Fetichism develops into Astrolatry: a point never reached by the animals. Still, without pronouncing upon the nature of these obscure differences, their reality cannot be denied. The fact that Man alone of the animals has the capacity for forming a distinct religious society points to the high value of this faculty; one of which the results accumulated through generations are even greater than its immediate value.

Accordingly, notwithstanding the long period of time before the Religious association was really established, it may be traced in germ in the earliest rise of civilisation. The constant rivalry between the priests and the warriors was the result of the absolute doctrines prevalent in thought and the absolute view about national activity then current. Yet sociological analysis still detects the real distinction between the two great social powers. They would not have ultimately separated, never to be combined, had they not been from the first radically distinct; even when the persons who exerted these two powers chanced to be the same. We must not mistake this complete separation when it has been accomplished as the cause, but we must recognise it as the result, of an inherent diversity between the two; to take it for the cause is but one of those shallow metaphysical notions, where the form is taken for the substance.

It is attained, so soon as a Priesthood arises.

So long as the development of the Social Organism has not reached the point where it founds a special Priesthood, it remains in a state too rudimentary to allow of any proper estimate of its collective existence. Its character, indeed, is not sufficiently formed, even when the required number of Families are settled in a permanent City. The truth is that, up to this point neither can the spirit of generality rise superior to the spirit of detail, nor social to personal emotions, for want of a fitting organ.   But to do both is the real mark of any true society.   Without this instrument of organisation found in a Priesthood, every society is exposed to the disturbances awakened by the continual course of specialisation in human employment.

The ultimate separation between Priesthood and Govern- It may be
ment accordingly is a mere deduction from the law formulated from Aris-
by Aristotle, when that admirable conception in Statics is carried social law.
out to its legitimate results.   For, when society is organised in active Cooperation, and this is the characteristic of civil society, this itself becomes a constant source of differences, mental and moral.   And these would ever tend to destroy the association altogether, were it not preserved by some apparatus adequate to maintain the organisation.   Accordingly, the ground plan of Social Statics as a whole ultimately rests on the principle of the Distribution of functions, as I stated in the previous chapter (p. 234).   Thus Sociology is finally furnished with an invaluable centre for its Statical work, and its Dynamical will be in reality nothing but the development of this central principle to its necessary conclusions.   In fact, the principle of Distribution of functions, usually employed to explain the earliest rise of civil society, has now been shown to be the ground, on which we may ultimately construct our entire theory as contained in the last chapter respecting the most important creation of society—Religious Organisation.   This connection is again strengthened by the fact that the Civil or middle form of society has been taken at the outset of this chapter as the natural centre of Sociology.   Since the Church must, like the Family, though in a different way, constantly refer to the City, the principle originally stated for civic life must finally embrace the larger and the smaller modes of association.

Although he, its incomparable founder, could little foresee the results of his work, far off as they were and so contrary to the civilisation of his day, Aristotle must be more and more regarded as the creator of Social Statics.   The only part in the ultimate construction of the final science exclusively due to myself, beside the systematic deduction of the leading laws, is my discovery of the double law of Evolution, which harmonises the theory of Progress with that of Order (see ch. i. pp. 70–74). But I trust that the entire Treatise, whilst bringing out the importance of this leading idea, will awaken fresh veneration for the immortal Prince of true philosophers; to whom Dante, expressing the thought peculiar to the Middle Age, awarded the place of honour.

The Church systematises the Family and the City.

It results then that the abstract theory of Social Existence will be best understood and illustrated, by showing how the Church systematises the Family, and the City. For this end can only be attained by a priesthood which will inculcate sound general views expounding the organisation of life secured by the Family and the State. The idea could only be reduced to a positive form in our own day. Yet, if it has so long been enveloped in Theological fictions, they were unable to destroy its principal work; though they certainly not a little impaired its completeness.

Religious formula of Positivism.

It would be wrong to attribute any essential novelty to the sacred Formula of Positivists, which sums up human existence individual and collective and each of its modes: *The Principle, Love; the Basis, Order; the End, Progress.* This programme is new only in the systematic form given to it. But its substance may be seen in the oldest germs of it, for its roots lie deep in the unchangeable nature of man. Thus the middle term, or Order, made its appearance as a principle in the ancient Theocracies, embracing in itself, without extinguishing, the other two. As to the first term, I have already remarked that the continuous influence of the benevolent affections long preceded the theoretic explanation which they have now received. Before they had any sanction from the teaching of Religion, their existence was fully recognised by all the minds emancipated from the system of official belief, and certainly by the poets of antiquity. We might even say the same thing as to the last term of the formula, Progress; although it was long a fixed dogma that the order of human life was immutable. As to home life, we have the continual search after moral Progress held up to us as the noble end of Humanity in the most ancient monuments of human wisdom, the admirable books of the Hebrew Theocracy. As to public life, a sense of the same high aim is at once manifest, as soon as any true collective activity has been formed under the inspiration of the military system, with its universal thought of growing Empire. In this way, we may say that the formula adopted in its explicit form by the adult stage of Humanity may be found in its implicit form associated with the infancy and the youth of Humanity, and investing both with a new meaning.

In the same way we may trace the normal institution of the Priesthood, late as its actual establishment has been, showing itself in the most ancient attempts to give system to human life. It fulfils a purpose ever present in social needs, and springs from the necessities of our nature. Each of its essential conditions was spontaneously recognised in early times ; it is the organisation of them all into a system which is now for the first time achieved. The most crucial of all the requirements of a true Priesthood, the sincere and habitual renunciation of Power and even of Wealth, was always unconsciously preferred either by the great types of the priestly character, or by the general instinct, as being necessary for the intellect no less than for the heart. Catholicism in the Middle Age, even when the course of events drove it to sacrifice this fundamental duty from the very fact that its own fine attempt to found a Spiritual Power was premature, saw in the possession of Wealth and Power a certain cause of inward degradation. Again, when the Priesthood under a temporary but unavoidable necessity, as the next volume of this work will show, imposed the rule of celibacy on itself, it felt even more forcibly how contrary to the natural law was this violation of principle ; for the domestic affections are at once the source and the guarantee of true social feeling. The wisdom of the Theocracies which had been popularised by ancient Poetry, had made this estimate of the Family familiar to men's minds.

Lastly, the very constitution of the Spiritual Power, not only in itself but in its two social allies, will show us how the characteristics of the final system, as set forth in the General View, were at all times spontaneously active. In spite of the state of civil subjection in which Women were placed by the ancients, the natural affinity of the affectionate sex for the contemplative order of men, and their common opposition to the ascendancy of material force, gave a continual and valuable aid to the Priesthood. Long before the Middle Age, which first gave woman her just position, the Theocracies of Egypt, of Chaldæa, and of India, as afterwards those of Peru and Mexico, availed themselves largely of this domestic help for the due fulfilment of their social functions. The same thing is true of the powerful help of the People, who have attained their full

Germs of the Priest-hood as an institution.

social position even later than Women.   From the earliest ages
of Theocracy, the natural decomposition of material force into
the concentrated force of Wealth and the dispersed force of
Numbers (*see* chap. v. p. 225) supplied the Priesthood with an
aid similar to that of the modern proletariat, only less developed.
The military system could not prevent an influence of the same
kind; for we see of old the soldiers rising against their officers,
under the instigation of the Priests; often, it must be said, not
without just cause.

On every ground, therefore, we ought to avoid the metaphysical tendency to look only at the appearance in regular
form of the different human institutions, instead of at their
earliest spontaneous germ; for these are as ancient as civilisation itself.   The rule of Positive thought on the other hand
will direct the new priesthood to represent every organisation as
founded upon a long period of previous existence in an empirical
form.   In its essence the true form of any Spiritual Power must
always be radically the same.   Its duty is to change the will
without compelling actions.   It is very late that it succeeds in
obtaining systematic shape, and can disengage itself sufficiently
from the mysticism and the fictions under which its social
purpose lies concealed.   In our time it is more direct and more
complete, and its character therefore may be more easily understood.   But having thus grasped its spirit in the instance which
is best adapted to display it rightly, we may properly use this
type as an instrument to guide us in the positive study of all
preceding ages.   There is a reason also upon the moral ground
which enhances the value of this logical expedient; for the
Positivist priesthood are bound by a generous sense of fellowship towards all their predecessors under Theological and even
under Fetichist systems.   The Religion, which most strongly
brings out the idea and the feeling of human Continuity, will
naturally incline its ministers ever to regard themselves as the
heirs of the various Priesthoods of old.   But for this habitual
attitude of mind and of heart, they would be powerless in the
present day, even to picture forth the Great Being as coextensive with man's planet; since its different regions present still
types of religion which recall those of the various social ages.

Use of the
complete
type.

Such are the reasons which induce me to make free use of
the full-grown type of Humanity as an instrument for the abstract study of its Social Existence organised by the Priesthood.

In my General View, I have described in outline the natural Order of man ; and I shall now apply it to the service of my Statical study; since in abstract Statics we must disregard all considerations of time and of manner belonging to concrete realisation.   At the same time, this normal order will be treated only in its essential features : those which concern the mere end of *preservation*, apart from the question of *development*, except only so far as this is the necessary object of existence.

In this organisation of social Existence by the Priesthood, the leading principle rests on the two positive conceptions : of Human Order individual or collective, on the one hand ; and of the Universal Order of nature controlling it, on the other. This was the foundation of every truly religious doctrine under the incoherent fictions natural to the societies of the long infancy of man.   Even before civilisation had existed long enough to call out a real need for any organisation, every Family and every City from its origin felt the pressure of two insurmountable forces, the one artificial, the other natural.   On every side Man was forced to recognise the continual influence over him of the external order of Nature ; and beside this, each generation experiences the irresistible pressure upon its life of the whole of the preceding generations.   The influence of the Past indeed is commonly perceived even sooner than the influence of Nature.   A doctrine which aims at affecting human wills is bound to offer an explanation of this twofold Necessity ; so that each adherent it acquires may learn therein his own relations to the Whole, which he unconsciously contributes to form or to maintain.   A religion which does not do this, and to do it involves a simultaneous study of the World and of Man, will never receive that free acceptance which is indispensable for its effect over society.   But when this task is fulfilled, as far as the civilisation then current permits, a Priesthood necessarily obtains a Spiritual authority ; and this becomes the natural base of its threefold function, as we described it in the preceding chapter (p. 248, &c.).   What it has then to do, is only to arrange and teach this fundamental doctrine, whereby it acquires its hold over society, so long as its conduct is worthy of its great mission.   Such an intellectual vantage ground enables a true Priesthood, even when represented by a single capable head, within its own province to overcome the most powerful material force, whether of riches or of numbers.   In fact it will thus call

ORGANISA-
TION OF SO-
CIETY, pp.
289–300.

Every
Priesthood
must explain
the relation
of man (1)
to Nature
(2) to the
Past,

out, as I shall presently show, those morai and mental influences which the preceding chapter showed to be necessary to form and maintain these material forces.

i.e., Material Order, and Social Order; especially the latter.

This principle shows us, that for the religious organisation of every human society, there are two conditions requisite, which must be properly combined in durable union. In the first place the Priesthood must sufficiently comprehend the laws both of Material Order and Social Order; and consequently of the Vital Order which forms the link between them. On the other hand, it must gain the requisite acceptance of this synthetic conception; so as to satisfy the universal craving for instruction and direction, which forms its influence upon society. This implies that it should present a Philosophy, higher than the untutored suggestions of general opinion; and secondly, a system of general Education to infuse the views of the Priesthood into the public mind. Thus every Priesthood, after forming the best theory it can of the universal Order of Nature, is brought face to face with the standing problem of Social Order; which, apart from its greater difficulty and its superior importance, is directly concerned with the chief sacerdotal function. So long as this sphere of Social Order remains to it, it still retains, though with serious loss, a real influence over society; even when it has given up, one by one, its other intellectual claims. In the Middle Age we saw Catholicism in this position. But when any Priesthood abandons the social and proper field of its labours, it speedily loses its credit in the State, and next its power within the Home; for it is proved at length to be incompetent to fulfil its proper offices: to *counsel*, to *consecrate*, and to *control*; and thereby to *classify*, and finally to *judge*. Thus the final blow was inevitably given to Theology, retrograde as it had been since the end of the Middle Age, when the establishment of my system of Sociology cut from under it its old title to teach Morality and direct Society, a title which my great predecessor, Descartes, was willing that it should retain. Neither in the Family nor in the City can men choose freely as guides of their conduct in actual life priests who are without any sort of knowledge of the laws which regulate the facts of human existence. Public confidence, the only real basis of a Spiritual Power, will naturally be accorded to any Priesthood which can show that it has this knowledge of social laws; always provided that its own moral position is equal

to its claims.   Hence we shall soon see the inevitable triumph
of Positivism over Catholicism throughout the West and all its
associated communities.

This, the Positive organisation of Social Existence, based
on the fundamental theory of the Order of Nature, may be first
regarded from the point of view of human society as a whole,
and may then be illustrated by special explanation of the main
elements of that society.

Each City, in its entirety, presents us with a continuous cooperation of three kinds of social function, answering to the three
elements of man's cerebral system.   The same are perceptible
also in the Families which form the units of each City ; only in
domestic existence, these functions are represented not by classes,
but by individuals.   In the City they are more marked and
more easily analysed, as soon as the classes are sufficiently separated ; and they may be traced by sound philosophy in very
early societies.   The theory of Social Existence is thus the same
as that of the last chapter as to the Structure of the Social
Organism, that is to say, the coordinate action of three natural
Powers: special organs, personal or collective, of the Intellect,
the Feeling, and the Activity.   In the smallest cities capable
of separate existence, we find these three classes : the Priests
who guide our speculations, the Women who inspire our highest
affections, and the practical Leaders who direct our activity, be
it in war or in industry.   Here the Priesthood comes in the
first rank, because it is a question of political, not of domestic
existence ; with an ultimate view to social organisation, which
is always an intellectual function.   But, as shown in my General
View, such is not the ultimate order which the Positive Religion
assigns to these three classes ; for then the Heart must be publicly recognised as superior to the Intelligence, according to
the principles of man's unity.   When I explain in the fourth
volume this, the true order of rank, I hope that all will see the
social necessity for placing the moral providence of Humanity,
the special part of Women, above the intellectual providence,
the allotted function of the Priesthood.   Both take precedence,
according to cerebral order, of the material providence of the
temporal Chiefs ; though the latter takes precedence in the
corporal order, the sole direct link between the order of Man
and the order of the World.   Thus the noble ideal of our pious
and chivalrous ancestors in the Middle Age finds its support in

Three social functions in every City.

philosophy, in spite of the sophistical attacks of modern criticism.

But this first general view of Social Existence requires as a supplement a further step. The three Providences of human society, moral, intellectual, and material, present, by virtue of the very peculiarity of their natures, some serious inconveniences ; and these would disturb the general harmony, unless something arose to temper them all. Thus women are ever ready to exaggerate the influence of Feeling ; undervaluing that of Reason, and even that of Activity. In like manner the contemplative class, whose task it is to insist. everywhere on generality of ideas, has a tendency to over-estimate Theoretic conditions, to the neglect of Practical necessities and the wants of the Affections. The danger is increased when the separation between the Priesthood and the Government is effected, essential though this separation be to the true influence of a Spiritual Power. It would be unnecessary to insist on similar abuses even more common in the Practical authority, since it is these which mainly require a special Priesthood to restrain them. Thus each of the providences which direct this world, whilst duly fulfilling its own function, has a tendency to overlook the other two kinds of human wants.

It is true that the three mutually counterbalance each other, and do something to restrain their respective defects. But this would not be enough to prevent or to subdue violent conflicts between them, were it not that the Social Existence of itself called out a new order of providence, in direct connection with each of the three principal ones, and well fitted to preserve the harmony that should reign between them all. This is found in the mass of the People ; for they are united to the affectionate sex by domestic ties, to the Priesthood through the medium of the education and advice which it gives them, and to the practical leaders through common action and the protection afforded them. So long as national action remained in the warlike stage, the consequent slavery of the material workmen limited the people, properly so-called, to the body of free citizens. Yet even then this fourth social providence already began its proper task by leading the other three from too engrossing attention to their special parts. The name which modern civilisation seems inclined to adopt to designate this last element of the City, is drawn indeed from the language of antiquity. But the complete abolition of personal slavery was evidently needed that the Proletariat, the element in question, should become really free to play its part. The fourth volume treating of the final order of Humanity will show the great part sustained by this general Providence, which is so well adapted to remedy the defects inherent in the three special Providences. The third volume will trace the history in the past of the rise of the industrial proletariat, and thus explain the features of its normal condition.

We have thus obtained by analysis the four elements always present in civil existence. But this division strictly holds good only for the society of coexisting families: that is to say, for the Present, united by mere objective Solidarity. Now this is in no way a sufficient or ultimate analysis of human association, the grand feature of which it does not take into account. Societies in the other animal races exhibit, at any rate in a rudimentary form, similar characteristics, in every case ending in cooperation between the members. The special mark of the societies of man is that they alone possess the faculty of co-operation between generations; and this is a power which cannot long be possessed by more than one of the races upon earth. The great principle of Aristotle in its full comprehensiveness always implies a combination continuous in time, as well as a combination effective in space. Thus understood, this luminous conception may really serve as the single basis of Social Statics, and explain Existence no less than Organisation. Positivism gives this principle systematic completeness; and in obedience to it places objective Solidarity second to subjective Continuity. It is the latter which it takes as the dominant character of the human City.

To these four, representing Solidarity, must be added Continuity, the influence of the Past.

In this prime duty, the genius of the ancient Theocracies was at once the herald and the teacher of the genius of modern Sociocracy. For in private as in public life, they showed a noble and unflagging anxiety to kindle the sense of the Continuity of Man. So soon as we get the first rudiments of the Spiritual Power within the home, we have the Elders, forerunners of a Priesthood, as the very word priest suggests, occupying themselves especially with preserving the traditions of their race, long before Writing, even in its hieroglyphic form, was established. The chiefs of the Theocracies, the heirs of this patriarchal power, gave great extension to this high social duty; and it is yet over vast populations the chief relic of that venerable primæval stage.

Continuity was neglected by all systems since the Theocratic.

The arrogance of Catholicism which claims for itself titles of merit, such as impartial judges must refuse to it, is little justified by its complete inferiority in this respect.   The more man's Continuity increases, the greater becomes the importance of cultivating it.   The transitional Catholic creed confessed its speedy decay, when it began by condemnation of the two orders of civilisation which preceded it, and anathematised the intellectual life of Greece and the social organisation of Rome; nay, even its own Hebrew ancestors.   During the whole of its existence, the Catholic Church showed itself utterly incapable of restoring the chain of Continuity which, in the spirit of ingratitude and lawlessness, it had begun by breaking.   There were noble hearts and great intellects then, whom this practice inspired with pathetic regrets; yet they could do nothing to repair an error inherent in the absolute and egoistic temper of every Monotheistic creed, one from which the illustrious Mahomet could not free his admirable system of religion. During the anarchy of modern times we have recovered, it is true, the sense of human Continuity as regards Antiquity; but it has been shattered afresh as regards the Middle Age.   Men revile this great epoch with an ingratitude as senseless as that which the Church once poured upon Polytheism.   Positivism at length comes forward to redress the errors of both at once ; it raises the spirit of Continuity to its true intellectual and moral level, giving it every development that its nature can demand, extending it even to the Future, and treating it as higher than the Solidarity of the living.

Social influence of Subjective Immortality.

The Religion of Humanity transforms once for all the fantastic and gross idea of Objective Immortality, which had a value for a time, though that value is now exhausted, into the grand and solid truth of Subjective Immortality awaiting every worthy human spirit.   Just as the original fiction was in its essence anti-social, when its defects were not corrected by the wisdom of the Priesthood, so the new idea of Immortality will have power to call out and foster our social instincts, which root themselves around the Past even more strongly than around the Present.

Empire of the Dead over the Living.

I asserted in the first chapter (p. 55), and I shall prove as a principle in the fourth volume, that the Living are always, and ever more and more, in essentials governed by the Dead.   The irresistible dominion of Subjective over visible Humanity forms in the social existence of each of us an element wholly incapable of change. This empire was felt and recognised in the oldest antiquity, but it naturally increases ever without end. Accordingly, the presumption of seeking to escape from it forms the main symptom of that chronic unsoundness of mind which seems to be falling on the West ever more and more since the Middle Age. It is this wholesome dominion of the Past which prevents the Insurrection of the Present from getting the head which is threatened. It is ever bringing the movement of Humanity into greater harmony; reducing the sources of discord, and it will soon succeed in making the course of civilisation clearer than is that of some planets. This is the explanation of the fact, that the laws of individual life are a study more complex than the laws of social life. The former is more exposed to the attack of forces transcending any prevision; and thus I make the study of the individual existence, or Morality, the seventh and the last of the series in the Classification of the Sciences.

The ascendancy over us which this cooperation of Past generations possesses, will be better understood when we see how it is multiplied by the extension of the cooperation between contemporaries in Space. When the Great Being is fully established throughout the human Planet, each City will be constantly subject to the pressure of authority from all preceding generations, and that not from the immediate local predecessors but from the entire human race.

Empire of contemporaries over the Living

A striking observation, suggested by the wise Franklin, shows us how under the merely physical aspect, no single family can ever be treated separately; and we may extend the observation from the Family to the State. As every one of us has two parents in the first degree, and as each of these had the same, the human populations would be, as we ascend the course of ages, infinitely more numerous if each of us had always had different persons as ancestors. The contrary, as reason and experience show us, is the truth. Thus, if we desire to trace simply the hereditary physical organisation of any individual existence, we shall have at once to extend our inquiries far beyond his particular Family, or even his particular City. This is an excellent illustration of the truth, that the spirit of generalisation is far more sound as a guide in social studies, than the spirit of specialisation.

Intermixture of Families.

Hence, in Sociology, the true point of view is to regard the

The Present
holds but a
subordinate
place in life. Objective Solidarity between men as ever of less importance than the Subjective Continuity of ages. The wisdom of the Theocracies discerned this truth; but Positivism finally reduced it to system. Continuity, not Solidarity, is the great moving force of man's destinies, especially in our modern times. The Present is but a vague and fleeting span which fills the interval between two immensities of duration, and binds them the one to the other. To live only, or even chiefly, in the Present, would be as irrational in philosophy as it is depraved in morality, and it must issue in interminable scepticism. In my first treatise in 1822 (see vol. iv. App. 1), I showed how we ought to qualify the celebrated aphorism of Leibnitz—' The chronological order of epochs is not their philosophical order: instead of saying the Past, the Present, and the Future, we ought to say, the Past, the Future, and the Present.' In fact, the Present, this middle term in mere order of time, can only be properly conceived by the aid of the two extremes which it unites and separates; following thereby a law of logic which I have frequently used before.

Continuity,
the chief
sphere of the
Priesthood; Such, therefore, is the main duty which the Priesthood is called on to fulfil in Society. Although necessarily the organ of the largest extent of Solidarity, its exclusive sphere is certainly Continuity with the Past and the Future; and this no temporal authority will be able long to dispute with it. Objectively, the City is no doubt superior to the Church, no less than to the Family; for otherwise strange tendencies to mysticism would set in, as I showed at the opening of this chapter. But in subjective existence the inherent superiority of religious society over the political, is as undeniable as it is over the domestic. Now it is the religious existence which must ultimately determine the character of our civilisation. Thus the superior dignity of the Priesthood has its foundation in fixed necessities of our nature, and this every government will more and more respect as these necessities are better understood.

But not
apart from
the External
World. For these reasons the Spiritual Power will be disposed, even by its own ambition, to regard the facts of society in the truly synthetic aspect; since its own influence on the Public or on the Family directly depends on this. But, though this twofold conception of the consensus in man's life, as due at once to the action of Solidarity and Continuity, must be the principal

object of religious education, it must never be conceived or studied by itself apart. For the conception of the social Order of Man ever depends on the universal Order of Nature, in its two sides of Inorganic and Organic.

From the first birth of society, the Priesthood felt the reality of this dependence of Man on Nature, even in the reign of Theological figments and Metaphysical subtleties. The chief use of these Gods and Entities, first intellectually and then socially, was to supply the place of real knowledge of this essential Order, impossible as this was, and to present Causes where Laws were not conceived. In fact, the general system of the Polytheistic Theology, as afterwards that of the Mono- theistic Creed, whether Catholic or Musulman, was in the main a provisional representation of the Economy of Nature, the natural foundation for any Economy of Society. If this latter had ever been conceived in the isolated way which our metaphysical extravagance would dictate, no religion would ever have obtained any real moral and social power. The instability natural to the human Order, the result of its ex- treme complexity of structure, everywhere awakens a general desire to unite it in thought with the more fixed and more in- telligible Order presented by the much simpler external World. Besides, every one feels himself in his own person under the direct yoke of this general Economy of Nature, first in its physical, but still more in its vital influence. Its prin- cipal pressure, however, is an indirect one, by the medium of the Social Order which it influences, and which in turn acts as a providence to temper this yoke to us, when civilisation is in full force. At the same time this is a fresh reason to study more carefully the order of Nature ; in order that we may sub- mit with true good sense to those conditions which cannot be modified, and that we may remedy those which can.

Every religion attempts to explain this World.

Our intellect is under a threefold necessity, on logical, scientific, and lastly technical reasons, to begin with a thorough study of the Order of Nature, as a preparation for direct study of the Order of Human Life, though the latter must ever be the goal of our ultimate speculation. Positivism has only given formal shape to this normal condition of thought, by showing its relation to the Scale of the Sciences; and thus is clothing with definite sanction one of the oldest maxims of human wisdom. The Subjective Synthesis of Positivism is

Dependence of the higher Order on the lower.

thus based upon a vast system of Objective Analysis, the great end of which may easily be lost in the prolonged education it involves. But the whole of this introductory scheme of science may be in its entirety summed up in a single law, at once objective and subjective : that the nobler Order invariably depends upon the lower Order. This is the most general law of the World and of Man : no other law can ever have this feature of universal applicability. If it be worked out on system, it will give to the entire scientific Education a true unity of thought, which ought to prevent or restrain all scientific wanderings after knowledge without an object.

The two great laws of Man and the World.

The two great laws whereby the Priesthood will explain social existence and its external basis are these :—first, the essential superiority of Continuity over Solidarity, and secondly, the dependence of the higher Order on the lower Order. The entire scheme of Scientific Education may be reduced to a mere development of these two correlative principles, which Positivism has established better than any form of Theology. But to make the religious Unity complete, it is not enough that it embrace the entire domain of Thought, and even that of the Activity. It must rule also in the Affective Existence, the true centre of human nature.

Both harmonised by the conception of Humanity.

This indispensable condition, without which there can be no religious unity, happily offered no difficulty in the spontaneous growth of primitive Religion. Fetishism indeed met the want of itself; and the Theological, especially the Polytheistic, systems were naturally even more favourable to it. On the other hand how to meet this condition is the grand difficulty of the final Religion, as we saw in the first chapter of this volume (p. 46). Positivism moving originally from without inwards, required a long preparation before it could raise the General Order of Nature into an object of universal and constant affection, instead of being a mere subject of speculation and action. And before this could be done, it needed that the most complex and noblest of all phenomena, the human, should be brought within the general Reign of Law. But for the immense difficulty which this involved, Positivism would long ago have replaced Theology ; for all great minds in turn, from Thales and Pythagoras downwards, have shown a settled bias towards positive methods of reasoning. The good sense of the public would have supported this tendency in the superior minds, and would have seen that the study of Laws was more adapted than that of Causes to supply real prevision capable of guiding action. All these difficulties in the way of the final establishment of Positivism have been now settled by the adoption of the doctrine of Humanity.

This doctrine was explained in the General View; it was then confirmed in the first chapter of this volume; and leaving to the third .olume the history of its development, the fourth volume will give the direct proof on which it rests. It is however already treated sufficiently to serve as the complete centre of the Positive Synthesis, in its affective as in its speculative or active side. It combines the idea of the Order of Man with the Order of the World, by representing the former as the necessary summing up of the latter. By means of this close connection between the two, the Order created by Man acquires the coherence of the natural Order, and inclines us to tenderness for the Natural, as the source of the Human, Order. It thus renews under a better form the Nature worship of Fetishism. This Positive Unity, being at once objective and subjective, meets the moral requirements better than its different Theological predecessors could do ; for they were all unable to take within their influence the dominant form of activity. Late as its advent has been, yet when it is fully established in its place, human existence will not ask how prolonged was the period required for its evolution.

Forming an Objective and Subjective unity.

With this conception of Humanity directly before us, there will henceforth be no necessity for the education of the individual to repeat the slow process of the education of the race; although the intellectual movement is at bottom the same in both. For, with this aid, the study of the External World may be recast from the Human point of view, as in my preceding volume I suggested for the whole of Science, and as I worked it out for Biology. Education thus will from the beginning have its goal marked out for it, and will thus never be wasted in useless academic studies ; for every science will serve only as the step to ascend to the next. Yet I have already remarked, that in the Positive education, the study of the Physical Sciences will always occupy more time than that of the final Science of Society, to which only the last two years of the seven years' course are devoted. But when once the school is quitted, the mind will easily restore the balance between the study of Nature

And this conception will give a paramount place to Sociology.

and that of Man, just as forty centuries ago was done by the
wisdom of the Theocracies. Sociology, absorbing within itself
Biology as its introduction, and Morality as its conclusion, will
necessarily overshadow Cosmology as a whole, first in the minds
of the Priesthood, and then in the instincts of the Women and
the People. The practical duties of Life will require the Temporal leaders to develop specially those branches of Cosmology,
which are directly concerned with their industrial operations,
as I have elsewhere explained (see vol. i. pp. 351, 385, &c.).

Three As-
pects of
Social Ex-
istence.
I. Moral,
pp. 300–308.   Such, in its entirety, is the substance of the doctrine which
the Priesthood will enforce as to Social Existence and the
general Order of Nature which governs it. This twofold conception, properly worked out and inculcated by the Common
Education, supplies the logical ground of the due authority of
the Spiritual Power. But this general view must be completed
by treating separately Social Existence under its three principal
aspects, Moral, Intellectual, and Material. Without this threefold complement, our conception of Existence would not adequately harmonise with that of Structure. And only thus can
we obtain a true estimate of the influence exercised by the
Priesthood over the whole of our real life : an influence which
is founded uniformly on the intellectual and moral effect of a
general Religious education.

The order in which these should be treated is naturally
determined by that in which the three human Providences
exert their influence. For although the influence of all is always
simultaneous, yet the ordinary course of life brings each of
them in turn into prominence. During the period of education,
we feel but slightly the regular power of the Temporal Authority ; because the Family and the City preserve us from the
cares which concern Government. Accordingly, our social
existence is mainly Moral up to puberty and is directed by
women. It becomes during youth mainly Intellectual, and is
directed by the priests. When these two phases of education
are completed, those who directed them finally lose their dominant influence. They deeply modify real life ; but it is henceforward under the power of the Material providence. This
natural order, in which the action of the three Social Powers is
applied to every existence, is the order also in which they stand
according to increasing energy and decreasing dignity. I omit
here any consideration of the temporal conditions needed for

the free play of the duties, whether of Women or of the Priesthood. These conditions I shall consider in treating the general duties of the material Providence, which principally consist in duly distributing the common means of support that it has in reserve. I only suppose a condition in the temporal sphere, most favourable to the proper fulfilment of the Affective and Speculative functions in society.

All human education is called upon to teach every man To Live for others, in such a manner that he may hereafter Live in others. This according to the Positive Religion is the constant end, as it is the necessary result, of the sum of our existence; and it is but the direct adoption of the indirect precepts left us by the Religions of the past. Under the early Theocracies, and then under Military Polytheism, every citizen was always educated with a view to take his part in the society in which he was born; and its grateful remembrance of his career was ever the highest recompense in death. Down to the Middle Age, the egoistic nature of the belief in Objective Eternity was wisely checked by giving force to the Subjective Immortality which the citizen received from the City; and this held good even under the Jewish Monotheism. Positivism therefore does nothing but reconstruct on system that which Theology had always spontaneously taught in its earlier forms. The final form of Theology, Catholicism, abandoned this appeal to Patriotism; but the real service of Catholicism was the admirable though premature attempt to institute the separation of the Temporal and Spiritual Powers. The reality peculiar to Positivism enables it for the first time to make the law of Happiness coincide with the law of Duty; for it teaches as a sacred truth the independent existence of man's sympathetic instincts, the sources at once of his Duty and of his Happiness. But the conception of the Order of Humanity is no new discovery of the final Religion, any more than is that of the Order of Nature. What Positivism has to offer towards a better knowledge of both, is only a theory more real, more complete, and more systematic than any offered by older religions. But a conception of both kinds of Order, the human as well as the physical, in forms less direct and less pure, was always the essential basis of Religious Doctrine during all the various phases of early civilisation. For each side of Social Existence, as we showed just now for Social Existence as a whole, the

The Positive view of it coincides with that of older religions.

picture we frame for the adult stage of Humanity will apply to the undeveloped age, though it be in that obscured by temporary fictions, such as any strong mind will now easily discard.

Moral Existence always commences in the Family,

Looked at in this light, Social Existence is at first moral; and of necessity it begins in the Family, under the teaching of the Mother, the source of all education. This spontaneous training with which life opens will always be in admirable harmony with the requirements of any real organisation of human life; for this will be based, and will be ever more and more based, upon the principle, that the Heart must hold the first place. Within the Home, we learn to love, and soon to understand, the Order that man creates, before we love or understand the Order that we find in the World. The Home calls out our affections first for our parents, who represent Continuity, and then for our brethren, who represent Solidarity. By all these ways, the Family trains us by easy steps to a sense of the Subjective Synthesis from the common centre of Man; and it lessens the dangers we may meet in the Objective Instruction in the Sciences, on which the Subjective Synthesis must ultimately be based. And thus, by a long cultivation of the various domestic affections, we found Religion on Love before it is crowned by Faith.

Under the influence of Women.

This admirable discipline of the Home, which nothing can replace, and which the entire course of our existence will continually deepen, forms the main function in society of the Affective Sex. But to perform it, Woman must be absolutely free from the necessity of labour without the family, and must be free to devote herself to her Providence within it. She must at the same time surrender all claim to temporal authority, even to authority within the house, and must content herself with that form of influence which comes from her moral superiority. These two conditions of Woman's life were from the first sought by instinct, though the theoretic reason for them is late in asserting its ground. Our social arrangements always steadily conformed to them, at least in the classes of easy circumstances; and no others are yet organised on any system at all.

It is enlarged by Marriage,

This Moral Existence within the Family is principally defective in that it limits our sympathies to too narrow a sphere. But this narrow sphere is at the commencement indispensable to their free growth; and sympathies would be nothing but vague and empty sentiment if the object of them were at first too remote.   However, this essential foundation once laid, moral existence acquires new proportions, when the influence of the City brings the various families into common relations, and the Priests put a ban upon the incestuous unions, which in early ages were customary.   Only on reaching this stage does Domestic life become the natural basis of Civil life.

There was on intellectual grounds even earlier evidence of the close relations between Domestic and Civil life in the fundamental institution of Language.   Though having its origin in the Family, Language only acquires any complete development, even in the type of it which we know among the smaller tribes, by the medium of a society, wider and less close than the Family.   Where this exists, the mother's teaching awakens in her child the idea of the City almost as early as affection for the Family.   But this gradual training of ideas would be inadequate to produce any profound connection between the Domestic and the Civic form of Moral Existence, were it not that our instincts of sympathy have a native power of self-expansion.   They give rise at length to that potent yearning for a mate, which urges the heart of man to find satisfaction beyond the limits of the primitive domestic circle.   But we must remember that this great step in progress, Marriage outside the pale of the family, a thing we nowadays regard as simply spontaneous, is in truth the first grand blessing which we owe to human wisdom ; for the difficult transformation of life it implies could never have been accomplished but for the untiring interference of society.   When we observe how incestuous marriages have received legal sanction, now that the anarchy of modern times has broken down the ancient religious discipline, we may learn how completely the great institution of regular Marriage is an artificial creation of human society. How to guarantee it, and how to perfect it as a practice, will soon engage the active care of the new Priesthood.

Essentially a Civic Institution.

This critical stage once passed, Moral Existence tends towards its true unity, which is not Domestic but Civic.   The noble institution of Marriage places the Family under the influence of the City ; just as in every individual life it generalises the affections, by giving a new weight to domestic ties, the result not of nature but of choice.   Domestic life only through

Family.

Marriage begins to display its main function, which is to free us from the early state of Personality, and then by degrees to raise us to the full sense of Sociability ; yet never so as to stop short at collective egoism. It is true that this spirit long seemed in danger of stopping at this point of national selfishness, whilst Military Activity held its inevitable supremacy ; yet, nevertheless, we may see in the most ancient poems, in the midst of their pictures of slaughter, clear traces of aspiration towards a life of Universal Benevolence.

Patriotism is the typical form of Social Feeling.

At the same time, Patriotism in its true sense, and even if limited to simple Civism, will ever be the most usual type of the true social feeling. For if, on the one hand, our instincts of sympathy have a native tendency to multiply their relations, our affections require for their full energy that the objects of them be constantly brought into presence with us. Were there not active and daily fellowship in common labours, and this is possible only in the City, there could be no expansion of universal Love ; for a close identity of Belief would not be sufficient to form it. The union between Citizens will always represent the most extensive group of those affections which appeal equally to every part of our existence, Material, Intellectual and Moral.

But the State must be reduced to its normal limits of the City.

Aspirations of the vaguest kind lead the modern admirers of Patriotism to look with contempt upon the narrow limits of the ancient City. But the regeneration of life at which Positivism aims, will soon reestablish the normal limit of extension of which this feeling of Patriotism is capable in practice. We shall restore the spirit of ancient manners by bringing into full harmony the different kinds of Civism under common subordination to the Great Being. The Middle Age gave us an admirable foretaste of this harmony, even whilst the Military life was still in the ascendant, by means of the fellowship which united nations in their acceptance of a common Faith. A permanent and complete union, however, between peoples can never be secured but by a general devotion to Industrial activity, which will bring about in all countries a sense of willing cooperation with each other. Industrial competition too often leads to bitter rivalries ; but the Priesthood will succeed in transforming these into a useful spirit of emulation. Under this system, the bond between citizens, like the love within the home, will foster of itself a true affection for society, without trenching on the Religious sense of harmony, for which these sentiments will form the final moral training. Were the spirit of Patriotism trained to aspire after grand nationalities, it would induce the coarser minds to attempt schemes of oppression, that they might everywhere realise a form of State centralisation and political bureaucracy far beyond the degree natural to free civic union. The principle, however, of separation between Government and Priesthood will naturally prevent these sources of disturbance, whenever the Positive Religion has obtained sufficient influence.

When thus restored to its proper place of first importance, the Civic sentiment will tend to act most happily upon the Domestic affections; it will strengthen, purify, and enlarge them. How this may be brought about, was fully shown by the genius of Rome for social progress. With her, Civism in its noblest sense served only to add fresh dignity to the principal duties of the Family ; whilst the opinion of Greece condemned the virtues of the Home as incompatible with those of the Citizen. *Rome shows us, how Patriotism may elevate the Family.*

To place our Public above our Private life is as useful to the one as to the other ; for thus only can we arrive at our true state of Unity. Our Domestic affections become at once stronger and nobler, when we feel that they inspire us with fresh energy for our Civic duties. This is the only manner in which the Providence of Women can take regular part in political life. A more direct participation in affairs would soon taint the moral superiority of the loving sex; for this moral superiority requires for its growth the sanctity of the Home, where alone there cannot enter the temptations of ambition or the engrossing cares of interest. Yet Mother, Wife, and Daughter gain fresh self-respect in their own eyes, and new dignity in ours, when they are felt to be the fountain where true citizens have drunk in the inspiration of an honest Patriotism. Such is the profound connection of our different sympathies, that women will soon perceive, how Civic enthusiasm is far from troubling the Domestic affections ; but, on the contrary, when well directed will give them consistency and elevation. For, each citizen feels towards this Moral Providence an instinct of lively gratitude which is soon augmented by consciousness that the same spirit animates his fellow-citizens. Private life becomes everywhere the necessary school of Public *Public life ennobles Private life.*

life, and naturally shares in the honour which is due to Public virtue.

Not only ought every true citizen to aspire *to live again in others*, but he should also aspire to procure a like immortality for the women to whom his moral character is so much indebted. Very exceptional cases apart, women have no other way of obtaining a Subjective Future life, outside the domestic circle. Yet this indirect immortality through others is a sufficient compensation to them, when sounder views of human nature have established the empire of the Heart over the whole of our existence. When we come to treat more particularly of the final worship, we shall show how the honour of the individual ought to be crowned by the just gratitude of the public towards all those whose influence has conspired to make him worthy of this reward. My own story, I hope, will afford an instance more marked even than the union of the name of Beatrice with that of Dante in the memory of the West. For as the great Religious System I have founded grows and increases, the hearts and the intelligence of my followers will tell them, what I express in the Dedication, how large and how profound a share in it is borne by my sainted Clotilda.

By this reaction, women share in public life.

Instances like this are far from being exceptions ; they point to the definite standard of regenerate Humanity, when a real and complete doctrine of life will confirm the judgments of the Priesthood, and this community of life will be familiar to all. But for the blind Metaphysical spirit which sees no close unity in the various functions of the Brain, there would be nothing strange that the mother, the wife, or the daughter of one eminent in action or in speculation should be publicly honoured as his colleagues. The Middle Age, in its own artless way, recognised this undoubted duty ; but the Positive Religion will give it a large development, by making generally known the true theory of human nature. It will be felt universally that if the direction in the world of Affection belonging to the loving sex is confined to the Domestic Existence, it is nevertheless Woman who disposes of the Moral Providence as a whole, even on the side of our widest social relations.

This sacred influence within the Home, whilst never departing from that sphere where only it is really strong, inspires in truth our whole civic existence, bringing out the moral disposition best fitted to each duty, whether in action or in specu-

lation. Properly extended, it becomes the chief base of the
only real solution of the great problem of Humanity, the constant
supremacy of Altruism over Egoism. Not only does it turn
each separate life on all its sides towards daily service of
Humanity; but it gives a charm to the smallest details by
throwing over them a moral purpose, without which many
social functions would be too repugnant to perform. We are
even in this way inclined towards a spirit of submission, partly
arising from nature, and partly from training, which we need to
regulate our conduct in life, and which assists in stimulating
our better instincts by curbing our personal desires. When
this moral education has been recognised as the source of true
happiness, public as well as private, it will be seen how right
Positive Religion has been to adopt a universal tendency of
mankind, by seeing in the affectionate sex the leading human
Providence. In accordance with the instincts of Chivalry,
Woman ought to possess for ever the privilege of supreme
Grace, which the godhead of old kept strictly to himself, in the
midst of all concessions to his representatives on earth.

For the perfecting of the sex itself, Women need no other
public care or protection, except that all scrupulously respect
the conditions of their proper part. Theirs is the only function
in society which, in its own limits, is not exposed to any special
degeneration. Nothing tends more to bring out our good
feelings than their habitual exercise in a right spirit; and it
will therefore be enough if we can secure to women the independence and the concentration needed for their part. In the
bosom of the Family they form instinctively a true Spiritual
Power, the earliest regular source of any modifying influence,
the precious private allies of the universal Priesthood. In
accordance with the principle of the superiority of the Heart,
Women in the normal system will have the superintendence of
the entire education, and even the exclusive direction of that
part of it which takes place within the home, leaving the
Priesthood only its ultimate systematisation. There are intellectual reasons for this distribution of parts, in that the highest
of all natural laws, those relating to our moral existence, will
always need woman's training. Not that Woman will ever be
able to give to this instinctive education that systematic
arrangement which belongs to the Priest. But he will learn

x 2

from the affectionate sex those special truths which need a purity and a delicacy beyond the scope of the male intellect.

II. INTEL-
LECTUAL
EXISTENCE,
pp. 308–318.

We have now completed our review of Moral Existence; and are naturally brought to consider Intellectual Existence, which must ever be regarded as dependent upon the Moral. Whether we study it in its special organs or in its general development, we may here limit our view of it to the General System of Education.

Its general
purpose.

The object of this Education, the indispensable complement of the training of the Home, is to direct us towards a general knowledge of the Order of Man, and of the Order of Nature governing that Order, with a view to discipline us to submit to both these Destinies over our lives, whilst actively seeking to modify them. But this object of Education would be disturbed by the dispersive character belonging to all abstract efforts of our feeble intellects, if we had not been previously disposed ever to place the end above the means. This is the reason why the Providence of the Priesthood should not be exercised over us until we have experienced the Providence of Women. This prolonged influence predisposed us to place the Heart above the Head. Of the different exercises of the mind, it taught us to prefer artistic training, as more closely allied to the impulses of the affection, scientific culture being limited to what was strictly needed for wise activity. Lastly, as I have just showed, it introduces us to Moral laws earlier than to Physical laws, though both in a practical not a scientific way; and thereby it exhibits the study of the Human Order as the principal object of every system of Truth.

Its limits.

For all these reasons, a domestic preparation of this kind, in complete accord as it is with the general centre of human civilisation, can alone preserve the education of the individual from the inherent evils to which the intellectual part of Education is so prone. The home introduction is the more proper, inasmuch as the dogmatic part of Education should proceed, as it did in the history of the race, from the World to Man. Education is thus ever in danger of giving too large a part to the introduction, Cosmology, at the expense of Sociology, its end; for the higher importance of this latter must be previously engrained into the mind by the force of habit, which cannot be secured by any philosophic exordium. Nor need we fear that the study of the Order of Nature will be cramped by that precept of General Philosophy which confines it to the limits of what is needed for the right conception of the Order of Man. For the first volume has shown us sufficiently how much the principal problems of Science gain by this essential limitation of its field. Without this no philosophic unity is possible, for Science is exhausted in academic specialism. We have also seen how fully this limit includes in Science all the ideas required for Man's active intervention in Nature, apart from the working out of special subjects, the place of which is in technical education.

Thus defined, the speculative domain of the Priesthood is essentially confined to the intellectual Laws, which in all ages have been theirs by special privilege. As to the moral and physical laws, the business of the Priesthood is really but one of systematisation; for the materials of both are furnished by that spontaneous education, in the first case given by Women, in the second case given by temporal leaders. In both departments the true speculative genius would gain by attending to this practical education, far more than modern savants suppose in their blind pride. Our best knowledge of moral and physical truth comes really from this source; and under a general system of Education it will be brought into closer relations with theory. The first chapter of this volume proved sufficiently (pp. 22–41) that neither moral laws nor physical laws alone admit of any separate systematisation, and that both sets of laws can only be coordinated by means of intellectual laws, holding the middle place between them. It is thus that we get the exclusive fitness of the Priesthood to establish any systematisation. In truth, although intellectual laws are imprinted upon all our studies, whether moral or physical, they are not easily seized by minds occupied with practice, and applying knowledge without a due sense of the value of its coordination. On the contrary, the class whose task it is to systematise our existence is bound to fix its principal attention on the laws special to the understanding; for the hold that these laws acquire over the thinking faculty necessarily determines the mode of every sort of Synthesis.

Intellectual laws the proper sphere of the Priesthood;

This great theoretic mission of expounding the Laws of Thought was always recognised by the Priesthood of the Theocracies, although it could only be duly realised by a Sociocratic Priesthood; for it required an indispensable basis, such as could only be secured by a long scientific evolution. But it enters into the very foundation of any true system of General Education, since there can be no systematic teaching without a knowledge of the laws of mind. Reciprocally, to make our study of mental science part of our general training, is better than to treat it as itself forming an abstract science. For it obliges us, under pain of practical failure, always to conceive our intellectual growth in its strict relations with the whole of man's existence, individual and collective. The utter emptiness of all attempts to constitute Psychology in metaphysical isolation as a substantive Science was seen in a practical way by the ancient Priesthoods, both Theocratic and Catholic. To direct minds to any purpose, they saw that it needed ideas more real and more complete than those which satisfied mere talkers.

Require long special study. A foundation for this study of Laws of Thought was laid in my early philosophical pieces (see vol. iv. App.), where I established the two connected laws which regulate human Evolution, whether for society or for the individual. But, even with this general foundation, the Positive Priesthood will need a long and difficult training in the history of the Progress of the human Mind. The organisation and development of universal Education will supply them at once with an unquestionable programme of study, and with a guide which cannot be misled.

They depend on the External and the Internal Order which govern our lives. With this end clearly in view, all will feel how completely our Intellectual existence depends, like the Affections and the Activity with which it is bound up, on the twofold destiny imposed on it, first by the Order of the World without, and secondly by the Order of Man within. Its dependence on these two Orders is indeed greater than that of the other sides of our nature, for the business of the Intelligence is to combine the two Orders in one.

The Brain must become an accurate mirror of the World. Since the object of every Theory is to represent the External with accuracy, our success in speculation depends on our fashioning our Subjective Conceptions into correspondence with our Objective Impressions. Although the intellect for a long period rejects this discipline as incompatible with its earliest efforts at philosophy, yet it is the only mode in which definitive results can be secured. Besides this, our original independence of thought is naturally restricted by the reaction of our practical necessities over our theoretic ideas; and these being strictly subjective are forced to yield to the influence of hard fact.

Perfect harmony, however, between Contemplation and Action can only be obtained in the completely Positive state. We then directly perceive that the most difficult and most important effort of our intellectual existence is the forming of the human Brain into an exact mirror of the Order of Nature. This is the sole mode in which Intelligence can become the direct source of our complete unity; binding the life of Affection and the life of Action in one common aim.

This transfiguration of Nature in Mind becomes possible by virtue of the necessary part played by the Order of Nature in our own Mental activity; for Nature ever supplies Mind with materials. Besides thus supplying Mind with its first food, Nature acts on it also as a stimulant, and indeed as a regulator, as it does in all the other vital functions, vegetative or animal. These three influences are closely associated, and all spring from a single cerebral law; which, though the facts it explains had been noted, has never been put till now into systematic form. It is this: that Objective Impressions have naturally a force superior to Subjective Results. Our outward sensations outweigh our inward forming Ideas. *Law that impressions are more potent than ideas.*

If our images formed within the Mind could become as intense as our sensations of the World without, our mental condition would never admit of stability, and, consequently, our practical existence would become incoherent, or rather incapable of control. In the first place, our conceptions of the World without would be utterly disturbed by the force with which ideas within would throng in beside them. But, further, the disturbance would be increased by the presence of a multitude of independent images at once, so equal in strength as to neutralise any mutual arrangement. It is only the ascendancy of the External Spectacle we observe over all our ideas whatever, that can give any order to our thoughts; for they thus find themselves subject to the weight of an unchangeable Power outside. When, under excitement in the brain, our mental recollections become more intense than our sensations of the facts, our reason is passing into a morbid state. However, when this morbid condition is confined to exaltation only of the observing apparatus, our reflecting apparatus is able to restore the balance. When, on the contrary, our reflecting processes overpower our sensations in energy, we reach the distinctive mark of actual insanity. *Otherwise, the mind could not act coherently.*

The human
Mind is
therefore
subject to
the World;

Thus, the necessary basis of mental harmony, and so of our whole cerebral economy, is found in this truth : that the Mind within be ever subordinate to the World without. Although this influence directly concerns only Observation, it affects indirectly Meditation by reason of their natural connection; especially when thought acts under conditions sufficiently fixed, and with the help of signs. The uniform presence before us of a Power Without cooperates in our mental development, however little we perceive it ; firstly, by recalling the Mind to its right purpose, through relations with reality more or less direct ; secondly, by restraining its subjective aberrations under the superior weight of the objective world. And so, sound Philosophy, completing and systematising the primary maxim of Aristotle, represents Man as subject to the World, not only as respects the body but also as respects the Mind.

And mental
are subordi-
nate to gene-
ral laws.

Each class of phenomena has doubtless its own laws not derived from the rest of the economy of Nature. But they are always subordinate to the laws of all the less complex and more general phenomena. If the intelligence were freed from this external influence, its aberrations would not be free from all limit. In the first place, it would be still under the force of the affective instincts, and consequently, of the reaction over them of the organs of vegetative life. Hence, to observe directly the laws of the understanding, we must get rid of this internal regulation. We shall, therefore, only get indirect ways of observing these laws, by means of their constant association with our chief ideas ; and the reaction upon these of the affections is very variable, and disappears at once in the progress of the race collectively.

Mind is de-
pendent on
Environ-
men ;

But this essential basis for our study of the Laws of Mind leaves in full force, and even brings out more clearly, the second invariable element of the great dualism, the External stimulus of Mind. The relative shares of the two are not fixed. Two observations, the converse of each other, serve to prove to us day by day the general dependence of the Understanding on the Order of Nature. Under very unfavourable surrounding conditions, the mind is incapable of any regular work. Again, the vagueness and incoherence of our ideas when we shut our eyes, without sleeping, is an evidence of this dependence of Mind on Fact ; although the objects we see are not those upon which the mind directly dwells. It is therefore impossible to dispute the natural tendency of our Intelligence to yield itself up to the Spectacle of the World without, so as ultimately to reproduce it to us in a systematic way. Still, this natural disposition is very late in becoming habitual, either in consequence of the difficulties of adequately explaining the External Order, or by reason of the vagaries of the Mind, springing from inexperience and maintained by our personal instincts. It is no exaggeration to say, that this harmony between the World and Mind, the chief product of our long civilisation, is hardly yet established even in the better understandings; and even then it is too often overthrown by the least burst of passion.

As to the other constitutional influence to which the intellect is subjected, that of the vital organs, it is no less indisputable henceforth in spite of the foolish assumptions of Metaphysicians to the contrary. Since Cabanis and Gall wrote, there is little need to prove that Thought is not an isolated function of our nature, having no part in the general consensus of vital phenomena. But the subordination of Thought to social influences is not so well accepted as its connection with organic conditions. Nevertheless, the former is just as certain as the power over Thought of the World without, when we regard it from the point of view needed for systematic estimate. That is to say, the laws of thought can only be understood by the aid of Sociology, as certainly as they are connected with the laws of Biology. And all of them are governed by the more general laws of Cosmology. *And further, upon Vital influences,*

The entire bearing of this work relieves me from the need of any explanation in detail of this connection, which was also fully treated in my Philosophical work. The direct proof of it may be found in the acknowledged influence which Language exerts over all other intellectual operations. For no one can doubt how much Language depends on the development of society, whether we regard it in the present or in the past; nor can we assign language to any individual origin, as metaphysicians crudely pretend. Viewed more directly, the same is true of all other intellectual functions. It is plain that the growth of any single mind is subject to the place and time of its development. The progress of science would admit of no consistency unless society thus acted upon intellect; and the same is true of the Fine Arts, which, less distinctly than Science, reflect *As well as Social.*

the changing points of view of the society in which they spring.

All mental action depends on social support.

For Observation as for Reflection, each mind constantly depends on others to furnish it with materials or to verify its results. In the morbid effect which the insane exert over the physicians devoting themselves to their care, we may see how the mind is shaken by earnestness of conviction, even when we know it to be mistaken. The boldest innovator rarely has full belief in his own discoveries, until they have won some amount of willing acceptance. And he cannot forego the sanction this gives him unless he feels a similar support in the general progress of humanity. In a word, the Order of individual life depends on the Order of Society as much in its details as in its entirety. But in these details, the superior influence of the Past as against that of the Present is more than ever conspicuous. Thus in the philosophic history of the sciences we may map out the field of discovery proper to each phase of progress, more precisely than specialists imagine. Accordingly, the intellectual empire exerted over the individual by the race is admitted now by all but Metaphysicians; and the ontological character of their speculations forbids at once any conclusive verification or any real progress. However, the very condition of their own minds exhibits the invariable truth of this law of intellectual filiation; since their discussions of to-day are obviously begotten by the controversies of Greek Sophists and Mediæval Schoolmen, which, if they were just as inane, had at least a better excuse.

Intellectual depends on moral existence.

This is a striking example of the general principle in question, and it explains the anomaly we see around us of so many minds shamefully ignorant of the main intellectual movement. We have here a new proof of the dependence of intellectual progress on the general scheme of human Order. For the main cause of this speculative anarchy is a want of a sound morality; and this the Priesthoods of old in their instinctive good sense used to perceive, both in the Theocratic, and still more under the Catholic system. Although the Sophists of our day have little ability except in turning language to bad account, they are quite capable of understanding the complete exposure now given to their empty speculations, and the growing need for scientific training, which until the last century no one denied. Their obstinacy in their own opinions can only be set down to a morbid egoism, causing them to repudiate the Positive, at least as much as the Theological discipline, and to cling to opinions which foster indolence and mediocrity, no less than pride and intrigue. We have in this a new proof of the uniform dependence of intellectual existence on moral existence.

The general result of this inquiry is, therefore, that the good or bad employment of our understanding depends mainly on the prompting of the affections. If it reject all guidance from without, this is due to the secret influence of the selfish instincts. As shown so often from the opening of this work, the intellect has a choice only of two masters: Personality, or Sociability. When it imagines itself free, it is only under the power of the less noble though the stronger of these two; which thus makes the Mind blind to the true ascendancy of the World Without, and turns its energies to the World of Self. The absolute and selfish character of the Provisional Synthesis taught the Intellect to place itself at the service of Force, which it hoped to control, though it rarely succeeded. Some fine natures, meeting with fit training, refused to fall victims to this vulgar ambition. And the scattered instances of such devotion to the service of the Heart left their traces deep, and foreshadowed unconsciously the final scheme of human intelligence.

The Intellect then has to choose for its master Personality, or Sociability.

The willing submission of the Intellect to Sociability is thus of necessity its normal state. It is only thus that Intellect can obtain its complete development, or even its due authority. For it becomes thus the organiser of our true unity, collective or individual. This unity, it is true, the Intellect bases on a twofold External Order; but it has by itself to discover the Objective laws on which both rest. Whilst systematising the Physical laws, Intellect recognises its relation to the Activity which discovers them, and which calls upon the Understanding to give them better application. When Intellect, again, comes to systematise the Moral laws, it is led to see how large a part it has in Man's principal progress. When it studies the constitution of the Mind itself, it perceives how much it gains in steadiness by having an external Power without, and how much it gains in force by the prompting of the feelings within. It then perceives that its own perfection depends mainly upon its wisely submitting to this twofold necessary yoke, which it bears with an increasing sense of gratitude. Under all these

Its normal condition is a willing service of the Social instincts.

aspects the normal condition of our Understanding is not yet sufficiently realised, even by the higher minds. But we are now in a position to show what that condition is to be, and we have explained the reason that its appearance has been so fatally delayed.

The knowledge of the laws of Mind reduces education to system,

We may learn from this brief inquiry how the Intellectual laws, which complete and coordinate the Moral and Physical laws, lead to the systematising of human Education, the great function of the Universal Priesthood. When concentrated upon this design, all our sound conceptions find a continual sustenance, even more than is needed for our moderate capacities, and the best preservative against the evils to which they are liable. The same discipline is extended, as may be needed, to the teachers and the experts, who are thus both alike fitted for their respective parts. According to their normal mission, the former fulfil the general function required by the nature of the Great Organism, which they have to complete and to direct. At the same time, the latter are trained for their special tasks, and learn how the part played by each of them contributes to the General Economy, which could not be carried on unless each, in their different careers, wisely seconded the influence of the Priesthood. The condition of this assistance, in fact, is this : that each besides his own business, should understand the entire course of civic existence, so as to have a knowledge of the various modifications of it ; and thus should be able to aid the Priesthood in duly awarding praise or blame.

And checks intellectual pride.

Although learning is not so commonly conducive to Pride as teaching is, still study will nevertheless expose the learners to kindred evils, moral as well as intellectual. For, we often find men growing as proud of what they know, as of what they teach, or even of what they discover. For both faults there is the same remedy, the complete realisation of the true facts : the recognition of the intellectual advantages of Humbleness of mind and a sense of Veneration, leading to the sincere subordination of the Intellect to the Heart. Besides, the generality of religious instruction at once brings out the extreme imperfection of every real study ; constantly comparing it with the truly manifold sum of general knowledge required for man's practical existence.

To understand the Order made by Man, by the light of the Order found in Nature on which man's Order depends ; with

a view to improve the former, and to submit oneself to the latter : such is the office, active in the Priesthood, passive in the Public, which both fulfil in universal Education, the natural centre of the entire Intellectual Existence of man.   This two-fold aim is fully marked by the two fundamental laws in which the picture of our mental state may be summarised.   The law of Filiation directly regulates the Human Order : the law of Classification completes and consolidates its fabric, by giving us the key to the Universal Order.

The preceding theory as a whole might seem at first sight to reduce our Intellectual Existence to the mere Culture of Science.   But we may be assured that it has no such narrow limits, when we remember that the same method will hold good in the Culture of Art, alike on the esthetic, and on the technical side.   In truth, the pursuit of the Beautiful, as well as of the Good, are necessarily dependent on our knowledge of the True. The object is the ideal, and then the real, perfecting of the Order of Man, and of the Order of Nature.   On every ground, therefore, we must first learn the nature of this twofold Economy around us, as well as the modifications that it admits.   Now, the systematic Education given to each individual, has as its sphere the ground common to all employments within the community. The artist and the industrialist, who apply themselves to special departments, have to carry out by a judicious course of practice the preparation which this Education has laid for particular vocations.   This practical continuation of the general education is, however, nothing but the extension of ideas previously mastered ; nor does it ever introduce any set of conceptions really foreign to the Encyclopædic course of the scientific training.

The object of Education is the perfecting of human Order for the improvement of the external Order,

Thus, from whatever side we study Intellectual Existence, it presents itself only as the proper complement of the Moral Ex-istence which introduced it.   For, the main work of the systematic Education is to cultivate and strengthen those promptings of the Heart, which the spontaneous education of the Family first implanted within us, to be a guide to the whole of conduct.   The Providence of Women thus enjoys the fruit formed out of the precious germs which it had handed over to the Providence of the Priests.   Just as our sympathies dispose us towards unity by surrounding us with natural ties, so do conceptions of unity strengthen those sympathies by teaching

Thus promoting the alliance of Heart and Mind.

us their true relations to our nature.   This sacred alliance between Mind and Heart is the only true foundation of cerebral
unity; for it effectually combines the two contiguous organs in
the brain, that of the Love which is the principle of that unity,
and that of the Order that forms its basis.   That alliance is even
of more importance to Social Harmony; since the feeling of
Solidarity, and even more that of Continuity, require a right and
familiar knowledge of all human relations, and the systematic
study of these is the chief business of Positive Education.

Thus the wisdom of the Priesthood, completing the influence
of Women, establishes a profound harmony between the Intellectual and the Moral Existence.   But this double training
suffices only for the age of preparation, wherein the true Providence, Humanity, preserves us by its care from the material wants
which rule over real life.   Throughout the rest of our career,
Education of every kind acts only to modify our Practical Existence, which, as we shall now see, assumes a direct preponderance.   Our general Education tends to make us first, more
sympathetic, and then more *synthetic,* to prepare us daily to
become ultimately more *synergetic.*

III. ACTIVE
EXISTENCE,
pp. 318–336.
The normal
state com-
pared with
our actual
state.

With respect to the Emotional and the Intellectual sides of
Social Existence, the picture of our normal condition in accordance with the true laws of human nature is indeed widely different from that which we see on all sides around us.   But the
contrast is even more melancholy and complete when we come
to the Active side of Existence, that which must necessarily be
dominant, whilst the others can only moderate.   Moral Existence, with all its actual maladies, is still the least affected by our
modern anarchy, for Feeling almost alone, in our time sustains
personal as well as social unity.   Our intellectual life has yet
deeper maladies, chiefly marked by the constant predominance
of the talkers over the thinkers.   At the same time, our Material
Existence is the main seat of disorder; for the two essential
elements of the controlling force, Numbers and Riches, have
passed into a deepening condition of mutual hostility, for which
both are equally to blame.

1. Workmen.

The former, the Workers, by virtue of the spirit of cooperation implied in the force of Numbers, are more disposed towards
sympathetic tendencies and ideas of unity; yet their ordinary
attitude is thoroughly subversive through intellectual and even
moral failings.   They accept greedily the most absurd utopias of

reorganisation; whilst rejecting real mental control, for the promises of quacks and visionaries. The height of their social aspiration is to place the necessary leaders of practical industries under the fetters of restrictive laws.

But the Employers, who hold the concentrated force of society, are even more in want of control than the Workmen who hold the dispersed force; at any rate their misdoings are more before us, since they are more constant. The early stages of civilisation aimed, it is true, at developing, rather than disciplining, the various social Powers; but they of their own accord always threw up some kind of controlling influence, at least as regards the most dangerous of all Powers, the Material. This continued so long as the intellectual supported the moral influence. During the long and splendid period of the early Theocracies, Wealth was subjected to strict social duties, and these were actively enforced. The great transitional period of Military rule maintained, and added to, these prescriptions of the Priesthood in the name of Public Safety, a plea often enough abused. The practice of controlling Wealth was brought to perfection under the Feudal System; and by the constant use of confiscation when Wealth was abused, the ground was laid for the Sociocratic character of property, it having had till then a Theocratic form.

2. Employers.

It is only since modern anarchy has destroyed all the provisional institutions of that admirable though imperfect system, that the employment of Wealth in the West has been left as a rule free from any control whatever. The cowardly selfishness which Dante in the name of the Middle Age excluded from the honours even of Hell (Inf. c. iii.) has been made in our day the legal and normal condition of the rich; nor does public opinion any longer impose on them any social duty. The official Priesthood, far from resisting this twofold source of degradation, has shared in it more and more; until it has come to direct against the poor its sacred mission of social guidance. Wherever abuse of Wealth has awakened indignation, this has taken the destructive form which I have just noticed. The habit of attacking Wealth springs too often not from a sincere desire of regeneration, so much as from the instinct of envy or the prompting of ambition. And thus it is that in the attempts to excite the poor against the rich, as in the sanction given by society to the indifference of the rich towards the poor, we may see in the Material sphere

Impotence of the existing Priesthood.

breaches of harmony more deep than any which affect Moral, or even Intellectual, unity.

It is not singular that we find this, the most complex form of existence, that which is most exposed to disturbing passions, to be the most seriously affected. Since the due regulation of this requires the constant cooperation of intellectual with moral influence, it shares in all the disorder which has befallen both. Lastly, it was natural that our modern anarchy should most deeply affect our practical system, since it has occurred precisely at the time when that system had entered on its greatest and most difficult crisis, the transformation of the Military into the Industrial form of activity.

Mission of the future Priesthood, to reorganise Industry.

Finally to reorganise this great reform will soon be the chief social mission of the new Spiritual Power ; and for this it must rightly direct opinion and custom in the West.   Thus to treat in a direct way of this great task of the Priesthood belongs to the fourth volume of this work, the third volume having given a theory of its historical growth.   This task will be a decisive test of the organic capacity of the Positive Religion; and will be only attempted here so far as to explain in the abstract the more general principles of man's Practical Existence. What we have just said upon its present condition has no other immediate object except that of preventing the attention in philosophy from resting on a state of things so abnormal.

The necessity for putting aside for the time all thought of this present condition, in order to lay down the essential truths of Material Order, much increases the difficulty of the Statical study which we must now commence.   At the same time, beside the general foundation supplied by the Positive theory of human nature, the study of material order will be aided by our previous study of the two modes of existence leading to, and modifying, the Material Existence, as well as by the valuable suggestions to be gathered from the early type of Material life.

Comparison of Industrial with Military Life.

Without doubt Military life need not now be regarded from the point of view of its characteristic features ; for this belongs to the Dynamical treatment of the laws of its evolution.   Yet, if we treat in its most abstract sense this primitive mode of civic activity, we may gain from it valuable, though perhaps indirect, suggestions as to the principles common to all forms of Practical Existence.   A further reason is that in Military

Activity, and none other has as yet been really organised, there is this admirable peculiarity, that it compels collective exertion and has no place for a merely personal career. On the other hand, Industrial life had its first origin in efforts essentially personal, and it still bears deeply the marks of this origin upon it. Thus, in order to get a real type of the general laws of Material Existence, we may make use in the abstract of its primitive or Military phase, whilst eliminating all those features of it which place it in antagonism with the final or Industrial phase. When the results of this Statical mode of treatment have been completed and developed by the general Historical survey of my next volume, the fitness of this theory to form an adequate and final discipline of modern activity will be more easily seen than is now possible.

In our systematic analysis of the three essential modes of Social Existence we have now taken a general view of its period of education, the great object of which is to discipline the ultimate activity of life. The emotional life, passed within the Family, fully establishes the essential superiority of the Heart; and then the speculative life, under the direction of the Priesthood, steps in to enforce the free submission of the Intellect to the feelings. When these two powers thus finally conjoin their influence first to educate, and then to guide human life, we must perceive at once the great end in view, which is: to bring under real control the dominant element of society, Activity. This period of education would, if taken apart, imply some such Material Existence as that which I supposed, by way of abstract hypothesis, in commencing the second chapter of this volume; that is to say, a life conceived without material wants, in order to get a better view of moral and intellectual tendencies. The care of the Family and of the City place each of us in this supposed condition, during the age of preparation which is to fit us for real life. Thus preserved from disturbing influences, we are able calmly to turn our spirit to live for others whilst we learn first how to cherish, and then how to serve Humanity. The next care is that this long and trying course of education may not break down, when it is brought to fulfil its true social mission. The Heart and the Mind must therefore be adequately prepared to bear their part without yielding in the critical battle that awaits them amidst the struggles of life.

Though Practical Existence, as I showed in my direct study

Practical existence is favourable both to Intellectual and to Moral Development.

of it in the second chapter of this volume, is necessarily the dominant element of life, yet this is perfectly compatible with Moral and Intellectual development. I have now to show how these may be reconciled ; and this must ever be the principal end of all human wisdom under the guidance of the true Priesthood.

In the spontaneous order of the three natural modes of association, the City holds the central place between the Family and the Church. For the City is a society less private and more extensive than the Family, more complete and less general than the Church. But a different order is required when we come to the systematic classification of these three elements of life. We come back to the great subjective law so often used in this work, as well as in my ' Positive Philosophy,' that the middle terms of a series ought always to be determined by the two extremes which include them. The present case will furnish a striking instance of this law. During the entire course of our education, we are in the hands first of our Family and then of the Church, though our ultimate destiny is to belong to the City. But this, the common object of the two other human societies, will only increase the direct and continuous influence of the last.

But for the disturbing causes, too natural to our imperfect cerebral constitution, Practical Existence would be excellently fitted to cultivate healthy feelings and sound belief, the result of all right education. It is certainly not at the moment when we become able really to live for others that we are likely to lose those qualities of heart and of head which trained us for this our natural career. On the contrary, the sense that we have this capacity in its maturity is very fit to strengthen and increase it. All that is needed is that, in the daily task of joint labour, each citizen should recognise in its true proportions his own personal share. An habitual sense of this share will be the natural result of a sound education ; first in its domestic, then in its religious form. The understanding finally systematises the tendencies of the heart to universal Love, by bringing home to every citizen a sense of his proper place in the great work of human Order, and his normal relations to all the other functions of society. Thus without any strained demand upon the emotions or the intelligence, a life of practical activity does much to develop the intellectual and moral germs of the laborious education which precedes it.

It is especially the want of such training which has made civic life so defective hitherto. The total absence of training has indeed only shown itself during the increasing anarchy which followed the Middle Age. Since then efforts have been individual, and consequently blind, inspired by merely personal motives, and seldom indeed directed with a view to the general whole; which no one then could understand, even by instinct. But the disorder of the West cannot furnish us with any type of the normal state of Humanity; it can only illustrate such general laws as we can gather from the more marked facts. These supply all that is needed in Social Statics to complete the picture given us by the Middle Age and Antiquity. In those epochs systematic Education was always most imperfect, even during the most splendid period of the Catholic and Feudal system. In Roman life the radical deficiency of the education was corrected by the naturally social spirit of the dominant type of activity, especially since the slavery of the producing class limited and simplified the range of civic life. The humblest citizen was enabled thoroughly to feel the share he had in the collective economy of a society which was so ready to exhibit a spontaneous unity. At the same time every one in it had an adequate knowledge of the essential duties of all the rest, and thus was able with good purpose to second his action, whether in the way of repression or of direction.

The system of cooperation, as defined by the great principle of Aristotle (p. 234), is not liable to any natural disturbance which cannot be prevented or remedied by the continual watchfulness of the City carrying on the education of the Family and the Church. The question next arises, whether this active discipline of the State which is both special and general, necessarily awakens vicious tendencies of a kind to affect seriously civic harmony. Careful examination leads to the conviction that this material form of Force is naturally more capable of improvement than the moral, if the Priesthood properly exercises its principal social function.

In truth Temporal Government has in itself nothing really oppressive, when both superiors and inferiors are inspired by a general education with a right sense of their position and of their duties. From the explanation given in the second chapter of this volume we learn that Command, although necessarily arising originally from personal instincts, may be made to combine with the active exercise of the social feelings. So delightful in practice are the benevolent affections that they will develop of themselves without our knowledge, when the situation is favourable for their exercise. When the true theory of human nature is properly understood, men will see that the great privilege of practical Power is that it puts us in a position to indulge our higher feelings; but there need be no bitterness in the regrets of those to whom it is denied. All will be accustomed to feel that the wise concentration of this Material Power is always indispensable to its true civic usefulness. Sincerely and habitually to feel convinced of the need society has of political chiefs, of the necessity which limits the active body of citizens to an existence as proletaries, this is certainly the great difficulty of social discipline. To understand it calls out a refined and complex process of reasoning; and this can only be sufficiently fulfilled by a sound religious education. There is no other power which can make the exact fulfilment of individual duties the true standard of life; instead of encouraging an empty discussion of the rights of persons: suggesting reaction to those who have power, and insurrection to those who have not.

But depends on its followers.

As to the converse and the correlative of this truth, it is much less difficult of apprehension. The Concentrated Force of the powerful is not likely long to forget its essential dependence on the Dispersed Force of numbers, of which it is the material providence. In the normal state of society, this mistake would be a result only of individual pride, for any leader who exhibited it would be easily restrained or constrained by his colleagues. It did not often arise during the long era of military activity, which is so well fitted to make the centre feel the importance of the mass. Industrial life will be just as well adapted to the same task, so soon as it has realised its proper social character. The independence of the inferiors will be even more striking, and therefore the superiors will be less ready to forget how completely their daily success needs the assistance it receives from the workers. Thus we may infer that the serious disturbances which modern anarchy has developed more and more on the side of both are in no way inherent in the nature of our practical existence, but are only the result of defects in our mental and moral discipline.

We come to the same conclusion if, after Command, we

examine the moral effects of Obedience. Although Military life, with its appeals to the evil instincts, would predispose men to insubordination, yet in its collective form, under the stimulus of Religion, it has succeeded in maintaining during a long course of years an almost unbroken discipline. On the contrary, since existence in the West upon the close of the Middle Age has tended to become finally industrial, the milder discipline which it exacts has undergone severe shocks. Such a difference can only be caused by total want of organisation in society in the modern state of transition. Peaceful industry must necessarily be more easy of discipline than warlike activity, for it calls out no passion of destruction. Modern existence is more favourable than the ancient was to the due subordination of the personal instincts to social duty.

The false theory of human nature, current during the long revolt of modern times against all authority, past or present, has given us entirely wrong ideas about the respective tendencies of obedience and insubordination. The latter has been the object of designing apologies, the former that of systematic abuse ; and yet the practical spirit of proletaries and women has remedied the sophistical mischief of the teachers of the day. The general laws of human nature are always felt before they are understood ; and by them men have been brought to perceive instinctively the moral superiority of submission over revolt. Since this universal instinct of obedience has been systematically explained by a sound cerebral theory, it appears that even in animals the qualities which form voluntary obedience, and no other obedience is permanent, are nobler than the instincts which reject discipline. We may recall the admirable maxim of the great Corneille :

> On va d'un pas plus ferme à suivre qu'à conduire,

and we may be assured that modern populations will not look upon themselves as degraded by the social destiny which imposes on them constant submission. On the contrary, each will feel the normal tendency of the situation to bring out our instincts of Veneration and Attachment, of all others the best fitted to found true human happiness, public or private. Whilst recognising the necessity of command, we shall come to look upon its special organs in high place as always exposed to serious moral evils by reason of their strong personal natures, and every healthy spirit will be glad to be spared their temptations.

Indeed, this fatal source of corruption, which is more contrary to private happiness even than to public good, can only be prevented or remedied by a vast expansion of social virtue, such as cannot form so long as temporal power is dispersed in so many hands.

Civic duty ennobles both Obedience and Command.

The natural remedy for the chief mischiefs of practical existence is to be found in its own development, as it passes into the social form towards which that existence ever aims. This civic character ennobles at once Obedience and Command, whilst at the same time it disciplines them under an active sense of different duties. The spontaneous growth of this civic loyalty was the finest quality of Military Civilisation, though found only in the Roman race, and then only under favourable conditions. On the contrary, this social discipline is the grand difficulty of our final existence, from the private form which industrial activity assumes and retains for so long. It is complicated by a serious question, as to the general use of human capital, the abstract study of which will complete the statical theory of active life.

Moral aspect of the Distribution of Wealth.

The question of the Distribution of Wealth grew to be a source of perplexity in the Military system, but its serious evils only became apparent under the industrial system. So long as the career of Conquest offered constant opening for new acquisitions, property was respected in the ancient world, apart from its consecration under the Theocracies; and this favoured the growth of vast fortunes such as became impossible in later times. Wealth in the civilised nations can no longer be accumulated by violence; and thus its slow accretion by the process of Grant or Exchange has given rise to serious social difficulties in securing its due distribution.

Wealth, the normal source of Power.

At the same time Wealth has acquired an importance in the Industrial existence, which it never had in the Military. In the latter, Wealth, if it was a symbol of Power, was so only as a consequence of Power, and not as being its essential basis. However, this decisive change in the nature of Wealth began in the Middle Age, under the system of Defensive War peculiar to that period, and when military functions were also localised. We have there, in fact, evidence of the great social importance which Wealth began to possess, at least in the form of Land, an importance such as often to eclipse the prestige of rank. This was the forerunner of the yet more dominant part which

it is destined to hold in the Industrial life. In this final stage
of civilisation, Wealth is not only the symbol of Material Power,
but also the chief and regular source of Power, by reason of the
influence it commands over the labouring masses. For this
reason I treated it in the last chapter (p. 226) as being the
real seat of aggregate power, contrasting it with the dispersive
form of power, arising from numbers.

In the Industrial, the ultimate phase of practical activity, *Even with out exceptional capacity.* the possession of Wealth is the main ground which entitles men
to take the lead in special industries. Only very rare unfitness
in the person will prevent this advantage from weighing more
than the greatest capacity for Industry without the essential
instrument of Capital. The growth of sound general education
ought to strengthen this natural tendency, by making cases of
this special unfitness less common and less injurious. Under
the Military system not only had Wealth less influence, but
personal merit was more indispensable in the leaders. In the
modern order of Industry, the chiefs are only the necessary
administrators of the Capital of mankind; and their duties
may be performed with moderate qualifications. When the
system is fully regulated, the effect of this will be to secure
greater unity, by diminishing the influence of personal character. However, so long as anarchy prevails in the West, this
fact will on the contrary increase the discord produced by
envious declaimers and unscrupulous rivals; for it diminishes
the respect in which this form of power ought to be held.

At the same time the danger, if constant, is yet one which *If only, it be active.* has its proper remedy in the wise reorganisation of society
under the Industrial system of life. For if the management
of the Capital of mankind requires no higher personal qualities
than the Socialist dreamers would have us suppose, this would
be but an additional reason for maintaining the managers in
their actual position, where permanence and safety are of such
importance to society. The worthless and idle Rich, like the
selfish spirits from whom Dante turns away in the vestibule of
Hell, alone need fear a strict judgment of their lives by Society.
But this class grows more and more rare, and will soon, we
may hope, disappear. We may also look for an easy mode of
transforming it into a useful class; which will obviate the
employment of any violent dealing with these parasites of
society. As to the active Employers of Wealth, who are the

only true Temporal leaders of modern society, they cannot but gain, both in estimation and in security, by acquiring a really social character under the systematic influence of Positive Religion.

Wealth to be subject to moral, not to legal, control. The new Priesthood, independent alike of the Proletariat and of the Patriciat, will invest with a sacred duty the essential function of the holders of Wealth, the true administrators of which will become the agents of that material Providence which the Great Being extends to all its servants. This Subjective consecration of Capital will be more respected, and the discipline it imposes will be more effective, when the Temporal chiefs are at once more powerful and fewer in number than they are in our present confusion, so that their work in society may be better performed. The heart-burnings and the invectives which the abuse of riches has awakened, since the final break-up of the old Faith at the end of the Middle Age, incline the hearts and minds of men, full of revolutionary ideas, either to sardonic distrust of or to oppressive interference with the natural power of Wealth. The masses of the People however, as well as Women, are really free from any designs on Property, at least in towns; and these feel, as do the small band of true Philosophers, that the service of the community requires great accumulations of Capital, as well as independence in its employment. According to the maxim given in the General View (p. 303), *great duties imply great powers.* The true spirit of the Future, in harmony with the Positive Theory of human nature, individual as well as collective, is marked by Confidence and Liberty, the natural conditions of a wise responsibility. This continuous check on abuse of wealth must remain essentially moral; and it only becomes political in extreme cases, which, as human nature is gradually perfected, will gradually tend to diminish in frequency. Under the wholesome influence of Positive Religion, metaphysical anarchy will finally fall into discredit, as alike incapable of sustaining searching criticism, or of supplying any real remedy. The Industrial Patriciat, becoming more worthy of its part and more respected by others, will feel how directly it is devoted to the incomparable happiness of a life of activity supported by the three social instincts: Attachment for the affectionate sex, Veneration for the Priesthood, and Benevolence towards the proletariat. Itself the temporal patron of every useful life, it

will honestly feel the religious superiority of the other three
human Providences which it surrounds with material comfort,
so that it may the better enjoy their moral, intellectual, and
social influence. It is the transitional classes, the Theologians,
the Soldiers, and the Metaphysicians, now interposed between
these four essential elements of the normal order, who cause
or prolong the main evils of modern society.

To give a firmer base to this final harmony, we may close
the abstract study of Practical Existence, by a brief analysis of
its leading function : the general Distribution of the Wealth of
mankind amongst the different classes. I shall in my fourth
volume enter into special explanations on this subject ; but this
is the place for some general observations on a statical doctrine,
much obscured by the ignoble metaphysics of Political Economy,
which pretends that the general laws of Material Order can be
studied, apart from other laws. This is now become the idle
expedient, whereby rhetoricians and sophists, hitherto with too
much reason, hope to conceal their shameful ignorance of
Science. The discipline of Positivism will easily succeed in
overcoming these subversive attempts by appealing at once to
Reason and to Feeling. *Distribution of Wealth amongst classes.*

In order to make this certain, we must give the principle of
Aristotle its due extension ; that is, we must make cooperation
in Space amongst contemporaries subordinate to cooperation
in Time with our predecessors, to which latter the progress of
civilisation gives ever fresh ascendancy. The Revolutionists of
the West all speak now in the name of the objective Solidarity
of the living. Positive Religion will reduce them all to order
by appealing to the subjective Continuity of the past, against
which no resistance can long be maintained. In Moral and
Intellectual existence, this subjective Continuity is already predominant ; it will be yet more so in Material existence, where
combinations, vaster and more enduring, are necessary to life. *In capital, as in other subjects, Continuity is more important than Solidarity.*

Whatever be the laws, yet little understood, by which the
Capital of the race is accumulated in particular families, we
cannot doubt that influences merely accidental, such as no one
can boast of, have usually had a great part in it. But this, and
the same criticism might be applied to all our modern aspirants
after Power, has no bearing on the main question, the Employment of Riches, putting aside all question of origin. It is
sufficient if, in acquiring fortunes, the laws imposed by the *The origin of Wealth unimportant.*

wisdom of society on their lawful acquirement have never been broken.   This is the proper and sole condition required as to the source of Wealth.   This satisfied, the social consecration of its possessors ought to depend on the use to which the Wealth is habitually directed, and it may be given in cases where they would not at once recognise themselves as the material ministers of Humanity.   Now, this guarantee is already sufficiently fulfilled for us to feel sure that all essential progress in the exercise of practical Power, depends on the right reconstruction of the Moral and the Intellectual Order.   For, those even who most loudly inveigh against the abuse of riches secretly envy the idle and selfish existence of the rich, and desire it as the main recompense of their own active labour, little as they dignify toil themselves.   If we are ever to get the true employment of material Power, we must begin by treating it with constant respect, save in any exceptional instances of fraud, such as those we have just mentioned.

Entire free-
dom of
testament-
ary disposi-
tion.

The Positive Organisation of society, far from restraining the liberty essential to Capital, will on the contrary much increase it, by introducing the one needful improvement which is required for the primitive mode. the Hereditary transmission of Wealth.   Since the definitive decay of the Caste system, Wealth ought not to be inherited by birth alone, though at first this was the best guide to its right use.   The Theocratic principle of the division of wealth amongst the Family was deeply modified by the admirable Sociocratic principle attempted by the Middle Age, when for social reasons estates were transmitted entire to the elder sons, charged only with portions for the younger.   Modern anarchy had no better device than the destruction of this preliminary system, without placing any better one in its place.   For the name of system cannot be given to the revolutionary practice of France, the rule of Equality of partition; a rude expedient dictated by blindness as much as by jealousy, and of which nothing lasting can ever be made, for all the praise which metaphysicians have given it. The good sense of a wise and conscientious economist, Dunoyer, led him to open an attack upon this principle in a memorable treatise, which ought to outlast the doctrines of his day to which it is devoted.   Positivism however will ultimately do justice to his advice, standing as it does in the true Social point of view.

The duties of the Rich towards their own families in the matter of Property will be smaller than we now suppose them, whilst their obligations as members of a community will be far wider.   They are the administrators of the Wealth of mankind acting as a Providence; and their duties to their sons are like those of other classes: to give them an education fitting for them, and the means of properly entering on a new industrial life of their own.   The rich would be abusing their social position, if they employed their fortunes in artificially creating mere parasites of society, a morbid growth which already encumbers the Great Organism unduly, owing to its complex organisation. The free transfer of this high function should crown the active career of the capitalist; ultimately in the form of a spontaneous choice of a worthy successor, taken from any family or any class. This involves complete freedom of Testamentary disposition. This is not the place to enlarge on this subject, of which special explanations will be found in the last volume.   Enough has been said to show the one fundamental change in principle, marking the Sociocratic method of transmitting human Wealth and the primitive method of the Theocracies.   The difference, we have seen, consists in developing the material power of the Head of the Family, who becomes morally, though not in law, a civil magistrate, whilst at the same time this greatly increases his proper responsibility.   If one of his sons seem to him worthy to succeed to his own social office he will be free to choose him. If, on the contrary, according to the ordinary bent of modern notions, he think that a better successor can be found elsewhere, Positive Religion will encourage him to place his choice there without hesitation.   Furthermore, the principle of Adoption, which will be largely developed in the ultimate system, will directly connect the Theocratic principle of Inheritance with the Sociocratic principle of Transmission, by duly incorporating in the Family the successor when properly selected.

This needful explanation at once avoids the only difficulty of principle which can interfere with the social duty of the rich, the claims of their families.   We can now easily follow out in its completeness the great function they perform; which is that, like central reservoirs of the nutritive apparatus of society, they constantly renew the material existence of the three other essential classes of apparatus proper to the collective Organism of Humanity.

Social function of Capitalists.

Materials are either, (1) Provisions, or (2) Instruments.

To make this clear, we must insist on the natural division of human materials into two very different portions : Provisions and Instruments. The part of the first is directly to sustain the existence of the social organs, whilst the second repairs the waste involved in each operation. Thus the mark of the one is dispersion, of the second is concentration.

In the second place, the parts filled by these two orders of materials are naturally distinguished into two essential classes, as they concern Spiritual existence, mental or moral, or as they concern mere Material existence. We come back to the luminous distinction suggested by Dunoyer between the arts which minister to Man's welfare, and those which improve the World ; a separation which in the preceding chapter (p. 261) I showed to have analogies with the separation between the two powers in Sociology. The importance of this distinction is now manifest ; for the proper mode of distributing Provisions or Instruments differs greatly in one case and in the other.

Positive theory of Wages.

Before treating it directly, I will revert to the fundamental principle of the Religious theory of Wages, which was stated in the first chapter of this volume (p. 63) and is now incontrovertibly established by the whole of the foregoing arguments. It is that the service of Humanity must always be looked upon as essentially gratuitous. Wages of any kind can really pay nothing but the material portion of each man's labour, by replacing the waste invariably required by the organ, and sometimes by the function it performs. As to the essence of the service, it never admits of any other real recompense beyond the satisfaction of having given it and the active gratitude which it spontaneously awakens.

All labour is gratuitous.

We cannot deny how truly gratuitous must be all real human service, when we reflect on the collective life of each generation, which without labour inherits the stores accumulated by the labour of preceding generations. In comparison with this Subjective Capital, its own objective share is always small, and becomes less with each age. Only, as it is formed of perishable materials, especially in the way of food, it constantly requires a laborious process of renewal, so as to transmit it to the next generation unimpaired, and even somewhat increased.

Public salaries.

This gratuitous character of Industry in each generation will serve to explain the same principle in the individual.

Great posts are no longer said to be paid for, though the salaries they receive are the highest ever given. The reason is that they are accepted as institutions of society. Now, it would be unreasonable not to extend the same notion to the professions less well paid, though their services in labour are the most necessary of all. This injustice is one of the consequences of our anarchical state of Transition, in which we have the empty distinction of civic duties into public and private. When we regard all citizens as being morally ministers of Society, and this is needed for any true human harmony, we shall have to extend to every useful profession the same respectful estimate of their material remuneration which we now give to the great offices of state.

The distinction we make between the *honorarium* of the great and the *wages* of the humbler worker is as unreasonable as it is immoral ; yet it rudely contains an abiding principle as to the natural distinction between the mode of distributing public support, as it is given to Spiritual or to Temporal functions. In the former case, the Spiritual service is so general, and the materials needed are so completely reducible to sustenance, that the salary ought to be paid by the public, and will not admit any taking into account of personal merit. By this an indispensable social office would be often degraded. *Spiritual stipends.*

This public institution, uniformity of stipend, need be followed however only for the Priesthood. If the Active body of society ought to support the Contemplative class, it is only collectively that this should be done. This need not exclude free private gifts to persons, such as are necessary in every first attempt of a system, and quite indispensable to restore the character of the Priestly order. I feel a pride in having myself at much personal sacrifice given a striking instance of this mode of maintaining life. Without it the Positivist Priesthood can never acquire its due social independence. Whatever be the form of this collective stipend, public or private, it ought always to be given directly to the functionary as such, and should not be measured by his success in the function itself. For it is important to retain intact the essentially gratuitous form of all Theoretic services, the fulfilment of which must be left to the conscience of each. *Voluntary gifts.*

As to the affectionate sex, the true source of our better Providence, Positive Religion is content to maintain the *Support of Women.*

sacredness of the natural principle, which arose with the dawn of civilisation, and has ever since been extended : *It is the duty of man to support woman.* In this case, striking as is the influence of woman over the whole of society, her value is so intimately impressed on the family, and there alone can it be fully known, that her material sustenance may without risk be left to the domestic care of the active sex. The father and the brothers in the first place, then the husband and the son, will fittingly perform this natural duty, in the well ordered State ; so that the City need only intervene in the exceptional cases where the Family do not suffice. Thus, this essential part of the distribution of the means of living comes properly midway between that public maintenance which belongs to the Priesthood, and that private remuneration by wages which is proper to the Proletariat.

Workmen : their private property in their homes.

We pass to this, the third general class of support. The industrial chiefs, whose duty it is to supply Provisions to the workers more than Instruments, ought further to secure every worthy citizen in the possession of that part of his temporal existence, which is independent of the special service he renders to the community. This is not the place to determine the extent to which this principle may be carried in the future. I will now only notice the leading rule to be observed, and point out the measure of property, which in the normal condition the Patriciat ought to secure to the Proletariat, in person or in family. The principle is : *that every one at all times should be entire owner of everything of which he has the constant and exclusive use.* This provision is evidently practicable ; and, at bottom, it amounts to this, that society combines the two ordinary senses of the root, *proper*, as meaning both aptitude and property. Now, though the rule is indisputable as a truth, in our times of anarchy we are far from observing it fairly, even in the case of moveables, and certainly we do not respect it in the matter of domicile. The situation is full of peril that the Proletariat should thus be encamped as it were in the midst of Western society, without having even quarters of its own. Yet surely no man would venture to assert this to be the type of the normal condition of society.

Classification of salaries of workmen.

Apart from such fair conditions as a foundation, and the temporal chiefs jointly should relieve exceptional cases of need or of unmerited neglect, the payment of the services of the workers will be left to the private decision of the employers. For no others can properly estimate the value of each special service. At the same time, Positive morality, duly enforced by the Priesthood, and supplemented by the feelings of Women and the opinion of the People, will lay on the employers obligations of a kind to prevent all abuse of this, their essential privilege. To sum up these civic duties of the Patriciat towards the Proletariat, they amount to this : *that every industrious citizen shall be secured in the means of fully developing his domestic life.* From this at present the larger part of the working population are debarred by low and irregular wages. For the fulfilment of this fundamental duty, every temporal Chief is morally responsible to his own subordinates ; and all besides, workers or employers, ought to regard themselves as jointly and severally liable together. When the City, under the preaching of the Church, shall undertake to make the Family safe from all unmerited disaster, the Proletaries will be the best guardians of harmony in the industrial organisation, for they will feel themselves to be members of it in the closest sense.

We have now but to consider the fourth class in society, the industrial Patricians. They who have to allot the material side of all functions, must also provide for their own. There is nothing really unreasonable in this apparent exception to rule, a class fixing its own place. The administrators of human Capital are not indeed the only order who fix the scale of their own material condition. Under the system of a healthy social competition, a similar rule will be universal ; so that every man will be left the sole natural judge of his real pecuniary wants. If he abuse this liberty, public opinion and individual competition will soon sit in judgment upon him ; and this holds good for the Priest, and indeed the Woman, as much as for the Workman. Now, the rich have indeed greater inducements to right conduct in this matter, for they naturally must have stronger desire to obtain general esteem. And this will never be won by such of them as consume upon their own enjoyments an excessive share of the Capital entrusted to their care by Humanity. The morality of Positivism must, however, be careful to avoid any exaggerated judgment, and indeed all affectation of frugality in the matter. We must remember that without peculiar energy of the personal instincts no one would

Incomes of Capitalists.

undertake the function of capitalist; and consequently this must involve a greater proneness in them to expensive forms of enjoyment. Positivists will be scrupulously watchful never to discredit the office filled by the rich by exhibiting a pedantic anxiety to improve the holder of it, heedless of the imperfect nature of man and the constant allurements of the patrician's position.

SOCIAL HAR-
MONY MAIN-
TAINED BY
THE PRIEST-
HOOD, pp.
336-345.

We have now shortly treated in the abstract the most distinctive and most complex of the three forms of man's social existence. And we may now conclude this chapter by showing, how the Priesthood, which originally organised them all, will maintain due harmony between them. We have already seen, and the thought will be worked out in detail hereafter, that if Material life is more exposed than either of the others to disturbance, it is able to give active assistance to the growth of Moral and Mental life, the business of which is to train and regulate the industrial. Thus the final organisation of human society is in strict conformity with the essential laws of our nature ; and thus it escapes those inherent self-contradictions, whereby every Provisional Synthesis of man's life broke down of its own accord. The Positivist Synthesis will be exposed to no such standing danger ; it will have to meet only the partial and temporary causes of disturbance which are inseparable from man's passions and his errors ; and these it will prevent or remedy with success unknown till now.

Relations of
orders.

All the essential elements of this type of society find in it naturally their highest satisfaction.

1. Women.

In it, Women find respect and tenderness together in the natural sanctuary of the Home ; for all will look on the Home as the direct and purest source of that principle of Love, which is the moving spirit of our entire system of life. The active care of their male relations, or at need of the State, will shield them from all material want, and thus leave them free to fulfil their natural office, that of guarding morality in the Home, and of superintending the first informal training of children.

2. Priests.

At the same time, the Spiritual Power, in the place of honour at the head of the civic hierarchy, exerts a social mission greater than that which it ever had in the days of absolute authority with all its corruptions. It will be more synthetic than any other power ; for it may be centred in the compass of a single brain, and will always originate in one : ever keeping within the region of the will, and never claiming authority over action; yet withal, the form of power most capable of wide diffusion. Its only natural limit will be that of the planet; and every part of this will feel equally its religious inspirations. The Priesthood, as the systematic director of General Education, will find this duty without effort give to it an influence of counsel, such as it may ultimately extend over the whole of real life, public as well as private.

In truth in the future, Women and Priests are alike debarred from all active command, and even from all wealth. But this self-denial of these orders is in no sense a defiance to the powerful or the rich. It is a condition, indispensable to any true devotion to affection or to speculation; and the just compensation of the constant care of relatives or of the State for the corporal life of the two orders which form the Spiritual Providence. The voluntary sacrifice of all inheritance by Women and Priests is moreover indispensable to the social concentration of Capital in the hands of the class which is specially charged to be the organ of general support to the community. When the institution by which these renounce Wealth is thus justified, it will give rise to no serious antagonism to Wealth, on the part either of Women or Priests; for of all classes it is they who by Heart or by Intellect are the best disposed to understand and to respect civic harmony.

Both have no part in wealth.

So also will it be with the industrial population. They will not be slow to see how the society thus organised will tend as a whole to secure their true happiness; and this, in truth, should be the centre towards which every society should aim. A sound education, the guiding spirit whereof will be a right knowledge of the laws of man's individual and social nature, will check any disposition to anarchy; and the workers themselves will respect and cause to be respected social classifications, of which they will feel the continual benefits. When their chief material wants are sufficiently guaranteed, they will value the concentration of the Capital of mankind in the hands of some, as the fundamental condition for making Capital of use to the community. When their hearts and understandings shall have become sensible of what true happiness is, the People will feel that they can taste it in larger measure than either their Spiritual or the Temporal chiefs; for happiness will be found

3. Workmen.

in the free expansion of family affection and social duty, and this the People can gratify better than any class in their fortunate exemption from anxiety. The Positive Religion, again, will preach to them of true dignity of labour, labour which Theology used to tell them was the consequence of God's curse on man. And in the matter of correction, the most terrible of punishments will be the sentence of compulsory idleness.

4. Industrial chiefs.

Lastly, the industrial Patricians, informed with a thoroughly new spirit, will feel continual gratitude for that arrangement of society, whereby they have ever before them active moral duties, conferring a civic importance of an entirely new kind. Their power will be increased, as their responsibility is increased. For the principle of all regular concentration of duty is this : *A single manager for the whole field of industry which one man can personally direct*. Thus temporal authority will be centred in a certain number of Families, scarcely one-thirtieth part of the entire population. It will thus have a truer sense both of its duties and its powers ; and will find a constant need to win respect for an authority having no conventional dignity, by a noble public employment of it. It will be only by a passing delirium or personal vanity that Patricians of this sort can ever be led to imitate the old Theological or Metaphysical tendency to look on themselves as absolute masters of the immense materials entrusted by the public to their care. There will be first the constant influence of the Positive education to enforce on every side the Sociocratic spirit in life ; but besides this, the perilous responsibility of their high office must check in them any such illusion of the past. As the personal instincts of the different orders of temporal directors will always be fairly gratified, so far as is properly compatible with the full vitality of the sympathetic feelings, there will be nothing in principle to bring them into conflict with the social system.

Resources for controlling social disorder.

Such a society will need, on the part of the Priesthood, far greater efforts to establish than to preserve it. However, to complete my Statical outline, I shall shortly notice the normal resources which the Spiritual Power will be able to use against partial and temporary disturbances of social order. When society is finally organised, no other disturbance can arise. We shall thus deepen the ample confidence we must all feel in the inherent stability of the mode of existence here figured. And we shall be convinced that society itself will create means of preventing or of rectifying any kind of disturbance, quite ample for the occasion.

Of these methods none is so pure, so direct, and so really efficient, as that which is the immediate result of the ascendancy obtained by the spiritual teachers over every intellect and every heart, as the directors of General Education. Unless they be much below their duty, they will thereby be invested with a confidence, capable of modifying the whole course of real life. Accordingly, individuals, families, and classes, even entire cities, will come to look on their instructors as the best counsellors of their conduct, the natural supporters of their just authority, and the true restorers of their mutual harmony. Positive worship as a whole will also much develop this native respect for the religious power ; for its moral teaching will be always founded on evidence, and will be looked upon by all as the ordinary source of Happiness and Progress. When this habit is broken under the force of some violent passion in public or in private life, the Priesthood will usually be able to restore order by appealing to the conscience or lastly the good sense of the offender.

1. By the teaching and preaching office of the Priesthood.

Should both of these fail, the Spiritual Power must have recourse to the second kind of expedient, the last that is left in the religious sphere. But they are measures less pure than the former, and also, in spite of their solemnity, really less efficient ; for they do not appeal to affection or conviction, but to a real force, controlling action without changing the will. At the same time, they are quite within the limit of sacerdotal authority ; for, force though it be, it is strictly spiritual, and is always free from material violence. It arises, in truth, from the impression which the acts of each produce o the hearts and minds of all his neighbours. The irresistible power of public opinion does at the same time create a really coercing force, because men submit to it, apart from any sense of wrong in the conscience or the understanding. Still, so long as it does not exceed the mere expression of praise or blame, no man can reasonably complain that his conduct is visited wit it. Were the public to be debarred from a fair judgment of his action, it would be the community which would most unjustly suffer an oppressive restriction on its liberty.

2. By the direction of Public opinion.

The second field of spiritual influence is therefore quite

3. Formal
condemna-
tion by Spi-
ritual au-
thority.

legitimate ; though the Priesthood ought only to resort to it on failure of the first.   It is of two kinds : domestic, or civic ; the latter consisting of three degrees, public blame, social excommunication, and reprobation after life, in the way to be described in the fourth volume.   Since the chief offences will be from abuse of material power, the Priesthood may count on the natural aid of the oppressed everywhere, to restrain its outbreaks or to redress its injuries.   In the Family, women will bring their influence to bear to the same purpose ; and the children may join in certain cases.   In the heart of the City, the Priests may call in the weight of the Proletariat. But besides these two unfailing sources of support, the Priesthood will always find valuable help in the centre of the Directing class ; and its better members will be eager to devote themselves to that honourable protection which the strong owe to the weak, with a spirit such as Chivalry essayed to establish in the Middle Age.   With these various kinds of aid united, the Priesthood will have very powerful resources in this indirect instrument for carrying on their regulating action.   Examples of the mediæval Church can give us but faint ideas of the force of such a public opinion, when it shall be based on an education completely Positive and strictly general.   Nevertheless, we are too apt to be blinded by the effect which Spiritual influence of this sort exerts over the imagination, and to attribute to it far too high an importance ; above all, we are wont to forget how much it is wanting in purity.   A control, to be truly Religious, should seek always to persuade or to convince ; never to force, even in a moral sense.   And thus, the direct influence of exhortation, though less impressive, is always of itself to be preferred, whenever it is possible to employ it alone.

4. By the se-
cular arm of
the Law.

This is, however, the extreme limit beyond which the action of the priest should never pass.   Across this borderland, the domain of Temporal authority begins, on which Religion must scrupulously avoid to trench.   Religion, if it can no longer touch the conscience or the reason of the offender, must appeal to the voice of the community ; and it may find there a force, truly coercive, though not ceasing to be moral.   If this indirect influence is also proved inadequate, there is no help but in material force.   But here the Church leaves the case to be dealt with by Government, whose duty it is to prevent or punish offences by its own material methods.   That these should ever be needed, and indeed they are needed less and less, is a blot on the constitution of human society. Nevertheless they will *Capital punishment.* never be wholly disused ; for there are vicious natures, such as Humanity can never hope to reform, and which it must put away for the sake of its own self-respect. It was a wise remark of Gall, that to abolish altogether the punishment of death, as some loose-thinking philanthropists dream, would be to go directly counter to the positive laws of our personal nature. I venture to add, that it would be still more abhorrent to the laws of our social Organism. At the same time, this last resource of Humanity against innate viciousness must certainly become more and more rare, amidst the increasing influence of a sound general education, and a wise organisation of society.

Temporal authority may more frequently employ another *Confiscation by Government.* class of the material methods of repression. It may take its stand on the principle that property is a civil institution ; and may *confiscate*, for a time or altogether, the capital of mankind, when those who possess it, prove unworthy of their trust. Yet withal, for property as for person, the Priesthood will ever advise the Government to prefer positive to negative measures, and to reward the deserving, rather than to punish the wrongdoers. This is a resource wholly unknown to our clumsy *Public rewards and grants.* legislation. Especially in the case of abuse of material property, it is better to raise the deserving to wealth than to reduce the evil to poverty ; to reform men by the force of example, not by that of fear. I have already remarked (p. 133), that the true wisdom of man, seeing how important it is to concentrate wealth, of old led vast populations to multiply possessions on popular leaders of the nation, even before the Theocracy gave any impulse to the practice. In the last volume I shall explain how in the normal Order of Society, these primitive tendencies of man may be systematised and developed ; by the practice of entrusting temporarily or permanently portions of public capital to workmen who have proved that they are qualified in character and intellect. These artificially rich men will become types for the gradual reformation of those who are naturally rich ; and we may thus avoid any frequent recurrence to confiscation, a practice which would seriously impair the security indispensable to the right employment of wealth.

This sketch of the means of remedying social abuses will *General consulting office of the Priesthood.* serve to give a general idea of the sacerdotal influence. Even at the point where its organised authority ends, it has a power of interfering morally; for it will possess a consulting voice in the whole of civic life.

Our social analysis shows that the Religious Power is amply provided by the scheme of Human Society with all the instruments needed for its office, to counsel, to sanction, and furthermore to regulate. And if the Priesthood does fall below the level of its proper mission, it will have nothing but its own shortcomings to blame; and its own weakness is more to be feared than the hostility of the Government or the indifference of the Public.

Danger of counsel degenerating into command.

The great temptation, against which it must ever guard, is found in man's instinctive tendency to command, when he ought to persuade and to convince. Any office of authority whatever, even when it springs originally from a purely spiritual source, leads us habitually to give men, in place of evidence which they can criticise, commands which they are to obey. We have daily instances of this in the arrogance of our literary politicians. Nevertheless, one must hope that the Positive study of human nature will preserve the new Priesthood from thus degenerating. Hitherto it has been found an inevitable failing in natures trained under Theology or Metaphysics, at least where there is not a rare moral greatness. However, if we turn to the personal instincts as placed in the cerebral scheme (vol. i. p. 594), we see that Vanity is higher in quality than Pride; and it follows that the theorician who yields to the bait of temporal ambition is lowered and not raised in the scale. On the contrary, when the man of action foolishly aspires to spiritual authority, however much he be to blame, still he is at least yielding to the impulse of a higher sentiment. A life of contemplation not of action is so necessary for maintaining the synthetic spirit and the social sentiment, that he whom idle ambition prompts to neglect this cardinal rule, shows himself by this for ever unworthy and unfit to enter the Priesthood. Perhaps he ought even to be thereby excluded from all serious share in Government: the State can choose its leaders better elsewhere. For this reason the spontaneous ban of Public Opinion, and the formal censure of the Church, should be expressed without mercy on all such crimes of ambition, which are the great source of disturbance to be feared in the final state of society. We may, in fact, be reassured that these two kinds of condemnation will never check the progress of any really great character. For, that tendency to Pedantocracy, which was formerly the ruin of so many great men, is in our day the best evidence of poverty of mind and heart. Nothing but loyal and constant rejection of Wealth and of Power can invest the Priesthood with the confidence both of the rich and the poor alike, which is required for any useful interference as arbiters in civil conflicts.

Next to this constant care, the true Priest must above all things strive to develop in himself the qualities concerned in active life. The powers of Heart and of Mind will have had a careful training throughout the two courses of education. The duties of the religious office give them an almost constant cultivation. But this is not the case with those which concern the Character strictly so-called. Yet these are no less indispensable to the social office of the Priesthood, who have often to carry on a struggle of principle with Wealth or Numbers. It was chiefly in order to give time for these qualities to ripen that I fixed the normal age for full priestly duty at forty-two, the period of man's perfect maturity of life. Many a fine nature, happily endowed with a synthetic intellect and a sympathetic heart, may often for want of due Courage and Perseverance collapse in the difficult positions in which the Priesthood may sometimes find itself. The third practical quality, Prudence properly so-called, seems less indispensable at first sight; but it is really as necessary as the other two qualities to the Priesthood; if only we look at it in its nobler form, animated with a social mission, and free from all traces of self-seeking. Indeed it is in the priestly class that true Prudence may be seen at its best, that is, deliberate forethought, uniformly enlightened by sound philosophy; and this is possible only in the public behalf. Everywhere men are too ready to give the honoured title of Prudence to the mere dictates of Selfishness. The successes of individuals in practical life are, in truth, too much intermingled with accidental circumstances to be the proper subject of calculation. On the contrary, the men who have ever in view the general welfare of Humanity, must naturally bring out all that man has of Prudence; for they will deal with subjects of a broader kind, almost wholly determined by regular laws, and those for the most part already ascertained.

Such, then, is the broad scheme of man's Social Existence,

Qualities essential to the Priesthood : Courage, Perseverance,

Prudence.

Slow prepa-
ration of
this social
harmony.

wisely organised by the Positive Priesthood. If we take all
that is said in this, with the concluding remarks of the preceding chapter, we shall see that this normal state, although
the one most in harmony with man's nature, could not be
established without a long and difficult course of gradual improvement.   Before the various forces of life could be regulated,
it was necessary that they should first develop of their own
accord, so that each should show its true character.   Now, any
premature discipline of them would have hampered this preliminary period of free growth.   We see this in the great
attempt of the Middle Age ; which speedily degenerated into
an oppression of the Intelligence and Activity, without being
at last favourable to Feeling, to which it devoted its thought
exclusively.   Before passing into the service of the Heart, so
as duly to control human life, Mind had long to be the servant
of Force, with a secret hope of becoming its master.   In this
way it established dominant Powers in society, the very abuses
of which showed their vitality.

However admirable were the ancient Theocracies, the only
types of a truly complete order which Man has hitherto
achieved, the rule of Intellect they set up was so charged
with evil, that we must not go to them for examples of man's
tendency towards a normal society.   We only began to work
towards it really, when the progress of civilisation first broke
the Theocratic yoke.   But then, as we saw before (p. 79), and
the next volume will expand the idea, all true harmony was at
an end.   No system of society could endure ; and thence began
the three stages of transition, intellectual, active, and affective :
the Greek, Roman, and Mediæval eras, which come between
the primitive Theocracy and the ultimate Sociocracy.   We see
now, in the vanguard of Humanity, the beginning of the end
of this long education of Man ; for we can clearly trace its
general features, now that we have founded the new Science of
Sociology, and as a deduction from Sociology, the Universal
Religion.   Five centuries of anarchy have passed even in the
West, since the last phase of the preparatory eras closed with
the Middle Age.   We must see in this how urgent is the need
of a new reorganisation : a new spiritual life first, and then a
new material life.

Summary of
the chapter
and its con-
nections.

This and the preceding chapters combined will give the
main characters of this final Order as deduced from the laws

of human nature.   Such is the method proper to Social Statics, where time is always put aside from the problem.   The task of Social Dynamics will be to explain the phases of Man's evolution, and to show the conditions which point to the advent of this final Order; a question not yet treated except incidentally.   This determined, we shall be in a position to complete our conception of the normal society, by direct and special discussion of its leading institutions.   Such is the scheme of the third and the fourth volumes to follow.   There still remains, however, one additional theory to work out in this volume, as I stated in the Introduction (p. 6).   The next chapter will give the best connection between the Statics and the Dynamics of Sociology, as dealing with the Limits of Variation to which human Order is subject under various reacting forces, natural or artificial.

CHAPTER VII.

POSITIVE THEORY OF THE GENERAL LIMITS OF VARIATION
IN THE ORDER OF HUMAN SOCIETY.

INTRO-
DUCTORY,
pp. 346–350.

It might seem that the Order of human society has now been treated in the abstract up to the point where begins the direct study of the natural laws of its evolution, with a view to show how far the actual development of society has gone.   But the circle of Social Statics will not be complete without a further inquiry.   To omit this would be to expose our conception of Dynamics to want of certainty, and even of clearness.   In fact, it will not be enough to recognise the cardinal rule, that Dynamical are governed by Statical laws; so that Progress must never be regarded as anything but the organic development of Order.   But to keep ever in view this great law, and even to apply it correctly, a further Statical law must be established.   What must first be done is to look upon this Order no longer as fixed, and thus specially to ascertain the necessary limits of the modifications of which it is capable.

Limits of
Social Varia-
tion.

Nor is this vast field of inquiry at all foreign to the scope of Social Statics.   For, the variations in question must always be there treated in the abstract, independently of time or place ; whereas time and place are the prime considerations in Dynamics dealing with events.   This is withal that side of Social Statics where they approach nearest to Dynamics ; and thus it forms strictly the transition from the first to the second half of the Science of Sociology.   If the laws of Progress were studied, before laying down the limits, within which alone modification is possible in society, the Philosophy of History would be confounded by the incoherent spectacle offered by man's Progress, and it soon would fall back into the state of chaos, from which I have drawn it.

Theoretic
elaboration
must be sub-

This addition to the field of Social Statics, and it is one no less difficult than it is new, is in necessary connection with the

study of the General Order of Nature, the original source of all changes in the Social Order. The entire subject is accordingly so vast that it can only be worked out properly in a separate volume, and this I must leave to my successor. I shall confine myself here to the essential ideas wherein such a work will find its spirit and its programme. In order to get rid of any pedantic subtlety or detail, we must keep firmly in mind that the use of theory whether for method or for knowledge, is to check those extravagances to which the study of Dynamics is naturally exposed. We must keep the inquiry therefore strictly to the cardinal object in view, that is, to trace out the Evolution of human society to the precise point where we may comprehend better the phase of it in which we are. In any further following out of the inquiry, we must hold fast to the same rule of keeping Theory in constant dependence on Practice, thus putting aside all premature speculations. Ever seeking to make this encyclopædic point of view familiar and consistent, I shall here note those concrete questions towards which will be directed the chief abstract studies involved in the immense field of thought surveyed in this work. When I gave it a practical rather than a theoretic title, my purpose was to keep ever before my own mind, as well as the reader's, the intellectual discipline necessary to found a Religion : *that the end be never absorbed in the means.*

ordinate to Practical object.

It has been shown throughout the first chapter of this volume that every sort of Order in Nature is of necessity liable to change, either by the intervention of Man, or by that spontaneous reaction, which is ever at work in the General Economy of things. The Order of the Heavens is in truth the only one really beyond the reach of our powers ; although our intelligence can easily conceive in it possible improvements. Every other sphere admits of modification, at once artificial and natural · so that Astronomy, far from giving us the permanent type of Natural Order, as it did in the infancy of science, really is an exception in that Man has no power over it. But, when in the chapter just cited I undertook to explain the normal law, according to which the Constant becomes compatible with the Variable, and this is the true scientific point of view, I took sufficient notice of the difficulty that the conception involves, the last great achievement of man's gradual mastery of Objective Science. The thinkers of our time are for the most part

Liability to Change is an essential part of any conception of Order.

little versed in this immense curriculum of scientific training, and, to them a Modifiable Necessity is a notion no less contradictory than it was thought to be thirty centuries ago, when the first rise of Astronomy gave to men the earliest systematic idea of the Order of Nature. However, the normal state of Positive conceptions ought to be maintained without reference to the anarchic attitude of minds which have never had any real Encyclopædic Education. Nevertheless, the regenerated intelligences are still so few, that we shall long have to resort to the measures of precaution required by the morbid state of minds in the West. For this reason, before entering directly on the theory of the Modifiability of Social Order, I shall add some preliminary remarks, addressed to minds of real power but of imperfect training.

Human Order is more modifiable than Vital, or Material Order.

Though less general, and thereby more complex, than the Material Order, and even than the Vital Order, the Human Order, collective or individual, is more modifiable than any other. Its real variations are so wide that they were naturally regarded as limitless: so wide are they that the antiquated philosophy, still in vogue in the West, is led by the spectacle of these changes to look on Social phenomena as exempt from all natural Law. The apparent incoherence of human affairs is such that the sages of the old Theocracies tried to satisfy man's craving for fixity by investing Social Order with a religious sanction of immutability, in harmony with their conservative organisation of life. But this dogma, however well adapted to that stage of civilisation, neither checked the energetic tendencies which continually urged men on to political and moral improvement, nor could it disguise the variations arising from the spontaneous growth of society.

Early notion that Progress was a return to Primitive Order.

The pride of the ruling order, whether Soldiers or Priests, could not recognise any social control in the World without, apart from Human will and force. There was the more reason for this misconception, in that political modifications allowed in olden times a wider range than in ours, and that personal influences played a larger part in social movements, as we shall hereafter see explained. In order to make any actual progress compatible with the religious immobility of society, it was asserted that every proposed change was a necessary return to Primitive Order. This spontaneous tendency, whilst it was readily accepted by the public as a practical guarantee of fixity, further offered this theoretic advantage, that it gave the first outline of the fundamental principle of Sociology (that Progress is the development of Order). However, the contradiction involved by the fiction was found in practice to be so glaring, that it satisfied neither the Practical wants of life nor the claims of the Intelligence.

The theory, indeed, but ill protected the society of Antiquity, even the Theocratic Society, from those unforeseen storms which so often convulsed it. At the same time, it was enough to prevent the human mind from reaching the true conception of social life, in which Progress must be brought into alliance with Order. It will give us a measure of the strength exerted over men's thoughts by these primitive dogmas, when we remember that the chief thinkers of the eighteenth century, not even excepting the illustrious Vico, thought that any alliance between Order and Progress involved an inherent contradiction ; and this, though they had before their eyes the decisive proof of revolutions actually effected. The truth is that the human understanding does not as a rule take into account any facts which it is unable to systematise. And in those days, for want of a due logical and scientific training, the facts of Progress were not yet in a state to be reduced to system.

Progress was an idea but slowly recognised.

However, now that I have founded the Final Science, Sociology, in its Statical and Dynamical branches, the normal condition of the problem, how to reconcile Order with Progress, is no insurmountable difficulty. If there be any minds to whom it is a stumbling-block, they must be of that unteachable temper to which Positive Religion would not assign the sphere of Theory. There is the less reason for any scruple in disregarding such objections, in that the arguments in the first chapter have shown that the necessary adjustment between Movement and Conservation is in no way special to the Social Economy. Throughout the General Harmony of thought, even including its basis in Mathematics, whence come our general formulæ, the Positive spirit always implies the union of Dynamic conceptions with Statical principles. The difference is only that this continual adjustment grows at once more difficult to effect and yet more important, in the degree that the facts before us become more complex, as they become more special. Still, true science does not begin until the two sets of ideas are harmonised. Up to this point, Science has only accumulated Objective Ma-

The true explanation may be found in Sociology.

terials, and waits the Subjective Coordination.   This is as yet complete only for Sociology, the only possible foundation for any Organisation of Knowledge.

Thus the general conception of a Modifiable Necessity, the unfailing note of the Positive doctrine, presents nothing special in the Human Order, beyond the greater difficulty of making it felt by reason of the increased amount of Variability.   The day is coming when all minds to which this habit of thought is not easy and familiar will find themselves shut out for ever from any part in Philosophy ; on the ground that their only influence on thought must be evil, and alike anarchical and retrograde. The judgment of the West will formally pronounce as incompetent : first the savants and specialists, who show themselves unfit for any really philosophic culture ; and next the so-called thinkers, who persist in addressing themselves to the social, the most difficult of all studies, with nothing but a literary or an ontological education.

This point determined, we may proceed directly to the Positive theory of Social Variations.   And I shall explain briefly the proper nature and the mutual relations of all its essential principles.

To give a better basis to this doctrine, it should be extended to the entire Encyclopædia of Science ; and it should be applied to the various elements necessary to the General Economy of Nature.   In doing this, the normal Classification which I have established must be followed.

Each order of the Great Economy which we know is subject to the constant influence of two sets of Variations : the first are direct, and are the spontaneous consequences of operations in the phenomena themselves ; the other are indirect, and spring from the reaction upon these phenomena of the whole Economy of Nature outside of them.   From both of these two ever active sources there may further arise exceptional variations ; which are called in Inorganic Existence, *perturbations* ; in Living Beings, *maladies* ; in Social Life, *revolutions*.   But, if we apply the luminous principle of Broussais (see p. 359) throughout the whole Scale of Thought, we always find that these anomalies differ only from the normal Order in the degree of their intensity : they never present a really new condition.

In any Order of phenomena, the energy of its own internal action at once introduces a series of changes.   An easy proof

may be found in the simplest of all the economics of Nature. der by its own proper activity.
For, the variations as yet ascertained in the Celestial Movement
are caused entirely by the reaction of the mechanical forces at
work throughout it ; and the perturbing action is always
similar, both in substance and in governing law, to the controlling action of the whole : differing from it only in place and in
degree.   Thus the normal type of the movement of any whole
is only to be found in an intermediate state, one rather ideal
than real, round which the actual system in fact oscillates; at
least so long as the aberrations of it do not exceed the limits
where the system ceases to be maintained.   The Order of Nature, therefore, apart from all external influences is no more
Eternal than it is Absolute.   But furthermore we have no need
to know it, except in the mode which corresponds with our own
existence.   Now, since Human Existence, as being more complex and more special than any other, is dependent on all the
other less noble and more regular existences in Nature, we have
continual assurance that the actual constitution of the Universal Order will outlast that of the Human Order.   Accordingly, the laws which we are unable to discover will ever of
necessity remain needless for us to know.   This is the reason
that our positive existence as a whole is so constituted that our
Theoretic resources naturally run parallel with our Practical
wants.

As to the second class of modifications to which every form 2. Variation is produced by the reaction of other Orders.
of Order is subject, the reaction from without, we must consider
this under the two heads into which it falls : Variations resulting from the Order preceding, or Variations resulting from the
Order succeeding it in the great hierarchy of the Universal
Order.   Every class of phenomena therein presents in the first
place its own laws, which would still subsist, if all the rest of the
Economy of Nature were to disappear.   But the Order resulting
from the aggregate of these laws is constantly dependent on the
simpler and more general kinds of Order, especially through the
medium of the Order next below it in the scale.   In its turn,
every Order is incessantly modifying the irresistible weight of
all the rest.   Now, these modifications necessarily react upon
itself, by reason of its own dependence on the existence so ope-
rated upon.   Thus, the variations of every Order in Nature are
due at once to the one which precedes it, and to that which
succeeds it.   It is only the two extremes of the Encyclopædic

Scale, which have each only one source of modification.   Accordingly, if this immense Classification of phenomena be grouped under its three leading branches, we find that the Material Order at the lower end, and the Social Order at the upper, are indirectly modified only by the Vital Order which separates them and unites them.   The latter, on the contrary, is at once subject to the two kinds of indirect Variations.   In the same way, in distinguishing the three successive modes of Material existence, we see that the Mathematical laws by themselves, that is Geometry and Mechanics, the great field of which is the Heavens, are indirectly affected only by the laws of Physics and Chemistry.   But the operation of Physical phenomena (properly so-called) is affected at the same time by the variations of the Astronomical and of the Chemical order, between which the Physical forms the natural junction.

Human Order divisible into 1. Social, and 2. Moral.
We must now apply to the Human Order these general principles as to the Limits of Variation.   For this purpose, we will first separate the Human Order finally into its two necessary modes : the one collective, the other individual ; forming respectively Social existence and Moral existence.   I introduced this distinction between Sociology and Morals in the first chapter of this volume as needed to complete my Encyclopædic Classification of the Sciences ; and this, the concluding chapter, may be now devoted to fill up and establish this prime doctrine ; whilst in the rest of the treatise it will be constantly applied, especially in implicit form.

Thus forming seven sciences.
This final conception of seven, instead of six, degrees for the Encyclopædic Scale of the Sciences was in my thought, when I sketched the general scheme of Positive Education ; so that of the two latter years of the seven years course, one year should be devoted to Sociology, and then one year to Morals (vol. i. p. 192).   That I should have suggested it in that connection illustrates the religious purpose involved in sound Philosophy, and further shows how real and opportune is the distinction itself.   Its value is further shown by the agreement between the subject closing the Encyclopædic course in the systematic wisdom of modern reason and the admirable instinct of the genius of Antiquity to regard Morals as the Master Science.

These are :— Mathematics, Astronomy, Physics, Chemis-
The venerable Theocracies with which civilisation opened, of which the spirit long survived in the Oracles of Greece, proclaimed forty centuries ago that the Knowledge of Man was the

true end of all science. Now that we have completed the immense Objective education in Science which has been accomplished since the date of this luminous aphorism, the Subjective Synthesis irrevocably brings us back to the same starting-point : for it gives us at once the general result of that Knowledge and the principle of the Synthesis. For Man, properly so called, when regarded in his essential reality, and not by the light of materialist or spiritualist dreams, can only be understood by means of a previous knowledge of Humanity, for on this Man necessarily depends. And it would be needless to enlarge any further on the view already familiar to the reader, that the Social Existence of Man is in necessary dependence on the Vital and on the Material Order. We thus obtain, if we decompose into its parts the Material Order, the seven essential stages of knowledge, Mathematical, Astronomical, Physical, Chemical, Vital, Social, and finally Moral. In the Positive system, these will henceforth be the steps in the great Encyclopædic Series of the Sciences.

try, Biology, Sociology, Morals.

If this series be made as compact as possible, it can be concentrated into the simple dualism between Cosmology and Sociology. In fact readers of the first volume must be already familiar with the condensation of the four groups of thought relating to Inorganic existence in the one general conception of Material Order (vol. i. p. 335). As to the fusion of the three Organic groups, all that we have to do is to regard Sociology as absorbing Biology by way of introduction, and Morals by way of conclusion. This simple philosophical dualism will finally be the most usual mode of conception, as the instrument by which theoretic wisdom will give system to practical wisdom. The various subdivisions of the group Cosmology, and even of the group Sociology, belong more to didactic education than to real life. For active life, Science has most urgent need of being condensed.

These may be condensed into two : Cosmology, and Sociology.

Nevertheless, it is of more importance to separate the parts of Sociology, than it is to keep distinct those of Cosmology. For, the distinction between Sociology and Morality is at bottom not less real and not less useful than the distinction between Sociology and Biology. It is simply the empiricism of science which prevents us nowadays from giving so much attention to the former distinction. Both of these distinctions must be kept in view, when the object is to represent, not the Statical

Or better, Sociology must be resolved into three : Biology, Sociology, and Morals.

condition of real science, but its Dynamical evolution ; so that the terms of the series will be : Cosmology, Biology, Sociology, Morals. These four terms, the first and last three of which exhibit a normal series, will form a very common mode of representing the hierarchy of the Sciences, elsewhere than in the Positivist Schools. However, the real subdivisions of Cosmology, which now absorb almost the whole of speculative attention, ought, on the contrary, to be limited more and more to the period of teaching, if we put aside their application to industry. At the same time, however serviceable may be the quaternary series which I have just stated, the binary classification of the sciences will always be the one most in use as a general arrangement of knowledge. It expresses, in fact, the utmost amount of concentration in the groups compatible with the necessary Dualism of sound Philosophy, by reason whereof there can be no Unity but a Subjective Unity (see vol. i. pp. 355–368).

Review of Objections.

This conception of Encyclopædic Classification is one to which I shall not again return, and we may clear up all difficulties as to it by a rapid examination of the two essential objections that it may meet.

1. First Objection : that Morals is not distinct from Sociology.

In the first place, this final subdivision of Human Order into the Collective and the Individual forms may be thought to be a distinction but slightly marked, if we compare it with the contrasts between the other grades in the Series of Seven Sciences. But, at bottom, the separation between Physics and Chemistry, which is still so much disputed by the specialism of the Academies, is less definitely marked ; yet withal no true thinker will be disposed to deny the distinction there. The same thing is true of the subdivision of Celestial Cosmology into Mathematics and Astronomy ; and it is the case also in the other distinction in Cosmology, that between Astronomy and Physics, a distinction which our savants hardly grasp in their vague conceptions of general Classification. We are yet lacking in habitual sense of the ultimate separation of Moral existence, truly so called, from simple Social existence. But it will soon be recognised that this last gradation in the grand Scale of Thought is completely in accord with the greater number of those which precede it.

Reality of the distinction.

I pointed out, when I first foreshadowed the distinction (vol. i. p. 142), that we come upon it directly if we extend to General

Classification of the Sciences the principle governing the Positive scheme of Classification : *decreasing generality and increasing dependence.* We may now add that this last term of the Abstract Series of sciences has as much importance as those which precede it. Unless a series of the kind were carried out to this its normal termination in Morals, the system of classification would be insufficient to group our concrete notions. The last term of the series has also the incomparable advantage of guiding the movement of Thought onwards to its ultimate object in Religion ; for by it the Encyclopædic curriculum of Science is crowned by the sacred doctrine of Morals, and we may leave pedants to dispute whether this be an art or a science. By this means the Series of Order is brought into better conformity with the Series of Progress; and thereby the whole Human Synthesis, speculative, active, and affective is really improved. At this point, the earliest science explored by the wisdom of the Priesthood may be brought into direct harmony with that peculiar to the philosophic reason, if we put aside the intermediate terms whereby a continuous chain of sciences is established between them. We have in the case of an eminent modern thinker, the weak and unfortunate Pascal, a memorable instance of the same mind with a native turn for Geometry as well as Morals ; and that in a time before it was possible to perceive the links which united them in a general chain of Classification.

The second objection to the separation of Morals from Sociology arises from a loose conception of Biology, on the ground that in the general laws of Vitality the science of man's individual existence was previously included. This objection is no doubt more formidable than the first; but, by following out the principles contained in the preceding volume, we may speedily find an answer to it.

2. Second Objection : that Biology includes Morals.

Biologists properly so called, whether theoretical or practical, always aim at the knowledge of Man with a view to his improvement ; but it is only in rare instances that both these objects are accomplished. For to do so is a direct impossibility to thinkers in a stage of materialism so complete, that they preposterously neglect the principal characters of human nature, the moral and intellectual. At bottom, what they study in mankind is not the man, but the animal. Of the essential attributes of the man as a rule they know nothing ; indeed they

But Biology at present confines itself to the animal nature.

know less than the unscientific public, because their observation is engrossed with the body alone. Our so-called physicians are really only veterinary surgeons, though for the most part worse taught than the latter now are in France. They are accordingly as little able to cure animals as they are able to cure men. The younger members of this decaying class begin to their honour to feel their false position, both socially and morally; nor can it cease, until the service of the Physician is again made an integral part of the office of Priest, as in the normal state it should be, and as in olden times it once was.

Besides, its subject is Life, not Man.

As was shown on scientific grounds before (vol. i. p. 474), true Biology has nothing to do with the Knowledge of Man as Individual, but with the general study of Life, as seen in the whole of the Beings enjoying life. Biology is accordingly a necessary precursor, first to the theory of Social Order, on which Vital Order is directly dependent; secondly, to the true understanding of Man, properly so called, so soon as the essential attributes of his nature are known. The study of Man, the normal conclusion of the Positive doctrine, is now irrationally parcelled out amongst three classes of thinkers : the Physicians, who study only the body; the Philosophers, who imagine that they study the mind; and the Priests, who specially study the heart. In consequence of this deplorable subdivision of labour no one of these three classes of mind really understands Human Nature; for this in its entirety must ever of necessity be indivisible, however much in our incoherent specialism we would break it into parts.

But the Cerebral Theory of Biology ultimately tends to an Anthropology, or science of Morals.

However, my eminent predecessor, Gall, at last opened a way which had been already prepared by Cabanis and Leroy. On this theory we may ultimately systematise the study of man; for it definitively unites our positive knowledge of the Soul with that of the Body. Physicians and Priests alike have hardly seen the bearing of this revolution in science. The consequences could not be seen, until, by founding Sociology, I was able to add the last group to the Encyclopædic series of the sciences. When this was effected, it was possible to have a systematic basis for an Anthropology, or true science of Man, though this science ought ever to retain its sacred name of Morals. Now that this last condition has been fulfilled, and now that it has already enabled me to construct on subjective methods a sound Cerebral Theory, the seventh and last gradation in the grand Hierarchy of Abstract Science is as distinctly defined as any of the others.

The science of Morals differs from the two preceding sciences in that it brings them into close combination. Biology may be looked at as introducing the study of Human Existence through that of the vegetative and animal functions; whilst Sociology only teaches us to know man's intellectual and moral qualities; for these can only be properly examined in their collective action. With this basis the true final science, that is Morals, is able to reduce to a system the special knowledge of man's individual nature, by duly combining the two points of view, the Biologic, and the Sociologic, in which that nature must be necessarily regarded.

Morals connects Biology with Sociology.

Besides this basis of deduction, Morals, like every other science, requires the direct inductions proper to it : observations, such as the instinct of the People and the perceptions of Women have always made without any teaching from Philosophers or Priests. Observations of the kind are necessary, precisely because in Sociology we must entirely eliminate the results of that continual reaction between man's Physical and Moral nature, arising from the organic relations of the Vegetative viscera with the Affective organs. These individual perturbations do not in fact sensibly affect collective existence ; and they are of less and less importance in proportion as that existence is developed. Facts peculiar to different individuals eventually neutralise each other : and thus they leave in Sociology only the permanent influence of such qualities as are really collective. This is true when we limit our view to mere objective Solidarity ; but the phenomena of individuals disappear more completely when we study subjective Continuity, ever more and more the dominant force in Social Order. For they neutralise each other in the succession of generations, more completely than they do in the union of individuals or of families. This is the main reason that Anthropology, in its strict sense, is at once more special and more complex than Sociology itself. Nevertheless, by the use of the term Morals, to denote the science of man's individual existence, we get a convenient reminder that this science is strictly confined to the normal grounds of human conduct ; for that reason it sternly rejects idle speculations about special idiosyncrasies which would prove in truth the most difficult of all problems.

It has to observe the more complex facts of individual life, which are eliminated in Sociology.

But this vo-
lume is con-
cerned with
Social, ra-
ther than
Moral Exist-
ence.

With this definitive subdivision of Human Order into its collective and individual sides, we are now in a position to apply the general principles already explained as to the Positive theory of the Limits of Variation. I shall, however, continue the examination rather of Social existence than of Moral existence, in its right sense, as belongs to the province of this volume. Moral existence, on the contrary, will take the first place in the fourth volume, which will treat directly the normal Organisation of human Life, determined chiefly by the Heart: it having been shown in the third volume that all the human forces are sufficiently developed to admit of systematic discipline.

Method of
procedure.

As the method of treatment which I propose, respecting the Limits of Social Variation, is based upon my system of general Classification, it will be clearer if I at once state, which mode of that classification I shall adopt. Out of all the arrangements, at once objective and subjective, which this Scale of the Sciences admits, it will be most convenient in this chapter to employ most commonly the quadruple method just stated; that is, to class the General Order under Material, Vital, Social, and lastly Moral. Nevertheless I shall take occasion, when convenient, to employ the simple ternary method; that is, grouping the last two terms of the series under the common name of the Human Order. When I proved just now the final separation of the Social and the Moral spheres, my purpose was simply to find a new instrument for carrying on the highest theoretic conceptions; and I had no intention of binding myself by any pedantic terminology, to be followed with blind and puerile servility.

Four sources
of Social
Variations:
Environ-
ment, Life,
Humanity,
Idiosyn-
crasy.

With this proviso, we must distinguish the modifications peculiar to the Social Existence, as in all other cases, into the direct and the indirect: according as they arise spontaneously from its own proper movement, or as they are induced by the reaction over this existence of the entire body of the real Order of Nature. This reaction again is of two kinds, first, the influence of the Order succeeding to the Social, that is the Individual; secondly, the influences of all the preceding modes of Order. Lastly, these latter influences must be again subdivided according to their origin, into the Material and the Vital. If we combine these three kinds of differences we come to perceive four general sources of social Variations: that of the Environment, that of Life, that of Humanity, and lastly that of Indi-

vidual Idiosyncrasies. The order in which these are stated is
also the order in which they ought to be systematically studied,
as it was also the order in which they respectively began to be
recognised. For, the fundamental principle of all Positive Classification, the principle of decreasing generality and increasing
complexity, is at once a historic and a scientific truth. However, for practical purposes this series may be reduced into its
binary form ; that is to say, grouping Environment and Life in
one term, and Humanity and the Individual in another term.
No real relation of phenomena is ignored by this logical artifice
of representing the series in two terms; if we refer it to the
primary distinction between the constant modifications ever in
operation throughout Space, and those progressive modifications
which can only be developed in Time. This therefore brings
us back to one general division into the indirect and the direct ;
that is, if we neglect the subdivision of the Human into the
Collective and the Individual. Nevertheless, the right understanding of this subject will be best promoted by using the
quaternary series above stated, wherein influences are grouped
in the order of their increasing intensity : the Cosmos, Life,
Humanity, Man.

But before treating the normal order of the series of modifi- *Governing principle of Variations.*
cations proper to the Social System, we must first establish the
fundamental principle running through their common nature.

This principle is established by duly following out as a *An exten-sion of the doctrine of Broussais : that the per-turbing forces are similar to the normal forces.*
general law the admirable aphorism struck out by the great
Broussais : *that the phenomena of Disease are homogeneous with
those of Health, but varying in intensity* (see vol. i. p. 527).
This conception, which has a value at once logical and scientific,
I there extended to apply to the Collective Organism, having
already applied it to the highest Individual functions. But
Intellects of a truly Encyclopædic power will have no difficulty
in acknowledging that this idea has even more bearing on
Material Order ; and that order ought even to have suggested
the idea previously, if only Cosmologists had been more familiar
with synthetic views of their sciences. In fact, I have already
noticed that the movement of the Astronomical world itself
everywhere exhibits essential likeness between the forces which
disturb and the forces which direct it, as was seen ever since
the formation of Celestial Mechanics as a special study. This
likeness between the two kinds of forces, may be less evident in

the Physical world, properly so-called, and especially as seen in Chemical action; but the reason of this is merely that Terrestrial Cosmology is in a more backward state, owing to its greater complexity. For the chief concrete application of its principles, that is the pretended science of Geology, has already shown the better intellects that it must be explained exclusively by normal forces, even in treating the phenomena which were once absurdly regarded as inexplicable catastrophes. The three modes or degrees of material existence might therefore have been sufficient to suggest an inductive basis for the general principle of Variability, but for the academic pedantry which made true scientific thinkers so few. It was in the more complex, but also the more modifiable form of economy, the Vital, that this principle was at length discovered by the genius of Broussais, a genius in the true sense synthetic, although badly trained. The principle, it is true, was more important in Biology than in the other sciences, and accordingly would awaken a more persevering effort to discover it; but on the other hand it required higher powers of abstraction, such as must fill us with greater admiration and gratitude for this luminous triumph of induction. We shall now carry out this thought into all the grades of the Encyclopædic series of Sciences; so that the primary aphorism of Broussais, still under the name of its immortal author, will henceforward stand for the true governing principle of the theory of Variability in phenomena of every kind. For, if, as this great thinker proved, there is a necessary identity between perturbing influences and the normal forces in every organism, even in the case of distinctly marked maladies, this will also hold good in the case of simple modifications. We may therefore pass to the general conclusion, that the difference between regular existence and any alteration in that existence, is entirely due to different intensity in the phenomena, either statical or dynamical, and does not proceed from any diversity in the laws which govern both. The principle of Broussais may be thus finally reconstructed; and in this form my own share of it is simply to have given it a complete general extension, and to have consolidated it into a system, by a judicious use of my constant rule to regard science in its Encyclopædic character.

Law that Progress is the develop-   It will serve more distinctly to define this fundamental law of Variability, if we compare it with the law which I propounded ten years ago (in 1842) at the close of my work on Philosophy. It will be found in the sixth volume of the Positive Philosophy (chap. 59, p. 685), where I showed, that in every order of phenomena the laws by which they are coordinated must govern all phases of modification; and that thereby, in every sphere alike, Movement is in strict relation with Existence. There is indeed this further point of resemblance between the principle set forth in the last paragraph, and the principle just referred to, in that as the former was adopted from Broussais, so the latter is but the celebrated Mathematical principle of d'Alembert made general and reduced to system. The principle may be found in the first volume of the Positive Philosophy (chap. 17, p. 491).

When in Mechanics he laid down, that the whole of the various motions lost and gained by bodies in mutual relation necessarily balance each other, he converted Movements into phenomena of Equilibrium, and thus reduced Dynamical problems to Statical questions. I was scrupulous to point out (Phil. Pos. vol. vi. chap. 59, p. 685), at the very moment when I first propounded this as a law of philosophy, that it was a development of the law of d'Alembert, and I thereby made its adoption more easy. But, when we compare carefully these two general laws, it will be seen that I should carry the abnegation of my own claims to the discovery too far, if I were to attribute to d'Alembert the principle whereby Movement and Existence may be coordinated in every group of phenomena, precisely as I have attributed to Broussais the first discovery of the law, that every state of Variation is only a phase of a state of Regularity. For d'Alembert, whose intellect was not truly synthetic, did not extend his principle beyond the simplest phase of material existence, that of Mechanics, without even conceiving that it applied to the Physico-Chemical Order, and yet more to the Vital World. The principle, in truth, seemed likely to have a simply Mathematical use, down to the time when Blainville attempted to extend it, though in a somewhat confused way, to the domain of Biology. When he proposed to distinguish the study of the external sources of modification in Life into special and general, the generalisation therein implied was more in words than in reality, but it led up to the principle of my own (see Phil. Pos. vol. iii. chap. 40, p. 215). My own meditations on this law were not finally consolidated, until by an induction in Sociology, that Progress is the development of Order, I had discovered a corresponding principle in a subject peculiarly fitted for reducing it to a definite system. It was only after completing the discovery that I was struck with its necessary agreement with the special aphorism that d'Alembert applied to rational Mechanics; though, having struck it out in this, he did not make it as general as he ought to have done. The principle of Broussais stands on an entirely different ground; for it was missed by the geometers who might have been expected to originate it, and then was directly discovered in the much more complex subject of Biology. For, when he was proving his principle for a form of existence so variable as the Vital, its author must have implicitly extended it to less variable phenomena; although the line of his studies would prevent him from stating explicitly this easy logical operation. It is unnecessary to carry this explanation any further; but it may be of use, if it point out to young thinkers, what is not easy in our age of anarchic thought, the steps of intellectual progress and also true philosophic merit. Since it is always absurd to teach Method apart from Doctrine, it is essential to seize every occasion when sound instruction in logic may be deduced from right procedure in science.

Combination of the two laws.

Without further discussing this point, which has both a historical and a scientific interest, I now proceed to point out how the true theory of every form of existence is necessarily comprised in a judicious blending of the two principles, which, as I have just shown, may be compared, but not identified. In fact, the law of Broussais— *that the phenomena of disease are varieties of the phenomena of health more or less intense*—implies that all kinds of modifications issue out of the normal state. On the other hand, my own law—*that Progress is nothing but the development of Order*—is an analysis of the normal state; and invariably connects its Movement with its Structure. When we put both laws together, therefore, we may secure in every subject of science a true logical unity. We shall obtain this, if after a simple Statical study of regular existence, we proceed, first to a Dynamical estimate of the evolution proper to it, and secondly to the further examination of its various modifications. We may even ultimately regard the principle of Broussais as a mere extension of my own, pushed to its extreme consequences. For, if Progress is everywhere the development of Order, Variation may be always reduced to Evolution, sometimes retarded, but most frequently stimulated. However, in spite of this undeniable connection between the two laws, both logically and scientifically, which it is quite right here to point out, we shall have for the most part to use these two principles in practice as if they were radically distinct, whenever the definiteness of the two conceptions they formulate is of higher importance than the agreement between them.

By virtue of this law, whether we regard it as simple or as double, all Modifications of the Social Order are necessarily limited by the whole body of fundamental rules, which in preceding chapters we have laid down, first as to the Structure, and then as to the Existence of the Collective Organism. Social Modifications, like all others, are a mere question of degree; and accordingly they imply simply varying intensity in Social Statics, and varying rate of speed in Social Dynamics; but they never affect the unchangeable conditions of Positive doctrine. In a word, the true scientific spirit will constantly tend to reduce apparent variations of Quality to simple differences of Quantity. The gradations in this series of modifications, insensibly lead us downwards from the most completely normal state, to the most profound anarchy; and this represents all the intermediate degrees as subject to the same essential laws as the fundamental type.

The laws of Variation are, therefore, corollaries of the laws of Structure and of Existence.

This conception of philosophy logically follows from the scientific ascendency which we have now given to true Positivity. For Invariability in the Order of Nature directly excludes any other explanation of the modifications of that Order but the one just given. If Quality were radically incapable of being stated in terms of Quantity, as, after Kant, the literary and ontological philosophers repeat, there would not really exist any general law, and the notion of laws of Nature would be upset. In a word, no rational Prevision would be any longer possible, and science would be limited to simple Empiricism, and would be stripped alike of induction and of deduction.

Otherwise, there would be no laws of Nature.

These general remarks, will emphatically prove the importance of the supplemental theory to which this chapter is devoted; and may suggest to some successor of my own one day, how the subject may be worked out in a special treatise on the Limits of Variation. But they will also serve to show the extreme difficulty of this vast study. It will be enough if I

Need of a special treatise on Social Variations.

here lay down the essential principles, and trace the general features in the subject of Society, the most decisive of all studies. The principle is this: always to refer to the Normal Type the Anomalies of every kind, be they natural or even artificial, which may be found in the most complex kind of existence. But, however difficult may be this theoretic condition in Sociology, the present treatise is already sufficiently advanced to give direct proof of the possibility of satisfying it even without the expectations indirectly afforded by its successful accomplishment in Biology. For even in the present state of anarchy I have frequently pointed to some special verification of laws proper to the normal type; although that state presents the most profound perturbation, at least intellectually, which is possible in the entire current of human destiny. In the third volume, we shall have many striking instances to confirm this; as we advance in the history of the transition, growing more and more revolutionary, which separates our age from the reign of the Theocracies, the only period of human life that has been entirely normal. Accordingly, if apparent anomalies cannot be duly reduced to phases of the normal type in the science of Sociology as in all other cases, where the study of these anomalies is really called for, the public will know that the weakness lies with the thinkers, and not with the science.

But it is at present premature.

But any general theory of Variations would be at present premature, were it carried beyond the point of suggesting systematically the different social Modifications, regarded as mere phases of the Normal State. I shall therefore here content myself with this methodical enumeration of them, since I have already explained the general order in which they arise. On the one hand, practical requirements do not at present call for more; on the other hand our theoretic resources do not permit us to proceed any further: it will be enough that this sketch for the foundations of the theory should serve as a guide to inquiries hereafter.

1. First or Material source of Variations : the Environment.

The ascending scale of Social Variability starts with the aggregate of material influences: first Astronomical, then Physical, lastly Chemical. These are the most easy to grasp, and the first of which human intelligence undertook the systematic study; a study which was commenced by the great Hippocrates in his admirable and unequalled Treatise upon Climate. The term Material Influences however, would have

to be somewhat forced if we extend it so as really to comprise
the whole of this first system of modifying forces. The word
Environment, already used as a general term of Biology, seems
to me the most convenient for the purpose. At the same time,
we must not confuse the theory of the Environment in Sociology
with that of the Environment in Biology, supposing the latter
theory were completed, whilst it is as yet hardly conceived. In
fact, the Social Order is indirectly affected by all the modifications which the material Environment produces in the Vital
Order. But the proper study of these modifications necessarily
belongs to the second system of modifying forces. In order
therefore to avoid the vice of studying the same subject twice,
we should in the first instance limit the Environment for the
purposes of Sociology to those material influences which directly
affect Sociality, without sensibly disturbing Vitality. For
man's Social existence, as being more complex, admits of many
celestial or terrestrial sources of perturbation, which need not
be taken into account in treating his Vital existence. It is for
this reason that in the Synthetic treatise upon Variability, when
it be written, there will need constantly to be kept in view the
aggregate Order of Nature, of which Human Order will be only
the principal instance, though placed in its proper rank in the
Encyclopædic Scale.

We may see from these reasons how premature it would be
to attempt the formation of any special theory of Environment
in Sociology, because there is as yet no theory of Environment
in Biology, which must serve as introduction and systematic
guide to the former. However, by reason even of this want, a
want which it is not my province to supply, it is the more necessary to state the two essential modes in which the Environment, Celestial or Terrestrial, modifies Social Order without
disturbing Vital Order. Were this omitted, the preceding
remarks would be left with a certain vagueness, and would thus
fail to present their full logical significance. At the same time
it is more easy for me to state both theories briefly, in that
they have been already worked out, though under another form
and for another object, in the last chapter of the fourth volume
of the Positive Philosophy. I shall not decide now, any more
than I did then, whether these two influences necessarily exclude
others, or are merely the principal influences; a point which I
think it idle to discuss.

The Modifications of the World may directly affect Humanity, although confined within limits which do not disturb Life. It will be enough that these influences, celestial or terrestrial, continuous or temporary, signally change man's longevity, or the state of human population, considered either as to its density, or as to its movements. Since we are yet so completely ignorant of the Biologic laws of longevity, we must conclude their influence to be of small importance in the Vital Order. But in the Social Order, as being more modifiable, we find on the contrary that the ordinary duration of human life is an essential element, either of its Statical consistence, or of its Dynamical evolution, where it largely decides the rate of progress. Since the Living are essentially governed by the Dead, the interval between generations, being always determined by the average longevity, directly affects the fundamental relation between the two influences, subjective and objective. Even if we limit ourselves to the consideration of the mere Solidarity of mankind, the greater or less period of each generation profoundly modifies it, for it increases or lessens the respective force of the Conservative instinct and of the Reconstructive instinct belonging to the old and to the young. As each population has greater or less density, it exerts a similar influence over the entire collective existence, domestic and yet more civic. This fact becomes, first in Space and then in Time, an essential condition of the normal rule : that the Country is subordinate to the Town. The same is true, lastly, of the greater or less period required for the ordinary doubling of the human population. For the reaction upon society of this more or less rapid multiplication, is in reality the same as the reaction produced by a corresponding change in longevity. Upon all these grounds, the Astronomical, Physical, or Chemical influences, which may be eliminated in considering Vitality, may seriously react upon Sociality. However, the aggregate laws of the World are as yet too little known to enable us to estimate relations so delicate, and I leave the proper study of them to my successors. If they would avoid entangling themselves in academic puerilities, they must be careful to frame the entire plan of their researches with constant reference to the gradual extension of the Great Being to the different portions of our planet, reaching outwards from its centre in the West.

We may now pass on to consider the second class of Variations peculiar to the Social Order; those which it experiences through the medium of the Vital Order. Although man's individual nature, certainly the vegetative, but also the animal, and even the cerebral is essentially fixed, so long as the form of the Environment is not greatly altered, it nevertheless presents minor differences, resulting from time and space. Now, these subordinate diversities in the Vital Order must largely affect Social Order, which is directly dependent upon it. Variations of the Vital may in the first place affect the Social Order by all the modes pointed out above as to material modifications. But, besides this, they have also a deeper influence; in that they change, first, the practical necessities which constantly control the whole of human existence, then our own resources for comprehending and reacting upon the External World.

The second source of Social Variations, that of Vital con- ditions, is therefore in general of a higher rank than that of the Material conditions. At the same time, we need not be surprised if it be even less understood, because it is closely dependent upon the first class of Variations; and these have been so imperfectly studied down to the present time. In fact, the most marked and the most permanent of these Vital differences, from which we get the irrational notion of *races*, appear to be due to local influences, slowly accumulated by inheritance, in such a way as to produce the maximum amount of organic variation (Phil. Pos. vol. iii. p. 247). At least, this happy suggestion of Blainville is the best hypothesis we can frame, and consequently is the one which sound Philosophy would have us use, so long as it is not opposed by plain and constant observations. We thus perceive that the principal influences which Life exerts over Society are themselves due to the reaction which Material Variations exercise over Life. To study them regularly, therefore, we depend directly upon the study of the Biologic Environment; and this is not yet reduced to system. But, besides these alterations rising from the World Without, the Vital Order, like every other sphere, is subject to spontaneous alterations of its own; and lastly to others arising out of the Order succeeding it in the series. Now, both of these, in their turn, react upon Sociality, itself dependent upon Vitality; and thus they modify Society in permanent ways with reference to places, and in a gradual way with reference to times.

Common ex-
aggeration
respecting it.

This outline will show the extreme complexity, and the greater difficulty of the theory of Biologic influences, which is still less understood than the theory of Material influences. Its effect is felt in a confused way in the vague principle of Races, just as the former theory was once represented by the theory of Climates. But both ideas alike are without any truly positive character. The so-called Philosophers who pretend to be authorities in Sociology, whilst ignorant of Arithmetic, now parade their views about Race, as their predecessors used to parade theirs upon Climate, and they thus get a cheap reputation for scientific profundity. The very men who criticise so sharply the irrational exaggerations of Montesquieu, as to the effect of Material conditions in modifying Society, themselves confidently lay down principles no less fallacious as to the influence of Vital conditions. Both of these kindred schools forget to apply that principle of Positive Logic : *that every examination of any kind of Variations, must be a corollary of fundamental laws found in the normal type.* Their error lies in converting simple differences of intensity and of rate of speed into radical divergences, each having laws of its own ; and they thus destroy anything like general conceptions, and make sound explanation impossible. When we see what deplorable confusion now reigns in the two theories, as to the effect on Society of Material or Vital conditions, it must strike all how urgent, and yet how difficult, is any really systematic handling of this subject.

3. Direct
reaction :
Sociologic
influences.

We now proceed to those influences which directly modify Society, that is to say, those which result from its own proper movement. We must note a fundamental distinction between them, or we shall be involved in a fruitless repetition running through our whole system of Sociology.

(*a*.) General
Social Evo-
lution is the
subject of
Historical
Sociology.

In fact, the Ordered Evolution of human life is continually modifying our normal existence, in the very act of giving it incessant development. We shall study this progressive reaction systematically in its proper place, in the third volume treating of Social Dynamics. In fact, there is no necessity for any special treatment of these direct influences of Variation ; for they are an integral part of Social Science, and their place in it is the most familiar side, the Philosophy of History. The variations which society itself throws up, forming the Dynamic Existence, whilst it develops the Statical existence, may be put aside for our present purpose, by reason in fact of their immense importance.   Unless we reserve them for their proper place in the Philosophy of History, the science of Sociology would be exposed to inextricable confusion.   But at the same time we have still left, the third class of Social Variations, mentioned above.

For, we ought to reserve the name of Modifying powers for the merely accessory influences; and under this head will come a second form of collective reaction: that of the sum of all societies upon each singly.

(b.) Reaction of the various societies upon each singly;

In abstract Sociology we conceive the Great Being as formed and as developed from a single nucleus.   In fact, the laws of Existence and the laws of Evolution, must be in essentials the same for all possible centres of this immense aggregate.   Whatever be the nucleus that finally preponderates, and whatever be the mode in which the others agglomerate around it, the fundamental conceptions of Sociology are in no way affected thereby; and my eminent predecessor Condorcet felt the logical necessity for this law.   It will no doubt be an important service of Social Science to determine both of these ultimate results; but they have no bearing on the formation of the science itself.   Even if the separate groups of Humanity were always to remain so numerous as to make the unity of the Great Being on earth impossible in fact, Sociology, whether Statical or Dynamical, would not be very seriously affected.   At the same time, when Condorcet, with an admirable instinct in logic, threw out his hypothesis of framing history as for a single people, he was well aware that this abstract conception, if indispensable as a starting point for historical science, involved the subsequently returning to consider the influence of nations on each other.   We may fairly compare this procedure in Social Science, with the working out of problems in Mechanics by using the artifice of *inertia*, as was done from the commencement of positive philosophy. It was then found necessary, in order to pass from the abstract to the concrete, to reintroduce forces which had been previously eliminated.   We know how difficult Geometers have found this process, and it has been the principal cause of their practical failures when attempting to give too great precision to the solution of some special problem.   The same is true in a higher degree, when we attempt in Sociology to state the abstract condition in terms of the concrete condition with an approximation closer than is needed for any practical purpose.

But must not be exaggerated in abstract Sociology.

Important in concrete and excep- tional cases.

The laws of Existence and the laws of Evolution, have always and everywhere the same essential character ; but, if their force together determines the main movement of each group of Humanity, they still leave any group exposed to the reaction of the rest.   Directly we attempt, in Statics or in Dynamics, to push our explanations beyond a given degree of precision, we find ourselves forced to consider these mutual influences of each group over others.   For the ordinary purposes of Sociologic theory we can fortunately neglect this kind of reaction ; but it is at times indispensable for the treatment of exceptional cases. In the third volume I shall note some striking examples of this, especially in respect to the Middle Age.   At the opening of this great transitional period the progress of the West was signally affected by political changes of very distant origin ; so that we find the general state of Europe depending on that of Asia, even of its most Eastern side.   At the same time, these influences, though essentially discontinuous in visible result, have in reality nothing accidental about them.   They could always have been foreseen by sufficient knowledge of the entire situation of mankind.

Third class of Social Variations is due to reac- tion of each group upon the rest.

The third class of Social Variations is, therefore, produced by the inevitable but intermittent reaction of the various groups, one upon another.   The judicious Ferguson was the first to hit upon the true principle of this latter source of normal Vari- ations (Phil. Pos. vol. iv. p. 289).   It is in fact implied in the law of Broussais ; inasmuch as it would represent Modifica- tions as being nothing but Varieties in intensity or in speed, according to our general law of modifiability.   These secondary influences over society are often so much exaggerated that they make any sound social theory impossible ; for when they are looked upon as governing forces, their number and their incon- sistency are such that no regular scheme of human phenomena can be framed.   Ferguson has however skilfully proved, that even in the case of conquest, the action of a foreign people over the conquered gives rise simply to modifications which would have developed of themselves a little sooner or a little later, the minor changes excepted.

These are either spon- taneous or systematic.

At the same time this explanation must be strictly confined to cases of original evolution, which of necessity are empirical, not systematic.   It is only the study of their spontaneous de- velopment which can suggest or establish the fundamental laws of man's Social Nature. When these laws have been discovered by the single energy of the most advanced group of mankind, it is quite possible for the leading people to exercise over backward nations a systematic action of much higher value. We have seen in the first chapter of this volume (pp. 70–119), the extreme importance of securing a sound theory of these Social Transitions. I shall not here anticipate the history of these which will be found in the third volume, or the mode of guiding them to their destined end, which will be considered in the fourth volume; but I may here point out, how vast and how grand a future is open to this third class of social changes : the influence of the leading groups over the rest. In spite of appearances, they are of much higher importance than either of those which precede.

I have now only to explain the fourth class of Variations in Sociology : those which are due to Individual action. This is the last indirect modifying force of the Collective Order, although in a sense the inverse of the more general modifying forces. If we consider separately each group of mankind, this kind of influence may often be found more important than any other ; and thus it attracted the principal attention of the public and even of philosophers, down to the foundation of Sociology. This puerile blunder, which took Individual forces for the sovereign arbiter of human Progress, often gave rise to violent and dangerous extravagancies ; for it fanned the pride of the great men and surrounded them with the illusions of the public. Nevertheless, the practical instinct of true statesmen usually taught them, by rude experience, the limits fixed to their power ; and showed them how completely it depended on the general conditions of society. *4. Fourth class of Social Variations : influence of Individuals on Society.*

It was nothing but his monstrous pride which could have suggested the belief in his own boundless power to the reactionary Dictator, who so long crushed France under his tyranny. The famous aphorism of Napoleon, that the power of a military chief is absolute, which was so rigorously branded by an honourable publicist, is a direct instance of the grossest of logical blunders, and displays utter ignorance of the laws as to how Force is formed and maintained. But this very man is an example which admirably shows the general limits of these individual modifying forces, so that, like all other cases, they may be referred to mere differences of intensity and of rapidity. *Merely affects the intensity or the rate of movement;*

For the retrograde tyranny of the Empire, though founded in a time of utter anarchy, so that the means of resistance in constituted society were almost neutralised, had yet no real result but to retard, at most for a generation, the natural march of the Revolution in the West.   We shall adequately prove this point in the third volume.   But there is no other case in history where individual influence could have had so mighty a scope.

But does not originate it.   The influence of the Individual, even when exerted on the side of Progress, as was that of the incomparable Frederic, is always restrained within similar limits ; although the great movement of society which it promotes, leads us to attach too high a value to personal genius.   If we were to throw the celebrated social axiom of the great Bossuet into a truer form, one which were he now alive he would adopt, it might remain of imperishable use.   Since the Living are ever, and ever more and more, governed by the Dead, the true priesthood will be able perpetually to remind the proudest tyrants : *Man troubles himself, but Humanity disposes of him.*   I make bold to prophesy, that the virtual result of the attempts now being made (1852) against the irrevocable establishment of the French Republic will ere long display the truth of this law: that Individuals cannot arrest a Social movement.

Maximum Limit of Variation.   I have now mentioned all the chief classes of Social Variations sufficiently to prepare for a systematic study of them hereafter.   And I proceed to consider them together with reference to the widest possible divergence from the normal Limits of Variation.   In the former cases, I have said nothing as to the degree of each minor influence ; and accordingly the principles which I have laid down apply to Modifications of all kinds, so long as they do not involve the disruption of the system itself.   At the same time, opinion in the West is in such a condition, even with the higher minds, that it is necessary to enter into some short explanation as to extreme cases ; in which the really fundamental laws must govern, as completely as they do elsewhere.

Series of intermediate stages between the extreme limits.   If we press to its consequences the admirable axiom of Broussais, (p. 359), we see that it destroys the old absolute distinction between Health and Disease.   Between the extreme limits of the two, we may always find a multitude of intermediate stages, not merely imaginary, but perfectly real, and together forming an almost insensible chain of delicate grada-

tions. I may give an instance of this necessity for an unbroken
series of change, in the alterations to be met with in Cerebral
existence ; where the Biologic point of view may be easily kept
subordinate to the Sociologic law. I shall also have further
occasion for the observation which I proceed to state.

If the reader recalls what I have already said (see p. 312)
on the nature of all human conceptions, as at once objective
and subjective, he will admit that the opposite states of Reason
and Madness differ only in the respective activity of the two
elements in every state of mind. In any act of thought, the
objective and the subjective process both enter in varying proportions. Should the balance of these proportions be seriously
disturbed, either may be exaggerated at the expense of the
other ; until it prepares the way for, and if persisted in, produces actual insanity. Excessive surrender of the mind to the
External World, with no due effort of the mind within, leads to
pure Idiocy. Madness, on the contrary, is an excessive activity
of the mind within, apart from special hallucination. It arises
from the apparatus of Meditation failing to correct the suggestions afforded by the apparatus of Observation.

Illustrated by mental Health or Disease.

This morbid state may be really better studied in the incomparable work of Cervantes than in any treatise on Biology.
We might even trace from it the great principle of Broussais ;
and might then apply it to Society, as I have now done for the
first time. In fact, the law of Continuity runs through the
whole current of Don Quixote, in the sound instinct with which
it marks the intermediate stages between Reason and Madness.
Cervantes indirectly expounds the primary principle of Positive
Logic : *that directness of mind consists in choosing the
simplest hypothesis which fits the case.* It would follow from
this, that the habit of resorting to complicated reasons to
explain facts is, in reality, a step towards Madness ; in that it
unduly stimulates the subjective action of the mind. A
vigorous brain once started on this course will know no bounds
to the extravagance of its arbitrary creations. Every time that
facts from the World without refute its hypotheses, such a mind
manages to evade conviction by still more elaborate devices to
explain them away.

Borderland between un-
sound logic and insa-
nity : Don Quixote.

The admirable picture of folly drawn by Cervantes also
points to the way in which the due proportions of Objectivity
and Subjectivity in each mind must vary in accordance with

Personal un-
soundness of
mind is rela-
tive to the
time and
place.

the state of society around it. The regular proportion of the two elements ought to follow the course of human civilisation. We shall state in the third volume the general law of these continuous variations: *that the subjective element of thought constantly decreases, and the objective element constantly increases.* If we compare states of mind in striking antagonism, either in widely different times or widely different places, we find that opinions and desires which are properly called *madness*, in one age or one place, are a perfectly normal state of mind in other ages, or other hemispheres. This is a signal proof of the nicety required in judging individual cases of Madness ; and it is a grave danger that in our day they are handed over to an ignorant, and often an immoral, Materialism. The truth is, that whatever the disturbance of reason, the positive laws of Cerebral Life, whether in mind or feeling, may be always traced by philosophic intelligence. And the great Cervantes instinctively pourtrays them, amid all the eccentricities of his hero.

Revolutions are simple cases of degree in change.

This identity in the elements of Health and Disease, the key of the entire law of Variability, holds good as much for the Collective Order as for the Individual Order. It is indeed more easily recognised in the former case, inasmuch as it is really less involved in complication. If they saw the whole bearing of this scientific truth, statesmen would not be so ready to believe that the normal laws of society cease to have any application in times of revolution. The truth however is that in revolutions the disturbance of society is always, as in every other case, a simple question of degree, either in the intensity of some fixed element, or in the rapidity of movement. I shall often have occasion to give specific instances of this, in describing the anarchy of modern times, in spite of the activity which distinguishes it, resulting from the profound breach in the sense of Continuity with the past.

Chronic unsoundness of the West due to a loss of any sense of continuity.

If we analyse the cerebral condition of the West we find it in a morbid state, amounting in reality to chronic unsoundness ; chiefly, it is true, Intellectual, but continually complicated by Moral disturbance, and often attended with Material agitation. The note of unsoundness, consisting in the fact that Meditation is unable to correct the errors of Observation, is only too conspicuous in our modern life, especially when we look to the law of subjective Continuity, the main source of Collective Order. Never was there a time when the term *mental alienation*, in its etymological sense, could be more truly applied than to this melancholy spectacle, of the entire race of the Living stolidly rebelling against the beneficent rule of the Past, even in the act of dreaming about the Future.   Now, however grave such a disturbance of society may be, we are never at a loss to detect in it the laws of the normal state; and some of them appear to me more striking than they do in situations of a more regular kind.   But when we see what different opinions are current on this subject, we may learn how completely relative all such judgments are; for they depend on the notion we form of the normal type.

In fact there are still many minds which are honestly unable to see in this state of things any disorder at all; because the negative phase of the eighteenth century is still to them the highest model of man's social nature.   At the same time, there is nothing arbitrary in the subject; and when we survey the destinies of mankind as a whole, we can always perceive the type to which they tend.   But in doing this, we gain a purer and profounder sense of Order; and we see how revolutionary are many epochs which philosophers are wont to regard as being quite as normal as they appeared to the generations who lived in them. *It is much older in date than is usually supposed,*

If we judge the anarchy of modern times by the light of the doctrines before stated on the Structure and Existence of the collective Organism, the whole era will appear to us as simply the last stage of an immense social perturbation.   The disorder in fact began, when the ancient Theocracies first dissolved; for they were the only complete type of Social Order which the world has hitherto seen.   As they broke up, there grew the principle, which is in all times and in all places revolutionary: that the Superior should be elected by the Inferior; and this dogma, gaining fresh force gradually for thirty centuries, now threatens political society with destruction.   The original purpose of this principle was simply that of modifying the system of Caste, which had become utterly oppressive.   But since it destroyed the ancient principle of transmitting power, whilst it substituted no new principle, the dogma could do nothing but dissolve societies, and ultimately overturn them. It is left for Positivism to put an end to this long disease in society; for in place of the Theocratic succession by Divine Right, it puts the Sociocratic succession by the choice of the *And really began with the downfall of the Theocracies and the introduction of the suffrage*

Superior; so that no break will be caused in the continuity of mankind. Be this as it may, the spectacle of such different judgments shows how necessarily relative is our normal state, and how essentially unchangeable are its abstract laws, whether collective or individual.

THEORY OF THEIR DE-VELOPMENT, pp. 376–382. Law of Development in the four classes of Social Variation.

This general theory of Social Variations will now be complete, when I have added one more essential principle, that of the continuous development traceable in the relative force of these four kinds of Modifying Influences. Since no one of these four can be always and equally intense as human existence advances, we have still to describe the common law of these inevitable changes. We may find the solution in the growing regularity of the Human Order, due mainly to the reaction of human society over the original imperfections of the Order of Nature, an influence which man exerts at first instinctively, and then more and more in systematic ways.

Growing regularity in Social existence, by internal effort.

At first sight it might appear that such a law contradicts the growing complication in social phenomena, due to the gradual extension both of Solidarity and Continuity throughout mankind. But through all the Hierarchy of Nature, the law of *inevitable increase in Complication in proportion with the decrease of Generality*, gives rise to two inverse consequences. And these tend to balance each other ever more and more; because *as liability to imperfection increases, capacity for improvement increases*. If we consider Material Order, and even Vital Order alone, notwithstanding this principle it is true that the real harmony of the system would become less perfect, in proportion as it becomes more complex; and the same rule would hold good for the Human Order if it were ever delivered over blindly to the natural consequences of its greater complication. Such a hypothesis, however, is fortunately out of the question; or at least it can only be realised for a season, at a moment when man's subjective experience from the Past is confounded or neutralised, by the anarchy of the objective Present. In the General View (p. 21), I showed how the inevitable conflict waged by Human Providence against the Fatality of Nature, gave our existence a regularity far beyond that which would otherwise belong to so complex an organisation as man's. I shall now reduce this suggestion to a complete law; that is to say I shall show a continuous progress in this conflict, whilst I treated it before as an unvarying phenomenon.

If we take the general sources of Variation just described, we may easily see in each of them the general law: *that man's activity is continually giving fresh ascendency to the normal state over the different modifications of it.*

In the first place this is obvious with regard to Climate; the active care of the Great Being, even in the beginning of civilisation, gradually reduces all the influences of Climate which are open to man's intervention, and it preserves us in a growing degree from all those which are beyond his resources. Thus it is that man's Planet tends to become uniformly habitable, if we except certain spots of extremely unpromising conditions. The permanent expedients of civilisation sometimes succeed in freeing the Vital conditions from their natural dependence upon Material order. For instance, the artificial warmth of towns in Russia often causes menstruation to take place as early as it does in India. The extravagance of those who dogmatise about Climate is, therefore, the more singular, inasmuch as its effects are in a very great measure neutralised by civilisation.

The same is true of Race, though this second modifying influence of society is more important than the former. The pretentious philosophers, who are ever ready with this fantastic explanation of social movement, are hardly aware that they are forcing the theory, at the very time when this kind of influence is being more and more confined to minor variations. Differences of race at no time did more than affect the rate of our social evolution, and they never changed its character or the course which it took; but the truth is, that the reaction of Race upon Society was formerly much greater than at present. In the first place, the continually increasing mixture of races, has a direct tendency to do away with this source of variety; but furthermore, the Progress of mankind in the mass, is gradually undermining the consequences of Race differences, even more completely than it overcomes the effects of Climate. And beside, as Cosmic influences are lessened in effect, this tends to diminish the varieties of vital conditions; for the latter were originally produced by the Environment.

If the three principal Races of mankind, the White, the Yellow, and the Black, are closely compared, and there are only three Races which present really positive distinctions, we must see how their respective qualities will tend to balance one another when the whole Human Family shall be completely assimilated, and all the forces of human nature called into active service.   Contrasting the two extreme types, it is plain that the Black Race is as much above the White, on the side of feeling, as it is below it on the side of intelligence.   So long as the main task of human life was *to develop* man's various resources, superiority of intelligence overpowered the respect for feeling; and thus it much exaggerated the difference of Race. This will not be the case hereafter ; when the group that leads the van of civilisation will be chiefly concerned with the *discipline* of all man's real powers, so as ultimately to

They will be
ultimately
harmonised. bring them into harmony for the common good.   Then the Heart will definitively assume its natural place of authority, and will incline the Mind to do justice to the qualities of the despised races, who are able to do such good service on behalf of the Great Being.   The middle race illustrates the same truth, though the contrast is less marked.   For the Yellow race appears to me to have the same superiority over the other two on the side of Activity as they have respectively on the side of Intelligence and Feeling.   When we shall all join in developing the resources of our domain the Earth, all these differences of organisation will be more and more made use of by the true Providence, which will transform hatred and hostility into new sources of universal harmony.   The same systematic wisdom, which will labour to associate with man's work all the animals capable of such training, will be directed in the first place to make all varieties of the ruling species work together in unison.   These ultimate modifications of the unity of mankind, by the gradual influence of its Environment, would necessarily develop in turn each of the three great cerebral regions, with more energy than the other two.   The theory of the Brain would in fact imply that entire harmony of the Great Being should call out into intimate cooperation with each other the three great races, the Speculative, the Active, and the Affective.

As we saw that the indirect and involuntary modifications of society are at once diminished and made regular by the expansion of civilisation, so also, the direct and more or less voluntary modifications are yet more subject to the same law of change.

3. Decrease
in the in-
fluence of No one can dispute this truth, as to international influences ; for we see that they interfere less and less with the spontaneous

evolution of each group of mankind. We are not to suppose one Nation on others.
that the subsidence of this source of disturbance in Society is
simply, or even mainly, due to the fortunate transformation
that has been going on in man's social activity : since Industry
took the place once occupied by War. The reason is rather to
be found in that progressive ascendency, which, by the laws of
human nature, the Subjective Continuity of Humanity is ever
acquiring over the Objective Solidarity of men. In presence
of this mighty Empire of the Dead, the petty turmoils of the
Living dwindle into less and less account. The immense populations, whether White or Yellow, who have most respected the
continuity of mankind, exhibit still decisive proofs of this law.
Neither Military violence, nor Industrial fraud, have yet been
able sensibly to change the characteristic manners and habits
implanted by Theocracy ; and these habits will never be broken
up by the influence of the West, so long as that influence shall
remain at once ignorant and self-seeking. The changes, which
beyond dispute have been introduced into such societies since
the commencement of our Middle Age, bear not the slightest
trace of any Monotheist intervention. I venture to assert that
a special study of these cases, rightly conducted, will show that
all modifications in the old Theocratic systems have been nothing but spontaneous results of local evolution. Even the
state of flux peculiar to our modern manners, rendering us so
sensitive to the reaction of other nations, brings into fresh
prominence the fact, that this third modifying force of society,
the International influence, is growing at once weaker and more
regular, and that in a way more distinctly than either the influence of Climate or of Race. Every day furnishes us with
evidence of this, in the small hold secured by those annexations
of peoples which are not spontaneous. For instance in France,
the case not merely of Algeria, but also of Corsica, and even of
Alsace, prove clearly the increasing impotence of a long foreign
domination to absorb any nationality really distinct.

Lastly in the fourth class of Social Modifications, we may 4. The in-
fluence of
Individuals
over Society
grows less.
trace yet more evidently than in the other three, the common
law: that they are becoming weaker and more regular. Both
of these results are yet more distinctly than before due to the
growing dominion of the Dead over the Living, a truth which
is at the bottom of all sound explanations in Sociology, as it is
at the bottom of all harmony in Practical life. In face of this

irresistible pressure of our ancestors, the agitations of our contemporaries grow more and more idle; even in situations where they have the greatest scope. The history of the past, supplies us with many decisive instances of this. However deplorable, for instance, was the retrograde tyranny of Bonaparte, it has had less influence over Europe than the domination of Attila, which indeed was of a nobler kind. And in like manner conversely, the excellent personal influence of Frederic was certainly less than that not merely of Alexander, but also of Cæsar, and even of Charlemagne.

Human Order grows ever more regular, by an increasing power of Self-modification,

The short analysis just given, amounts therefore to this: that it gives us fresh assurance of that consolatory law, which a synthetic view of civilisation suggested at the outset. *Human Order exhibits a course of increasing regularity*, by virtue of man's ever growing power to affect the sum of his destinies. Although all the forces modifying society grow less and less intense, the reaction of the Great Being over the Fatality upon which it depends, grows ever more and more complete. We thus dispose of that serious difficulty which threatened us, when the conclusion of Social Statics seemed to point to a constantly increasing complication of society. A complete answer is given by means of the universal law that explains all variations in nature. Phenomena of all kinds, whilst they are growing more and more complex, at the same time are growing more and more capable of modification. Where development takes place, in like manner complication is multiplied as evolution is effected. But at the same time, the highest class of phenomena, which are also the most complex, tend to exhibit an Order more and more regular, which almost recalls in its symmetry the higher types of Celestial Movement. This balance in favour of Regularity is due to the wisdom and energy of the grand agent of Progress. For Humanity is ever at work to assert its own high freedom of action, and thus triumphs over the blind Fatality encompassing its life.

Under the increasing ascendancy of Humanity.

To ameliorate man's Condition or man's Nature, not to make an idle display of man's Power, is the spirit in which we must labour without ceasing to modify the Universal Economy of things. It matters little, therefore, that the normal Variations of Human Order, are growing positively weaker, if in doing so they are constantly growing more orderly. This tendency in the Modifying forces to grow weaker is far from diminishing our true empire over our own destinies. On the contrary, this much increases our power, and even renders it far nobler; for it keeps man's action pure from any arbitrary motive. In truth, if the laws of Nature in the aggregate work up to this end, it is mainly the result of the gradual perfecting of Man's wisdom, as man's powers are more and more devoted to secure his highest destiny. Our cares and our energies were long confined to the improvement of the Physical World; they were next absorbed in Intellectual Progress; and they are lastly concentrated upon Moral Order, by which the great issues of human life must finally be judged. It would seem as if the long anarchy in which we live, might for ever debar Civilisation from reaching this sacred end of all effort; but we may reflect how, without our wills, we are being called back to it by the growing power of the Great Being; even before it has yet attained to a full sense of its supremacy.

The growing weight of the Past is ever silently ordering the course of the Future: and no Material variations, and no Vital modifications, and neither Social nor Individual perturbations, can ever arrest its work. Forty centuries ago, the genius of the Theocracies had an instinctive sense: *that the Dead govern the Living*; and we see this spirit in the system of Caste, and in the pathetic ceremonials with which they celebrated the sacred rites of Burial. Although the West has so far lost its reason, that, for the time, it ignores this supreme law of Human Order, the constant ascendency of the Past, the law itself is continually growing in importance, by reason, first, of the perpetual strengthening of the forces that control human life, and then by the perpetual weakening of those forces which disturb it. Of the three powers which control the Living, the Material, the Affective and the Intellectual, the two latter which are most adapted to feel, and to transmit the action of the Dead, that is to say, the influence of Women and the authority of the Priest, are ever tending to an importance higher than that of the Practical government, which is least in sympathy with the Past. *Growing ascendency of the Past over the Present,*

Spirits new-made by our Religion will henceforward accept, knowingly and willingly, the ennobling dominion of the Past; whilst the rebellious spirits endure it blindly and perforce. But the good will bless it, as the source of man's highest perfection, as that which guides to good all personal desires, so that they are insensibly lost in the harmonious working of feel- *Will become the spirit of Religious Duty.*

ing and of reason.   With the full assurance that Happiness, like Duty, is to be found only in the more perfect surrender of self to the Great Being, in whom the Universal Order is transfigured, the wise will strive ever to devote their lives more truly to its service.   Man's prudence and energy only bring out with all their resources man's natural state of dependence; so that they force him to seek outside himself the only foundations on which he can give stability to his life.   It would seem as if these fixed grounds were wanting as regards man's highest functions, those of Social life, which are most in need of regulation, by reason of their greater complication.   But Death, the natural issue of Life, is converted into the principal instrument by which Life is reduced to system.   It was with reference to private existence, that my sainted and eternal companion uttered that profound sentence : ' There is nothing in Life irrevocable, but Death.'   Nevertheless, this truth has a still higher meaning when applied to the Social System.   It then coincides with the primary law of human organisation.   For the subjective influence of the Dead predominates over the objective energy of the Living, only by virtue of the fact, that the first is irrevocable, and thereby, it ultimately bends everything changeable before it.

Growing assimilation of Languages.   The impressive truth to which this chapter has brought us may be illustrated in a very striking way, if we apply it to the institution of Language, the most social of all institutions, and yet the one best fitted to develop personal qualities.   Under the increasing pressure exerted by subjective influences, human Language is perpetually tending to full and ultimate symmetry, in the degree that man's Solidarity and Continuity broaden ; notwithstanding the objective varieties in it due to Climate, to Race, and to Nationalities or Individualities.   This destined state of Unity is at once a consequence and a condition of a Universal Religion ; and it will justify by reason that instinct of each man's heart to bow down before the revered will of the Great Being, whose controlling authority is ever guiding our lives in spite of ourselves.

CONCLUSION OF THE SECOND VOLUME.

HUMANITY is so far above all other known beings that it finds itself compelled to work out its own destiny, with no general type as a guide to direct its natural tendencies, until it has reached that point in its evolution where the Laws of Progress can be grasped. It begins by attributing its own existence, like all other existences, to Absolute Powers; and these it involuntarily endows with all the attributes of wisdom and of goodness which in that stage it is able to conceive; and in so doing, it sets up these Powers provisionally as the guides of its conduct. But, as all such religious institutions can never be anything but subjective, they always fall short, whether for theory or for practice, of an objective ground of action and belief; such as man finally works out for himself by studying the laws of human progress.

To be able to direct our destinies on system, instead of submitting blindly to their weight, is the principal mark of the full maturity now reached by the Van-guard of mankind. Henceforward, this central nucleus of the true Great Being will follow its natural course, with a just sense of the goal set before it, as well as of its own available resources. Thus wisely directed, the less advanced groups of men will be better able to adapt their career by the light of the common laws; and thus all may be brought up to the Normal State, with fewer difficulties and with greater speed.

This full manhood of the race, can only be attained when it has accomplished two great works in Philosophy, or rather in Religion. The fundamental type of human existence must be determined first, and then the laws of its development. The first of these conditions has been the subject of this volume, the latter condition will be the subject of the next.

The foundation of both was worked out in the type in the theory of Human Unity and of its slow preparation (chap. i.).

With this as a starting point, I laid down the Positive theory of man's elementary existence ; treating first the Activity which dominates it, next the Family ties of which it is made up, and then the Language which permits it to extend (chaps. ii., iii., and iv.). Having done this, I was able to construct a systematic and abstract programme of Human Order ; dealing successively with the Structure of the great organism, its complete Existence, and lastly the Limits of its different Modifications (chaps. v., vi., and vii.).

The scheme of this volume may be summed up and illustrated by simply tracing the history of the elementary term of Statics ; inasmuch as Language has an inherent tendency to reflect man's entire nature. If we compare the two general senses of the word, *Order,* we find that it always connotes at the same time *commandment* and *arrangement.* During the whole course of previous civilisation, the purpose of which was rather to develop man's various forces than to regulate them, Command was thought more important than Arrangement ; and indeed Arrangement could not even begin in any other way, for want of an external base. The adult state of Man, on the other hand, is distinguished by the higher importance of Arrangement ; when, Order being directly founded upon its objective type in External Nature, it merely requires Command as a subsidiary instrument, wherewith to turn our decisions into practical action. Thus the contrast between the Absolute synthesis and the Relative synthesis may be represented as the mere reversing of the places held, now-by one, and now by the other sense of the word, *Order.* In fact the inversion which is thus naturally brought about between Command and Arrangement is at once a formula to express the fact : that Laws have taken the place of Causes; and an indication of the growing tendency to make Spiritual Discipline of higher import than Temporal Government.

It might be thought that the fundamental laws of Human Order would be sufficient to give a systematic form to the destiny of man : which must ever consist in a closer approach to the primary type. But we may gather from all that has been said in this volume, that, however necessary is this body of theory, it is in no way all that we require ; for it has left undetermined the manner, and the time, in which the typical Order may ultimately come about, simply explaining the conditions which inevitably prepare the way. The most complete Statical theory therefore is never adequate as a guide to social action; although it is always an element necessary for action. To rely upon the Statical type alone, or even too largely, would usually involve us in serious mischief; for it would give to our political designs too absolute a character, and too vague a direction.

A comparison drawn from Mathematics will serve to give a good general idea of these two dangers, and it will illustrate the true use of the Statical half of the science of Sociology. The Statical theory is, in Social phenomena, what the various right lines are to the geometer, in working out the problems of a curve, especially in determining its asymptotes. When a curve has many asymptotes, as may often be the case with a very simple equation, we may obtain from the sum of them as a preliminary valuable indications as to the general figure of the curve; and we may get from these data approximate results of considerable value. But no use of these right lines will ever supply the place of direct and specific treatment of the orbit described by the curve; for it will always leave many important questions undetermined. The same error would be still more marked in Political Science, if we attempted to trace the course of Progress by applying directly to Social Statics; for Statics can only supply us with a vast group of asymptotes, necessarily common to a multitude of different courses. Yet we have to choose one course out of many.

To assist us in this ultimate choice of a course to be adopted, and the decision must be made before action can begin, we have nothing to resort to, but Social Dynamics. Although, in studying Progress we must always treat it as a mere development of an already defined Order, the more precise methods of Historical Science alone can teach us, what are at each epoch the practicable paths towards the given Type, and by what course of procedure they may be found. Not only are our notions of the Normal State made clearer and more consistent by knowing the laws of Movement; but this knowledge points out the only highway, where we are safe both from Reaction and from Anarchy; for we should be continually oscillating between these two, were we to confine our view to Statical conceptions where questions of Time are eliminated. The more necessary that it was for this volume to put aside this question of Time, for, as in Mechanics, it would otherwise have been impossible to build up any general law, so much the more necessary is it for the philosophy of history to bring the element of Time to the front, in order to place on a settled footing the relations of the Abstract and the Concrete.

Amongst numberless examples which history can supply of dangerous illusions due to the use of Statical views without their dynamic corrective, it is enough to mention how all the great men of antiquity utterly misconceived the gain to civilisation, which the Middle Age had in store. I pointed out (p. 87), how the best spirits of the ancient world long committed the blunder of rejecting Catholicism in its birth, as it seemed to them to be directly diverting Humanity from the noble social end which towards the close of antiquity seemed to be opening to mankind. Now we can easily perceive how this mistake, inevitable as it was, was produced; it was owing to their complete ignorance of any historical movement, which could enable them to see the necessary stages through which they must pass in order to reach this Statical Type. From the time of Scipio and Cæsar down to Trajan and Constantine, philosophers and statesmen were both coming more and more to perceive, how the entire advance of the whole Roman world was implanting Positive knowledge in place of Theological or Metaphysical creeds, and Industrial activity in place of a life of War. But, as they had no clear Knowledge of human Progress, they utterly failed to see how necessary to civilisation was the stage of Monotheism and of Feudalism. The best amongst them were thus too often led to sully their names by savage persecution of the Christians, who unconsciously were working out the lofty Organisation of Life, towards which also the greater Romans were struggling after an abstract, and therefore impossible, type.

Such a catastrophe may warn us how urgent is the need for the true Philosophy of History, for want of which the Intelligence of modern times may again think it necessary to break with the Past, and for fifteen centuries to seek a new course for human progress. It is true that in the act of conceiving aright the normal order in Social Statics, we make a necessary approach to the period of its actual advent; for the imagination never can be very far in advance of reality, especially in such a case as the ultimate state of Humanity. But the general conviction that we are approaching this type will not enable us to dispense with a third volume on History, to show in detail how in fact this result may be attained; and then a fourth volume on Practice will be needed to develop that general Faith wherein the Progress of mankind will be finally embodied in a system.

END OF THE SECOND VOLUME.